IFÁ DIVINATIO
AND PERFORMANCE

IFÁ DIVINATION, KNOWLEDGE, POWER, AND PERFORMANCE

Edited by Jacob K. Olupona and
Rowland O. Abiodun

Indiana University Press

Bloomington & Indianapolis

This book is a publication of

Indiana University Press
Office of Scholarly Publishing
Herman B Wells Library 350
1320 East 10th Street
Bloomington, Indiana 47405 USA

iupress.indiana.edu

Manufactured in the United States of America

Library of Congress Cataloging-in-Publication Data

Ifa divination, knowledge, power, and performance / edited
by Jacob K. Olupona and Rowland O. Abiodun.
    pages cm — (African expressive cultures)
    Papers from a conference held March 13–16, 2008
at Harvard University.
    Includes bibliographical references and index.
    ISBN 978-0-253-01882-3 (cloth : alk. paper) — ISBN 978-0-253-
01890-8 (pbk. : alk. paper) — ISBN 978-0-253-01896-0 (ebook) 1. Ifa
(Religion) 2. Yoruba (African people)—Religion. 3. Divination.
4. Orisha religion. 5. Afro-Caribbean cults. 6. Ifa (Religion)—Art.
I. Olupona, Jacob K. (Jacob Kehinde), 1951– editor. II. Abiodun,
Rowland, editor. III. Series: African expressive cultures.
    BF1779.I4I347 2016
    299.6'8333—dc23

                                                            2015033418

1 2 3 4 5   21 20 19 18 17 16

Dedicated to a distinguished scholar of Ifá Studies,
Professor Wándé Abímbólá,

and in memory of a pioneer of Ifá Studies,
Professor William R. Bascom (1912–1981)

Ifá ló l'òní
Ifá ló lòla
Ifá ló l'òtúnla pèlú è
Òrúnmìlà ló n'ijó mérèrin Òòsà d'ááyé.

Ifá is the master of today
Ifá is the master of tomorrow;
Ifá is the master of the day after tomorrow.
To Ifá belongs all the four days
Established by Òòsà on earth.

Wándé Abímbólá, *Ifá: An Exposition of Ifá Literary Corpus*

Contents

Foreword

I AM DELIGHTED TO know that this book—the result of a fascinating three-day conference on Ifá tradition at Harvard University in 2008—will now be available for all to read and enjoy. As the Ooni of Ife, it was indeed an honor for me and my fellow Oba—including the Owa Obokun of Ijesa Land, Oba Agunlejika, and the governor of Osun State, Prince Oyinlola—to be active participants in the deliberations over many important aspects of Ifá by a worldwide gathering of distinguished scholars, practitioners, and devotees of Ifá. There was not a dull moment throughout the conference; we all left with the feeling of giving credence to the beloved Ifá lyrics, "Ifá will not perish from the face of the Earth."

Traditional rulers and priests of Ifá in Yorùbáland have long recognized Ifá's multicomplexities—its religious, philosophical, and cultural traditions—and have, within their power and resources, supported efforts to enlighten the world about Ifá and its relevance to all facets of life, irrespective of race, color or people's religious persuasion. Perhaps the most alluring and delightful aspect of Yorùbá religious tradition and culture bequeathed to us is the comprehensive oral narrative comprising the 256 odú Corpus of Poetry—an encyclopedia of knowledge. Equally impressive is the artistic legacy associated with Ifá divination practice. Artifacts used in Ifá divination can now be found in major museums in the West and many parts of the world. For example, in the Ulmer Museum in Ulm, Germany, there is a most beautiful Ifá divination tray that was collected as early as the eighteenth century.

The patron divinity of the Ifá divination system is Orunmila (with aliases that include Agboniregun, Okunrin-kukuru Oke-Geti, Agiri-ile-ilogbon), who made Ile-Ife his home, and he is celebrated to this day at Oke-Tase with elaborate annual festivals that attract Ifá priests from all over the world. Orunmila was the only witness at creation, which means that his own creation must have preceded those of other orishas. More importantly, he has the unique advantage of knowing the destinies of everyone and is equipped with the language to express them. Orunmila is a polyglot, which has earned him the praise name, Afedefeyo ("one who speaks and understands all tongues"). He is also capable of resolving conflicts and bringing peace and order into the universe, for which reason he is called and known as Agbayegun. Despite their sometimes nominal conversion to Islam and Christianity, the Yorùbá continue to cherish Ifá traditions, which play pivotal roles in daily life and govern the social and economic fabric of traditional and modern Yorùbá society.

The chapters in this volume touch on various themes and topics providing deep-seated knowledge of Ifá traditions. Together they point to the rich depth of scholarship of the presenters. From discussion of myths and rituals to the intersections of Ifá and Islamic traditions; from historical accounts to artistic performances of Ifá in the Caribbean and throughout the Americas—Ifá has endured. All these legacies point to the global reach and significance of Ifá tradition, confirming what scholars of Yorùbá cultures have been saying all along—that their own tradition is a world culture deserving to be placed alongside other world cultures in the "global cultural hall of fame." Of course, UNESCO's recognition of Osun Osogbo Sacred Grove as a World Global Heritage Site testifies to the richness of Yorùbá culture and traditions. I wholeheartedly recommend this volume to readers and scholars everywhere. It provides numerous platforms from which young scholars can now launch their future research projects on Ifá.

I am most pleased that the Harvard conference provided an opportunity for the world community of scholars to honor two most influential scholars of Ifá tradition: Professor Wándé Abímbọ́lá, whose Ifá chieftaincy title, "Awise Awo Agbaye," attests to his exalted position among members of the king's inner circle of palace senior diviners (Awo-Ooni), and the late William Bascom, anthropologist at the University of California, Berkeley, whose pioneering research opened up Yorùbá studies for others to follow. Professor Abímbọ́lá remains the most knowledgeable scholar-practitioner of Ifá in his generation. This is a most valuable and illuminating work on an African divinatory tradition and practice.

His Royal Highness Oba Okunade Sijuade Olubuse II
Ooni of Ile-Ife, Enu Owa Palace
Ile-Ife, Osun State, Nigeria

Preface

Jacob K. Olupona and Rowland O. Abiodun

THIS BOOK EMANATES from Harvard University's interdisciplinary conference, "Sacred Knowledge, Sacred Power and Performance: Ifá Divination in West Africa and the African Diaspora" (March 13–16, 2008). We organized this event in response to a request from academics around the world that we bring together scholars, scholar-practitioners, and practitioners to analyze Ifá's multidimensionality and to chart Ifa scholarship, today and into the future. The conference aimed neither to streamline various discourses in Ifa studies nor to give credibility to any one strand of scholarship. Rather it strove to give contemporary research on Ifá a new and energized hearing, thereby promoting future investigations on the subject. In exploring Ifa divination and its practices, many authors pursued ideas, theory, and practical performances of its rich traditions, highlighting its arts, aesthetics, rituals, literature, science, religion and philosophy. This book, therefore, launches critical questions about the Ifá diviniation corpus and should be seen as an advanced introduction to the analysis of Ifá in Africa, the Caribbean, and the Americas.

The lively conversations that ensued among scholars and participants who came from Africa, Europe, South America, the Caribbean, and North America likely remain fresh in the minds of the contributors. "Sacred Knowledge, Sacred Power and Performance" was not only judged a successful academic meeting of the minds, but also hailed as a model for strong partnership among practitioners and scholars. The Ooni of Ile-Ife, Oba Okunade Sijuade, Olubuse II, and the Governor of Osun State, Nigeria, Prince Olagunsoye Oyinlola, emanating from the ancestral homelands of Ifá, enlivened the proceedings. Nigeria's colorful contingency, its traditional *Oba*, elders, Yorùbá intellectuals, and state officials infused the conference with vibrancy and vitality. Each session began with traditional dancing inspired by a dynamic ensemble of drummers accompanying our Yorùbá dignitaries. The audience witnessed the beauty and charisma of Yorùbá culture, dress, and life in action. As each drumming session ended, our guests quietly took their seats, listened to the presenters, and participated in the discussion with deep interest. It was a model that many of our colleagues present promised to replicate whenever they have the opportunity to host such a global conference.

This volume's success follows upon the hard work of many whose labor and contributions we acknowledge here. We thank Adam McGee of Harvard University, who assisted with planning and organizing the conference that produced this volume. His assistance made it possible to enjoy such a successful meeting in Cambridge. We are indebted to former Harvard students Lisanne Norman, who read the early draft of the project, and Venise Battle (who is at the University of Pennsylvania now), for her diligence in completing the project. The staff of the Department of African and African American Studies and Harvard Divinity School provided significant assistance and support for the necessary logistics to hold the conference. Giselle Jackson, Josiah Epps, and Melissa Huser deserve our immense appreciation. The dean of the Harvard Divinity School, Professor William Graham, and the chair of the Department of African and African American Studies, Professor Evelyn Higginbotham, gave us moral and financial support that counted so much in our success. We appreciate deeply the financial assistance of Professor Henry Louis Gates, Jr., director of the Du Bois Institute at Harvard University, who has an active intellectual interest in Yorùbá and Ifá Studies.

It remains for us to thank wholeheartedly several distinguished visitors who traveled far from Nigeria to Harvard, beginning with the *Ooni* of *Ile-Ife*, the governor, and traditional rulers, *A mo ri yin ba o, ASE,* the *Owa Obokun* of Ijesaland, the *Apetu of Ipetumodu*, the *Olojudo* of *Ido Osun*, the *Agbowu* of *Ogaagba*, the *Adimula* of *Ifewara*, the *Owamoran* of *Esa-Oke*, the *Olumoro* of *Moro,* the *Timi* of *Ede*, the *Orangun* of *Oke-Ila*, Professor Babatunde Osotimehin of UNESCO, Prince Ayo Aderemi, Mr. Femi Adelegan, Professor Bade Ajuwon, Chief S. K. Ajayi, Professor Akinrinade, and Ms. Ike Fayemi.

This volume is like a kaleidoscope in which Ifá passes through the lenses of various disciplines, theories, and experiences. We hope the ideas presented here demonstrate Ifá's continuing relevance to contemporary society and inspire a new generation of interdisciplinary investigations into the endless depths of Ifá divination.

IFÁ DIVINATION, KNOWLEDGE, POWER, AND PERFORMANCE

Introduction

Jacob K. Olupona and Rowland O. Abiodun

with Niyi Afolabi

IFÁ DIVINATION, KNOWLEDGE, POWER, AND PERFORMANCE focuses on a number of themes germane to the study of Ifá today. Our contributors show scholarly interest in the collection, transcription, translation, and interpretation of the Ifá divination corpus. In general, Ifá divination is a geomantic knowledge system through which specialized interpreters diagnose, explain, or predict current and future fortunes (or misfortunes). In Nigeria, Benin, Togo, and throughout the African diaspora, Yorùbá people and their descendants use an ornate circular or rectangular *opon Ifá* (divination tray) for divination. It is carved with the image of *Esu*, the deity who interprets and delivers messages between heaven and earth. After coating the tray with a sacred powder, the babalawo (diviner) casts palm nuts onto the tray and interprets the binary code produced by their markings. Most importantly, the diviner recites by heart the stories, poems, herbal remedies, and recommended sacrifices associated with the pattern on the divining board. The essays gathered here operate under the premise that Ifá divination encompasses a body of knowledge that has not been fully explored.

The authors approach divination from an interdisciplinary perspective and illustrate Ifá's pertinence beyond religious studies to philosophy, performance studies, and cultural studies. A desire to generate new theoretical and hermeneutic questions and to extend the superb scholarship of two pioneering scholars on Ifá, William Bascom and Wándé Abímbọ́lá, propelled us to organize a conference at Harvard University. The following essays are glimmers of the current scholarship and they point to the future of Ifá research. This book will serve a variety of readers, including practitioners of Ifá, scholars of Ifá studies, and students of African and African diaspora religions, as well as readers interested in African art, performance, and culture.

Our volume intervenes several issues in the current state of Ifá studies. First, it seeks to debunk existing scholarship that treats Ifá oral narratives as timeless and ahistorical. It highlights the ways that Ifá narratives and their brokers are dynamic and ever changing, shaped by politics, cultural histories, and social rituals. Second, though Ifá divination texts are classified as indigenous narratives, a close examination of the texts reveals the underexplored influences of modernity and outside traditions, especially Christianity and Islam. Third, most available collections pay little attention to the intricacies of translation, particularly the process of transmission and the performed structure of the text. As a result, these collections fail to capture the poetic and dialectical significance of Ifá divination. Several of the essays included in this volume examine these problems of translation and transmission while rethinking the symbolic and discursive politics of language use in ritual contexts. Fourth, a few of the essays make bold reference to the historical and social contexts in which the corpus was produced. Whereas several earlier works in Ifá divination focused on regions outside the two central and western Yorùbá city-states, this volume presents some findings from lesser-known parts of Yorùbáland. Finally, this volume addresses the travel and spread of Ifá knowledge and cosmologies, and contributes to the development of a theoretical and empirical language for advancing the state of Ifá scholarship.

Since most, if not all, contributors in this volume have Wándé Abímbọlá and William Bascomb's classic studies as their point of departure, it is important to comment on this scholarship in Ifá studies.

Wándé Abímbọlá: His Contributions to Ifá Studies

To reflect on Abímbọlá's contribution to the study of Ifá, we would like to make three points. First, Wándé Abímbọlá initiated Ifá studies in the department of African Languages and Literature at Obafemi Awolowo University in Ile-Ife, Nigeria. Even though there was an institute for African studies on that campus before he joined the faculty, he was indeed the one that gave Ifá studies their tone and identity—so much so that the department began to hire diviners and practitioner scholars to teach the Yorùbá language and Ifá divination. Abímbọlá more than anyone else gave this field the credibility it assumes globally. Second, he was also responsible for taking Ifá studies to places outside Nigeria, particularly to universities in the Americas. As a result, he developed an academic framework for its pedagogy and also for construing it as a body of knowledge available to scholars in various disciplines, such as philosophy, religion, literature, and the arts. Third, on a practical level, he spoke as a modern apostle of Ifá divination, in the sense that he championed what would later become the World Congress of Òrìsà Tradition—an organization responsible for convening conferences and defining a new role for Òrìsà tradition as a global religion. As a public intellectual, Abímbọlá engages the Ifá body of knowledge and uses a new hermeneutics derived from these texts to engage in discourse on larger issues of culture and society. For example, he speaks on issues such as moral character and interreligious communication by applying oral Ifá divination texts, to give Ifá concepts and ideas new meaning and to reveal their relevance to modern societies. The climax of Abímbọlá's engagement with Ifá can be seen in his establishment in

2008 of the Ifá Heritage Institute, which is a two-year college in Oyo, Nigeria. It offers a curriculum founded upon Ifá and Yorùbá indigenous epistemology, and all courses are taught in the Yoruba language. This establishment was born with UNESCO support after Abímbọ́lá received the UNESCO Proclamation of Ifá as one of the Masterpieces of the Oral and Intangible Heritage of Humanity in 2005.

We should note that several of the scholars who contributed to this collection reference Wándé Abímbọ́lá's schema for exploring Ifá divination texts. His works, particularly those that have been translated into English, have become the standard texts invoked by scholars in Ifá studies. He is well known for isolating the eight components that comprise the structure of ẹṣẹ Ifá:

> Nearly all ẹṣẹ Ifá have a maximum of eight main parts. The first part states the name(s) of the Ifá priest(s) involved in a past divination. The second part states the name(s) of the client(s) for whom the divination was performed. The third part states the reason for the divination while the fourth part contains the instructions of Ifá priest(s) to the client(s) after the divination. The fifth part then tells whether or not the client(s) complied with the instructions. The sixth part narrates what happened to the client(s) after he carried out or refused to carry out the instructions. The seventh part contains the reactions of the client(s) to the joy or sorrow that resulted from the process of divination while the eighth part draws a fitting moral from the story as a whole.[1]

Abímbọ́lá uses this observation to argue that ẹṣẹ Ifá link historical recollection with divinatory contexts. He states: "Every ẹṣẹ Ifá is . . . presented as a historical poem. Each ẹṣẹ is believed to be an accurate account of what once happened or what has once been observed in the past. . . . In this way, every Ifá priest makes his client see what happened or was observed in the past so that his client may learn from the experiences of the past. History is the language of Ifá divination, and 'histories make men wise.'"[2] This observation guides several of the authors' arguments in this volume.

Abímbọ́lá's works not only contain extensive Ifá divination poetry but also point to diverse methods of interpreting the texts and explicating their connections to metaphysics, worldviews, biological science, and history. His works have become a springboard for integrating Ifá into various epistemologies. One classic example is Olu Longe's inaugural lecture at the University of Ibadan in 1983, titled "Ifá Divination and Computer Science." Another significant and more recent example is Olusegun Folorunso, Adio T. Akinwale, Rebecca O. Vincent, and Babatunde Olabenjo's article, "A Mobile-Based Knowledge Management System for 'Ifá': An African Traditional Oracle," published in 2010. Folorunso and colleagues have created a digital Ifá consultation application for mobile phones. In the future, this application will enable people to receive a mobile consultation, including an odù, the codified message that appears to the babalawo in a divination session, and the appropriate ẹṣẹ Ifá. This development presents an opportunity for analytical discussions about Ifá's adaptability to the cultural and technological advancements in our new-millennial society.

William Bascom: A Groundbreaking Ethnographer of Ifá

Bascom was a trained anthropologist who conducted extensive field research in southwestern Nigerian (particularly Ile-Ife). His book *Ifá Divination: Communication Between Gods and Men in West Africa* became a classic. It was the first major volume on the Ifá divination system. It is based on his field research in 1937–1938 and on his data from later research in the 1950s and 1960s. This book is a critical starting point for understanding the divination process, the Ifá oral narratives, and Ifá itself as a body of knowledge. In this text, Bascom's most famous intervention is his tripartite outline of the structure of ẹsẹ Ifá, in which he identifies: "(1) the statement of the mythological case which serves as a precedent, (2) the resolution or outcome of this case, and (3) its application to the client."[3] Bascom notes that not all ẹsẹ Ifá conform to this structure, but these common traits surface in most. As with Abímbọlá's observations, Bascom's conclusions heavily inform the authors' arguments in this volume.

During his lifetime, Bascom helped establish the University of California at Berkeley's master's degree program in folklore.[4] His ethnographic work in Nigeria and later in Cuba allowed him to play a pioneering role in the overall creation of folkloric studies in the American academy. He was the mentor of a long line of accomplished folklorists, including American anthropologists Alan Dundes and Daniel J. Crowley and the Nigerian anthropologist Niyi Akinnaso.

Sixteen Cowries: Yorùbá Divination from Africa to the New World builds on the goals established in Bascom's groundbreaking book, *Ifá Divination*. In this seminal publication, Bascom presents the entire orature of a single merindinlogun diviner. Merindinlogun, a condensed and expedited form of Ifá divination, is practiced throughout Cuba, and has taken root more recently in the United States. But Bascom was more than an ethnographer. He was the first to theorize the connection between verbal and ritual arts. Also, he wrote about the intersection of folklore and anthropology. Toward the end of his life, he developed a comparative study of oral tradition whereby he examined African oral narratives and their manifestations in the Black Atlantic diaspora, especially in Cuba. Overall, his publications and theoretical reflections have advanced folklore studies and in the process have integrated Ifá studies into Western academic disciplines. A collection of his papers deposited at the Bancroft Library at the University of California, Berkeley, evinces his untiring interest in not only Yoruba divination but also numerous African and African-diasporic religions, arts, and cultures. We provide this brief reflection on Wándé Abímbọlá's and William Bascom's works in Ifá studies to show the state of the field, to indicate what spurred the contributors to this volume to explore various dimensions of Ifá divination, and to point to unexplored research areas for future study.

Major Themes and Organization

This book is divided into four conceptual, analytical, and theoretical categories or sections, each approached from an interdisciplinary angle. The four sections are: "Ifá Orature: Its Interpretation and Translation," "Ifá as Knowledge: Theoretical Questions and Concerns," "Ifá in the Afro-Atlantic," and "Sacred Art in Ifá." *Ifá Divination* has the following intellectual objectives: (i) to show that Ifá chants and narratives and their repositories are dynamic entities shaped by political, cultural, historical, and social realities; (ii) to recuperate the performative and dialectical nature of the tradition by exploring translation and transmission studies; (iii) to explore the symbolic and discursive politics of language in ritual contexts; (iv) to make visible the lesser-known parts of Yorùbáland where the tradition equally thrives; and (v) to explicate the spread and diffusion of the Ifá knowledge system and cosmologies across the diaspora through empirical and paradigmatic formulations that will make the practice more enduring in the advancement of Ifá scholarship. Each chapter is a cogent statement about and celebration of Ifá oracular and ontological mysteries and mythologies.

The first section, "Ifá Orature: Its Interpretation and Translation," presents Ifá as a body of oral narratives and a genre that is amenable to deep hermeneutics, as in similar traditions such as biblical, Qur'anic, and cultural narratives across the globe. In chapter 1, "*Ayajo* as Ifá in Mythical and Sacred Contexts," Ayo Opefeyitimi classifies sacred-mythical texts into three categories, namely, "luckbringing," "neutralizers," and "spells," while using *narrasobeneutics* to theorize about the efficacy of words when the invocator believes in his potent activation through spiritual invocation. Narrasobeneutics combines narratology, sociology of literature, metaphysics, and hermeneutics into a hermeneutical tool by which one may best comprehend *ayajo*. Drawing upon varied cogent theories advanced by Gennet, Duncan, and Dundes and their contributions to the typology, mythology, and efficacy of words, Opefeyitimi raises many questions about what he calls "verbal law" and how it can validate in practice.

In chapter 2, "Continuity and Change in the Verbal, Artistic, Ritualistic, and Performance Traditions of Ifá Divination," Wándé Abímbọ́lá addresses the tensions between continuity and change in Ifá oral texts and ritual practices in Africa and the African diaspora. For example, he observes that babalawo in the diaspora divined with cowrie shells instead of kola nuts because the latter were not available in the Americas. The freedom and creativity of the babalawo in Ifá recitations have further enriched the variety of Ifá divination practices, while Christianity and Islam have caused the theft of Ifá divination treasures and artifacts. Abímbọ́lá argues that what is resisted is not change per se but falsification or vulgarization, especially interpretations imposed through an agency external to the tradition that priests may consider foreign. Abímbọ́lá correctly points out how neighboring languages, the use of music, and the effects of becoming written shape the renditions of Ifá verses. He also highlights how the effects of Christianization and Islamization have led to the sale or theft of Ifá treasures. As a result, indigenous technologies for producing Ifá arts have virtually collapsed—causing changes in the colors used in beadwork, for instance. Finally, dance is another arena of innovation. Abímbọ́lá notes that while Ifá drumming and dance have grown in popularity throughout the world, these traditions are dying out in Yorùbáland. But he concludes that while much has been lost, a sizable part of Ifá traditions has been preserved and new innovations advanced.

While chapters 1 and 2 focus on origin, typology, tradition, and change, chapters 3 through 6 deal with the performative and referential nature of the sacred knowledge system. In "Recasting Ifá: Historicity and Recursive Recollection in Ifá Divination Texts," Andrew Apter examines historical narratives in Ifá divination, arguing that consultations from the primordial past appear in the contemporary recitation of ẹsẹ Ifá in order to explicate a client's present situation. He expands on Bascom's research by developing an ethnomethodological framework for theorizing Ifá and identifying recursive recasting as a form of historicity.

In chapter 4, "Ifá, Knowledge, Performance, the Sacred, and the Medium," Olasope O. Oyelaran's central concern is not just the eight-part structure of the poem as consistently postulated by Wándé Abímbọ́lá; he is equally concerned with noting the preservation of the tradition in Brazil and Cuba. Oyelaran surmises that both recitation and creative expression are vital in the preservation of the Ifá tradition as established structure. To this end, he suggests that while Yorùbá oral performance requires ingenuity, most rules regulating a babalawo's mastery of Ifá demand recitation. The words themselves do not change, but the style applied to the recitation may vary from one performer to the next.

On the other hand, in "'Writing' and 'Reference' in Ifá," Adéléke Adéẹkọ́ argues that "the referential antecedence of the Ifá story is the inscription and not the event of the story," that is, the odù constitute unchanging reference points in Yorùbá divination and cannot be conflated with either the present that the client presents before divination or the past associated with either the diviner's retrogressive analysis or the diviner's future-directed predictions or solutions. In summary, Adéẹkọ́ advocates a more rigorous scrutiny of the claims and methodologies of Ifá divination. He also examines how references occur within the text. Adéẹkọ́ suggests that the odù qualify as "writing," a resilient and unchanging signification system. Moreover, this writing is mythographic in that the odù connect to narratives rather than phonemes. The odù emerge apart from any diviner's influence; thus they become a written message between Orunmila and the client. Objectivity remains intact throughout the consultation, because the diviner references Orunmila as the keeper of these divine texts and the distributor of *odù* for the client. Importantly, by referencing a consultation from the past (as discussed in Apter's essay), the person divining in the present-day context minimizes his or her input and emphasizes the prognosis's divine source.

Part 2, "Ifá as Knowledge: Theoretical Questions and Concerns," focuses on a perennial question: how does Ifá constitute a major epistemology and worldview? Most Ifá scholars who explore and interpret Ifá narratives do so mainly out of the conviction that Ifá ritual, as a body of knowledge, rivals similar ancient traditions across the globe, such as the Hindu Puranas, the Bhagavad-Gita, the Bible, the Qur'an, and Confucian texts. What deep meaning does it hold on various existential questions of our time? In the sixth chapter, "Ifá: Sixteen *Odù*, Sixteen Questions," Barry Hallen lays out a Socratic approach to methodological issues in Ifá research. Rather than presenting a discourse on one specific question, Hallen offers sixteen thought-provoking questions in order to raise critical issues for scholars and practitioners. Among these questions are: (i) Who should divine—the initiated or the uninitiated? (ii) Whose voice bears more weight in Ifá discourse—the scholar, the babalawo, or the academe and initiate? (iii) Can a single methodology be representative of the entire Yorùbá divination system? (iv) How does the Trindadian Ifá discourse differ from the West African? (v) What are the consequences of Ifá as a transnational current or movement? These questions are just that, without any attempt to answer them. It is as if the author leaves the reader with the burden of returning to the Ifá knowledge system in order to locate the answers.

Like Barry Hallen, Olúfẹ́mi Táíwò in chapter 7, "*Kín N'Ifá Wí?*: Philosophical Issues in Ifá Divination," and Rowland O. Abiodun in chapter 8, "Diviner as Explorer: The Afuwape Paradigm," transcend the limits of interpretation by engendering debates on hitherto simplistic claims and assumptions about Ifá. Based on questions raised in the volume edited by Jacob Olupona and Terry Rey, *Òrìṣà Devotions as a World Religion* (2008), Táíwò explores how the *ebo* (sacrificial rites) is a part of the divination process and how without it the act or art is incomplete. Abiodun examines the journey motif or itinerancy, typical of the babalawo and suggests it is a pretext for the acquisition of knowledge across timeless spaces. Abiodun relates his argument to the history and anthropology of Ifá art as discussed by other scholars in this volume by describing the horse-and-rider motif in Ifá sculptures. While this motif functions as an *oriki* of Ifá, Abiodun's writing on the subject endeavors to showcase how "journey" became a cardinal motif in Ifá texts. Along these same lines of knowledge quests and questionings, the remaining chapters of this section theorize on the limits and transcendence of knowledge.

In chapter 9, "'The Hunter Thinks the Monkey Is Not Wise. The Monkey Is Wise, But Has Its Own Logic': Multiple Divination Systems and Multiple Knowledge Systems in Yorùbá Religious Life," Mei-Mei Sanford argues that, though partial and far from perfect, Yorùbá knowledge is a progressive and unending database that is locked within an innovative historic tradition. She presents short accounts gathered from her encounters with priests in Iragbiji town in Osun state, Nigeria, in order to illustrate the various knowledge sources in Ifá religious practice including *obi* (kola divination), *owo merindinlogun* (sixteen cowries), *orogbo* (bitter kola), dreams, and visions. Sanford's main goal is to complicate the sources of knowledge we investigate when researching Yorùbá religion. She argues that binaries limiting Ifá's validation in the academy—such as "privileging verbal over ritual knowledge; direct teaching over indirect, kinesthetic, and relational knowledge; men over women"—will continue restricting our scholastic reach if they remain unchecked.

Chapter 10, Wyatt MacGaffey's "Dagbon, Oyo, Kongo: Critical and Comparative Reflections on Sacrifice," challenges scholars of the Ifá tradition to reevaluate the terms "sacrifice" and "ancestral worship" with respect to African religions. He utilizes research by James Lorand Matory and Karin Barber to argue that dealings with spirits mirror transactions with Big Men, that is to say, wealthy men with massive social capital. The economic exchanges benefit both the supplicant and the receiver, since the òrìsà needs "food" in order to maintain his or her power and petitioners need the òrìsà's blessings in order to continually provide offerings. This leads MacGaffey to question long-standing theories about sacrifice; he disagrees with how Western thinkers separate religious, economic, and social relations when theorizing about religion. For this reason, he concludes that we must return to Marcel Mauss's word, "prestation," which unifies the religious and economic components integral to African religions.

In the eleventh chapter, "Ifá: The Quintessential Builder of Our Bank of Images," Akínwùmí Ìṣọlá suggests that proverbs, myths, and folktales are discourses to aid members of a society to live in harmony with each other. He identifies Ifá as a source of orature whose imagery offers useful models for today's society. Chapter 12, "*Odù Imole*: Islamic Tradition in Ifá and the Yorùbá Religious Imagination," is where Jacob K. Olupona discusses how Ifá orature contains many references to Islamic beliefs, and discusses an issue that has made scholars speculate about the relationship between the two traditions. One factor is clear, and that is that Islam entered Yorùbáland several centuries before Christianity; Islam and Yorùbá remained the only two Yorùbáland traditions until the arrival of Christian missionaries in the nineteenth century. The long interaction between Islam and the Ifá tradition inevitably led to significant borrowing, especially from Islam by the Ifá cosmology. This process seems inconsistent with Yorùbá's inclination to domesticate other traditions it encounters.

From the fifteenth to the nineteenth century, people from West Africa were taken to the Americas as slaves. They traveled with their knowledge of traditions, particularly Ifá. In the New World, this divination system took on new meaning and functions, and became a unique epistemology. It is this historical and cultural reality that makes the work of William Bascom on divinatory practices in Cuba useful to contemporary scholarship.

The third section of this volume, "Ifá in the Afro-Atlantic," explores the diasporic diffusion of Ifá divination across the Atlantic. Seven case studies cover spaces such as Brazil, Cuba, Trinidad, and the United States. Chapter 13, Velma Love's "Ifá Divination as Sacred Compass for Reading Self and World," investigates how African Americans in New York City and South Carolina became invested in Yorùbá religion. Deploying Margaret Drewal's notion of "Yorùbá ritual performance" as well as Victor Turner's conclusions, Love argues that Ifá is an instrument of spiritual and cultural relocation, while its practice empowers the participant to transcend separation and liminality to become reunited in the cyclic space of life's journey. Love concludes that Ifá divination operates "as a sacred compass locating self," a tool by which African Americans have relocated themselves spiritually and culturally. Ifá also can assist an individual to understand his or her "self" more accurately, by reinterpreting patterns and problems in his or her life. This essay opens a window on how Ifá tradition appeals to African Americans and the subsequent function it plays in one's personal development.

In chapter 14, "Ìtan Odù Òní: Tales of Strivers Today," John Mason traces the historical foundations of the Ifá corpus while drawing connections between sacred myths and historical records. Sacred myths in Ifá include the narratives associated with the concrete signs, called odù, that manifest via divination. Òdí Èjìogbè, one such odù, recounts a battle between Oyo kingdom and Dahomey, in which the Oyo warriors distract their opponents with ceremonious festivities in order to smite them in their defenseless drunken stupor. Interestingly, Mason offers an account from the odù Ifá Ìròsùn-Òsé to demonstrate Ifá narratives' relevance to African Americans. The last story mentioned here, odù Ifá Òsé-Èjìlá, explains how cowrie shells and brass money entered market spaces as valid compensation for trade. Mason pairs this account with historical records regarding cowrie and brass exchanges in Yorùbá markets. Overall, for scholars and practitioners Mason's chapter demonstrates the interconnections between sacred myth and historical record, between distant past events and our acute modern experiences.

In chapter 15, "Orunmila's Faithful Dog: Transmitting Sacred Knowledge in a *Lucumí* Orisha Tradition," Joseph M. Murphy undertakes a hermeneutic analysis of a *pataki* narrative about Orunmila and his dog in order to illustrate the principle of secrecy in Yorùbá divination. Murphy locates himself as an initiate and a scholar; he notes the restraints he faces when wearing either hat. For an initiate, *secrecy* means some knowledge ought not to be shared, because an inexperienced recipient may not comprehend it, making the knowledge dangerous to the hearer. On the other hand, teaching university students about Ifá demonstrates how some knowledge remains secret, "incapable of being transmitted because information without experience is not sacred knowledge." In effect, Murphy presents a methodological and ethical conundrum, one with which all students of Ifá must wrestle.

For Ysamur M. Flores-Peña, in chapter 16, "*Mofá* and the *Oba*: Translation of Ifá Epistemology in the Afro-Cuban *Dilogún*," sacred narratives in the *odù* corpus not only validate authority but also reinforce hierarchy. The transatlantic slave trade dislocated babalawo from practitioners in the new world, causing devotees in Cuba to create a more accessible divination technique: *dilogún*. The Lucumí *ẹsẹ Ifá* contains fewer stories than those found in the *ẹsẹ Ifá* of Nigeria. Modifications to the text also included the removal of characters and verbal adornments that proved irrelevant in the Atlantic world. Flores-Peña explains that "*Mofá*" abbreviates "*omo Ifá*," meaning "child of Ifá"—a direct reference to babalawo. It contrasts the *oriaté*, who emerged to provide services the babalawo would normally render. Babalawo must exist in tandem with *oriatés*, but the opposite is not true. Consequently, it becomes difficult for babalawo to maintain rank in Cuba's ever-evolving Creole culture. Flores-Peña concludes that researchers must study *Lucumí* with attention to how commonalities with African cultures are addressed in Cuba, while paying especially close attention to the role of the *obá oriaté*.

Whereas Flores-Peña discusses conflict between *oba oriatés* and babaláwó in *Lucumí*, in chapter 17, "The *Pai-de-santo* and the Babaláwo: Religious Interaction and Ritual Rearrangements within Orisha Religion," Stefania Capone investigates how the reintroduction of Ifá worship in Candomblé causes tension between the pais-de-santo (heads of spiritual societies) and the babalawo (masters of secrets). Capone explains that establishing a religious genealogy depends on mediumship—that is, one's ability to fall into trance. Only those who fall into trance may initiate new members. Yet babalawos claim that their authority rests on an ability to interpret Ifá. In the end, the movement to "Africanize" Candomblé caused historic rifts between religious houses. Capone admonishes those studying the globalization of Yorùbá religion to consider analytically the intracommunal tensions new ritual arrangements may ignite.

M. Ajisebo McElwaine Abimbola turns our attention to gender dynamics in Ifá traditions in chapter 18, "The Role of Women in the Ifá Priesthood: Inclusion versus Exclusion." McElwaine Abimbola argues that women can and must serve as Ifá priests. She grounds her argument in Ifá literature, claiming that because several verses identify female diviners, it is impossible to exclude women based on their sex. McElwaine Abimbola also argues that women are integral to Ifá practice. She cites an *ẹsẹ Ifá* in which Òsùmàrè, a female rainbow deity, divines for a client. In addition, she notes that certain *odù* themselves bear a specifically female identification. Above all, "Odù" refers to both the text and to Orunmila's wife, who has died but remains living on earth. McElwaine Abimbola's essay is transformative in that it reveals profound sources for women's crucial roles in Ifá traditions. She confirms that women are indispensable, and that restrictions on women's involvement demand deconstruction.

In chapter 19, "Transnational Ifá: The 'Readings of the Year' and Contemporary Economies of Orisa Knowledge," Kamari Maxine Clarke argues for connections between capitalism, diaspora identities, and religious consciousness that differ tangentially from the rootedness of the homeland's localized articulations. Clarke analyzes civic divination readings within the village, showing how interpretations of Ifá seek to explain global and national sociopolitical happenings rather than locate ancestors lost in the transatlantic slave trade. She suggests that the diaspora's identity now stems from post–Cold War consequences rather than the slave trade. The reading of the year, then, contextualizes African Americans in larger discourses about world events. Thus, the key theme in Clarke's essay is what she calls "diasporic technologies of religious consciousness."

While the previous sections focus on verbal arts, the final section, "Sacred Art in Ifá," explores visual arts and Ifá divination. These readings investigate the retention of the old with rapidly changing new media and its implications for sacrality in the digital age. In chapter 20, "The Creatures of Ifá," Philip M. Peek questions the meanings behind animal imagery in Ifá. Numerous mammalian, amphibian and semiamphibian, and avian creatures adorn divination boards, Osun staffs, and babalawo's satchels. But the literature in religious studies and art history stops short of explaining the cosmological significance these creatures represent. In his review of numerous essays from several fields, Peek expected to find common denominators among the animals, if not a universal significance. Surprisingly, his review of the literature reveals a lacuna. The parallel meanings between sacrificial animals and those that are meant as symbols of authority and *àse* or empowered speech, as in the Yorùbá case, require greater research. As a result, Peek's essay opens a new direction for ethnographic investigation in Ifá studies.

In chapter 21, "Of Color, Character, Attributes, and Values of Orunmila," Bolaji Campbell presents an authoritative piece on colors in Ifá, where the tripartite categories of *awo dudu* (black), *awo pupa* (red), and *awo funfun* (white) signify different meanings and ambiguities: for example, black may mean death or evil; red danger or sacrifice; white peace, goodness, and tranquility. Campbell describes colors applied to honorific ritual objects in order to suggest that each bears a particular meaning and thereby communicates distinct ideas about Orunmila and Esu. Campbell examines colors as they pertain to both deities.

Careful summaries of Yorùbá color spectra and applications allow the author to interpret the meanings contained in the colors on a diviner's bag.

In chapter 22, "Signs, Doors, and Games: Divination's Dynamic Visual Canon," Laura S. Grillo argues that the *odù* themselves comprise Ifá's canonical texts. Her idea shifts attention from the *ẹsẹ se Ifá* to the signs of Ifá. For Grillo, *ẹsẹ Ifá* are subject to innovation, but the *odù* determine what is normative. Grillo demonstrates how this visual canon contains discourse about divinities, the cosmos, and human beings in relation to their spiritual and physical environment. She shows how this information manifests itself in art and ritual. She compares Dogon and Ifá divination systems in order to strengthen her argument that signs constitute the visual canon in West Africa. Grillo's conclusion points to an equal and opposite dynamic in Yorùbá and Dogon divination: the signs establish the normative order, but diviners, clients, and artists put them into play through art and ritual.

In chapter 23, "Ifá: Visual and Sensorial Aspects," Henry John Drewal identifies seven senses at play in Yorùbá sacred art. The common five form the core components. The additional two, motion and "extrasensory perception" (ESP), are the author's theoretical intervention. *Sensiotics,* he argues, enables researchers to incorporate movement and trance in their examination of Yorùbá art. The cardinal points preoccupy Yorùbá beliefs. As such, they emphasize "positioning and movement—orienting oneself in order to move forward in life's journey." Motion, then, becomes critical to any researcher's tool kit if he or she seeks a well-rounded understanding. ESP, on the other hand, points to intuition and to the indeterminacy of synaesthesia. Essentially, Drewal's theory enables scholars to comprehend how Yorùbá sacred art projects an integrated African worldview in which balance, temperature, aural, oral, tactile and extrasensory perceptions allow one to know and be known in the world.

The final chapter is Akintunde Akinyemi's essay, "Art, Culture, and Creativity: The Representation of Ifá in Yorùbá Video Films." Akinyemi invokes Ifá's image in video films in which divinatory tools such as *ikin, iyèròsùn,* and *ibò* are replaced with an *opele* as a more convenient divination chain. Akinyemi argues that through the incorporation of Ifá in Yorùbá video films, the filmmakers are critiquing the politics of corruption as well as questioning the accuracy of divination. He wonders what methods there are to challenge the validity of Ifá divination. Akinyemi's essay challenges scholars in Ifá studies and African studies to consider carefully the ways in which new media reproduce indigenous African orature for social and political purposes.

While the papers in this volume have been written from different disciplinary perspectives, there is a unifying force within this compilation that can be summarized. First, all of the essays are concerned with exploring new areas of knowledge that Ifá espouses. Second, as a collection, this book is an exercise in applying Ifá epistemology to existential, pragmatic, and ontological questions facing our millennial societies. Third, the essays experiment with Ifá's applicability to interdisciplinary studies. Scholars from various disciplines articulate not only how their methodology interacts with Ifá, but how it connects with methodologies and theories advanced in other disciplines. Fourth, the Ifá conference at Harvard enabled these scholars to explore Ifá narratives in depth. While it is assumed that Ifá embodies 256 chapters of *odù*, it has not been clear how these oral texts can become a useful resource for hermeneutics. If it is assumed that Ifá is an encyclopedia of knowledge, then this edited volume enables scholars to show how different oral narratives can lend themselves to in-depth interpretations that can lead to new meanings. For example, Olupona's essay discusses how Ifá engages Islam, and he argues that virtually all the key issues that pertain to the understanding of Islam are discussed in Ifá—a non-Islamic text. Ultimately we are talking about intertextual, intercultural studies as they relate to Ifá scholarship. All the chapters in this volume point to one clear thing about Ifá: Ifá is not limited to a theoretical or ethnographic discourse; it shows how the performative is intertwined with academic explorations of Ifá divination.

Notes

1. Abímbọ́lá (1976), 43.
2. Ibid., 46.
3. Bascom (1969), 122.
4. Crowley and Dundes (1982), 465–467.

References

Abímbọ́lá, Wándé. 1976. *Ifá: An Exposition of Ifá Literary Corpus*. Ibadan: Oxford University Press Nigeria.
Bascom, William. 1969. *Ifá Divination: Communication Between God and Men in West Africa*. Bloomington: Indiana University Press.
Crowley, Daniel, and Alan Dundes. 1982. "Obituary: William Russel Bascom, 1912–1981." *Journal of American Folklore* 95: 378, 465–467.

PART I.
IFÁ ORATURE:
ITS INTERPRETATION AND TRANSLATION

1   *Ayajo* as Ifá in Mythical and Sacred Contexts

Ayo Opefeyitimi

IF *AYAJO* (MYTH-INCANTATION) is Ifá in the mythical and sacred contexts, the best angle from which to begin this essay is the definition of myth. In *Sacred Narrative: Readings in the Theory of Myth*, Lauri Honko gave a definition of myth that he regarded as descriptive and concise, and in which the gods, fundamental events, nature and culture, order, and continuity are foregrounded. According to Honko, a myth is "a story of the gods, a religious account of the beginning of the world, the creation, fundamental events, the exemplary deeds of the gods as a result of which the world, nature and culture were created together with all parts thereof and given their order, which still obtains." (1984, 49). Honko believed that this definition was "built on four criteria: form, content, function and context" (ibid.). Here, form is explained in terms of myth as sacred and symbolic narrative. Its content implicates the articulation of figures and deeds as verbalized in a narrative or poetic medium. The functions of myth are predicated in its ontological view of the world as it describes aspects of life and the universe. And the context of myth is ritualistic, wherein events once possible and operative can be exerted anew.

To complement the above, Harold Scheub wrote that:

> The ancient myth has to do with the supernatural, with gods and with transcendental wisdom, with mystical behavior, and awesome activities. . . . Regularly, ritualistically, through the theatrical re-enactment of the myths, we revisit the ancient times . . . the contexts for our lives. What we do occurs within the context of the ancient myths. Nothing is new; we only routinely re-enact the ancient myths, moving in the paths of our gods. (2002, 185)

Special attention is called to the issue of awesomeness and reenactment (implicating performance) as the wisdom of the great beyond. These issues are reflected in *Ayajo* myths of Ifá. In the following discussion, attention is given to salient passages where the nature, content, functions, and theoretical angles of *Ayajo* evince it is a Yorùbá type of sacred myth.

Specifically, the case of *Ayajo* as Ifá in "sacred" contexts concerns the use of symbols—verbal symbols and objects or materials—in the performance of the genre. O'Keefe described the material objects as "'anointed'—to symbolize that old feeling, that immanent excitement of power . . . objects that have become symbols of society" (1979, 248). According to Duncan (1961), they relate to the order of the society itself. Whoever controls such symbols must be obeyed, for in obeying we uphold the structure of our society. Thus, it can be said that one reason for the awesomeness of the contexts of *Ayajo* performance is the use of anointed symbolic objects and utterances.

Preliminaries to the Text of (*Ayajo*) Myth-Incantations

In Ifá divination contexts, the diviner uses the sacred chain (*opele*) or palm kernel (*ikin*) to find *odù* in connection with an inquirer's request. The verses of the *odù* (as related through the signatures of the material objects used in Ifá) are chanted in full. More often than not an appropriate sacrifice is performed; this depends on the urgency, prejudice, and readiness of the inquirer.

After the performance of the sacrifice, the diviner and inquirer assume that all will be well as far as the treated case is concerned. Meanwhile, if the inquirer keeps complaining about the same or a similar issue, the diviner arranges to tackle the problem the *Ayajo* way. Here, the diviner arranges with the inquirer to invoke the mythological events as contained in the original *odù*, since it contains the initial sacrifice performed. In other words, the process of borrowing (*yiya*) the events of a (primordial) day (*Ojo*) for use (*lo*)—that is, *yiya + ojo + lo* = ayajo (*lo*)—begins. This is premised upon the belief that any problem facing an individual in contemporary times has an equivalent in the past life of our ancestors, as read by Òrunmílà who was the first literary expert on earth in the Odù of Ifá.

Ayajo Myths as a Case Study

In Yorùbá orature scholarship, Afolabi Olabimtan has defined *Ayajo* Yorùbá sacred myths partly as "a word generally used to refer to the past in relation to the present . . . attachment to a divinity—Òrunmílà, associated with a particular odù-ifá, relate to an incident in the past, feature some lines of ofo in some instances . . . ancient Ifá priests are appealed to in Ayajo to help the reciter to achieve the purpose of the incantations" (1971, 4). In this excerpt Òrunmílà, the corpus of Ifá, relationships between past and present incidents, and the pragmatic achievement of purposes are mentioned. However, as I stated elsewhere:

> *Ayajo ni Imo asiri oruko, isele, Itan Iwase, majemu ayeraye ati ijinle akiyesi nipa iwa ewe, egbo tabi eda miiran, ti a n lo lode oni fun ifare, atubi ati abilu, gege bi a ti se awon asiri wonyen lojo sinu odù-Ifá, eyi to fa a ti a fi n kape Òrunmílà bi eleriiki o le fase si atubotan ti a n lepa.*

Myth-incantations are the knowledge of secret names, events, myths, old covenants and deeply rooted discoveries about the essence of herbs and roots or any other creatures, which are recounted in contemporary times for luck, as neutralizers and for evil, as those secrets are kept in the corpus of Ifá, which accounts for why we call upon Òrunmílà as a witness to accent the desires in view. (2010, 10)

This statement incorporates a number of aspects of the same genre, but does not reflect that the narrative is usually poetic in presentation.

Because the academic study of *Ayajo* is still in its infancy, this essay will undertake a proper definition of *Ayajo* so that readers can identify it whenever it is found or heard. Taking an example of *Ayajo* from the three broad types, this paper also aims at a critical analysis of representative examples. Specifically, the articulation of the following themes in the example under analysis will be treated: power of invocation, precedence, symbolic objects and covenants, the place of *Ayajo* in the *odù* of Ifá, the typology of *Ayajo*, the essence of primordial origin, verbal law, and the babalawo as a personification of the word in the society.

Typology of Ayajo (Myth-Incantations)

Broadly categorized, there are three types of *Ayajo*: luck attractant, neutralizers, and spells. Under the luck attractant are subtypes such as those meant for quick sales, soliciting love, and so on. The neutralizers comprise three major subtypes: cases (*Aforan*), protection against spells (*Isasi*), and witchcraft (*Eleye*). Each of the three subtypes has its own subgenres. The third major type is the one used for "spells" (or "evil-works" to employ Verger's [1977] language) to designate.

A close examination of the names in each category reveals their functionality. In other words, Yorùbá myth-incantations are typologically categorized and named in accordance with the notion of the functions performed.

The Thematic Content of an Ayajo

Of the three subtypes of *Ayajo*, witchcraft will serve as a case study. In the Yorùbá cultural worldview, once you are in sociological tune with the witches, you stand the chance of living a good long life and getting rich. This is in light of the fact adduced by O'Keefe that "a great deal of 'magic' (which I prefer to call 'myth-incantations') is little more than a defense against witches . . . the very opposite of every value the group stands for" (1979, 550).

Ayajo Atubi Eleye

Ela ro waa
Ela ro waa
Ela ro waa
Alagada-nla loruko a a paye
5   *Arabatasi loruko aa pele*
Bi a ba fi efun fun aye

Ara aye a ya gaga
Bi a ba sepe so Ogun
Ara ogun a le koko
10 *Ogun a sege*
Omo won nile Ife
Oun ni o bi Atepe
Bi o ba wa ri bee
A je wi pe:
15 *Omode lo ni n ma tele yii pe*
Ko ku bi afe ti n ku
Toun togboni, toun togboni
Agbalagba lo ni n ma tele yii pe
Ko ku bi aguntan se e ku
20 *Toun ti bolobolo enu re*
Bo ba se pe:
Iyami aje lo ni n ma tele yii pe
Ko ku bi adiye-opipi se n ku
Toun ti apada esee re mejeeji
25 *Omode lo ni n ma tele yii pe*
Ona-odi ni ko maa ba rorun, ona-odi
Agba lo ni n ma tele yii pe
Ona-odi ni ko maa ba rorun, ona-odi
Eye seye, fapa seye
30 *Eye seye, fese seye*
Eye be, fese be omowu-alagbede
O di wo o
Eye wole Alara
O pa omo Alara
35 *Eye wole Ajero*
O pa omo Ajero
Eye wole Orangun Ile-Ila,
O pomo Orangun Ile-Ila
Won ni nibo ni awon alawo tun ku si?
40 *Won lo sile Olori-aja-n-gbo-wewe.*
Awo ile Alara
Eye pa a
Won lo sile Boo-boo-laguntan-wo
Awo ile Ajero
45 *Eye pa a*
Won wole Afikori-oke
Ti n sawo Orangun Ile-Ila
Ogan ganke, awo pa a
Won gbera lo odo Òrunmílà

50 *Won ni kee gbo, kee to, aboru-aboye o baba*
    Won ni awon yoo pa o
    Awon yoo pa awon omoo re
    Awon yoo pa aboyun ilee re
    O o ni I se aseyori
55 *Òrunmílà wa dawon lohun pe,*
    E o le pami
    E o le pawon omoo mi
    E o si le paboyun ilee mi
    Emi yoo si se aseyori
60 *Won bi Òrunmílà pe,*
    Bawo ni oo ti se aseyori
    Òrunmílà ni mo ti mo oruko tiyaa eyin aje n je
    Emi yoo si soruko tiyaa eyin aje n je
    Awon aje ni haa haa haa!
65 *Ase o tun ku awon to moruko tajee n je laye*
    Òrunmílà ni Atinusoro loruko iya eyin aje n je
    Atedojokan loruko ti baba eyin aje n je
    Eyin aje gan-an ni Owawa-lakaka
    Awon aje ni o di eewo
70 *Ani se, o di oro eewo;*
    Won ni ki Òrunmílà wagbin-in apinnu meji
    Ki o ko sefunsefun lowo si i,
    Ki o pe Osa-meji lowo.
    Nitori oun ni odù to mawon aje waye
75 *Ki won bura Òrunmílà*
    Enikeni to ba je ninu aseje yii
    Ninu awon omo Òrunmílà,
    Awon yoo yonu si i
    Awon yoo si maa bowoo re
80 *Emi lagbaja omo lagbaja deni owo latoni lo*
    Nitori berin ba jeko,
    A bowo faluki
    Befon ba jeko,
    A bowo faluki
85 *Aje kan ki i gboju*
    Ko bale igi ajeofole, o seewo
    Osa meji waa lo ree sa ire gbogbo.
    Ti ni be lode aye wa femi lagbaja
    Ki ona owo nlanla si funmi
90 *Ki n gbo*
    Ki n to; ati bee bee lo

Ayajo (To Neutralize Witchcraft)

Ela descend fast
Ela descend fast
Ela descend fast
Life is called Owner-of-a-big-cutlass
5   The Earth is called Owner-of-garner-in-which-to-shine
If the whiting is given to life
Life will be very healthy
If we place a curse on Ogun
Ogun will become hardened
10 Ogun will relax
Their offspring in Ife
He was one who begot Longevity
If it were so!
It then means that
15 If the young is against my living for long
May she die as of a witch
With cultism, with cultism
The aged who is against my long-life
Should die as the sheep
20 With the dirt of its mouth
If it is
My-mother-the-witch who pronounces death upon me
She should die as the featherless fowl
With the curved sections of its legs
25 The young who is against my living for long
Should die the wrong way to heaven, the wrong way
The aged who says I should not grow old
Should die wrongly, wrongly
Birds are birds by virtue of their feathers
30 Birds are birds by virtue of their legs
The bird jumped, hit its legs with the blacksmith's anvil
Destruction resulted
The bird entered Alara's house
Killed Alara's son.
35 The bird entered Ajero's house
Killed Ajero's son.
The bird entered Orangun of Ila's house
He killed the son of the king of Orangun of Ile-Ila
He asked where else to find other cultists?
40 They went into Olori-aja-n-gbo-wewe's house
The priest in Alara's house

Birds killed him
They went into Boo-boo-laguntan-n-wo's house
The priest in Ajero's house
45 Birds killed him
They entered the house of Afikori-oke
Who was priest of Orangun-ile-Ila
He became lifeless, cultists killed him
They made for Òrunmílà's house
50 They greeted him as tradition demanded
They said we would kill you
We would kill your children
We would kill the pregnant in your house
You will not accomplish your goals
55 Òrunmílà answered them that,
You can't kill me
You can't kill my children
Neither can you kill the pregnant in my house
And I will accomplish my goals.
60 They asked Òrunmílà that,
How would you succeed.
Òrunmílà said because I know the mother of witches by name
And I will pronounce the name
The witches were astonished
65 Saying, so some still know witches' secret names!
Òrunmílà said that mother of witches are Atinusoro
Atedojokan is name for the father of witches
You witches are Owawa-lakaka
Witches said henceforth it became forbidden
70 And insisted, henceforth it became a forbidden issue
Òrunmílà was asked to procure two big snails.
Plus that which produces whiting
And invoke Osa Meji corpus alongside
Because "he" is the corpus that brought witchcraft to life
75 So as to covenant with Òrunmílà
Whoever eats out of this stuff
Amongst Òrunmílà's descendants
They will be merciful unto him/her
They will honor
80 I, So, child of So, becomes honorable henceforth
Because if the elephant vegetates,
It honors aluki leaves
If the buffalo feeds
It honors aluki leaves

85 No witch can be so daring
    As to alight on ajeofole tree, it is forbidden
    Osa Meji-go and gather the good things
    On earth for I, whose name is So
    For me to experience momentary breakthrough
90 For me to live long
    To live to old age.[1]

Exposition

It has been noted that genres such as the mythological types were created, propagated, and utilized for sociological reasons. For instance, Duncan noted that the practice of literature is concerned with specific social problems (1961, 59). This particular *Ayajo* is used for a long life. This is the preoccupation of line 12 in particular and lines 13–28 in general. Second, Duncan noted that "no one can finish a study of the sociology of literature without feeling deeply how much he has not said about words . . . for words are wondrous things. They evoke great power for evil as well as for good" (ibid., xi–xii). This observation was reechoed by Pettazzoni, who suggests that "the efficacy of myths . . . lies in the magic of the word, in its evocative power, the power of mythos in its oldest sense . . . as a secret and potent force" (1984, 103). To be sure, invocation of appropriate powers in the context of each *Ayajo* is intimately connected with belief in its efficacy.

Living on earth (lines 4 and 5) depends on the prejudice of the young (line 15), the old (line 18), and the witches (line 22). What makes this *Ayajo* so powerful is the coded messages, especially against witchcraft, that implicitly contain warnings. They include the secret names of the extended family members of witches. This is revealed in lines 66–68, and the issue of covenant between Òrunmílà (on behalf of his offspring) is revealed in lines 71–78. Succinctly put, the idea of coded words of metaphysical power, which some scholars translate as "magic," achieves the desired results. This is because "the magic of words is of the same stuff as the world that made us, and so it can go *straight into* us . . . spells can go *right into* a person's psychic organization, because it is itself constituted out of words" (O'Keefe 1979, 58, 63).

The thematic aspect of naming as a symbolic and powerful weapons of attack in the context of these myth-incantations cannot be underestimated. It is the basis of the "success" expected in this genre. The secrecy attached to the names accounts for their success. It is stressed in the discussion of the covenant, lines 69–75, and is so vital it must be sealed with the signature of the corpus of Osa Meji (line 73) for life. In the words of O'Keefe, it is through this connection that the orature piece can be considered a "charter myth" (1979, 301). This idea is what Olatunji (1984) regarded as "verbal law."

The interaction between the performer and the audience constitutes a reciprocal relationship. The performer of this *Ayajo* is the chanter, while the audience includes Ela (lines 1–3), Osa Meji (line 87), and the human participants in the context of performance as the querent. Notably, apart from the repetition in lines 1–3, the use of the verb "come" (*wa*) in line 87 is indicative of invocation. The phrase "go and gather" is a direct reference to the issue of errand, conditioned by the device of personification. Considering the aspect of narrative plot structure, Genette's (1972) consideration of the "order," "analepsis," and "prolepsis anticipation" are crucial to the present analysis. For instance, in the context of this poem, the issue of order implicates its separation into the beginning, the middle, and ending.

The first three lines constitute the beginning, an invocation to Ela who has the power to create order out of existence in the contexts of *Ayajo* performances. The middle of the poem can be found in lines 14 through 79. This section can be further subdivided as follows: lines 14–28, where the enemies of the *Ayajo* reciter or recipient were cursed; lines 33–54, where the activities of witchcraft are highlighted; and lines 55–79, which treat the theme of covenants made for the offspring of Òrunmílà. The ending consists of lines 80–91, where the performer of the myth uses the language of *ofo* (herb-incantations) to state what has transformed him or her into a "touch-me-not-oh-you-witches" as well as to reiterate the good things desired of life.

The above tripartite division should be expected; as Powell has said, "myth is a traditional story . . . which is to say, it has a plot (a threefold narrative structure consisting of a beginning, a middle and end)" (1995, 2). Furthermore, Dundes notes that for scholars of myth such as Claude Lévi-Strauss, "it is the underlying 'schemata' rather than the 'sequences' of myth that is more important" (1976, 83). It is the "tension" (Scheub 2002, 15) created by the connection between those sections of the mythological poetry that is more important for the efficacy for which the poetry is tagged "*ewi-awise* (efficacious poetry)" (Bamgboṣe 1984).

In discussing the narrative plot structures, the analeptic portion of this poem is the section that states the precedence (the initial event recounted) in lines 34–89, upon which the solution for the present desire of overcoming witchcraft (in the context of this particular myth) resides. The prolepsis is the section that deals with the expected desire of the performer of these myth-incantations. This is especially revealed in lines 87 and 88, where the symbolic personality of Osa Meji was involved in the act of bringing the good things of life, apart from the issue of victory over witchcraft depicted in lines 15–28.

Apart from the narratological discussion above, there is a need for a hermeneutic explanation of the more difficult words, phrases, or sentences. For instance, the allusion to Ogun (god of war) as their "offspring in Ife" is crucial because Ife is the original place where Òrunmílà composed *Ayajo*. In this context, Ogun becomes a divinity symbolic of victory, because according to Froman "origins are a part of the language of power" (1992, 15).

In lines 29–32, the *Ayajo* employs many stylistic devices that invoke repetition, parallelism, phonaesthetics, and onomatopoeia; they present a kind of ominous imagery aimed at standardizing the originality of the narrative poem. The rationale behind the use of language in this sense can be found in Smith's statement that "in the execution of literature, precision and secret knowledge becomes vital, its mystique is frequently impenetrable to non-initiates, the numinous is often invoked and terror instilled as a means of defamiliarization" (1982, 5). Thus, the reference to a blacksmith's anvil (line 31) in this context is a mystical way of invoking the numinous to defamiliarize, while the imagery of destruction (line 32) is meant to inspire terror. In the same vein, personifications and animations such as are observed in lines 40, 43, 46, and especially in 68 where the name given to witches connotes mockery, are "where we must compete with sacred power, [and] begin at once to reduce this power. Magical art initiates this through mockery, raillery, derision and scorn . . . As we attach ludicrous symbols to a role, we neutralize its power" (Duncan 1961, 23). Clearly the desire to neutralize the atrocities of witchcraft is the essence of this piece of the narrative poem.

The Issues of Filial Relations, Authority, and Efficacy in *Ayajo*

So far, our analysis has been premised upon the integration of aspects of four theories into one. These theories are narratology (Genette 1972), sociology of literature (Duncan 1961; Bamidele 2000; Baldick 2004, 238), hermeneutics (Eagleton 1983; Heidegger 1962; Gadamer 1976), and the metaphysical theory of myths (Preminger and Brogan 1993). In my dissertation, "A Literary Analysis of Ayajo in Yorùbáland," these theories have been synchronized and realized as "Narrasobeneutics" This new theory can be split into the following:

Narra	+	So	+	Be	+	Neutics
1	+	2	+	3	+	4

1	"Narra"	is a shortened form of "narralology"
2	"So"	is a shortened form of "sociology of literature"
3	"Be"	is the most important verb in the shortened sentence, "So be it" which represents, describes or implicate the notion of "metaphysics"
4	"Neutics"	is my own way of representing "hermeneutics" in this context

While 1, 2 and 4 have been taken care of, 3 implicates the issue of efficacy and explains why *Ayajo* poems are regarded as an incantation or as efficacious poetry; it therefore requires further explanation.

Babcock suggested that "we use the term *metanarration* to refer specifically to narrative performance and discourse and to those devices which comment upon the narrator, the narrating, and the narrative both as message and code" (1977, 67). The following metanarration poem, recorded from Chief Esegba of Il-esa (a town in Osun state, Nigeria), will serve as an example:

> Tumisi ni omo Ewi
> Seere ni omo Osu
> Osoorowo ni omo iyami-osoronga
> Lorun ni won ti n pin opon
> 5 Igba ti won pe leyin
> La fi n debo nideyin won
> Nigba ti won de
> Won lawa ta lo n debo nideyin awon
> A ni awa
> 10 Tumisi omo Ewi
> Seere omo Osu ati
> Osoorowo omo iyami-osoronga ni
> Won ni bawo la se n da a?
> A nib o bah u meji
> 15 A o tekan
> Bo ba hukan
> A o te meji
> Won ni ki la n pe e?
> A ni Oyekulogbe!
> 20 Won ni ki awa maa je
> Ewi awo ode isalaye
> Won ni awon yoo maa je
> Egba awo ode-orun
> Eyi ewi aye ba wi
> 25 Oun naa legba orun n gba
> Dandan ni

> Tumisi is the son of Ewi
> Seere is the son of Osu
> Osoorowo is the son of witches
> The tray [object of Ifá] was shared from heaven
> 5 It was because they were late
> That we divined in their absence
> When they arrived
> They asked about those who divined in their absence
> We answered that we were
> 10 Tumisi is the son of Ewi
> Seere is the son of Osu

> Osoorowo the son of Iyami-Osoronga are the ones
> They asked about how we'd been divining
> We said if we perceived two signatures
> 15 We marked one
> When we perceived one signature
> We marked two
> They asked about the name we gave to such an arrangement
> We said Oyekulogbe
> 20 They asked us to be known as
> Sayers—the secret keeper on earth
> They would be known as
> Receivers—the secret keeper in heaven
> That which the Sayers of the earth say
> 25 Is what the Receivers of heaven will sanction
> So-be-it

In this poem, issues of filial relations (lines 1–3), test and measurement (lines 13–19), conferment of oratory authority (lines 20–23), and efficacy (line 24–26) are implicated.

In the context of the *Ayajo* Atubi Eleye cited earlier, however, the issue of filial relations is more assertively stated in lines 76–79: "Whoever eats out of this stuff / Amongst Òrunmílà's descendants / They will be merciful unto his descendants / They will honor." To buttress this point, Abímbọ́lá noted that:

> *Niwon igba ti onibeere yi ti ti rubo, o ti di omo Ifá . . .*
> *Idi niyi ti o fi y e ki eeyan o maa rubo, ki oluware o*
> *le je omo awon oisa, ki Òrunmílà o si le ro ejo nipa*
> *oluware . . .*

> Since this client had performed the sacrifice, s/he
> had become the offspring Ifá . . . Hence the need
> for one to constantly perform sacrifice, so that the
> person can be adopted by the divinities, to enable
> Òrunmílà to solicit on one's behalf . . . (1977, 120–121)

As far the issue of authority is concerned, the chanters of *Ayajo* are usually the babalawo. In the context of the metanarration poem, the "sayers of the earth" and "Òrunmílà's descendants" are the babalawo, or other people who have been let into the secrets of *Ayajo* by virtue of which they have become adherents or followers of Òrunmílà. This is one of the reasons Eric Dardel refers to chiefs as "the word of the clan" (1984, 233).

Now, apart form the last line realized in Yorùbá as "dandan ni," translated as "so-be-it," efficacy in *Ayajo* depends not only on the symbolic objects but also on the notion of authority. For instance, as Ray described it: "The question is not a matter of the words themselves as mere sounds, but the culturally defined authority, which is exercised in the act of uttering them. Thus the notion of powerful speech is based on the socio-linguistic fact that when authorities speak, things usually happen" (1973, 28). This explains the status of those who pronounce "charter words" in the society.

With specific reference to the genre of *Ayajo* apart from the issue of authority, some other intertwined variables in the efficacy of the poetry are evident in the words of Abímbọ́lá:

> *Awon Yorùbá gbagbo pupo ninu ofo paapaa ofo Ifá tabi ayajo. Won gba pe Ifá mo oruko asiri ti gbogbo aisan n je. Bee naa ni ifá se mo oruko ewe ati egbo kookan, o si tun mo oruko asiri awon ebora ati irunmole ti n gbe ile-aye. . . . Ifá mo gbogbo majemu ti awon ebora, aje ati aisan orisiirisii ba gbogbo awon oosa da. Leyin igba ti Ifá ba pe . . . oruko . . . yoo na an lo si inu Odù ti o so idi re . . .*

The Yorùbá believe strongly in incantations especially Ifá incantations or ayajo. They agree that Ifá knows the secret names, which all ailments bear. In the same way, Ifá knows the names of each herb and root, and equally knows the secret names of supernatural beings and divinities who live on earth. . . . Ifá knows all the covenants which supernatural beings, witches and ailments covenanted with all divinities. After Ifá might have invoked . . . names . . . he will refer to the appropriate *odù* which narrate the reason(s) . . . (1977, 120)

Evidently, variables in the efficacy of *Ayajo*, such as revealed in the above quotation, include the knowledge of secret and sacred names of human, animate, inanimate, or supernatural beings, primordial covenants, and appropriate *odù* corpora of Ifá.

This chapter began with a review of the definitions of myths in world mythological scholarship by notable scholars. This was followed by consideration of the views of some Yorùbá scholars on *Ayajo*, which was designated as "myth-incantations." After providing a contextual definition, the place of *Ayajo* in Ifá divination systems was considered. In trying to advance the typology of *Ayajo*, four categories were tabled to demonstrate the many types. In treating the thematic content of *Ayajo*, an important type was selected and its structure was subjected to the tools of "narra-so-be-neutics"—a new theory incorporating five existing theories of myth. Through the use of the theory, the sociological functions, narratological plot structure, style of hermeneutical import, and efficacy of the narrative poetry of focus were clearly explicated in order to evince how this theoretical approach has shown the variegated aspects of *Ayajo* as a tale of power in the Yorùbá cultural worldview.

Notes

1. All translations are mine unless otherwise indicated.

References

Abímbọ́lá, Wándé. 1977. *Awon Oju Odù Mereedinlogun.* Ibadan: University Press.
Babcock, Barbara A. 1977. "The Story in the Story: Metanarration in Folk Narrative." In *Verbal Art as Performance,* edited by Richard Bauman, 61–79. Prospect Heights, IL: Waveland Press.
Bamgboṣe, Ayọ, and Oladele Awobuluyi. 1984. *Yoruba Metalanguage: A Glossary of English-Yoruba Technical Terms in Language, Literature, and Methodology.* Vol. 2. Lagos: Nigeria Educational Research Council.
Baldick, Chris. 2004. *The Concise Oxford Dictionary of Literary Terms.* Oxford: Oxford University Press.
Bamidele, Lawrence Olanrele. 2000. *Literature and Sociology.* Ibadan: Stirling-Horden Publishers.
Dardel, Eric. 1984. "The Mythic." In *Sacred Narratives: Readings in the Theory of Myth,* edited by Alan Dundes. Berkeley: University of California Press. 225–243.
Duncan, Hugh Dalziel. 1961. *Language and Literature in Society: A Sociological Essay on Theory and Method in the Interpretation of Linguistic Symbols with a Bibliographical Guide to the Sociology of Literature.* New York: Bedminster Press.
Dundes, Alan. 1976. "Structuralism and Folklore." *Studia Fennica* 20, no. 1076: 75–93.
——, ed. 1984. *Sacred Narratives: Readings in the Theory of Myth.* Berkeley: University of California Press.
Eagleton, Terry. 1983. *Literary Theory: An Introduction.* Oxford: Clarendon Press.
Froman, Creel. 1992. *Language and Power: Books I & II.* Atlantic Highlands, NJ: Humanities Press.
Gadamer, Hans-Georg. 1976. *Philosophical Hermeneutics.* Translated by David E. Linge. Berkeley: University of California Press.
Genette, Gérard. 1972. *Narrative Discourse: An Essay in Method.* Ithaca, NY: Cornell University Press.
Heidegger, Martin. 1962. *Being and Time.* Translated by John Macquarrie and Edward Robinson. San Francisco: Harper.
Honko, Lauri. 1984. "The Problem of Defining Myth." In *Sacred Narrative: Readings in the Theory of Myth,* edited by Alan Dundes, 41–52. Berkeley: University of California Press.
O'Keefe, Daniel Lawrence. "A General Sociological Theory of Magic." PhD diss., New School for Social Research, 1979.
Ọlatunji, Ọlatunde. 1984. *Features of Yorùbá Oral Poetry.* Ibadan: University Press.
Opefeyitimi, Joseph Ayo. 2010. "Itupale Alawomo-Litireso Fun Ayajo Ni Ile Yorùbá: A Literary Analysis of Ayajo in Yorùbáland." PhD diss., Obafemi Awolowo University.
Pettazonni, Rafaelle. 1984. "The Truth of Myth." In *Sacred Narratives: Readings in the Theory of Myth,* edited by Alan Dundes. Berkeley: University of California Press, 98–109.
Powell, Barry B. 1995. *Classical Myth.* Englewood Cliffs, NJ: Prentice Hall.
Preminger, Alex, and Terry V. F. Brogan, eds. 1993. *The New Princeton Encyclopedia of Poetry and Poetics.* Princeton, NJ: Princeton University Press.
Ray, Benjamin. 1973. "Performative Utterances in African Rituals." *History of Religions* 13, no. 1: 16–35.

Scheub, Harold. 2002. *The Poem in the Story: Music, Poetry and Narrative*. Madison: University of Wisconsin Press.

Smith, Allan Gardner. 1982. "The Occultism of the Text." *Poetics Today* 3, no. 4: 5–20.

Verger, Pierre Fatumbi. 1977. "Poisons (*oró*) and Antidotes (*èrò*): Evil Works (*àbìlù*) and Protection from Them (*ìdáàbòbò*). Stimulants and Tranquilizers. Money-Wives-Children." Seminar Series 1: 296–353. Ilé-Ifè: Department of African Languages and Literatures, University of Ifè.

2 Continuity and Change in the Verbal, Artistic, Ritualistic, and Performance Traditions of Ifá Divination

Wándé Abímbọ́lá

IN MANY PARTS of Yorùbáland,[1] it is quite common to witness how an assembly of Ifá priests sternly and sharply denounce their colleagues who ascribe an incorrect *ese* (verse of Ifá) to a particular *odu* (chapter of Ifá sacred literature). One may also be chastised for omitting a significant part of an *ese* in the course of the verbal rendition of an Ifá text. Such acts of omission are rarely forgiven. These ritual techniques are taken seriously and punished immediately by alerting the culprit to his errors, stopping the performance and thereby putting him to ridicule.

I vividly remember my first lessons of Ifá with Ifádayiiro, the late Oluwo (chief priest) of Akeetan Oyo in 1963. I had recently been appointed as a junior research fellow in Yorùbá studies at the University of Ibadan. As part of my role, I was charged with the responsibility of collecting, transcribing, and translating verses of Ifá for the Institute of African Studies where I was working. Later, I returned to visit Ifádayiiro, a great friend of my father's and an accomplished babaláwó, with whom I had studied Ifá briefly twenty-two years earlier.[2] On this occasion, I brought a tape recorder and recorded a few verses of the *odù Eji Ogbe* recited by my teacher. I then stopped the tape and played it back to find out if my recording was good. Ifádayiiro heard his voice on tape and warned me gravely never to record his voice again! I then turned off the tape recorder and started to write down his information in an exercise book. But my teacher was not comfortable with that either. It took the intervention of my father for him to agree to continue teaching me. In the end, my apprenticeship with him did not last more than a few days.

One early morning, he came to our house and told my father that he could no longer continue to teach me because he was afraid that I would record his voice or write down his information. He would agree to continue to teach only if I agreed to study without a tape recorder or an exercise book—that is, if the teachings only took place completely through an oral medium. I continued my research with Ifádayiiro, but never made the mistake of using a tape recorder or writing down information in his presence. Fortunately, other priests agreed to my recording them and writing down their material (though at times reluctantly).[3]

I have narrated these incidents to demonstrate how very stoutly Ifá priests of Yorùbáland have resisted certain aspects of change and how very faithfully they believe they have kept the tradition, which is essentially an oral tradition. The interesting thing is that change or deliberate creativity is built into and has become an integral part of the tradition of Ifá. A closer examination will reveal that what is being resisted is not change per se, but falsification or vulgarization. This is especially the case when the change is imposed from outside through a medium or an agency that the Ifá priest considers alien or one which, for one reason or another, he may not find trustworthy.

In this essay, I examine the issue of continuity and change in the traditions of Ifá divination, ranging from the retention of oral/verbal texts to changes in the rituals as practiced in both Africa and the African diaspora. I also focus on how these divination traditions become modified in the context of performance before an audience or with the accompaniment of music.

Continuity and Change in Ifá Verbal Arts

I begin with an examination of Ifá as a verbal art and with the elements of continuity and change in the process of chanting, rendition, or transmission of Ifá as an oral literary form. In the eight-part structure of *ese Ifá*, which are the sacred oral narratives recited during divination, there is a moment where the Ifá priest can use his own words to render the plot of his story the way he wants. However, there are also certain parts of the same structure where he is not allowed to deviate from the text as it was given to him by his master.

In previous studies, I attempted a detailed analysis of the structure of *ese Ifá*, especially in my book *Ifá: An Exposition of Ifá Literary Corpus* (1976), which contains a chapter on the subject. The structure of *ese Ifá* reveals a startling combination of a constant attempt to preserve and retain a given oral text while providing the babaláwó with a degree of creative innovation with regard to the structure of *ese Ifá*. Thus, the first part of *ese Ifá* enumerates the name or names of previous babaláwó who first chanted the particular *ese Ifá* in question, while the second part mentions the names of the previous clients for whom the divination was performed. The third part mentions the occasion or reasons for the divination. The Ifá priest must try as much as possible to render these first three parts exactly as they were presented to him by his teacher. He is not permitted to make use of his own words to create anything new in this part of the structure. The same is also true for the last part, part 8, where the Ifá priest draws a fitting conclusion or moral to his own story. With part 8, however, he has the freedom to chant the section as a song or to render it in poetry or sometimes in free verse tending toward prose. Most accomplished babaláwó render this part in verse or sing it, depending on their audience and other circumstances that may affect their creative decision.

Broadly speaking, these four parts of *ese Ifá* structure in particular are obligatory for the babaláwó to chant as he learned them from his teacher. But even here, nuances of his own personal use of language or the dialect of the Yorùbá language that he speaks may vary his material to some extent. Such variations, however, are predictable once the researcher becomes familiar with the babaláwó and the dialect he speaks. We can therefore conclude that these four parts of the structure of *ese Ifá* (parts 1, 2, 3, and 8) are not only obligatory, but fairly conservative with regard to innovation.

This, however, is not the same with the remaining parts of the structure of *ese Ifá*, parts 4 through 7. The fourth part contains the instructions of the babaláwó to his client, while the fifth part indicates whether or not the client complied with the instructions. The sixth part reveals what happened to the client after he or she carried out or refused to carry out the instructions. The seventh part contains the reaction of the client to the joy or sorrow that has resulted from the process of divination. In these middle parts, a babaláwó is permitted to render his material in his own words, while of course being faithful to the plot of the story as he learned it from his teacher. Here, a babaláwó can employ ordinary prose to share the divinatory message. Only accomplished priests render this part in poetry or free verse, as this part of the structure of *ese Ifá* does not easily lend itself to chanting. Indeed, some babaláwó do not deliver these four parts at all, in which case the *ese* becomes a short one.

We can thus conclude that parts 4 through 7 of the structure of *ese Ifá* are optional to a certain extent. If the babaláwó wants to tell a complete story, he may chant parts 4 through 7, and he is further entitled to use his own words in chanting them either in poetry or free verse, or in speaking them in ordinary prose. If parts 1 through 3 and part 8 are conservative, we can say that in contrast, parts 4 through 7 are far more dynamic and provide greater room for creative interpretation. As such, we can ascertain that within the structure of *ese Ifá* (any *ese Ifá*) there is a constant struggle between tradition or continuity and creativity or dynamism. As we shall see, a true *ese Ifá* and an accomplished babaláwó must pass both tests; the babaláwó must maintain a balance between what was handed over to him by his master and his own genius as a storyteller and master of the Yorùbá language.

Other factors that may affect continuity and change include contact with some other neighboring languages such as Nupe, Fon, Ewe, Gun, or Gan. This leads to the inclusion of lines, phrases, or sentences from the languages of the neighbors of Yorùbá peoples in some parts of the *ese Ifá* structure. This happened in the past and may still be happening today in the twenty-first century, because priests of Ifá from neighboring West African ethnic groups traveled in large numbers and still travel to a lesser extent today to Yorùbáland to study the tradition of Ifá.

The use of music at times also contributes to the productivity and creativity of recitations of Ifá verses. In some instances, one performs before a knowledgeable audience with the accompaniment of musical instruments such as *agogo, ipese (aran), bata,* or *dundun,* in which case the babaláwó may have to present his repertoire in the form of *iyere,* singing or chanting the entire *ese.* Needless to say, only an accomplished master priest can attempt this.

Finally, with regard to continuity and change in *ese Ifá* as an oral tradition, what happens when the verses are written down? Indeed, how might the corpus of knowledge have been transformed if all *ese Ifá* became inscribed as well as recounted? Certainly the language of *ese Ifá* would have become fixed; creativity in the use of language in the process of rendering *ese Ifá* would have become circumscribed and stifled. Is this the reason why Ifádayiiro was afraid of having his material recorded and written down? I cannot explore this important point in detail here, but suffice it to say that writing down a divinatory material like Ifá has its own consequences, both good and bad, for the future of such a sacred and oral literature.

Continuity and Change in Ifá Visual Arts

I now turn to the visual arts to examine the nature of continuity and change in this arena. Of all the numerous *òrìṣà* of the Yorùbá, none has more artifacts than the spirit of Ifá. That is why it is referred to as *Baba alohum ola ju egbee lo* ("father who has more treasures than his colleagues"). Most of these treasures of Ifá have found their way into museums and private collections all over the world, as a result of large-scale Christianization and Islamization of Yorùbá peoples. Unfortunately, for the greater part of the twentieth century, many of these transactions have led to the outright sale or theft of these treasures. The interesting thing is that more and more artifacts, such as the *opon Ifá* (divination tray), *iroke* (divination tapper), *agere Ifá* (wooden dishes for the sacred palm nuts), and beaded bags of Ifá, are once again being created for ritual use. This reveals that there is still a need for many of these ritual implements in the contemporary age, and that they also have significant implications for the collecting world, as they demonstrate the cultural and social relevancy of artifacts that are being created anew today.

In traditional Yorùbá society, a babaláwó was allowed to use all sorts of beaded objects, such as sandals, bags, necklaces, bracelets, and even crowns worn by high-ranking priests. Most of these beads are no longer being produced on the African continent. They are now produced in the Americas and in Europe, because the indigenous technology virtually collapsed in Africa. The most important beads of Ifá are the traditional green and maroon beads known as *otutu* and *opon*, which all devotees (*omo isode*) and priests of Ifá wear as necklaces or bracelets. In Cuba and the rest of the African diaspora, the color for Yorùbá initiates has been changed to light green and yellow. Generally speaking, babaláwó in the diaspora make greater use of beads than their counterparts in Africa. This is true of the priesthood of the other *òrìṣà* as well.

The use of wooden objects is less common in the diaspora than in the West African context. Most babaláwó of Yorùbáland hold a wooden, beaded, or ivory *iroke* (divination tapper) in their hands regularly as part of their regalia. Babaláwó also make use of the *opon Ifá* (divination bowl) for divination purposes. This practice is becoming more popular in the diaspora, where it had gone into virtual extinction in the past due to the lack of artists and materials with which to produce them.

I was pleasantly surprised to see some of the wooden objects of Ifá, such as *iroke* and especially *opon Ifá*, still being used in Cuba during my first visit there in 1987. I was presented with a unique wooden divining bowl by the Acasa de Africa, which I still cherish.[4] It is round and about ten inches (twenty-five centimeters) in diameter. The interesting thing about this object is that it has a tiny head of Esu on four of the five parts usually recognized by babaláwó as:

Iwaju opon
Eyin opon
Olubu lotuun
Olokanran losi
Aarin opon nita orun.

Front part of *opon*
Back part of *opon*
Olubu on the right
Olokanran on the left
The middle of *opon* is a forecourt of heaven.[5]

In the diaspora, there are no decorations around the fringes of *opon Ifá* as is customary in Yorùbáland. Furthermore, the middle part of the *opon* is less hollow than it is on the African continent. Very likely, it was carved from a wood native to Cuba, as it is heavier than any other *opon Ifá* of its size that I have seen in Yorùbáland. It appears that production of such wooden objects was not widespread in Cuba and probably died out long ago. Most babaláwó of the diaspora (including Cuba) now buy their *iroke* and *opon Ifá* from vendors in the Americas, who sell contemporary and ancient objects of Ifá from West Africa.

In the past, the *opele* (divining chain) was made from coconut shells in the diaspora, since the *opele*—the natural fruit of a tree in Yorùbáland that bears the same name—from which it is obtained does not grow in Cuba. Nowadays, *opele* are being imported to the Americas and other parts of the world where Yorùbá-derived religions are practiced. Metallic *opele* made of brass, copper, or certain other metals produced on the African continent are also regularly sold in the Americas.

An interesting change has occurred with respect to *opa orere,* also known as *osun,* handled by senior babaláwó. In Yorùbáland, this staff is usually made of iron. Rattles, also made of iron, are attached to the sides of the staff in order to create a particular musical effect. Babaláwó typically use these staffs as walking sticks, and when the staff lands with its pointed base on the ground, the rattles produce the sound "*jin-win-rin-rin.*" When people indoors or on the streets hear this sound as a babaláwó walks down the street, they salute the babaláwó from wherever they are (even inside their own rooms) with shouts of *aboruboye* (may your sacrifices be accepted and blessed). In Africa, the top of an *orere* staff is crowned by *eye kan* (the lone pigeon), who watches over the affairs of a babaláwó even in his absence. The following Ifá chant originates from one of the chapters of the Ifá divinatory orature. The purpose of chanting it is to invoke the power of the *orere* staff to protect the diviner and members of his household.

> *Oloniimoro tunle se demi o*
> *Eye tunle se*
> *Erukuku tunle se demi o*
> *Eye tunle se.*

> Oloniimoro, look after my house in my absence
> Bird, look after my house
> Erukuku, look after my house in my absence
> Bird, look after my house.[6]

In Cuban *Lukumi* and *Santería,* the Osun (also the name of a deity) is a ritual object given to new initiates of any *òrìṣà,* and unlike in Yorùbáland, the object is not restricted to a babaláwó. Furthermore, it is made of a zinclike material, and does not function as a walking stick. The Osun is about ten inches (twenty-five centimeters) high compared with the West African type, which can be in excess of three feet (ninety centimeters), depending on the height of its owner. Moreover, the top of a Cuban Osun is dominated by a rooster rather than a pigeon. However, the Osun, in both Yorùbáland and Cuba, is highly regarded as a ritual, sacred object. In fact, in both regions, it is believed to be an *òrìṣà* in its own right. It must never be allowed to fall with its sides lying on the ground. Hence the babaláwó keeps it in a sacred corner of his shrine and makes sacrifices to his Ifá. If it accidentally falls on the ground, a special sacrifice must be made to restore its ritual potency. That is why we have the following saying among Ifá priests: "*Ooro gan gaan gan la a bosun* (Osun is to be found standing erect at all times)."

Changes in Ifá Rituals

Another area of continuity and change in the traditions of Ifá divination is the transmission of particular rituals from Africa to the diaspora. The African diaspora seems to be more conservative than continental Africa with regard to the practice of rituals and ceremonies. It seems that having lost a good part of the sacred orature and also the Yorùbá language as an everyday vehicle of thought, the diaspora has focused greater attention on observance of the innumerable details of rituals. As a result, the Yorùbá religion appears to be much simpler and less costly in West Africa than it has become in the Americas. The commitment of diaspora devotees to detailed observance of rites seems to have led to something of a preoccupation with ritual prescription. From this particular interpretation of religion, one might infer that members of the diaspora propose that the most essential aspect of òrìṣà religion is the observance of minute rituals and the acquisition of numerous vessels of the òrìṣà. However, many other devotees in the diaspora maintain that these rites are simply one component of worship and belief.

One can still observe significant areas of change that have come about over the years as a result of transmissions to the diaspora. A few examples will suffice. In the diaspora, coconuts are used instead of *obi* (kola nut) for ritualistic purposes, including divination. This is due to the simple fact that the kola nut tree does not thrive in the Americas. Attempts have been made to plant it in Brazil, but where it thrives, it does not produce any fruit. Hence, in Brazil, Cuba, Trinidad and Tobago, and elsewhere, coconuts were used instead of *obi* until recently, when the latter became more accessible by importation.

There also seems to be a greater emphasis on blood sacrifice in the diaspora than in Yorùbáland, where *epo pupa* (red palm oil) is sometimes used to symbolize blood. That is why people say: "*E tapo si i, ko debo*" ("pour palm oil on it so that it becomes a sacrifice"). There seems to be a greater emphasis on feeding the òrìṣà with dishes of well-known food items in West Africa. Except when animals are used to cleanse the sick or for some other cleansing work, most animals—such as goats, rams, sheep, fowl, birds, fish, and rodents—that are slaughtered for the òrìṣà are cooked and eaten instead of being thrown away.

Some of the food items of Yorùbáland have been preserved in the diaspora. A good example is *akara* (bean cake), a popular food item used for rituals in West Africa and also sold on the streets of Brazil. It appears that *olele,* popularly known as *mom-mom* (another pudding made with black-eyed peas) is not well known in the diaspora, although it is now being introduced. Contact with European and Amerindian cuisine as well as with cuisine from other parts of Africa seems to have had a radical effect on the food culture of Yorùbá religious communities in the diaspora.

As far as food is concerned, cuisine and materials for its preparation have not simply been influential from east to west; Africa has also borrowed from its own diaspora. An important example is a dish made from cassava that Yorùbá peoples in West Africa call *gaari,* a grainlike flour made by grating cassava, fermenting it, and frying it. This food, which is known as *farofa* in Brazil and which originated from the American Indians, is now the staple food of Yorùbá peoples in West Africa. Even the name of the flat metal implement used in grating the cassava has been adopted in the Yorùbá language from Portuguese. The Yorùbá call it *gareta,* and the original Portuguese word is pronounced almost the same way but spelled *garreta.*

Nourishment is at the very center of Yorùbá religion. Feeding a person or an *òrìṣà,* even an ordinary object of nature, is a means of serving that being or entity, nourishing it, saluting and respecting it, and proclaiming its right to exist and flourish in the world. The Yorùbá believe that when we feed a person or an *òrìṣà,* or any other ritual objects or creatures of nature, we can reasonably expect them to be on our side or even serve as our "messengers" in communicating our needs and desires to the unseen world of spirits. It is for precisely this reason that sacrifices made of food items prove so essential in Yorùbá rituals and ceremonies.

Continuity and Change in Ifá Performance

One final area of this examination of change and continuity is the issue of performance, which is a highly developed area of Ifá tradition. The most important form of performance in Ifá tradition is the chanting of *iyere,* with or without the accompaniment of instruments. *Iyere* is a special chant in Ifá rendered by the most accomplished babaláwó. The Yorùbá word used for "to chant," *iyere si sun,* literally means "to cry." The same word is used for *ijala,* the poetry of hunters and devotees of Ogun. So we say *"sun iyere"* ("chant *iyere"*) and *"sun ijala"* ("chant *ijala"*). This means that both *iyere* and *ijala* are elegies chanted with considerable emotional expression. This aspect of Ifá has largely been lost in the diaspora.

Where *iyere* is chanted in Africa, it is often accompanied with music made with *agogo* (iron gongs beaten with sticks) or *ipese* (also known as *aran*), which is a special drum used only in the worship of Ifá. Neither *agogo* nor *ipeses* are currently used in the diaspora, though other ritual instruments play an important role in sacred ceremonies. Ifá priests also make use of *dundun* and *bata* talking drums. *Dundun* is not used in the diaspora, but *bata* is well preserved, even though the ensemble has diminished from five drums to three. Cuban *bata* based on its Yorùbá original, a drum of Sango from the ancient capital of the Oyo empire, is becoming more and more famous throughout the world.

Some of the dance steps of Africa have been kept in the diaspora, though many others have changed dramatically. In recent years, the particular, stylized dances of the *òrìṣà* have become more and more popular in the Americas. So also have the indigenous music and dancers of other parts of West Africa, especially of Senegal, Mali, and Guinea. The whole Western world seems to be greatly fascinated by African music in general. In almost every major city in the United

States, for example, there are academic institutions as well as art and cultural centers where African music and dance are taught. The contribution of the *òrìṣà* religion in this regard cannot be overlooked.

Today, the number of babaláwó in Africa has diminished and their patrons and audiences have become Christianized, Islamized, or marginalized by modern economic trends. While twenty years ago festivals and large performances by Ifá priests involving the entire community could be witnessed in almost every Yorùbá town, they have deteriorated so much that there are now some small towns without any babaláwó, let alone Ifá festivals. However, some important towns have kept their traditional yearly festivals. Such festivals can be seen in Oyo, Ibadan, Osogbo, Iseyin, and Iwo, among others. This writer was responsible for reintroducing the Agboniregun annual festival in 1981 after more than twenty-five years, when the babaláwó of the rest of Yorùbáland walked away from Ile-Ife because of conflict with the Araba of Ife. It is very interesting to note that the same Araba, Awosope of blessed memory, presided over the new Agboniregun festivals from 1981 to 1986, when he broke his *osun* sacred walking stick and departed to the great beyond.

Since 1981 when I was made Awise Agbaye, Ifá priests from the whole of West Africa and also sometimes from Cuba, Brazil, Puerto Rico, and the United States have congregated in Ile-Ife to observe the annual Agboniregun festival. More than a hundred towns are represented by a large delegation of their babaláwó every year. Each delegation arrives with its own instruments, drummers, and chanters, who are both young and old and who take turns entertaining the large crowd congregated in the most important Ifá temple in the world. This temple is situated on Itase Hill, the highest point in the geographical center of Ile-Ife, from where one can see the rest of the city and beyond. During this annual festival celebrated in honor of Agboniregun, the identical twin brother of Orunmila, the Araba of Ife invokes all the *òrìṣà* of Ife in a celebration of poetry that is uttered in Ife but is evoked in honor of the whole world. At this time, a special midnight divination is made for the world, during which the congregation of babaláwó foretells the future of the world as revealed from the cast. As if to celebrate the theme of continuity and change, the Awise Agbaye, a university professor and babaláwó, is called upon at midnight to say prayers on behalf of the whole world.

Even though much in the diaspora has changed (with many verses of Ifá and recipes of medicine forgotten), it is true that a sizeable number of Ifá traditions have been kept in literature, art forms, rituals, and performances. One interesting and salutary development is the interest now being taken by young men and women in the traditions of Ifá on a worldwide basis. Ifá has traveled quite far in the Americas, where many people are being initiated as babaláwó and *santeros* every day. Unfortunately, due to the lack of a central and universal authority, many religious leaders who do not have solid grounding have emerged—some of them Africans from the continent as well as Americans—who think that a single initiation can transform a person into a knowledgeable and well-respected babaláwó. In actuality, no number of initiations can make a person a babaláwó. It is experience acquired by many years of training that transforms a person into a babaláwó imbued not only with the sacred knowledge of the verses, herbs, and medicines, but also with good character, which is the most important attribute of a priest of Ifá.

The language of Ifá is full of images and metaphors. The mountain is a symbol of immortality. Dew is a symbol of peace, healing, and gentle interaction. Sacrifice is a means of giving respect and salutations to supernatural powers, since nutrition is necessary for all humans and for all things to survive and interact among themselves. The world of Ifá is, in that sense, eternal and timeless. But change as a dynamic and creative process is also a part of this world order. This allows Ifá to speak to each age in a language that can be understood. What matters is neither continuity or change. Change we will always have. As for continuity, there will always be ups and downs. What matters is the context, the agents, and the medium of change. What is also important is the attitude of the agents themselves. Only change that is carried out through a medium of respect and standing, that is not imposed or vulgarized, will stand the test of time and lead to a multiplier effect of greater creativity.

There is a constant tension between the principles of continuity and change in the traditions of Ifá divination. But as in the wider world of Yorùbá belief, conflict and resolution are necessary for peace and progress. In the twenty-first century, a balance must always be struck between the principles of continuity and change, as Yorùbá religion travels around the world to take its place as an important world religion.

Aboru
Aboye
Abosise Ogbo
Ato
Asure, Iworiwofin.

May our sacrifices be accepted
May our sacrifices lead to long life
May our prayers/sacrifices come to pass
Blessing of long life
Blessing of good health
Blessings of *Iworiwofin.*

Notes

An earlier version of this chapter appeared in *Insight and Artistry in African Divination*, edited by John Pemberton III (Washington, DC: Smithsonian Institution Press, 2000), 175–181.

1. Yorùbáland includes modern-day southwestern Nigeria and parts of Benin and Togo.
2. Ifádayiiro was a great babaláwó. He died in 1980 at the age of 125.
3. I later studied Ifá with the late Animasaun Oyedele Isola of Beesin compound, Paakoyi, and later with other babaláwó of Oyo town, Ife, Osogbo, Ilobu, and Ikoyi.
4. The Acasa de Africa was about eighty years old in 1987 when he presented the divining bowl to me. He had inherited the bowl from his father, who had in turn inherited it from his father. Hence the bowl must have been carved sometime between 1830 and 1860.
5. All translations are my own unless otherwise indicated.
6. Part of a verse of Eji Ogbe.

References

Abímbólá, Wándé. 1975a. *Sixteen Great Poems of Ifá*. Paris: UNESCO.

———, ed. 1975b. *Yorùbá Oral Tradition: Poetry in Music, Dance and Drama*. Ile-Ife, Nigeria: University of Ife.

———. 1976. *Ifá: An Exposition of Ifá Literary Corpus*. Ibadan: Oxford University Press.

———. 1977. *Ifá Divination Poetry*. New York: Nok Publishers.

Pemberton, John, III, ed. 2000. *Insight and Artistry in African Divination*. Washington, DC: Smithsonian Institution Press.

3 Recasting Ifá

Historicity and Recursive Recollection in Ifá Divination Texts

Andrew Apter

THE PLACE OF "history" in Ifá divination has generated a fair amount of debate about Ifá's origins, contents, politics, and poetics, reflecting a putatively fixed body of verses that somehow represent and incorporate change. Ifá has been seen as an Islamic import, a coded history of kingdoms, a primary "document," a repository of secrets (*awo*), even the computer program of Yorùbá culture—all within an interpretive system that caters to clients by disclosing the future.[1] What is historical in Ifá divination, and how do we access its hidden histories as a textual and performative archive of the past? I approach this question by examining a specific form of historicity that is recursively embedded in Ifá divination—not only referring to external events, but to original divinations that are "recast" and "recollected." I argue that what Ifá reveals about the Yoruba past, in addition to particular events and migrations, are the recursive forms of temporality and historical consciousness in which the secrets of the past are located. The deep histories or *ìtàn jinlè* that characterize the "archive" of Ifá divination emerge, in this form of recursive recollection, not from a hidden transcript of fixed sacred texts, but from dynamic instabilities of situated readings that sustain multiple interpretations of the past.

Wándé Abímbọ́lá was in fact the first to see Ifá as a viable and valuable primary source for Yorùbá historiography. The structure and historicity of *ese Ifa* summarized in the introduction to the present volume set the stage for the perspectives presented in this paper.

From Abímbọ́lá's concise formulation we see how history is built into the very logic and language of Ifá divination as a prescriptive system of revelations and disclosures. If the client is concerned with pressing problems of the present, it is only by recourse to a hidden past that his or her situation can be accurately diagnosed and resolved with an appropriate sacrifice.

Abímbọ́lá is quick to point out that despite the ideology of fixity ascribed to *ese Ifá* as faithful renditions of a sacred textual corpus, and despite the strict conditions of transmission (*iyere Ifá*) imposed to maintain accuracy and prevent "adulteration," Ifá texts do in fact change over time, reflecting local conditions and historical trends. From the cognomens or *oríkì* of past diviners mentioned in the texts, Abímbọ́lá identifies such archaic technologies as the crossbow (*àkàtàn-pó*) and the throwing spear (*èsín*) that predated the introduction of firearms, as well as heritable domestic slaves (*erú*) that were later proscribed by the British (1973, 50–52). From place names Abímbọ́lá discerns traces of population migrations, references to famous towns, markets, quarters, and even compounds, as well as glosses on the political organization of abandoned kingdoms such as Ìká, with its four civil chiefs, storage barns, and maskers in attendance (52–55).

Equally illuminating are the *ese Ifá* associated with the founding of historic kingdoms. From Ose Méjì, the *odù* believed to have been cast at the founding of Ibadan circa 1829, Abímbọ́lá adduces evidence that gunpowder was already in use to kill predatory bushpigs (55–57). And finally, from epic verses contained in *odù* such as Òtúá Méjì, echoes of the advent of Islam into Yorùbáland reverberate from the past, including the violent exploits of one Àlùkáádi (Al-Kadi) and his eventual decapitation through the intervention of Eshu (57–59). There are of course many ways of reading these references to artifacts, events, institutions, and places, ranging from empirical designations to veiled mythic allegories, as Abímbọ́lá himself acknowledges. However, I would like to propose an alternative approach to the historical significance of Ifá divination—one equally foregrounded in Abímbọ́lá's discussion—pertaining less to concrete objects and events than to the recursive forms of historicity in which they are embedded. It is not my aim to jettison the evidentiary base of Ifá divination as an historical archive, but rather to illuminate the recursive logic of recollection through which it operates, and thus the forms of historical consciousness that it actively generates.

Recasting Ifá

Let us return to the more formal dimensions of Abímbọ́lá's account of Ifá's historicity. If every *ese* provides an "accurate account" of a past event or activity, as befits the Yorùbá concept *itàn*, it does so within a particular structure, as embedded within a prior, indeed original, divination: "The past event is presented as an accurate record of a past divination involving a past priest of Ifá and his clients" (Abímbọ́lá, 1973, 46). It is important to note that the *ese* contains not only the occasion and results of this prior divination but also the names of those originally involved. In this basic sense, then, every casting of Ifá contains within itself a prior, originary casting, one that occurred in the past and that returns to illuminate the present situation. Every casting is always a recasting. Every divination contains within itself the original divination—and its associated sacrifice—which it recursively instantiates, presumably tracing back to *láílái* (time immemorial).

How are we to understand the historicity of these recursive recastings, or metadivinations? Is the efficacy of the past divination reactivated in the present, to perform the same illuminating work? Or is the present to be seen as an extension of the past, a contemporary rerun, as it were, of a primordial drama? Does the accuracy of Ifá's revelation derive from the invocation of "original speech," as one *onísegùn* characterized the power of *àyàjó*, or do past divinations simply serve as proactive guides for protective sacrifices and courses of action? Insofar as original divinations invoke the hidden histories of deep knowledge (*imo ijinlè*), must their references remain opaque, or can they be recovered to mobilize rival political claims? Such questions are not exactly foremost on the minds of anxious clients seeking immediate solutions rather than insights into the mythic past. But if the efficacy, indeed the truth value, of Ifá divination rests on the logic of prior divinatory revelation, then the historicity of recursive recollection remains central to Ifá as a social practice and ritual technology.

Turning to Bascom's *Ifá Divination: Communication Between Gods and Men in West Africa* (1969), we find much valuable material on prior divinations characteristically embedded in Ifá texts, but relatively little discussion of recursive recasting as a form of historicity. In his tripartite characterization of Ifá verses, Bascom distinguishes: "(1) the statement of the mythological case which serves as a precedent, (2) the resolution or outcome of this case, and (3) its application to the client" (1969: 122). From the practical perspective of the babalawo and his clients, the historical status of the original divination invoked in the opening of the *ese Ifá* is less important than its role as a mythic charter or precedent for the client's predicament at hand. The first portion names the diviner or diviners of the primordial casting "in quotation marks," the mythic figure who consulted them, and often the sacrificial items prescribed. The second section recounts what happened to the mythic figure, who either followed the sacrifice to great advantage or in failing to sacrifice suffered dire consequences. Many see this as a warning not to treat Ifá's prescriptions lightly. The third section relates the mythic precedent to the client's problem and situation, predicting a negative outcome should the sacrifice be avoided and a positive outcome should it be fulfilled. Not all *ese* Ifá follow this tripartite structure to the letter, Bascom notes, but generally it prevails.

If the mythological precedent appears fairly straightforward, its semiotic structure is quite complex. As Bascom notes, the naming of the original diviners "in quotation marks" is understood as a form of *oríkì* (praise name) commemorating a former diviner by his cognomen, but it is typically expressed as a proverb converted into an *oríkì*. Thus a simple example from the *odù* Oyeku-Edi reads: "'The road is very straight, it does not turn' was the one who cast Ifá for Oye when he was going to bring home a bride from his ward" (1969, 265). As an *oríkì* of an original diviner, the name does not refer to a historic personage but functions more as an incantation that is nominalized and personified, and which actually—in the larger context of the *ese*—refers to Oye's sexual impotence and by implication to that of the living client. In the more favorable and complex precedent of Ogbe-Oyeku, the proverbial name of the original diviner accompanies the more elaborated *oríkì* of his client, identified specifically as a former king of Ofa:

> "The head that should not go naked will find a cloth seller when the market opens" was the one who cast Ifá for "The King of Ofa who sells a box full of velvet," child of "One who coughs 'gbinrin' like the trumpeting of an elephant," child of "One who uses the top of a calabash to measure out beads for his mistresses," child of "One who enjoys the world wet and soggy, like someone licking honey." (169)

In this precedent, the original diviner personifies a proverb in which a person with good character will be recognized (will cover his head, wear a crown). The proverb refers to the original client, who becomes King of Ofa, and who is located genealogically through additional *oríkì* that denote royalty (elephant), wealth (beads), and worldly success (honey).

Whether this elaborate precedent refers to a specific dynastic transition in Ofa's history, or to the dynamics of political succession more generally, there are questions that can be better pursued by specifying referential strategies within the texts themselves. Let us begin with conventions of naming. It is a well-known characteristic of Yorùbá names such as Ògúndélé, Oládiméjì, Babatúndé, Abíodún, not to mention Táíwò, Kéèhìndé and Ìdòwú, that they incorporate mythic references, family relations, and circumstances surrounding a child's birth into their morphology, including birth order, festivals, chieftaincies, or even the "return" of an ancestor (Akinnaso 1980). My first-born son is thus Babatúndé in Yorùbá, because he was born exactly a year after the death of his grandfather—thus his "father" returned. He is also Abíodún because he was born on the day of a festival, the Fourth of July. My twins are of course Táíwò and Kéèhìndé, indicating the "second born" twin's seniority because he sent his junior brother out to see the world first. Yorùbá proper names thus incorporate significant aspects of their sociocultural contexts of production. With *oríkì* this process of contextualization is extended. Praise names of men and women not only locate them genealogically in relation to important ancestors and affines, but also historically in relation to kingdoms, events, migrations, or even scandals. The allusions, however, are typically oblique. Like suggestive tags, they invoke pieces of larger histories and stories, *ìtàn* that are in many cases hidden or repressed, but that can be supplied by knowledgeable listeners and elders. Without its implied and often hidden history, the meaning of the *oríkì* remains a mystery (Barber 1991, 19 et passim; Babalola 1966). Seen in relation to a primary proper name, an *oríkì* thus represents a double coding of context, a secondary elaboration of a primary designation that already registers context in the first place.

Seen in relation to proper names and *oríkì*, the name of the primordial diviner in *ese Ifá* registers a different kind of context. In the two examples discussed thus far, "The road is very straight, it does not turn," and "The head that should not go naked will find a cloth seller when the market opens," there is no already-named person receiving an *oríkì*; rather, the incantation or proverb functions as an *oríkì* to create the person so named. Unlike proper names, proverbs do not generally register contexts of birth, but they do resonate with the performative contexts from which their socially situated significance derives. Just as a proverb only makes sense, often as veiled criticism, in relation to those present at the speech event, so the original context of the primordial divination is manifest in the name of the first diviner, representing the transfiguration of text (proverb) and context (original divination) into flesh. This capacity of discourse to nominalize actions and verbalize nouns is a characteristic of ritual power, or *àse*, that has been noted in diverse ritual language genres, and in the mythological precedent of *ese Ifá*; it transforms text into the agency of a named diviner. In many *ese Ifá*, many diviners are so named by a succession of proverbial enunciations and quotations. In one of the verses of Òtúrúpòn Méjì, recorded in Oshogbo in 1966, an opening precedent, "Where it is 'The wonderful groundnut that stays in the farm and menstruates' was the one who cast Ifá for Òtú who was going barren, who bore no children" is followed by what appears to be a second opening precedent, "Where 'Ìtóbólò was the Priest of Ìtóbólò, Ìtòbòlò was the Priest of Ìtòbòlò, indeed!' 'It is the snail whose chest is smooth (but still) climbs the tree,' 'It was the wife who, informally, called her husband by name,' 'An elder does not accept a bribe and complain of abusive speech,' were the ones who cast Ifá for Banregun who was a queen, a queen in Olofin's palace'" (Armstrong et al. 1978). This *ese* constructs a parallelism between two original divinations—one for a barren woman seeking issue, the other for a queen seeking peace and prosperity in her palace. But barring further exegesis for now, it is enough to point out that naming of the original diviner or diviners transforms an original mythic or proverbial context into the personified agency of original divination.

Similar transpositions of text and context identify the original or primordial client. In the Oyeku-Edi verse quoted above, the client is named Oye, the unfortunate groom who could not satisfy his bride. But who is this Oye, a mythic figure, an Ekiti town, or simply a placeholder for any potential client? The *ese* itself gives us a hint—its second part, the resolution or outcome of the mythological precedent, identifies Oye in a condensed account, or *ìtàn:* "When Oye brought his bride home, he was not able to sleep with her. They said, 'What kind of Oye is he?' They said, 'He is Oye who has died at his waist.' From this time on we have been calling him Oyeku-edi" (Bascom 1969, 265). Bascom notes the pun or folk-etymological connection between Oye's name, "Oye-die-waist" and the very name of the *odù*, Oyeku-Edi (265n3). In this transposition, the mythic figure of Oye personifies the very *odù* it manifests. Nor are such co-implicative relations between mythic figures and associated texts limited to the names of clients. In an earlier verse of the same *odù* recorded by Bascom, it is the diviner, not the client, who shares a name with the Ifá divination figure: "'Oyeku-Edi' was the one who cast Ifá for Snail" (263). Thus within different *ese* of the same *odù*, the names of the original diviners and clients are transposable, thereby shifting the implicit contexts, the hidden and expandable "histories," that illuminate their implicit meanings.

* * *

What this preliminary examination of "mythological precedents" reveals is that those original castings embedded within every divination are themselves entangled within labile mythohistories (*itàn*) that are mobilized by the poetics of naming. If the name of the primordial babalawo personifies a proverbial text or mythohistorical context, transforming text into performative agency, his client counterpart is similarly implicated within associated mythohistories (*itàn*) that in many cases identify political titles and historic kingdoms. Such invocations of prior contexts inform the histories associated with the mythological precedent that itself establishes a prior "historical" context for the current divination at hand. The structural formula that identifies the mythological precedent within the text follows the convention "X was/were the one/s who cast Ifá for Y," where X and Y represent the original babalawo and client, as in "X *a d'ifá fún* Y."[2] In this syntactic formulation, X and Y are indeed variables that not only shift actual names between different recitations of the "same" verse; they can also expand or contract as *oríkì*. As Amherd notes, "For the material that comes before and after, [*a d'ifá fún*] plays an important role in projecting the identity of the *ese Ifá* as well as *acting as a pivot* around which the surrounding parts, which are open to *expansion, contraction,* or *lexical difference,* can coalesce" (2005, 68n11, emphasis mine). If, as Amherd argues, such built-in flexibility allows *ese Ifá* to be modified and adapted to accommodate local variations within performative contexts, it also sustains a corpus of repressed historical allusions and associations within every recursive recasting of Ifá. In this preliminary exploration of recursion within Ifá divination texts, I have identified a model of Yorùbá historicity that provides an ethnomethodological framework for approaching Ifá as a living historical archive. It is through this framework that Ifá's illuminations of the past can be most accurately assessed and pursued.

Notes

1. The scholarly and practical literature on Ifa divination is vast. Representative hallmarks of Ifa scholarship and documentation include Abímbólá (1975, 1976), Akinnaso (1995), Amherd (2010), Armstrong et al. (1978), Barber (1990), Bascom (1969, 1980), Epega and Niemark (1995), Fatoogun (1987), and Gleason (1973).

2. Or alternatively, *"difa fun," "lo difa fun,"* or *"a da fun"* Amherd (2005, 68n11).

References

Abímbólá, Wándé. 1973. "The Literature of the Ifa Cult." In *Sources of Yorùbá History,* edited by Saburi Oladeni Biobaku, 41–62. Oxford: Clarendon Press.

———. 1975. *Sixteen Great Poems of Ifa.* Paris: UNESCO.

———. 1976. *Ifá: An Exposition of Ifá Literary Corpus.* Ibadan: Oxford University Press.

Akinnaso, Niyi. 1980. "The Sociolinguistic Basis of Yorùbá Personal Names." *Anthropological Linguistics* 22, no. 7: 275–304.

———. 1995. "Bourdieu and the Diviner: Language and Symbolic Power in Yorùbá Divination." In *The Pursuit of Certainty: Religious and Cultural Formations,* edited by Wendy James, 234–257. London: Routledge.

Amherd, K. Noel. 2005. "Ifá Texts: Diversity and Discourse." In *Orisa: Yorùbá Gods and Spiritual Identity in Africa and the Diaspora,* edited by Toyin Falola and Ann Genova, 23–73. Trenton, NJ: Africa World Press.

———. 2010. *Reciting Ifá: Difference, Heterogeneity, and Identity.* Trenton, NJ: Africa World Press.

Armstrong, Robert. 1978. *Ìyèrè Ifá: The Deep Chants of Ifá at the Ile Awo Osogbo.* Ibadan: University of Ibadan Institute of African Studies.

Babalola, Adeboye. 1966. *Àwon Oríkì Orílè.* Glasgow: Collins.

Barber, Karin. 1990. "Discursive Strategies in the Texts of Ifá and in the 'Holy Book of Odù' of the African Church of Orunmila." In *Self-Assertion and Brokerage: Early Cultural Nationalism in West Africa,* edited by P. F. de Moraes Farias and Karin Barber, 196–224. Birmingham, UK: University of Birmingham Centre of West African Studies.

———. 1991. *I Could Speak Until Tomorrow: Oríkì, Women and the Past in a Yorùbá Town.* Washington, DC: Smithsonian Institution Press.

Bascom, William. 1969. *Ifá Divination: Communication Between Gods and Men in West Africa.* Bloomington: Indiana University Press.

———. 1980. *Sixteen Cowries: Ifa Divination from Africa to the New World.* Bloomington: Indiana University Press.

Epega, Afolabi, and Philip John Neimark. 1995. *The Sacred Ifá Oracle.* San Francisco: HarperSanFrancisco.

Fatooga, Babalola. 1987. *Isedale awon Odu Ifa.* Edited by S. O. Biobaku and O. O. Adekola. 4 vols. Ibadan: University of Ibadan Institute of African Studies.

Gleason, Judith. 1973. *A Recitation of Ifa, Oracle of the Yorùbá.* New York: Grossman.

4 Ifá, Knowledge, Performance, the Sacred, and the Medium

Olasope O. Oyelaran

THIS ESSAY IS programmatic about the task ahead of us as culture bearers who are conscious of the Yorùbá epistemological system encapsulated in Ifá and in the context of the human reality at this moment and beyond. The essay runs the risk of making invalid or erroneous assumptions about the subject matter before us; of being inadequately informed about how much others have done or are doing in tackling the task before us.

The essay assumes, nevertheless, that this volume presents us with tremendous opportunities—perhaps more opportunities than challenges. I am aware that a volume of this type, addressing one single culture, one particular trend that interests that culture, or one of its institutions, is not unprecedented. It is fair to assume further that the subject matter of this volume, namely Ifá divination, has uniquely survived among identifiable modes of prognostics among people of African descent for example, in the Americas.

I would like to suggest that decisions made concerning the direction we go from here and their consequences for Ifá at home and abroad may depend on the realism with which we address Ifá as a "poetic" phenomenon. This essay's use of the term "poetics" abstracts from Aristotle's *Poetics* and mines the Greek verb *poieo*, which means "to do" or "to create." Aristotle could be interpreted as predicating artistic productivity exemplified in tragedy, comedy, and attendant deployment of language by the artist—for example, Euripides's use of agents and elements of language—onto the creative capacity and imagination, which the artist must presume to bring to representations that move the audience and society as experiencers and end users. My point of departure, therefore, is that when Aristotle is said to have proposed that art imitates life, we must understand that proposition as suggesting that the artist creatively deploys his or her imaginative competence to re-present objects of his or her consciousness. From this point of view, I wish to propose that to deny the babalawo the capacity for and disposition toward imaginative creativity implies that *ese Ifá*, and thus the *odù*, are generated only through memorization and regurgitative capacities. One unfortunate conclusion from such a point of departure denies Ifá the capacity to account for new situations in the human condition, new phenomena, and hence any and all explanatory possibilities.

Of Ifá and Ọ̀rúnmìlà

I take to heart Abímbọ́lá's disciplined canon that the names "Ifá and Ọ̀rúnmìlà refer to the same deity. But while the name 'Ọ̀rúnmìlà' refers exclusively to the deity himself, the name 'Ifá' refers both to the deity and his divination system" (1976, 3). In accepting the first proposition, I do not have to account for how 'Ifá' acquired the compendium of information that made Ọ̀rúnmìlà in Ogbèdí (Oyèláràn 1988, 2008) custodian of exhaustive information about all objects of consciousness.[1] In order to understand Ọ̀rúnmìlà/Ifá's preeminent status in the context of the current information technology explosion, it follows that it is necessary to conceive of "him" and look to Ifá as the source for confirming every emerging object of consciousness and what we observe and experience. Because of the nature of our existential reality, we must also look to Ifá for explanations about each phenomenon and condition, for prognostics of what lies ahead, and for how we ford the stream of life ahead. For the purpose of this essay, I propose that any being that has the capacity to use a system as capacious as Ifá must also possess creative originality.

Èdè (language) is also in Ogbèdí (Oyèláràn 1988), the Òjíṣẹ (commissioner) of Olódùmàrè. It appears fair, therefore, to suspect that in that role Èdè conveys all the information of which Ifá now stands as custodian from Olódùmàrè to Ifá. This information is not normally readily accessible, and therefore remains a mystery to ordinary human beings. The human being who has or acquires the capacity to access the mystery through language, Èdè, is referred to as babalawo, master in matters of the mystery,[2] to whom we will interchangeably refer as "exponent" in the rest of this essay. This raises the question of the nature of the exponent's relevant capacity and attributes. Is it poetic in the sense of being imaginatively creative, or is it merely recitative? In order to answer this question, we must first inquire into the nature of the form in which Ifá's message is usually couched.

The Medium

For heuristic purposes, we must keep in mind Abímbọ́lá's summary presentation of the structure of *ẹsẹ Ifá* cited in this book's introduction.

Parts 1, 2, 3, and 8 are normally present in all *ẹsẹ Ifá*. They are often allusive and recondite. If we assume that the knowledge of a language implies the capacity to generate and understand expressions freely generated in that language, the following questions arise with respect to the medium of Ifá. Do all ẹsẹ Ifá have a set of parts (such as parts 4, 5, 6, and 7) expressed in ordinary language that is more intelligible to the audience than the other parts? Do these parts form a continuous sequence in the structure of ẹsẹ Ifá? To paraphrase Tambiah (1968), do they collectively convey living knowledge related to technological and social activities? If these questions can be answered affirmatively, it becomes necessary to consider looking for a babalawo's creativity in the sequence and language of these parts.

Babalawo and Poetic Competence

Unlike Yai, we disagree with Manfred Bierwisch's definition of "poetic competence" as a "'recognition grammar,' and 'a differentiating algorithm which determines whether or not a given sentence is poetic'" (Yai 1999, 13).[3] For us, poetic competence also inheres in the imaginative potential for creative, expressive representations of experiential reality in language. This position is inspired to a degree by Aristotle's *Poetics*.[4] The language style and genre for re-presentation depends on the predisposition of the poet. Yai (1986) clearly appreciates this implication of the notion of poetic competence, as he demonstrates in his appraisal of the trailblazing program that the Department of African Languages and Literatures at the University of Ifẹ̀ incorporated in its degree program. The program made it mandatory that students acquire at least a modicum of ability to perform in at least one of three oral poetry genres of Yorùbá, for which the department engaged exponents.

Certain idiosyncratic properties of each genre of the Yorùbá orature call for particular nuclear predicative formatives, for which they may serve as propositional complements. For example, the genre *iyẹ̀rẹ̀* corresponds to the performance voice *sun iyẹ̀rẹ̀*, which means to chant *iyẹre*; the genre *ewì* corresponds to the performance voice *ké ewì*, meaning to shout *ewì*; and the genre *oríkì* corresponds to the performance voice *kì oríkì*, meaning to cite *oríkì*. The awareness of this informed the department's instructional program for students' learning experiences. The program aimed to cultivate the students' creativity in the performance style of the genre they chose to study.

In the performance of each of these genres, imaginative creativity and originality that must meet its artistic exigencies are the rule rather than the exception. Any artist who falls short of expectation is considered to be lacking in poetic competence, not just by his or her own peers, but by the general public who already inculcate the performance standards.[5]

Now, consider the "performance" predicates for Ifá: *dá Ifá*, meaning to create/craft/design *Ifá*; *tẹ̀ Ifá* (*tẹ̀ alẹ̀ Ifá*), meaning to print (Greek "graphein") *Ifá*; and *kì Ifá*, meaning to cite *Ifá*.

Does it make sense to adduce poetic consideration in experiencing the babalawo in his acts, to which all of these predicates apply? In other words, is originality normal in the performance situation that involves any and all of the predi-cates? Does the saying "*a tẹ̀ ọ́ nífá tán, kí o tún ara à rẹ tẹ̀*" ("we have completed imbuing you with competence in Ifá; [it is up to you] to reindoctrinate/inform yourself"), apply to all of the predicates? Does this saying address the heart of the matter, because it encapsulates the expectation of imaginative creativity and originality after training? Is it admissible to extend to babalawo Yai's (1994) con-cept of creativity, which he explores in the studied term *àrè* (the artist)?

Both of the predicates *dá Ifá* and *tẹ̀ Ifá/tẹ̀ alẹ̀ Ifá* (print/mark the emerging sign on the surface meant for Ifá) apply to the process of creating and graphically presenting emergent combinatorial configurations that signify the *odù* during the consultative session of divination. Since each particular configuration is id-iosyncratic to an individual *odù*, and Ifá counts only 256 (2^8) *odù*, there is a finite number of configurations that the exponent must learn to recognize. The expo-nent's competence may, accordingly, be judged by whether or not he or she casts, *dá*, the *ọ̀pẹ̀lẹ̀* competently, or whether he or she can compose/print, *tẹ̀*, the emerg-ing combinatorial configurations accurately—and also recognize each when the divinatory process involves *ikin*, cowries, or *ọ̀pẹ̀lẹ̀*, the two-to-the-fourth-power (2^4) divining chain. In any of these cases, one expects very little to no originality or creativity. The judgment of poetic competence does not, strictly speaking, ap-ply to these processes.

However, the predicate *kì Ifá* may involve effusive verbal performance in the divinatory process—the generation of *ẹsẹ Ifá*—even when minor *odù* appear and are being "hailed."[6] Does this predicate *kì* admit of spontaneous, imagina-tive, creative originality on the part of the babalawo? The kind of originality that is relevant here must be distinguished from the originality of the bard reciting a Homeric epic or the Epic of Sundiata. It also must not be confused with the insight and originality of the exegete contemplating a given text, whatever the medium. In each of these cases, a measure of fidelity to the archetype is an im-perative. Therefore, what do proposals for the training of a babalawo allow us to come away with when it comes to originality?

The Training of a Babalawo

Of particular interest in the training of babalawo is their preparedness to *kì Ifá* to the level where they can serve with probity, in the words of Abímbọ́lá, as veritable "guardians, counsellors, philosophers, and physicians of their various communi-ties" (1976, 18). Also of critical interest are the personal attributes required of a trainee to have a chance to succeed. Since most expositions of Ifá that address the formation of an exponent present, at least, the attributes and expectations found in Abímbọ́lá (1976),[7] I will cite from his seminal work liberally in the following.

1. "If the training goes well, and if the trainee has *a retentive memory*, the training lasts not more than ten to twelve years" (18, emphasis mine).

2. "The most important [factors] are firstly *mental rigor* and secondly the extremely hard conditions of living involved in the training" (18).
3. "The ẹsẹ are *memorized* at the steady rate of one per day" (20).
4. "Each ẹsẹ is *learnt in the form of recitation* in the first instance. The master-priest says one complete sentence at a time and the trainee *parrots* the words after him several times *until he is able to retain the whole sentence in his memory*" (20, emphasis mine).
5. "According to many of my informants, after a trainee has properly *memorized* the first sixteen ẹsẹ the task of *learning Ifá verse by heart* becomes relatively easy for him" (20, emphasis mine except for italics on the word ẹsẹ).
6. "The ẹsẹ is *memorized* with such great reverence that *not a single word is missed.* It is considered extremely sacrilegious for anybody to add or subtract anything from the corpus. The *ẹsẹ must always be learnt in the very form in which it is has been preserved and disseminated from ancient times.* It is believed that in this way the texts in the Ifá literary corpus have been kept free of errors" (20, emphasis mine except for italics on the word ẹsẹ).[8]
7. "Learning how to chant the ẹsẹ is reserved for a much later part of the training. A clever trainee, however, acquires the art of chanting Ifá verse by imitating his master when chanting ẹsẹ *Ifá* everyday [sic] during the process of performing Ifá divination. A trainee could also learn the art of chanting Ifá verse by attending the regular assemblies of Ifá priests. Ifá priests could, however, specialize in chanting as a part of their post-initiation training" (20).

Presumably, since each ẹsẹ *Ifá* is an idiosyncratic component of a particular Odù, ascertaining the ẹbọ, "sacrifice," that each ẹsẹ *Ifá* calls for must be mastered in the process of learning to *dá Ifá* or *tẹ̀ Ifá*. It need not allow for any originality on the part of babalawo. From the foregoing it would appear that for accomplished babalawo, the performance described by the predicate *kì Ifá* also appears to exclude any imaginative or creative originality attributable to poetic competence, but originality is not excluded for the predicate *sun ìyẹ̀rẹ̀*. This is an inaccurate conclusion.[9]

For communicating through babalawo, what implications does the conclusion distilled from the above passage have for understanding and explaining the medium deployed by Ifá? How does this conclusion account for the manner and scope of the survival of Ifá in certain contexts of verifiable encounters by people of Yorùbá descent and of the Yorùbá culture outside the Southwestern Nigeria–Benin-Togo enclave, but not in others? How does the performance of Ifá literary text at home and in the diaspora lead to the exclusion of poetic competence in the recitation of the text? Finally, what kinds of obligations do plausible answers to these questions impose on those of us who are stakeholders in the fortunes of Ifá?

Òwe ni Ifá ń pa (Ifa Speaks in Proverbs)

Òwe is accepted to be the fulcrum on which eloquence, effective discourse, and speech communication generally in the Yorùbá language critically balances.[10] I take the position that, from all evidence at my disposal, the genre Òwe has been underappreciated. Thus it has been variously rendered as "parables" (Abímbọlá 1975, 388–410), as "proverbs" (Owomoyela 1988, 2005, 2007), and by countless scholars and users of the now almost hackneyed saying "Òwe lẹşin ọrọ, bọrọ bá sọnù, òwe la fii wá a" ("Òwe is the horse of discourse, when the discourse is at risk of miscarrying Òwe is best brought to its rescue").

For the purpose of this chapter, I take Òwe to apply to figures of speech or tropes in the most comprehensive sense of each of these terms. "Trope," which for all practical purposes includes all imaginable figures of speech, involves graphic representation with language as the medium for desired effects. This may relate to perceptual and experiential entities on the one hand, and propositions in the discourse on the other. In poetry or in prose, a figure of speech could be a pithy expression, a dramatic setting, or a narrative of any length. In order to be effective, Òwe and all instances of trope call for an epistemological commonalty between the speaker and the addressee, as all symbolic systems do. Otherwise, communication breaks down.

A material homologue of Òwe in the Yorùbá tradition is àrokò (Olaniyan 1975; Olomola 1979, 1991).[11] In the past, royalty used to send àrokò as symbolic diplomatic yet graphic messages, using specific material objects in ways that would convey the intended meaning of a secret message. It is also well known that names and naming among the Yorùbá are loaded with meaning and experiential references.

In order to appreciate the real import of the proposition "Òwe ni Ifá ń pa," we take a critical look at the predicative nuclear pa that invariably collocates with it, and which it serves as propositional complement. Consider the following usages:

- *pa obì:* to split a kola nut
  This refers to the splitting of a kola nut into its constituent cotyledons, usually for the purpose of offering them to members of the present company, for propitiation, for divination, or for invoking unseen powers.
- *pa ọmọ; ẹyin:* to bring forth, as in birthing a child, or hatching an egg
  Interestingly, *pa* assigns inherent àşẹ to the egg as in *ẹyin pa* "an egg hatches"; but *adìẹ pa(ọ)mọ* "a chicken hatches" (that is, chicks)."
- *pa irọ:* to contrive and deliver a falsehood/a tortuous and empty speech act
- *pa àlọ:* to contrive and deliver a riddle, or a tale with plots with twists, turns, and suspense
- *pa eyín:* to reform or reshape dentition, usually for cosmetic purposes

- *pa òwe:* to contrive, depict and deliver a graphic, imaginative, imaginable presentation of an experientially informed situation, setting, or narrative, usually involving dramatis personae, real or fictive, in order to effect a desirable transactional outcome

Thus each of the instances above uses the medium of language to present a transactional process graphically. In each case, the interpretation assignable to *pa* invokes attributes inherent in the complement metonymically. Some would like to refer to the inherent "attributes" as referential features determining of the semantic content of the propositional complement of *pa* in each case. This explains why this argument and explanation also applies to *"pa ìtàn/pìtàn* (spin, tell, weave, a story/narrative)," since it is not infrequently encountered in *ẹsẹ Ifá*.

As with *àrokò* or *ìtàn*, *òwe* calls for originality and for imaginative creativity in coming up with new narratives or in the use of existing narratives. This suggests that if *"Òwe ni Ifá ń pa"* ("Ifa speaks in proverbs"), it would be counterintuitive to expect that the originality of babalawo could be held in check, by reason of their training, in contexts that are conducive to effective use of figures of speech to convey meanings. Similarly, it seems one should not expect a babalawo to withhold creativity when playing the role of a guardian, counselor, philosopher, and physician of his or her various communities. Otherwise, it becomes difficult to sustain Ifá's attribute as *akọnilọ́ràn-bí-ìyekan-ẹni* (one who counsels like one's next-of-kin). To put it more clearly, we could borrow from Tambiah, and suggest that Ifá constantly "exploits the expressive properties of language, the sensory qualities of objects" (1968, 190) and the experiential and perceptive capacities of members of the communities and supplicants.

Ẹsẹ Ifá, as *òwe*, presents the client/supplicant and everyone present in a *dá Ifá* session with a dramatic setting in which the dramatis personae include Ọ̀rúnmìla, all previous babalawo, and all antecedent clients/supplicants involved in predicaments and existential conditions. If the client identifies with his or her homologue in the *òwe*, obligations for the way forward and for the most favorable outcome to the predicament are in his or her hands.

Factors influencing the outcome include the perspicacity with which the client apprehends all the elements of the predicament presented and the level of consciousness and sense of responsibility he or she exercises in that apprehension. It is only on the basis of this premise that Èṣù, the consummate arbiter and custodian of the primordial *aṣẹ*, may exercise his office, to which the babalawo almost never fails to return in the coda of an *ẹsẹ Ifá*.

If we now return to *ẹsẹ Ifá*, as has been painstakingly explicated in many studies of far-reaching consequences by Abímbọ́lá, the first three parts are more often than not allusive. These include:

- Part one: Usually an epithet, attributive or graphically descriptive, for which Amherd (2010) felicitously suggests the French term *devise*
- Part two: Client of reference, usually in citation, *oríkì*, format
- Part three: Reason or context for the *ìdá Fá* of reference

Where any of these involves antecedents that are no longer within the shared epistemological radar of the babalawo and of the supplicant or supplicants, as well as all others present at the session, the parts are apprehended as indicative of the mystery of Ifá. These parts may be seen to serve as a "broadcast" to the audience in the sense that Tambiah (1968) remarks for homologous parts of the Trobriand ritual session. Expressions and propositions in any of these parts do not have to be archaic to escape being classifiable as ordinary language. Where, as is often the case with Ifá, they are tropes, they may not be readily intelligible to the audience.

Still, that in no way suggests that they may not be attributable to the babalawo's imaginative creativity and be seen as products of his originality. As Amherd puts it: "While ẹsẹ Ifá have standard structural units, when it comes to actually uttering the text, there clearly exists room for differently mobilizing the narrative materials. . . . The ẹsẹ Ifa is accepted as legitimate as long as a devise form is used that evokes recognition even when altering the syntax when using various discourse strategies" (2010, 249). Parts 4 to 7, where they occur, more often than not appear to be in nonheightened, ordinary language that is readily accessible to ordinary listeners. One would expect this sequence to provide the widest scope for the exponent's imaginative creativity. Again, Amherd argues in accord with this view: "Once he utters the devise, the babaláwo can construct the ìtàn in multiple ways . . . Since the ìtàn section of ẹsẹ Ifá can be expanded or shortened, the possibility of metonymically linking to other texts and even incorporating particular signs from them can be effected, and a form of discourse and commentary implied through these chains of association" (2010, 249). Clearly, if our argument for the active agency of babalawo and their implied creative originality is sustained, future research into and about Ifá should be more fruitful.

Ifá in the Americas: Implications for Poetic Competence

The Context of Cultural Contact

By all accounts, between 1785 and 1850 a considerable number of enslaved individuals and indentured workers from Southwestern Nigeria and the Benin-Togo enclave of West Africa who spoke one dialect or other of the language now known as Yorùbá found themselves in locations now identified as Brazil, Cuba, North Carolina, Sierra Leone, the South Carolina Sea Islands, and Trinidad and

Tobago. Of these places, excluding the community of Ọ̀yọ̀túnjí founded in Beaufort County in 1973, no tangible survival of the Yorùbá culture coherently associated with Ifá has been registered.

In North Carolina, I have reported (Oyelaran 1993) that the Egúngún tradition was confirmed to have been vibrant on plantations, including those in the Eno River valley until the Cape Fear Rising (also known as the Wilmington Riot) of 1898. We have not ascertained the geographical location of High John De Conquer, the African American traditional figure described in the chapter of that name in Zora Neale Hurston's *The Sanctified Church*. "High John De Conquer" replicates the myth of Ifá who returns to ọ̀run but leaves or sends the sixteen *ikin*, "nuts of the sacred tropical oil palm tree," to his people as a means by which they could gain access to him in times of need. In terms reminiscent of the Yorùbá myth of Ọ̀rúnmìlà (Abimbọla 1976, 5-7), Hurston writes of High John De Conquer:

> He is not so well known to the present generation of colored people in the same way that he was in slavery time. Like King Arthur of England, he has served his people, and gone back in mystery again. . . . High John De Conquer went back to Africa, he left his power here, and placed his American dwelling in the root of a certain plant. Possess that root, and he can be summoned at any time (Hurston 1981, 72-73).

In Sierra Leone, there appears to be no trace of Ifá; however, on research trips there in 1978 and 1980 (Oyelaran 1989), I encountered very lively traditions of Ọ̀jẹ̀ Egúngún (a cult for the ancestors); Gẹ̀lẹ̀dẹ́ (a cult to honor women exclusively); and Ògún (the divinity of the arts, identified with iron as a medium of artistic expression, especially for making implements). Fúnṣọ Aiyejina (pers. comm.) reports a continued vibrant Ṣàngó tradition in Trinidad and Tobago, particularly strong on the island of Tobago where the term Ṣàngó covers the entire gamut of the survival of the Yorùbá tradition. But there is no Ifá heritage to be found. This leaves only Brazil and Cuba as locations in the diaspora where it appears there is a strong Ifá tradition.

What is the nature of the relevant ecology of the cultural evolution—to borrow a perspective from Mufwene's paradigm-shifting book *The Ecology of Language Evolution* (2001)—that resulted in the survival of the Ifá tradition in both settings? It appears that both in Brazil (Verger 1977; Voeks 1997) and Cuba (Brandon 1997) a critical factor was the socialization of enslaved Yorùbá mature culture bearers by Spanish and Portuguese colonial populations who brought with them the Counter-Reformation Catholicism of the Middle Ages, complete with its ritual of the sacraments and a rich pantheon of saints. These culture bearers were not serving as field hands in Cuba and Brazil. It appears that given the incorporative nature of the Yorùbá tradition (Oyelaran 2001, 2008),[12] the Yorùbá who served in the homesteads of plantation owners in Bahia and Cuba had no difficulty incorporating both the Catholic rituals and saints into the Yorùbá system of òrìṣa and ẹbọ (rituals and sacrifices). This acculturation apparently excluded enslaved individuals who lived in extremely mixed populations in rural settings. The proactive enslaved Africans in the homesteads of plantation owners became change agents who acculturated both the new arrivals from West Africa and the Spanish or Portuguese settler population with whom they lived, bringing up the creole generations of European descent at the same time.

The following passages illustrate the ecological contexts that suggest the beginnings of Candomblé in Brazil, echoing those of Santería in Cuba:

> All slaves had been converted to the Catholic faith right on their arrival in Brazil. The domestic servants would accompany their masters to church for Sunday mass with pomp and pageantry, the footmen dressed in beautiful garb, the chamber-maids and nurses covered in showy jewelry for the greater glory and ostentation of opulence of the masters, but one cannot be too sure whether these conversions were always very genuine. (Verger 1977, 222–223)

> The polytheistic nature of Brazil's Catholicism was complemented by a series of other structural similarities to the religion of the Yoruba. Whereas the simple rituals of North America's Protestant churches, dominated by the Methodist and Calvinist ideals, stood in sharp contrast with the complex structure of African religious practice, "the pomp and display of the Catholic liturgy gave the Africans a basis for identification and correspondence." Elaborate rituals and offerings, belief in magic and divinations, ancestor worship, votive offerings and sacrifices, and the adjuration of gods to deal with real world problems—all fundamental to African religious structure—found their ready parallels within Catholicism. (Voeks 1997, 157–158, quoting Camara 1988)

The Nature of Ifá in Cuba and Brazil

We have had access to limited collections of texts and not more than half a dozen systematic studies of Ifá in Cuba and Bahia. In both settings, only the Dílógún (Ẹẹrìndílógún) appears to have survived and to be thriving. Hopefully further study will enable us to explain the relative portability of Dílógún compared to other Ifá divinatory systems, processes, and paraphernalia.

It does appear that selectional factors (Mufwene 2001) under the ecology of culture contact sketched above may have resulted in the structure of Ifá divinatory texts, which have strong similarities in both Bahia and Cuba. In both settings, names of the sixteen major *odù* (complete with their aliases) and the ẹbọ prescribed at the emergence of particular signature configurations have survived with surprising fidelity. Parts 1, 2, and 3 of ẹsẹ *Ifá* have survived in vestigial versions, where they have survived at all. Part 8, obligations for the client, has survived robustly. The equivalents of parts 4 to 7 have survived as revered informative narratives in both Brazil and Cuba. It is interesting, however, that narratives such as the *pataki* in Cuba (Cabrera 2000; Furé 1985; Sandoval 1975) and the *caminhos de odu* in Brazil are rendered as tales and stories when translated into English (Feuser and Carneiro da Cunha 1989). They are, in fact, dramatic narratives complete with characters in sociological settings engaged in transactional processes.

A comparison of *patakin* and *caminhos de odu* of homologous *odù* in Cuba and Brazil with *ẹsẹ Ifá* from *odù* of the same names in Nigeria points very strongly to a tendency towards creative imagination on the part of exponents across the board.[13] Comparative texts of the same *ẹsẹ Ifá* by and from different babalawo in Nigeria reveal similar suggestions of imaginative creativity on the part of the exponents. In support of this view, compare Ọ̀sá Méjì in Agboọlá (1989, 136–137), partly versified, with Abímbọ́lá (1975, 295, 297, 299, 301), entirely versified. This leaves us with a strong inclination to pursue our inquiry about manifestations of poetic competence and creative originality in any component part or sets of parts of *ẹsẹ Ifá*.

Nevertheless, I do not wish to give the impression that I am minimizing the rigor in the training of a babalawo; nor do my arguments set at naught the indispensable role that memorization and reiteration play in the cultivation of the competence of the agent and mouthpiece of Ọ̀rúnmìla, the babalawo. Rather, I hold steadfastly to the important role of creative originality and generative competence in the babalawo in the performance of *ẹsẹ Ifá* at all times. Indeed, I subscribe to Amherd's instructive way of putting the matter:

> The apprenticeship of babaláwo requires the utmost conformity to the conservative practices of the profession where recitations should conform to the master's teaching. Nearly every researcher who has dealt with babaláwo has commented on their high ethical behavior, reinforced by the fact of a babaláwo's being immersed in a community, locally and extensively, which provides a checks-and-balance conservatism that inhibits the gratuitous invention of texts by those who are unable to live up to the intellectual and ethical rigor that Ifá requires. (2010, 223)

Implications

Our inquiry so far invites us to weigh the consequences of the nature of our commitment to the various ways we may have for promoting Ifá. If, as we strongly suspect, plausible conclusions supported with experiential data lead to the entertainment of creative originality as an essential attribute of babalawo, then the transmission to the up-and-coming generations and the propagation and dissemination of essentials of Ifá will enable us to benefit from all the available information technology at our disposal. If, on the other hand, we accept the role of rote learning, exclusive of any inkling of poetic competence on the part of the babalawo, then perhaps all we need do is compile, order, and provide a search mechanism for the "exhaustive" compendium of ẹsẹ *Ifá*. That done, all we need do is put these at the disposal of the babalawo, or of anyone, for that matter, to use whenever the signature configuration of a specific *odù* emerges in the process of divination. That will, without a doubt, enable us to ensure that Ifá continues to be transmitted "free of errors," most certainly with the highest fidelity to a finite recoverable set of texts. Of course, the challenge will remain how to also preserve Ifá's generative capacity for *òwe*, for trope, and indeed for coping with new and emergent human experiences and predicaments. This question persists because it is unclear how to preserve the long-standing tropes of Ifá when Ifá must develop new *òwe*, a new way of speaking, in response to our contemporary experience.

Notes

1. In the ẹsẹ *odù* of this reference, Ọsanyìn accompanies Ọrúnmìlà to Olódùmàrè in order to acquire "essential" information about and understand the essence of all objects of consciousness. Èdè (language) is the Òjiṣẹ́ of Olódùmàrè, and mediates, for all conscious beings with speech, access to and acquisition of the information they seek.

2. Plausibly from "*baba-ní-awo*." We have chosen to understand "*baba*" to stand for "one who has precedence and authority," "*ní*" for "in respect of," "*awo*" for "mystery" rather than "secret." Access to a secret is "concessional," whereas one may gain "access" to a mystery through systematic inquiry or learning.

3. Yai cites Bierwisch and Heidolph (1970), 105.

4. Imitation, then, is one instinct of our nature. . . . Persons, therefore, starting with this natural gift developed by degrees their special aptitudes, till their rude improvisations gave birth to Poetry.

 The poet being an imitator, like a painter or any other artist, must of necessity imitate one of three objects—things as they were or are, things as they are said or thought to be, or things as they ought to be. The vehicle of expression is language—either current terms or, it may be, rare words or metaphors. There are also many modifications of language, which we concede to the poets. (Aristotle 1997, 53)

5. A reviewer remarked quite appropriately: "It is significant what you have left out. None of the genres respecting [sic] gods/deities and other religious elements. Ṣàngó pípè is a good example. How much improvisation in this genre? Shouldn't we separate religions from secular pursuits in this regard?"

 I owe this felicitous interrogation to Femi Taiwo. The predicative nuclear "*pè*" may be glossed as "to call; to invoke." It may take any and all of the divinities, òrìṣà, as predicate. In essence, the core of òrìṣà pípè is "oríkì," which suggests invocation by and through the means of citing the primordial essence of the divinity for whatever purpose, including descending to ride, *gùn*, his or her horse, the devotee, ẹlégùn òrìṣà. There is, therefore, no way to exclude "Ṣàngó, Ọya, Ògún, [etc.] *pípè*" from any consideration of creative originality.

6. The babaláwo and all "cognoscenti" present at a divinatory session literally salute an emerging *odù*, because the *odù*, indeed, have the status of royalty, as they do of divinity.

7. These include Cabrera (1980).

8. But of note is the following excerpt from the same source, which appears to apply only to the predicate *sun* as in the genre *ìyèrè* and the performance voice *sun ìyèrè*.

9. William Bascom (1969), earlier than Abímbọ́lá (1976), is more nuanced in attributing the training of babalawo without exception to rote learning. He limits memorization to only "the 256 figures," to which the predicates *dá Ifá* and *tè Ifá* properly apply. He goes on to say of the remaining process to which the predicate *kì Ifá* appears appropriate that:

> As for the working of the system of divination, these verses are of far greater importance than either the figures themselves or the manipulations from which they are derived. The verses form an important corpus of verbal art, including myths, folktales, praise names, incantations, songs, proverbs, and even riddles; but to the Yoruba their "literary" or aesthetic merit is secondary to their religious significance. *In effect these verses constitute their unwritten scriptures.* (Bascom 1969, 11, emphasis mine)

This nuance allows Bascom (1993, 26–28) to remark on evidence of performance variation from one babaláwo to another, and by the same babaláwo from session to another.

Kọ́lá Abímbọ́lá (2006, xviii), on the other hand, appears to wedge his position between these earlier scholars, leaving his reader groping for meaning when he writes that:

> Given the fact that the Odù Ifá is to a large extent "fixed" and "given," the situation becomes somewhat analogous to that of professional philosophers who interpret, analyse and reflect critically on any major philosopher such as Plato, Immanuel Kant, Martin Heidegger. . . . The Odù Ifá are (relatively) fixed and given, but there is considerable room for different critical reflective appraisal of them when Ifá priests and priestesses make use of the Odù Ifá as heuristic action principles on the basis of which they counsel and advise people.

10. For the enormous literature on *Ówe*, a good point of departure for anyone in the Americas is Oyekan Owomoyela (1988, 2005). I wish to register here that the loss of Oyekan Owomoyela is irreparable for the study and advancement of the Yorùbá tradition and culture. May his generous soul rest in peace! I do and will miss a dialogue with him on every position taken in this chapter and its future sequel both for my own edification and for the advancement of learning for others.

11. See also Opadotun (1986) and Sheba (1986, 1997).

12. Compare also the existence of "*odù Ìmàle*" (Abímbọ́lá 1971).

13. For Brazil, this is confirmed by the texts of Ọ̀bàrà Méjì (Feuser and da Cunha 1989, appendix III-1). For Nigerian references see Abímbọ́lá (1976, 96–97), and Bascom (1993) 494, 496, 498, 500).

References

Abímbọ́lá, Kọ́lá. 2006. *Yorùbá Culture: A Philosophical Account.* Birmingham, UK: Ìrókò Academic Publishers.

Abímbọ́lá, Wándé. 1971. "Ifá divination poetry and the coming of Islam to Yorubaland." *Pan-African Journal* 4, no. 4: 440–454.

———. 1975. *Sixteen Great Poems of Ifá.* Paris: UNESCO.

———. 1976. *Ifá: An Exposition of Ifá Literary Corpus.* Ibadan: Oxford University Press.

———. 1977. "The Yoruba Traditional Religion in Brazil: Problems and Prospects." In *Seminar Series*, no. 1, part 1, edited by Ọlasope O. Oyelaran, 1–63. Ilé-Ifè: University of Ifè Press.

——. 1997. *Ifá Will Mend Our Broken World.* Roxbury, MA: Aims Books.

Abiọdun, Rowland, Henry J. Drewal, and John Pemberton III, eds. 1994. *The Yoruba Artist.* Washington, DC: Smithsonian Institution Press.

Agboọlá, Àgbà Awo A. Faṣínà. 1989. *Ojúlówò Oríkì Ifá.* Lagos: Project Publications.

Amherd, K. Noel. 2010. *Reciting Ifá: Difference, Heterogeneity, and Identity.* Trenton, NJ: Africa World Press.

Aristotle. 1997. *Poetics.* Mineola, NY: Dover.

Bascom, William. 1969. *Ifa Divination: Communication between Gods and Men in West Africa.* Bloomington: Indiana University Press.

——. 1993. *Sixteen Cowries: Yoruba Divination from Africa to the New World.* Rev. ed. Bloomington: Indiana University Press.

Bierwisch, Manfred, and Karl Erich Heidolph, eds. *Progress in Linguistics: A Collection of Papers.* The Hague: Mouton, 1970.

Brandon, George. 1997. *Santeria from Africa to the New World.* Bloomington: Indiana University Press.

Cabrera, Lydia. 1980. *Koeko Iyawó: Aprende Novicia.* Miami: Colecion del Chichereku en el Exilio.

——. 2000. *El Monte: Igbo, Finda, Ewe Orisha, Vititi Nfinda.* Miami: Ediciones Universal.

Drewal, Henry John, John Pemberton III, Rowland Abiodun, and Allen Wardwell. 1989. *Yoruba: Nine Centuries of African Art and Thought.* New York: Center for African Art in association with H. N. Abrams.

Ẹlẹbuibọn, Yẹmí. 1999. *Ìyẹ̀rẹ̀ Ifá (Tonal Poetry, the Voice of Ifá).* San Bernardino, CA: Ilé Ọrúnmìlá Communications.

Feuser, William, and José Mariano Carneiro da Cunha. 1989. *Dílógún: Brazilian Tales of Yorùbá Divination Discovered in Bahia by Pierre Verger.* Ibadan: Shaneson C.I.

Furé, Rogelio Martinez. 1985. "Patakin: Littérature sacrée de Cuba." In *Culture Africaines: Documents de la réunion d'experts sur "Les survivances des traditions religieuses africaines dans les Caraibes et en Amérique latine,"* 43–68. Paris: UNESCO.

Hurston, Zora Neale. 1981. *The Sanctified Church: The Folklore Writings of Zora Neale Hurston.* Berkeley, CA: Turtle Island.

Law, Robin. 1996. "Ethnicity and Slavery: 'Lukumi' and 'Nago' as Ethnonyms in West Africa." Paper presented at the annual conference of the African Studies Association, San Francisco, November 23–26.

Mason, John. 1992. *Orin Òrìṣà: Songs for Selected Heads.* Brooklyn: Yorùbá Theological Archministry.

Mufwene, Salikoko S. 2001. *The Ecology of Language Evolution.* Cambridge: Cambridge University Press.

Ọlaniyan, Richard. 1975. "Elements of Yoruba Diplomacy in Oral Tradition." In *Yoruba Oral Tradition,* edited by Wándé Abímbọ́lá, 292–332. Ile-Ifẹ̀: University of Ifẹ Press.

Olomola, Isola. 1979. "Atroko: An Indigenous Yoruba Semiotic Device." *Odu: A Journal of West African Studies* 19 (January/July): 78–102.

——. 1991. "Alile: Traditional Security System Among the Yoruba." *Africana Marburgensia* 24, no. 2: 50–61.

Opadotun, Olatunji ("Elewi Odo"). 1986. *Aroko: Awon Ami ati Iro Ibanisoro l'Ate Ijeloo.* Ibadan: Vantage Publishers.

Owomoyela, Oyekan. 1988. *A Kì í: Yoruba Proscriptive and Prescriptive Proverbs.* Lanham, MD: University Press of America.

——. 2005. *Yoruba Proverbs.* Lincoln: University of Nebraska Press.

———. 2007. "Preservation or Mummification? The Implications of Subjecting Traditional Texts to Modern Processes." *Research in African Literatures* 38, no. 3: 170–182.

Oyèláràn, Olasope. 1988. " Ìtàn Ìdàgbàsókè Ẹ̀kọ́ Ìmọ̀ Èdè Yorùbá Láti Ìbẹ̀rẹ̀rẹ̀ Pẹ̀pẹ̀." In *Yoruba: A Language in Transition; J. F. Ọdunjọ Memorial Lectures*, edited by Ọlatúndé O. Ọlátúnjí, 16–58. Ibadan: J. F. Ọdunjọ Memorial Lecture Series.

———. 1989. "Of Roots and Transplants: The Case of Yoruba Institutions in the Krio Culture." Paper presented at the conference "Cultural Vibrations: Transformations and Continuities in the Yoruba Diaspora," Center for African Studies, University of Florida, Gainesville, April 27–28.

———. 1993. "West African Languages: A Window on African American Contribution to the Uniqueness of South Carolina." *Research in Yoruba Language and Literature* 4: 10–35.

———. 2001. "The Intension of Yorùbá Pantheon of 401 Òrìsà." Paper presented at the conference "Aguda: Aspects of Afro-Brazilian Heritage in the Bight of Benin," Ecole du Patrimoine Africain, Porto Novo, Republic of Benin, November 26–30.

———. 2008. "In What Tongue?" In *Òrìsà Devotion as a World Religion: Global Yorùbá Religious Culture*, edited by Jacob K. Olupona and Terry Rey, 70–83. Madison: University of Wisconsin Press.

Oyèláràn, Olasope, and Lawrence O. Adewole. 2007. *Ìsẹ̀mbáyé àti Ìlò Èdè Yorùbá.* CASAS Book Series no. 30. Cape Town: Centre for Advanced Studies of African Society.

Peek, Philip M. 1991. *African Divinatory Systems: Ways of Knowing.* Bloomington: Indiana University Press.

Pessoa de Castro, Yeda. 1985. "Les religions d'origine africaines au Brézil: Dénominations, origins, cultes noveaux et cultes peu connus." In *Culture Africaines: Documents de la réunion d'experts sur "Les survivances des traditions religieuses africaines dans les Caraibes et en Amérique latine,"* 129–143. Paris: UNESCO.

———. 2008. "Towards a Comparative Approach of Bantuism in Iberoamerica." In *AfriAmericas: Itineraries, Dialogues and Sounds*, edited by Ineke Phaf-Rheinberger and Tiago Oliveira de Pinto, 79–90. Madrid: Iberoamericana-Vervuert.

Pierson, Donald. 1942. *Negroes in Brazil: A Study of Race Contact in Bahia.* Chicago: University of Chicago Press.

Sandoval, Mercedes Cros. 1975. *La Religion Afrocubana.* Madrid: Layor.

Sheba, Eben. "Aroko: A Symbolic Communication among the Yoruba, and Its Potentials for Modern Graphic Design." MA thesis, University of Ifẹ̀, 1986.

———. 1999. "Aale: A Deterrent Symbol and Communication Device Among the Ikale Yoruba of Nigeria." *Ife: Journal of the Institute of Cultural Studies* no. 7: 10–17.

Tambiah, S. J. 1968. "The Magical Power of Words." *Man* 3, no. 2: 175–208.

Thornton, John. 1992. *Africa and Africans in the Making of the Atlantic World, 1400–1680.* New York: Cambridge University Press.

Vega, Marta Moreno. 2000. *The Altar of My Soul: The Living Traditions of Santeria.* New York: Ballantine.

Verger, Pierre. 1977. "African Religions and the Valorization of Brazilians of African Descent." In *Seminar Series*, no. 1, part 1, edited by Ọlasope O. Oyelaran, 217–241. Ile-Ifẹ̀: University of Ifẹ̀ Press.

———. 1995. *Ewé: The Use of Plants in Yoruba Society.* Sao Paulo: Fundação Pierre Verger.

Voeks, Robert A. 1997. *Sacred Leaves of Candomblé: African Magic, Medicine, and Religion in Brazil.* Austin: University of Texas Press.

Yai, Ọlabiyi Babalọla. 1986. *Towards a New Poetics of Oral Poetry in Africa*. Ilé-Ifẹ̀: University of Ifẹ̀ Press.

———. 1994. "In Praise of Metonymy: The Concepts of 'Tradition' and 'Creativity' in the Transmission of Yoruba Artistry over Time and Space." In *The Yoruba Artist*, edited by Rowland Abiọdun, Henry J. Drewal, and John Pemberton III, 107–115. Washington, DC: Smithsonian Institution Press.

———. 1999. "The Path is Open: The Legacy of Melville and Frances Herskovits in African Oral Narrative Analysis." *Research in African Literatures*, 30, no. 2: 1–16.

Yemonjá, Mãe Beata de. 2002. *Roço Dendê a Saberdoria dos Terreiros*. 2nd ed. Rio de Janeiro: Pallas Editora.

5 "Writing" and "Reference" in Ifá

Adélékè Adéẹ̀kọ́

In JULY 1897, Bishop Charles Phillips, a leading member of the Yorùbá-speaking clergy of the Anglican Church in Nigeria, praised Reverend E. M. Lijadu's commentaries on Ifá divination stories as a bold first step towards understanding the basis of the disappointing result of evangelization in the Yorùbá missionary field. Thinking of conversion work in warfare terms, Bishop Phillips believed Lijadu's collection and commentary to be a brilliant reconnaissance:

> *Bí a kò bá rí ìdí ibi tí agbára ọ̀tá gbé wà, a kò lè ṣẹgun wọn. Bí àwa Kristian kò bá mọ ìdí ìsìn àwọn Kèfèrí àti àwọn Ìmàle, a kì yóò lè gbé ìhìnrere Kristi síwájú wọn lí ọ̀nà tí yóò fi ká wọn lára.*

> If we do not locate the source of our enemies' strength, we cannot defeat them. If we Christians do not fathom the foundation of pagan and Islamic devotion, we will not be able to present Christ's gospel to them in the most appealing form. (Lijadu 1972 [1898], 4)[1]

The bishop also decried the unfortunate attitude that misled Christian missionaries in Yorùbá-speaking regions to forget how the mastery of pre-Christian practices helped conversion in biblical places and times.[2] Bishop Phillips rebukes fellow soldiers for their intellectual arrogance in not acting early enough on pre-Christian Yorùbá religion. He finds unconscionable their belief in their ability to preach effectively and convert sufficiently without understanding the basis of thought among the people they are charged to persuade about the gospel:

> *Ṣùgbọ́n àwa ńja ogun àti-fi ìhìnrere Kristi múlẹ̀ ni ilẹ̀ wa láì wá ìdí ìsìn àtọwọ́dọ́wọ́ àwọn bàbá wa tí ó ní agbára tóbẹ́ẹ̀ lórí àwọn Kèfèrí. Nítorí náà ni iwààsù wa kò ní agbára tó bẹ́ẹ̀ lórí wọn. Òmíràn nínú wọn rò pé àìmọ̀ ni ó jẹ́ kí àwa máa sọ ìsọkúsọ sí ìsìn wọn.*

> We strive to plant Christ's gospel in our country without researching the very strong, albeit pagan, ancient beliefs of our fathers. Our preaching produces

little impact for that reason. Unknown numbers among them believe that we deride their religions because we know nothing about them. (ibid.)

Perhaps the most important observation Bishop Phillips made in that short preface concerns the effect he believed publishing Ifá stories in book form would have on unbelievers:

> *Nígbà tí àwọn tí ó ńkọ́ Ifá sórí bá mọ̀ pé wọ́n lè ka Odù Ifá nínú ìwé, mo rò pé yóò ṣí wọn lórí láti kọ́ ìwé kíkà, àti láti fi ọ̀rọ̀ inú Bíbélì wé ti Odù Ifá. Wọn yóò sì rí èyí tí ó sàn jù fún ara wọn.*

> I believe that when rote learners of Ifá stories discover that they can read the Odù in a book, they will seek literacy eagerly, gain the capacity to compare the Bible to Ifá stories, and discover on their own the merit of the superior text. (ibid.)

By casting Ifá stories in a comparatively permanent medium, Christian workers would be creating a self-reflection apparatus for the literate nonbeliever. It would become a tool with which to critically examine thought spheres hitherto controlled by the guild of divination priests (the babalawo). Taking divination stories to be Ifá's main tool of mind control, Bishop Phillips recommended print dissemination of these narratives as a means of freeing up the critical faculty of non-Christians against the shroud of secrecy (*awo*), with which Ifá priests have deceived Yorùbá people through the ages. Print technology, he thought, would separate *awo* from its curators (babalawo). For Bishop Phillips, the deep secret of pre-Christian Yorùbá worship lay not in sculptured icons but in the reasoning that inspires divination stories. The theological errors of Yorùbá religion could be easily pointed out if the stories are converted to portable packages comparable to the Bible, the only book authored by the true God. In a palpable, scripted shape indigenous religious thought could be quoted, disputed, and its false teaching exposed.

Within Bishop Phillips' manifest desire to accelerate conversion through a literacy campaign there is a noticeable "nationalist" displeasure at the condescension of fellow missionaries who mistook the historical lack of printed scriptures among the Yorùbá as a sign of backwardness:

> *àwá fi ojú kékeré wo àwọn kèfèrí ilẹ̀ wa nítorí pé wọn kò ní ìwé. Bẹ́ẹ̀ ni àwa mọ̀ pé ó ní iye ẹ̀kọ́ tí ènìyàn ńkọ́ kí a tó gbàá bí babaláwo. Èdè Ifá jìnlẹ̀ gidigidi.*

> We belittle the intelligence of the pagans of our country because they do not have written scriptures, when the situation shows that babaláwo training truly involves extended and rigorous training. Ifá discourse is very profound. (ibid.)

Bishop Phillips seems to be insinuating that if the situation were considered without prejudice, it would be realized that the unbelievers of "our land" have

authored "books" waiting to be transcribed and analyzed. Although this essay
stops short of saying that Ifá stories constitute a book, my characterization of Ifá
discourse as revolving around writing shares Bishop Phillips's representation of
the storytelling elements of Ifá divination infrastructure as an instituted, durable
signification system.[3]

Bishop Phillips isolates two questions that still persist in academic studies of
Ifá: (1) Does the divination infrastructure, especially the contents of the stories,
elaborate a unified Yorùbá theological or philosophical viewpoint? (2) Are Ifá
divination stories oracular utterances or fancy-driven poetic inventions? These
questions reflect the concerns of two tendencies in Ifá studies. First, the insiders—professional custodians of Ifá divination stories who lean heavily on literal
assertions of the stories, and who claim divine origins for the narratives upon
which they base their authority to make proclamations on the nature of all things
and ideas across time and space. This includes ideas and thoughts about things
and ideas. Second, from the outside, there is the radical polytheism of religious
identification in Yorùbá traditional societies that encourages skeptics to question
Ifá's exclusive arrogation of theological centrality to itself.

As the contemporary scholar Karin Barber's (1990) study implies, scholars
make Ifá the central divinity in Yorùbá religion because they accept too easily
Ifá's elaborate self-justifications, particularly its stories about itself. Scholars and
divination practitioners speak as if the illustrative stories used in Ifá consultation
are patently guileless and their divine authorship therefore ascertained. Wándé
Abímbọ́lá's plain reporting of his informants' view that the source of the disclosure system he supervises during divination is the first-hand knowledge that
the divination God, Ọ̀rúnmìlà, gained exclusively by virtue of his presence at
creation (Abímbọ́lá 1977, 1) illustrates Barber's point very well. In Abímbọ́lá's accounts, Ifá's divination procedures are retrieval mechanisms for accessing the
corpus of primordial knowledge stored in (and as) divination stories. He declares
in *Ifá Divination Poetry*, for example, that "Ifá was put in charge of divination
because of his great wisdom, which he acquired as a result of his presence by
the side of Olódùmarè [the Almighty] when the latter created the universe. Ifá
therefore knew all the hidden secrets of the universe. Hence, his praise-name
Akéréfinúṣọgbọ́n (the small one who is full of wisdom)" (ibid.). Although he does
not trust the truth claims of Ifá's self-justifying narratives as Abímbọ́lá does,
Lijadu does not question Ifá's centrality, even in the largely antagonistic first volume of his studies. Lijadu contests the theological basis of many stories, but accepts the placement of Ọ̀rúnmìlà next to the Almighty:

> àwọn bàbá wa mọ̀, wọ́n sí ní ìmọ̀ náà lí èrò nígbà gbogbo, wọn kò sì ṣe tàbítàbí kí
> wọ́n tó jẹ́wọ́ ìmọ̀ yìí pé Ẹni kan mbẹ tí í ṣe Ẹlẹ́dàá ohun gbogbo, tí í ṣe Olúwa ohun
> gbogbo, tí ó sì ní ipa, ọlá àti agbára gbogbo, Olúwa rẹ̀ náà ni wọ́n ńpè lí Ọlọ́run
> Olódùmarè tàbí Ọba ọrun . . . Olódùmarè ti fi Ẹni kan ṣe ibìkejì ara Rẹ̀, Òun à sì

máa pe Olúwa rẹ̀ sí ìmọ̀ nínú ohun gbogbo, Òun á sì máa fi ohun gbogbo hàn án, Òun sì fí i ṣe ẹlẹ́rìí ara Ré ninu ohun gbogbo, tóbẹ́ẹ̀ tí kò sí ohun tí Olódùmarè mọ̀ tí Olúwa rẹ̀ náà kò mọ̀, kò sì sí ohun tí Olódùmarè rí tí Òun kò rí. Ẹni náà ni wọ́n ńpè ní 'Ọ̀rúnmìlà, Ẹlẹ́rìí ìpín, ibìkejì Olódùmarè.' Lọ́dọ̀ ẹni yìí nìkan ni wọ́n sì gbàgbọ́ pé ènìyàn lè gbọ́ òdodo ohùn ẹnu àti ìfẹ́ inú Olódùmare.

Our forefathers knew, always had the knowledge in them, and did not waiver in witnessing that there is a being by whom all things were made, the Lord whose might, glory, and power surpass all. That being they named as God Almighty or Heavenly King . . . God has by his side a second entity to whom he discloses the knowledge of all things and in whom he reposes all confidence such that everything the Almighty knows this person knows, and everything the Almighty sees, he too sees. This person is the one called "Ọ̀rúnmìlà, the witness to the allotment of destiny, second to the Almighty." This person is the only true source of Almighty God's plans. (Lijadu 1972 [1898], 17–18)

Although understandable professional interests could have caused the preference of Abímbọ́lá's informants, the admiration of indigenous Christian missionaries suggests that more than selfish goals are involved in the way Ifá is thought about.[4] Phillips and Lijadu seemed to value the promise Ifá stories hold for systematizing Yorùbá theology.

While I do not share the prosecutorial inclination of Barber's essay, I am sympathetic to her materialist, text-oriented analysis of the incorporation mechanisms with which Ifá discourse presents its operations as unquestionably pantheistic; Ifá discourse definitely does not disguise it. I am proposing in this paper that Ifá divination discourse holds the attention of its operators because it foregrounds an objective, graphematic approach to what constitutes intellectual problems, the methods of analyzing them, and the means of teasing out solutions. I begin with a brief explication of the divination processes, the underlying reasoning, and the general problems of inquiry the system raises. My ensuing analysis of the relationship of storytelling to inscriptions shows that the referential gap between these two main elements of the Ifá divination system is the location from which practitioners derive their authority for creating narrative motifs and making commentaries. This essay concludes with a discussion of how the same referential gap enables a view of time that allows divination clients to manage a coherent relationship to the past and to the ostensible source of the solutions to their contemporary problems.

Writing in Ifá

The foundation of analysis in Ifá is the systematized graphic translation of the results of the random presentation of the divination objects, among which the chain (ọ̀pẹ̀lẹ̀) and palm nuts (*ikin*) are the two most prestigious. To divine with nuts, the priest holds sixteen ritually sanctified palm nuts in his or her enclosed palms, shakes them well, and takes off a bunch with the right hand. If two nuts remain in the left palm, the diviner makes one short vertical fingertip imprint on the fine sand spread on the divination tray. If one nut remains two imprints are made. A remainder of more than two or none does not yield any sign. When the chain—which consists of eight half divination nut shells with four each attached to two sides of a string—is the preferred instrument, the diviner holds it in the middle and throws it four times. The presentation of each throw is transcribed on the tray. A nut that falls with its concave inner surface upward indicates one imprint; the one that falls with the convex side up indicates two imprints. Producing readable inscriptions is obviously faster with the chain method. In either method the priest reads the imprints, top down, right side first, to identify which of the sixteen basic units of the Ifá graphemes (odù Ifá) is presented. Identifying the presented units gives the diviner clues as to which stories to tell to illustrate the problems revealed by the divination god and to decipher what ritual sacrifices or behavioral changes to prescribe. The casting, imprinting, and narrating process typically starts after the client has whispered his or her purpose into some tokens, which could be money mixed with the divination objects. The sign revealed and the illustrative stories told must bear some allegorical relationship to the problems the client wants to solve.

Virtually all Ifá scholars agree on the names, visible appearance, and order of the characters that make up the basic notation system (the graphemes), with Ogbè in the first position, Òyèkú in the second, and Òfún in the sixteenth. In practical counseling, the basic units must double to produce a diagnosis and prognosis. A pattern that signals Òyèkú on the right and Ogbè on the left will be named Òyèkúlógbè—it will be Ogbèyèkú, if the other way round—and one Òfún on both sides will be Òfún Méjì (Doubled Òfún).[5] The inscriptions issue from a grid that is structured so systematically that naming errors can be fixed with little difficulty.[6]

The foundational role of the inscription system in the Ifá divination process distinguishes it as a "literate" learned means of inquiry—Ifá is commonly called alákòwé (operator of the scribal discourse)—and not a séance or some other kind of intuitive, magical, or gifted fortune telling. The practitioners' rigorous and lengthy training further enhances Ifá's image of honest dedication and discipline. References to the profession in everyday speech extol honesty and straightforwardness. The saying "a kìí ṣawo ká puró" ("The person sworn to the divination profession cannot lie") attests axiomatically to the diviner's truthfulness. Of course, professional practices and rituals lend an air of mystery, if not mysticism to the inscription system. To the untrained observer, the link between palm-nut manipulation (or string casting) and readable, visible imprints is thoroughly occultic. Nonetheless, the credit for the aura goes largely to the discourse's consistent association of named, visibly embodied signs to oracular revelations. Diviners gain respect and command attention because they operate as disinterested agents of a disclosure system anchored by an inscription sign system whose production is outwardly indifferent to the "writer's" time- and space-bound will. The mute sign's lack of passion one way or the other about the case presented, and its theoretical ability to repeat the same signification for all clients consistently, cannot but induce trust. The notation system, in theory and perception, removes the individual priest's influence and will from the intercourse between the client and the witness to creation, Ọ̀rúnmìlà, who inspirits its knowledge in the presentation of the material divination instrument. The notation system, and not the human diviner, arbitrates the most important steps in the discovery and disclosure processes. I do not believe humility motivates diviners, including the most accomplished, who attribute their acumen for making correct findings to Ifá—"*Ifá ló wí bẹ́ẹ̀*" (Ifá renders it thus); they tout the superiority of their instruments of discovery.

Lijadu's work offers evidence of the importance of "writing" to Ifá's prestige. Although his Christian priestly calling demands that he should reject Ifá as idolatry—and he does—Lijadu initiates his Ifá studies because Ifá discourse involves etiological stories that are tied to an inscription system presumed to have originated from Orunmila, a deity believed to have been physically present at the beginning of all creation. Genealogy in Ifá discourse goes directly to the Supreme Being after passing through only the divination god and the system of honest inscriptions instituted in his name. In the second chapter of Ifá, Lijadu asks, "*Kínni a lè pè ní Ìfihàn-Ọ̀rọ̀ Ọlọ́run? Kí sì ni ẹ̀rí tí a lè fi mọ̀ ọ́ yàtọ̀ sí ọ̀rọ̀ mìràn* ([W]hat is a divine revelation? And what proof distinguishes it from others)?" He answers the question thus:

> *Ọ̀rọ̀ Ọlọ́run ni èyí tí a bá lè jẹ́rìí pé Ọlọ́run tìkára rẹ̀ li ó sọ ọ́ fún gbígbọ́ tàbí tí ó kọ ọ́ sílẹ̀ fún kíkà àwa ènìyàn. Lẹ́hìn èyí—Ọ̀rọ̀ Ọlọ́run ni èyí tí ẹnikẹ́ni sọ, tàbí tí ó kọ sílẹ̀, ìbá à ṣe nípa àṣẹ tàbí nípa ìmísí Ọlọ́run tìkárarẹ̀.*

> God's genuine revelations are the ones for which we can truly testify that he either spoke directly to us or wrote down for us to read. God's genuine revelations could also be those spoken out or written down by those directly ordered or inspired by the Almighty to do so. (1972 [1898)], 30)

The Godhead is the original writer and speaker, who directly delivers his wishes in inscribed or spoken words. He could speak to favored listeners or dictate to chosen scribes who would send the words forth. Either way, the medium—words, writing surfaces, or the inspired individual—must be touched directly by God in order for the message they bear to be valid.

Ifá divination protocols are the closest means an "oral" society can devise to fulfill the basis of genuinely divine writing and speaking, as Lijadu conceived it. Ọ̀rúnmìlà was copresent with the Almighty at the beginning of things. The divination god, skilled in inscriptions, reduces everything the Almighty has done to 256 symbols. Ọ̀rúnmìlà does not create things. He only transcribes the

Almighty's creations and designs. People trained to access Ọ̀rúnmìlà's significations portray him as capable of correcting mistakes (*atórí ẹni tí ò sunwọ̀n ṣe*) not because of an independent inventive power, but because his transcriptions of the Godhead's directions give clues to the right path. I would like to speculate that Lijadu's very close study of Ifá as a specimen of pre-Christian Yorùbá theology is based on the prominent role of direct writing in the disclosure system. Lijadu does not condemn Ifá as a system of direct divine revelation, probably because of its close ties to a minimally mediated writing system. He rejects Ifá because its stories—and not its graphic encoding—about God's true nature, true worship, true human nature, and God's relationship to humans do not quite agree with Biblical tenets. Lijadu is dissatisfied with Ifá teachings on human nature, especially regarding divine truth, the love of God and of fellow men and women, holiness, and Ifa's disinterested search for divine grace, because the teachings are too lax and therefore unmeritorious in comparison to Christianity.

Reference in Ifá

Divination continues when the priest, after completing the transcription of the revealed sign and following the set structure of the Ifá story unit (ẹsẹ), recites a narrative whose central motif addresses a situation similar in some respect to the predicament that the client seeks to resolve. All the stories pose a problem and a protagonist, usually in the form of an original client believed to have been the person for whom the indicated story and inscription were first devised. The stories also construct at least one antagonist, a set of resolutions or an escalation, and the reaction of the entity that first experienced the problem (Abímbọ́lá 1976, 43–62; Bascom 1969, 120–137; Olatunji 1984, 127–134). Death (ikú), disease (àrùn), loss (òfò), curse (èpè), paralysis (ègbà), general misfortune (òràn), incarceration (ẹ̀wọ̀n), accidents (eṣe), and witchcraft (àjẹ́ and oṣó) are the most common antagonists. These problems can afflict a person at any time. One's enemies could also cause them through some diabolical machinations. Opposed to the antagonists are the highly sought general blessings (ire) of wealth (owó), child bearing (ọmọ), good health (àlàáfíà) and longevity (àìkú). The antagonists represent forces of illness and the protagonists represent those of wellness. The two groups fight for control of the client's body and social existence. The story unit (ẹsẹ) has no independently verifiable embodiment, in that it does not attach directly to one graphematic sign. In effect, the divined inscriptions generate stories and not phonemes. Ifá writing is mythographic and not phonocentric. To use Derrida's words, it "spells its symbols pluri-dimensionally" and its referents are "not subject to successivity, to the order of a logical time, or to the irreversible temporality of sound" (Derrida 1976, 85).

T. M. Ilesanmi's schematic analysis of Ifá inscriptions and narratives reveals a deep-seated binarism—"*agbára méjì tó so ayé ro*" ("the two poles on which existence suspends") (2004, 132)—which Ifá diviners use to manage the "pluri-dimensional" significations of their writing method. According to Ilesanmi,[7] Ifá priests ascribe positive or *ire* (good, desirable, highly sought) values to some elements and negative or aburú (bad, undesirable, abhorred) values to others. They tie these values to the order of temporal appearance: the first to appear is the most positive, the next one less so. The positive values are indicated with an imprinted one and a negative value is indicated with a two. The sixteen primary figures of the *odù* are valued according to how imprinted signs (ones and twos) and the ordinal rank of the presented odù (first, second, and so on) add up. Thus Ogbè, signed with all ones (and no twos) is relentlessly positive (*bẹ́ẹ̀ ni*) and Ọ̀yẹ̀kú, all twos (and no ones) is frighteningly negative (béẹ̀ kọ́). These two signs are ranked first and second in the ordinal system.

> *Àwọn odù méjì yìí ló ta ko ara wọn jù nínú àbùdá oníbeji bẹ́ẹ̀-ni-bẹ́ẹ̀-kó. Ọ̀kan kò ní bẹ́ẹ̀-kọ́ rárá; èkejì kò sì ní bẹ́ẹ̀-ni olóókan. Kò sí ìgbà tí àwọn méjèèjì jọ wí ohun kan náà. Gbogbo àwọn odù yòókù ló ní bẹ́ẹ̀-ni díẹ̀, bẹ́ẹ̀-kọ́ díẹ̀ nínú. Nínú ọkan, ire le pọ̀ ju ibi lọ, nínú òmíràn, ibi le pọ̀ ju ire lọ. Wàyí o, ipò tí ibi àti ire wà ta ko ara wọn. Iye ire àti ibi kan náà ni Èdí àti Ìwòrì ní ṣùgbọ́n wọ́n fi ipò ta ko ara wọn.*

> These two odù are polar opposites in the positive and negative binary structure. One has no negative at all; the other has not one positive. At no point do the two odù express the same attributes. All the other odù signs express a little of positive and negative values. In some, positives outnumber negatives, in others negatives outnumber positives. The positioning of the attributes might oppose each other. Èdí and Ìwòrì express equal number of positives and negatives but in different positions. (Ilesanmi 2004, 134–135)

According to Ilesanmi's very useful charts of the *odu* (2004, 136), Ọsẹ́ (in the fifteenth position) and Ọ̀fún (in the sixteenth position) have the same number of positive and negative values, but they are placed in opposite positions. The pattern of values in the sign of Ọsẹ́ is: a negative, a positive, a negative, and a positive. Ọ̀fún consists of the inverse of this pattern. Ilesanmi argues that the assignment of values operate references in the *odù* inscriptions. The "inner" oppositions of the *odù* system seem to be twofold: first, the contrasting patterns of positive and negative values comprising the inverse pairs of *odù*, and second, the revised ordinal ranking that progresses from one to fifteen by odd numbers and then sixteen to two by even numbers.

Ilesanmi offers no speculation on why the public, outer, ordinal ranking differs from the inner order. He also does not say why Ifá priests do not usually speak of the underlying binary with which they operate their system. The language of his conclusion suggests, however, that they might have been protecting their guild's secret: *"méjì, méjì ni Ifá ṣe ìgbékalẹ̀ èrò rẹ̀ lórí ayé; tibi-tire ló jọ ńrìn pọ̀ nínú ètò Ifá. Ìmọ̀ àbùdá oníbejì ló lè ṣí aṣọ lójú eégun Ifá"* ("The Ifá thought system turns on a binary structure in which positives and negatives walk hand in glove. Only the knowledge of how binary structures work can unmask Ifá") (2004, 146).

We should not forget that even the outer order the priests present to the uninitiated is not universal. Bascom recorded ten variations in Nigeria alone, eight in Benin and Togo, and two in Cuba. Moreover, the primary *odù* units do not carry any readable significance in practical, problem-solving divination until doubled or paired with another. This means that each consultation would involve ordering and decoding a minimum of thirty-two negative (-) and positive (+) values. A double Ọ̀fún, for example, would have to be arranged thus in the priest's mind: +-+-+ +-+-+; to the client only the ordinal appearance—the two columns of ones and twos—is visible: | ‖ | ‖ | ‖ | ‖.

Ilesanmi's sketch of the foundation of reference in Ifá's mythography is very stimulating and absorbing. However, there is no evidence that the temporal order implied in the sequence of positives and negatives is repeated in the narrative plots of the illustrative stories (*ẹsẹ*). That is, the imprinted signs do not appear to govern the story units. In order for Ilesanmi's "revelations" to work for practical criticism, we need to have an idea of how the values affect narrative sequence and the relation of plot details to the ordering of values.

The only evidence I have seen that thematic coordination along imprinted signs is possible for the stories occurs in the Epega and Niemark collection (1995). Stories in this book demonstrate an inscription-governed thematic unity that one does not find in earlier published collections such as Bascom's (1969) or Abímbọ́lá's (1969, 1977). Stories gathered under the Ògúndá sign, for example, show judicious adjudication to be Ògún's forte. In the narratives, Ògún, the god of iron, creates (dá) the path to being (ọnà ìwà) and acts as the guarantor of biological reproduction and progeny (isẹdá). In the same manner, the resolution of Ọ̀sá stories generally upholds the literal glossing of the root word, sá, as having to do with fleeing for refuge. Ìká narratives also support the etymology of ká in multiple references to encircling, circumscription, circumspection, reaping, bending, limiting, and so on. It is not clear to me whether the thematic unity of the Epega/ Niemark stories reflects regional (Ìjẹ̀bú) variations or whether the coordination is a result of editorial selections guided by a more "literary" sensibility.

While future studies might reveal a closer relationship between the inscription details and the illustrative stories, such a discovery will not diminish the importance of inscription in Ifá divination. Arriving at the right sign opens up channels of meaning to diviners and clients. The client's whispering his or her desires and concerns into the divination object brings the past of the client into the presence of the priest and engages the attention of the divination god's representative, which is either the palm kernel or the chain. The inscriptions revealed by the objects present traces of the emblematic primordial events to which the divination god was a witness. The signs also instigate deliberations about what future actions the client should take. In this order of events, the generated inscriptions regulate the relation of the past, the present, and the future. The client's concerns and problems belong, like the divination god's archetypal knowledge, in the past; the priest's verbal articulation of such knowledge belongs in the present; the realization of the agreed-upon solutions derivable from the present interpretation of the divine codes belongs in the future.

The sample solutions modeled in the narrative have a chance to work if the client's disposition allows it. Actionable reference, as the story unit or as the directive resulting from it, comes after the inscription; it belongs in the future of the "letter." Things could not be otherwise, because the past (the "historical" referent) of the entity I am calling the "letter" belongs in the experience of the deity who witnessed creation at a moment that now lies permanently outside of immediate cognition. This process reveals that Ifá practice distinguishes voice from graphé without separating them; the "letter" does not correspond to a sound but to a stand-alone problem unit. Ọ̀rúnmìlà, the original writer, does not read his text verbally; the transcribing diviner (the deity's "stenographer") who can verbalize the contents of the inscriptions does not "write." He invents solutions, but these are not original to him.

The space and time left empty by the discontinuity between the *odù*'s regimented notations and the free-floating themes they generate in stories warrants critical analysis. In that location, "implicit significations" are teased out, "silent determinations" are made, "obscured contents" are rendered manifest (Foucault 1979, 145). The considerable time and intellectual expense that pioneer Yorùbá Christian missionaries devoted to that location is instructive. Believing that Ifá stories are theological on the bases discussed earlier in this paper, Lijadu found evidence in the narratives of admirable Godliness comparable to Christianity, but Lijadu is exasperated by the sheer humanness of the Godhead in Ifá texts— an entity who would not command a simple kola nut at will for his personal use and who fails to detect that one presented to him by a sacrifice carrier was picked up from a crossroads offering. Lijadu exclaims *"ẹlẹ́yà ni gbogbo ìtàn yií"* ("These stories are utterly contemptuous") (1972 [1898], 32), because the Almighty they portray is not that mighty. *"Irú Olódùmarè wo ni eyi ẹ jàre?"*("What a puny God this is?"), he declaims (ibid.). For nontheological reasons, Karin Barber finds something untoward in how "Westernized members of the Yorùbá elite," including Lijadu, monumentalized Ifá by collecting, transcribing, and annotating the narratives recited by chosen priests. She observes how they then misrepresent the texts, perhaps unwittingly, "as a fixed body of knowledge" (Barber 1990, 197). The elite allow themselves to be seduced by the inbuilt incorporation strategies of Ifá discourse that cast its priest as someone who espouses a storied "body of wisdom conceived of as anterior and external to his own existence" (202), independent of his or her will. The only divination element that either Lijadu (the Christian, elite monument maker) or Barber comments on critically is the Ifá story's relationship to the inscription it supports. The written notations' anteriority to the priest, the client, and the story is never questioned. I would like to think that both Lijadu's project and Barber's critique are possible because the site of commentary making is deliberately constructed and preserved in Ifá discourse so that the initiated and the uninitiated can interact over the meaning of the fundamental inscriptions of being.

A Story of Origin in Ìwòrì

One story that one of Wándé Abímbọ́lá's informants associated with Ìwòrì Méjì, the sign that balances ones and twos on each side of the readable inscriptions, deals with the origin of the Ifá divination system (Abímbọ́lá 1969, 34–40). Ìwòrì pairs twos and ones symmetrically: a two on top and bottom and two ones between them. To use Ilesanmi's language, polar negatives are separated by two middle positives. For using the Ifá story type to present the origin of the system, this ẹsẹ acts like an autobiography of its own devices.

The story begins with the names of the four priests who coordinated the original consultation, two of whom are *Apá Níí Gbókoó Tan Iná Oṣo* ("The mahogany bean tree takes to the bush to kindle its wizard red fire") and *Orúrù Níí Wẹ̀wù Ẹ̀jẹ̀ Kalẹ̀* ("The orúrù tree dons the blood red garment from top to bottom"). The third is named *Ilẹ̀ Ni Mo Tẹ̀ Tẹ̀ẹ̀ Tẹ̀ Kí Ntóó Tọpọ́n* ("For a long while did I cut ordinary earth before I began to cut divination tray sand"). The fourth is *Ọ̀pẹ̀ Tẹ́ẹ́rẹ́ Erékè Níí Yà sí Ya Búkà Mẹ́rìndínlógún* ("The slender uphill palm tree divides into sixteen branches"). To reflect the tonal counterpoint principles that governed the poetic performance, Abímbọ́lá breaks the names of the third and fourth diviners into two lines each:

> Ilẹ̀ ni mo tẹ̀ tẹ̀ẹ̀ tẹ̀
> Kí ntóó tọpọ́n;
> Ọ̀pẹ̀ tẹ́ẹ́rẹ́ erékè
> Níí yà sí ya búkà mẹ́rìndínlógún
>
> I cut the earth for a long while
> Before cutting the divination tray sand
> The uphill slender palm tree
> The one that divides into sixteen branches
> (Abímbọ́lá 1969, 34)

The four cast their objects and disclosed to Ọ̀rúnmìlà that he will be barren in Ifẹ̀. But their findings were mocked.

The ensuing narrative does not specify the *odú* inscription that indicates it, and the only authority we have for that classification is the transcriber. Abímbọ́lá does not identify which of Pópóọlá Àyìnlá (of Ìkòyí, near Ògbómọ̀ṣọ́), Oyèédélé Iṣọlá (of Bẹẹṣin compound, Pààkòyí quarters, Ọ̀yọ́) and Adéjàre (of Pààkòyí quarters, Ọ̀yọ́) recited the story. In practical terms, Ọ̀rúnmìlà's four diviners completed their brief after they had related their findings. They could not have participated in the details contained in the rest of the story; logic dictates that we attribute its collation to succeeding observers and other diviners, including Abímbọ́lá's informants.

But the story of the original diviners is not that simple. According to Abímbọ́lá, the named diviners (with which all Ifá stories open) led the first consultation session recounted in the story. He adds that the names are either fragments of praise epithets (oríkì) or pseudonyms (1977, 19). The names, as such, historicize the narratives and make them accounts of something that actually happened.[8] It is not hard to disagree with Abímbọ́lá: if the priests existed in time and place, succeeding diviners who acknowledge their activities do not seem interested in identifying them as historical figures. From a more realistic viewpoint, the names are specific to a story and never repeated even when the motif of events addressed in one ẹsẹ appears in another. Most often, the names summarize the topic of the events in the consultation scenario. Abímbọ́lá himself admits that the names could be personifications of animals or plants devised for narrative unity. This implies that the names are a story element—more precisely a characterization strategy—and that they do not identify people whose lineage oríkì a listener can recite, or whose compound or hometown one can always locate precisely. From the beginning of the narrative, the names hold together the activities of the coordinators of an Ifá consult and serve as a textual resource for brokering attribution. Invoking antecedence by using the original priest's names helps place the contemporary performer in a discursive line of descent.

The motif of the importance of patience for overcoming barrenness, the central theme of the Ìwòrì narrative under discussion here, inhabits every facet of the story, including the names of the original diviners. The first diviner's name insinuates the beautiful efflorescence of the hardy mahogany bean tree draws the attention of malevolent forces. Although the tough apá wood is very useful for building construction, its hardiness also attracts witches and wizards who gather around it for their nightly deliberations (Abraham 1958). Apá seeds are also used by Ifá priests as active ingredients in protective amulets. To name the second diviner, Abímbọ́lá's informant pairs the scarlet flowers of the formidably tall orúrù with that of the apá, to juxtapose threat and ultimate victory. The witches' malevolence has no effect on the trees' florescence. The victory theme is also present in the colorless but forbearing nature given to the other diviners. In time, it seems, the person who begins cutting divination signs in mud will graduate to professional-grade divination tray sand; with time, the slender palm tree located in the tough uphill landscape blooms into sixteen full branches.

Events narrated in the next section of the story contradict the four wise diviners' prognostication, a development that shows divination's fallibility. Ọ̀rúnmìlà, contrary to predictions, has children who became kings in various regions, but in various regions of Yorùbáland such as Alárá, Ajerò, Ọlọ́yé, Oǹtagi and Ọlọ́wọ̀. Alákégtu and Ẹlẹ́jẹ̀lúmọ̀pé assumed the thrones of two territories that are not identifiable on a contemporary map. Ọwáràngún-àga became the leader of a diviners' guild. Further analysis of these names reveals more about the circumstances of their birth and the feelings of the parent who named them: Alárá ("Companionship") colloquially translates as "I would make a companion of my child"; Ajerò ("Communality") translates as "Children's causes warrant collective deliberations"; Ọlọ́yé ("Harmattan") implies that having a child weathers the body. Others are identified by their father's professional activity at the time of each child's birth: wood cutting, wood selling, and dye making. According to their birth order, the older children represent the parents' ambition of youth, the middle four denote phases of material strivings for the sustenance of life, and the youngest two—Ọwáràngún and Ọlọ́wọ̀—commemorate the accomplishments of old age. The children's names signify different stages of a life span, from the search for companionship to respectful regard. Reproduction is more than procreation; it entails companionship, bracing the elements, physical work, participation in the exchange of goods and services, and rest.

The next section, which consists of thirty-five lines, further expands the meaning of reproduction to include the need for devising instruments of managing contacts and sustaining relationships. These lines describe how the father of the far-flung kings and master professionals manages his extended family under central influence by instituting an annual pilgrimage to Ifẹ̀ during the Ifá festival. On one such occasion, Ọlọ́wọ̀, the child imagined at birth as the symbol of respectful regard, shows up determined to publicly topple the father's authority. This person dresses up in a replica of the official outfit of Ifẹ̀'s chief diviner—then Ọ̀rúnmìlà—and refuses to pay proper homage. When asked to pay due respect, Ọlọ́wọ̀ remains adamant. The confrontation is dramatized as follows:

Ó ní òun ò lè pábọrúbọyè bọ ṣiṣẹ.
Ọ̀rúnmìlà ní èé ti jẹ́?
Ọlọ́wọ̀ ní ìwọ Ọ̀rúnmìlà sọ̀dùn kọ́, o sòdùn kọ́;
Òun Ọlọ́wọ naa sọ̀dùn kọ́, òun sòdùn kọ́
Ìwọ Ọ̀rúnmìlà fòsùn idẹ lọ́wọ́;
Òun Ọlọ́wọ náà fòsùn idẹ lọ́wọ́
Ìwọ Ọ̀rúnmìlà bọ sálúbàtà idẹ;
Òun Ọlọ́wọ náà bọ sálúbàtà idẹ
Ìwọ Ọ̀rúnmìlà dádé,
Òun Ọlọ́wọ náà dádé.
Bẹ́ẹ̀ ni wọ́n sì ní
Ẹ̀nìkan kìí forí adé balẹ̀ fẹ́nìkan.

He said he cannot wish him good tidings
Ọ̀rúnmìlà asked why?

Ọlọ́wọ̀ said you, Ọ̀rúnmìlà, are in raffia garments
He the Ọlọ́wọ̀ too dons raffia garments
You Ọ̀rúnmìlà carry a brass staff of office
He the Ọlọ́wọ̀ too carries a brass staff of office
You Ọ̀rúnmìlà wear brass slippers
He Ọlọ́wọ wears brass slippers
You Ọ̀rúnmìlà wear a crown
He Ọlọ́wọ has a crown on
And it is known that
One crowned head does not prostrate to another.[9]
(Abímbọ́lá 1969, 36)

A rival chief diviner exists now, the determined Ọlọ́wọ̀ wants to say. The angry father, probably realizing the redundancy of his presence in the reflection mounted in Ọlọ́wọ̀'s appearance, exiles himself into a tall sixteen-branch palm tree.

It looks like Ọ̀rúnmìlà holds the key to some reproduction essentials, because all motion within the cycle of life stopped after his departure; the pregnant could not deliver, the barren continued fruitless, the infirm remained bedridden, semen dried up in men, women ceased to menstruate, yams refused to grow, peas did not flower, chickens pecked at the few rain drops that fell, and goats mistook sharpened blades for yam peels and munched on them. The community went seeking divination help from unnamed diviners who prescribed what sacrifices to make and counseled them to assemble at the foot of the palm tree into which Ọ̀rúnmìlà had disappeared. The people gathered around the tree as instructed and chanted the self-exiled priest's praise epithets, believing that they could coax him to return "home." But Ọ̀rúnmìlà stayed in exile and offered sixteen palm nuts as his proxy:

Ọ̀rúnmìlà ní òun ò tún relé mọ́
Ó ní kí wọn ó tẹ́wọ́,
Ó wáá fún wọn ní ikin mẹ́rìndínlógún.
Ó ní bẹ́ ẹ bá délé,
Bẹ́ ẹ bá fówóó ní,
Ẹni tẹ́ẹ́ mọọ bi nù un.
Bẹ́ ẹ bá délé
Bẹ́ ẹ bá fáyaá ní,
Ẹni tẹ́ẹ́ mọọ bi nù un.
Bẹ́ ẹ bá délé
Bẹ́ ẹ bá fọ́mọọ bí
Ẹni tẹ́ẹ́ mọọ bi nù un.
Ilé lẹ bá fẹ́ẹ kọ́ láyé,
Aṣọ lẹ bá fẹ́ẹ́ ní láyé,
Ẹni tẹ́ẹ́ mọọ bi nù un.

Ire gbogbo tẹ́ ẹ bá féẹ́ ní láyé,
Ẹni téẹ́ mọọ bi nù un.
Ìgbà tí wọ́n délé,
Gbogbo ire náà ni wọ́n ńrí.
Ọ̀rúnmìlà afèdèfẹ̀yọ̀,
Ẹ̀lààsòdè
Ifá relé Olókun kò dé mọ́.
Ó lẹ́ni tẹ́ ẹ bá rí,
Ẹ ṣá mọọ pè ni baba.

Ọ̀rúnmìlà says he will never return home
He asked them to open their palms
And handed to them sixteen palm nuts
He said, when you get home
If you desire wealth
That is the person to ask
When you get home
If you desire a wife
That is the person to ask
When you get home
If you desire children
That is the person to ask
Should you want to build a home
In case you want clothes
That is the person to ask
Any other comfort you might seek
That is the person to ask
When they got home
All the blessings became theirs
Ọ̀rúnmìlà, the polyglot
The redeeming deity of Ìsòdè
Ifá left for Olókun's abode
He said whoever you see
Call upon him.
(Abímbọ́lá 1969, 39)

The presentation of one divination as a function of an antecedent divination in this story reveals a characteristic of Ifá processes to which scholars do not usually pay attention: Ifá divination sessions are a consultation of a consultation. The first divination session in the origin-of-divination story summarized above concerns Ọ̀rúnmìlà's engagement with the four diviners and the details of the client's success in spite of contrary oracular predictions. The second divination session describes the Ìfẹ̀ people's failed attempt to bring back Ọ̀rúnmìlà from exile, a situation that arose because he could not manage his children. The third story, the one that presents the other two, is told by Abímbọ́lá's informants, probably as it was handed down to them from other diviners. The third story supplements the other two, one of which involves the birth of the discursive practice that governs all the stories. All divination sessions involve the use of at least the first and the third types of stories; but only the first type is marked as a story, because the diviner in charge of the present moment has to efface the importance of his or her own active material input. The babalawo, as it were, has to spirit away his or her own presence by not marking the story of his storytelling.[10]

Ethnographic studies of Ifá will not suffice for analyzing this narrative of presence, absence, doubling, writing, designating, conjuring, and responsiveness. The story describes the irremediably occultic nature of signification; bare meaning as embodied in what Ọ̀rúnmìlà knows, details of the allotment of destiny, have disappeared permanently. Ọ̀rúnmìlà is never coming home with us! However, life continues in the exchange of traces of the instituted codes that bear fragments of Ọ̀rúnmìlà's record. Ọ̀rúnmìlà's permanent disappearance signifies that meaning, in itself, is gone; the search for recovery launched by Ifẹ̀ people left behind in the material world shows that continued existence revolves around the anxiety of what is yet to happen. According to this narrative, the structure of meaning production named for Ọ̀rúnmìlà construes being as the continuous coaxing of useful means of approaching the present from tokens of the unrecoverable past, which is in the future of that past.

It is significant that the story categorizes the reference of divination writing as material well-being in all its aspects (*ire gbogbo*) and more concretely as money (owó), spouse (*aya*), childbearing (ọmọ), shelter (ilé), and clothing (aṣọ). The authority (or spirit) that controls the knowledge of the distribution, use, and acquisition of these blessings, being none other than the eyewitness to creation, cannot be accessed directly. It is instead accessed through its occult proxies, which in practice exist as a structure of appellation: "*ẹni tẹ́ mọọ bi nù un* (that is the person to ask)," the oracle instructs. The permanently absent Ọ̀rúnmìlà offers the palm nuts (and the writing generated through them) as his principle of "being there." Operators of the divination infrastructure make their best efforts to ensure that the palm nuts transmit the spirit's reply to their labors of enquiry accurately.

In the calculus of material existence worked out in this story, the spirit is in permanent exile and cannot return home. This spirit's irreversible alienation and the trace forms in which it partially appears when properly invoked are essential for the procreation of life in general, and they are a good part of the story unit. The palm nuts and the remainders constitute the "masque" of the spirit that has become un-present-able.[11] The spirit mitigates the effect of its absence with the mute palm nuts that are signs of its absent-presence. The inscribed signs transcribe patterns of the knowledge Ọ̀rúnmìlà gained as a result of its one-time presence at the time of destiny. The ẹsẹ Ifá connects and translates the significance of the traced-out presence (which is a sign of an irremediable absence) as stories to be interpreted for the present moment, with the collaboration of the client who is seeking insights into a fragment of general existential difficulty.

In theory, meaning in Ifá discourse is the approximation of what Ọrúnmìlà witnessed at the distribution of destiny.[12] Divination therefore involves probing into the inner reaches of essential occultation (awo) for the main purpose of making it yield fundamental knowledge (ìmọ̀) about life. Divination hermeneutics as instituted in Ifá practices requires efforts to draw plain knowledge out of the occult. Stories are used to translate inscribed codes of Ọrúnmìlà because the record of the events witnessed at the distribution of destiny cannot travel as events any more. Those events happened only once; even if Ọrúnmìlà did not disappear into the palm tree he could only relate narrativized versions of what he witnessed. Events survive beyond happenstance only in stories or ìtàn.

The Ìwòrì Méjì story shows that several translations occur between the priest's transcription of the signs emitted by the nuts and the client's response to counseling. Ọrúnmìlà's four priests probably recited a narrative whose contents Abímbọlá's informants summarized in one line about barrenness. Ọrúnmìlà's curt reaction to the diviners' conclusion indicates that while the client can follow his or her own will, the priest is not free to do as he or she wishes and must be guided by the inscription-story. After interpretation, priests can conclude their briefs and depart, while the client begins to exercise his or her intelligence and will. Ọrúnmìlà laughs off his counselors and ends up inside a palm tree!

The Past and Present in Ifá Writing

Early Yorùbá Christian clergymen believed that divination priests led an "oracular cult" that made "hegemonic claims to a special relationship with the Supreme Being, with a key theme—the powerful precedent—which presents a highly refracted memory of the vanished greatness of its sacred centre" (Peel 1990, 344). The pastors invested much interest in the diviners, as I observed earlier, because the former held sway over the non-Christian population based mainly on the mystique of their graphematic practice. Befriending and converting powerful local divination priests netted not just an individual pagan for the Christians but a truth-regime leader. Converting a divination priest brought the pagan mythography under the authority of a phoneticized and allegedly more democratic writing system. The missionaries did not attack the mythography, but exploited the commentary-making space. This was the space between inscription and action manipulated by missionaries to discredit the divination priests as selfish charlatans who used the mystical basis of their techniques to do just as they wished—which, they suggested, resulted in diviners misleading their clients. In the words of Lijadu:

Lára jíjẹ àti mímu ni olóri aájò àwọn babaláwo kulẹ̀ sí; níbẹ̀ kan náà ni ti àwọn olùsìn tìkárawọn náà mọ pẹ̀lú. Síbẹ̀síbẹ̀ a wá ọ̀pọ̀lọpọ̀ ìtàn asán jọ láti já àwọn ọ̀gbẹ̀rì lí àyà tàbí láti yá wọn lórí, tàbí láti fo àwọn adéjàá lí ẹyẹ, kí wọ́n má ṣe lè ṣe ọrùn líle, ṣùgbọ́n kí wọ́n fi ohùn sí ibi tí àwọn babalawó bá fí i sí.

Subsistence interest is the be-all and end-all of the divination priests; the same goes for their followers too. Jejune tales are gathered to either scare or enthuse the uninitiated or to mislead the inquisitive so that they will cease asking questions and agree with the priests' self-serving conclusions. (1972 [1898], 66.)

Lijadu addresses more than theological facts here. He construes the use of narratives in Ifá as a barefaced "presentism"; that is, a system by which divination priests construct the past to suit only today's needs. The babalawo's claims for the past cannot be verified.

Karin Barber also focuses on the postinscription elements of the divination protocols for her analysis of Ifá discourse's incorporation of multiple others to position Ifá strategically as the governor of the Yorùbá intellectual universe. Barber does not question the consistency of the odù inscriptions. Her concern is how the priests' stories use verifiable "techniques of argument" to place Ifá above all else. The strategies include "narrative positioning"; that is to say, the unrestrained thematic range of the contents of the Ifá story authorizes diviners to appropriate tales from all sources, all domains, and about any topic, consign them to the past, and then retrieve them as ideas activated by the odù. Barber caricatures Ifá's "narrative positioning" in words similar to Lijadu's. According to Barber, "The 'moral' is always the same, whatever the origin of the story: 'Ifá knows best . . . Do what Ifá tells you and you will prosper; disobey Ifá and disaster will ensue'" (1990, 208). Another incorporation strategy Ifá uses is "preempting time": each story reports an event as having taken place in the distant past, and the diviner comments on the events as if Ọ̀rúnmìlà constructed and handed down a model of future action from patterns observed in the past. The cleverest part of this presentation of the all-encompassing model, Barber says, is that the divination god himself appears as a bewildered client in many of the stories: "Ifá the deity himself appeals to a body of wisdom, encoded in precedents, which must be seen as outside his consciousness and antecedent to him. Nothing can go behind this paradox: the argument of the precedent is arrested at that point in a permanent and unresolvable deadlock. This has the effect of enhancing the authority both of Ifá as system and as spiritual being" (209). Ifá's third main discourse-making technique is "lexical layering," or the invention of "strange names" for familiar acts and objects. For example, Ifá stories commonly refer to the part of the body called *ẹnu* (mouth) in every day language such as *"olúbọ́bọ́tiribọ́ baba ẹbọ* (the insatiable gobbler of all sacrificial offerings)."

Barber evaluates Ifá stories in the way we currently think of histories—as reports of past events in proportions narratively scaled to reflect how persons interacted with themselves and their environment in verifiable specified spaces and time. But this model of the past would apply to Ifá only if the graphic-notation stage of the divination process is treated as an extraneous element with no significance at all. To follow the reading I suggested above, Barber neglects the significance of the mythographic inscriptions that stand for the permanent barrier to our capturing past events in their "true" proportions. The commentary space in Ifá diviniation protocols would also have to be completely disregarded in order for "presentism" criticism to be fully accepted. But we cannot speak about Ifá discourse or extract significance from its practices without considering "writing" and "commentary." The central axiom of Ifá practice that enjoins critical listening and acting on the client was recorded by Lijadu himself: "*Bí o bá tẹ'fá tań, kí o tún 'yè rẹ tẹ* (When you're done consulting Ifá, be sure to reconsult your gumption)" (1839: 37). A person counseled in Ifá is duty bound to recounsel him or herself and decide to what extent instructions and prescriptions will be followed or rejected; Ọ̀rúnmìlà mocked his diviners in the story discussed earlier. The self-recounseling injunction means that while every story unit gives an allegorical account of how things were and how similar they might be in the present (although not in mimetic proportions), the priest's retelling must generate a directive, evince a pledge, articulate a feeling, or change the status quo. These are all gestures of àtúntẹ̀ (reimprinting, recounseling).[13] In other words, the client is not to make the past present as it was. Even Ọ̀rúnmìlà could not perform such a feat. As records of divination sessions show, the priest and the client, voluble readers of Ifá's mute signs in the commentary space, are not absolved from the responsibility of contemplation and self-reflection. Ifá's clients might have been authored by precedence; they are not therefore exempted from answering to genuinely new responsibilities.

Ifá narratives are not like simple, constative oríkì or descriptive charters whose primary referential relationship is to an event, a moral goal, or the performers' other vested interests. In the *ese Ifá*, convention bound as it is, in theory the priest is obliged to not pursue a detectable personal interest—except that of proving to be a competent, honest broker of the revelations of destiny—in the problem addressed by the story. This is why, I would suggest, the referential antecedence of the Ifá story is the inscription and not the event of the story. It is something that, in theory, only the disappeared Ọ̀rúnmìlà experienced. At any rate, the instigator of the story's contents is not the priest, but the nuts (or chain). Ifá clients do not just seek a reading, they also look for a "correct" writing.

How does Ifá practice actualize a theory of time and history and elaborate how the past influences (or does not influence) the present and the future? In *Ifá Divination Poetry* Abímbọ́lá asserts that the "*ẹsẹ Ifá* is a type of 'historical' poetry" (1977, 20). Peel's explanation of the past's relationship to the present in mythical narratives is better nuanced: "present practice is governed by the model of past practice and, where change *does* occur, there is a tendency to rework the past so as to make it appear that past practice has governed present practice" (1984a: 113). I would emend Peel and say that the expectation that the client should act willfully upon the reports of the events presented by the diviner demonstrates that the stories constitute and do not just report the events. The client can forestall the portentous past from repeating itself or allow it to fulfill its propitious potential. In Ifá, that the past is in exile does not mean that the present stands alone. The past is not the present of the living client who still has to make the labor of sacrifice. That sacrifices and offerings (*ẹbọ*) made in the past do not offer protections against present and future peril indicates a clear notion of how the past differs from the present. Living clients are responsible for their *ẹbọ*, sacrifices and offerings made not to the past but in the present for the smoothing of yet-to-be-trodden paths. Were Ifá stories merely constatives of past events, in theory history would have ended with the disappearance of Ọ̀rúnmìlà and no new narratives would be possible. But Ifá stories recount the basis of belief in Islam, explain the peculiarities of Christian beliefs, and even divine the significance of the coming of railways. In Ifá practice, the inscription system physically marks what Peel calls the "otherness of the past."

Notes

1. All translations are mine unless otherwise indicated.
2. His examples include Paul's learning of Jewish traditions under Gamaliel and his studying Greek idolatry at Tarsus. Bishop Phillips also attributes Moses's success in the Exodus to his intimate knowledge of Egyptian religions.
3. These are the terms Derrida uses to describe general writing in *Of Grammatology* (1976).
4. James Johnson declares Ifá "the great Oracle of the Yorùbá country" (1989, 19).
5. For details of the inscription of process, see Bascom 1969, 13–12 and 49–59; Abimbola, 1977, 9–11. Epega's practitioner manual lists by name and visual illustrations all of the 256 possible units in the system, from Ejiogbé to Ofúnṣèé (1987, 7–38).
6. For example, an obvious typographic mistake in Abímbọ́lá's *Ifá Divination Poetry* records similar graphic marks for both Ìròsùn (the fifth basic unit) and Ọ̀bàrà (the seventh). An attentive reader, without being a trained babalawo, can correct the mistake simply by following the order of twos and ones. See also Bascom (1961) for a discussion of the principles that can be used to correct variations.
7. Ilesanmi, like Lijadu, Phillips, and Johnson, is a Christian priest—an ordained Catholic priest—and professor of Yorùbá studies.
8. Bascom says that the only autochthonous section of the ẹsẹ Ifá are the names of the diviners. Other parts could be sourced from folktales, myths, legends, and the like.
9. My using the male pronoun here is to manage readability and not to reflect Ọlọ́wọ̀'s anatomical sex, which the Yoruba language pronominal system does not mark.
10. Ọ̀rúnmìlà here institutes a system of iteration: "the possibility for every mark to be repeated and still to function as a meaning mark in new contexts that are cut off entirely from

the original context, the 'intention to communicate' of the original maker of the mark. That originator may be absent or dead, but the mark still functions, just as it goes on functioning after the death of its intended recipient" (Miller 2001, 78).

11. It should not be forgotten that the "*odù*" writing practice is literally operated by remainders; in the palm-nut divination system, for example, only remainders express portentous inscription.

12. *Ìpín* (literally "allotment" or destiny in colloquial Yorùbá) is what Ọ̀rúnmìlà reveals through (and in) the divination process. But in practical divination terms, *ìpín* is what recurs in narrativity. The ẹsẹ Ifá contains what has happened at least once in the past.

13. See Searle's (1979) taxonomy of illocutionary acts, in which he discusses directives and commissives, classifying pledges as a form of commissive.

References

Abímbọ́lá, Wándé. 1969. *Ijinle Ohun Enu Ifá, Apa Keji*. Glasgow: Collins.

———. 1976. *Ifá: An Exposition of Ifá Literary Corpus*. Ibadan: Oxford University Press.

———. 1977. *Ifá Divination Poetry*. New York: Nok.

Abraham, R. C. 1958. *Dictionary of Modern Yoruba*. London: University of London Press.

Austin, J. L. 1975. *How to Do Things with Words*. 2nd ed. Edited by J. O. Urmson and Marina Sbisà. Cambridge, MA: Harvard University Press.

Barber, Karin. 1990. "Discursive Strategies in the Texts of Ifá and in the 'Holy Book of Odù' of the African Church of Ọ̀rúnmìlà." In *Self-Assertion and Brokerage: Early Cultural Nationalism in West Africa*, edited by P. F. De Moraes Farias and Karin Barber, 196–224. Birmingham, UK: Center for West African Studies.

Bascom, William. 1961. "Odu Ifá: The Order of the Figures of Ifá." *Bulletin de l'Institut Français d'Afrique Noire* 23, no. 3/4: 676–682.

———. 1969. *Ifá Divination: Communication Between Gods and Men in West Africa*. Bloomington: Indiana University Press.

Derrida, Jacques. 1976. *Of Grammatology*. Translated by Gayatri Chakravorty Spivak. Baltimore: Johns Hopkins University Press.

———. 1994. *Specters of Marx: The State of the Debt, the Work of Mourning, and the New International*. Translated by Peggy Kamuf. New York: Routledge.

Epega, Afolabi A. 1987. *Ifá: The Ancient Wisdom*. New York: Imole Oluwa Institute.

Epega, Afolabi A., and Philip J. Neimark. 1995. *The Sacred Ifá Oracle*. San Francisco: HarperSanFrancisco.

Foucault, Michel. 1979. "What is an Author?" In *Textual Strategies: Perspectives in Post-Structuralist Criticism*, edited by Josué V. Harari, 141–160. Ithaca, NY: Cornell University Press.

Ilesanmi, T. M. 2004. *Yorùbá Orature and Literature: A Cultural Analysis*. Ile-Ife: Obafemi Awolowo University Press.

Johnson, James. 1899. *Yoruba Heathenism*. Exeter, UK: James Townsend and Son.

Lijadu, E. M. 1972 (1898). *Ifá: Imọle Rẹ ti i Ṣe Ipilẹ Isin ni Ilẹ Yoruba*. Ado-Ekiti, Nigeria: Omolayo Standard Press.

———. 1972 (1908). *Ọrúnmla! Nipa*. Ado-Ekiti, NG: Omolayo Standard Press.

Miller, J. Hillis. 2001. *Speech Acts in Literature*. Stanford, CA: Stanford University Press.

Ọlatunji, Ọlatunde. 1984. *Features of Yorùbá Oral Poetry*. Ibadan: University Press.

Peel, J. D. Y. 1984a. "The Past in the Ijesha Present." *Man* 19, no. 1: 111–132.

———. 1984b. *Religious Encounter and the Making of the Yoruba*. Bloomington: Indiana University Press.

———. 1990. "The Pastor and the Babalawo: The Interaction of Religions in Nineteenth Century Yorubaland." *Africa* 60, no. 3: 338–369.

Searle, John R. 1979. *Expression and Meaning: Studies in the Theory of Speech Acts*. Cambridge: Cambridge University Press.

PART II.

IFÁ AS KNOWLEDGE:
THEORETICAL QUESTIONS AND
CONCERNS

6 Ifá

Sixteen Odù, *Sixteen Questions*

Barry Hallen

ALTHOUGH OVER THE course of my career I have had occasion to write several papers related to Ifá, I have made a point of concentrating on methodological issues. My sixteen questions are primarily methodological in character.

1. Is someone, myself included, privileged to speak knowledgeably about so complex—and, to some, foreign—a system of knowledge as Ifá if that person has not been formally initiated into it in some sense?

2. If you do not have such firsthand experience and knowledge of Ifá, is it a safe or hazardous undertaking for you to set about reducing it to, or analyzing it in, discursive terms?

3. We are all familiar with a variety of supposedly standardized, cross-cultural, and methodological approaches to the study of non-Western systems of thought: structural-functionalism, structuralism, symbolism, phenomenology, hermeneutics, conceptual analysis, and so forth. Has any single specific methodology been identified as *the* one that can do justice to the Ifá system? I suspect that the consensus, even if tacit, regarding the answer to this question is no. No methodological key other than Ifá itself has as yet been found. What might this mean, and how then should one proceed?

4. I become concerned when I note the regularity with which scholars resort to metaphor, to analogy, to ambiguous comparisons ("It's an African *I Ching*"), to excessively technical and therefore even more confusing methodological terminology ("metadiscursive unpacking") as a basis for providing informative insights into the Ifá system of knowledge. Is this something about which we should be concerned?

5. Yet, Ifá in its inimitable way persists; indeed some might even say it is flourishing in places in our world where only decades ago it was unknown or

minimally acknowledged as some form of exotic foreign "cult." How and why does it continue to be of such persistent international appeal?

6. Ifá persists in a physical, geographical fashion as well as in an intellectual one. If that is the case, is it relevant to ask about the location of its "control center," its hub or nub? Is a place like Ife-Ife today primarily a symbolic but now essentially historic home of Ifá? Is it a primary and outstanding place of pilgrimage perhaps, but not the heart of a functioning international infrastructure?

7. Since the Yorùbá scholars of Ifá with whom I am familiar have always stressed the tolerance, the flexibility, the adaptability, and the creativity of the Ifá system as well as its stability, how is it possible to reconcile what might become contradictory tendencies? What are the consequences for the Ifá corpus if the ẹsẹ Ifá in Cuba or Trinidad differs from the ẹsẹ Ifá in places like Ife-Ife or Oyo? Does this mean that Ifá will or does accommodate ẹsẹ Ifá that are of local origins and therefore not a part of the "original" corpus? If so, what are the consequences for Ifá as an international movement? Does it become somewhat denominational (to use an inadequate Western-derived term), in that the corpus in one place may not replicate the corpus in another? To repeat, what then would be the consequences for Ifá as a truly international movement?

8. In order to facilitate the academic exegesis of the Ifá corpus, by which I mean the *odù Ifá* oral texts, must the whole corpus first be transcribed into written form? Must it be translated into one of the so-called world languages, such as English? What would be the consequences for the Ifá corpus as a vibrant, flexible system and expression of knowledge if it were to become reduced to the more or less permanent format of the printed page in what is supposedly either a definitive Yorùbá edition or a definitive English-language translation?

9. Could this be a groundbreaking opportunity for a long-term process of study of an African system of knowledge—carried out and expressed by scholars who themselves write their analyses in Yorùbá, thereby doing greater justice to tonal nuances, word play, and the like? If there were a demand for such studies to be communicated to a wider international audience, they could then be selectively translated into one of the so-called world languages, such as English, including the relevant ẹsẹ of course, perhaps as a form of text and commentary.

10. Ifá divination as a whole is a *process,* as well as a corpus of oral texts or verses. What could be the negative consequences of sundering or extracting the corpus from the divination process and subjecting it to independent analysis? Do the ẹsẹ Ifá derive part of their meaning from and during the actual divination process in which they play a part? How might their academic exegesis then come to terms with giving due consideration to the divination process as a whole?

11. In 1977, Professor Wándé Abímbọ́lá and I gave a joint presentation at the Annual Meeting of the African Studies Association in Baltimore, on the role of secrecy in Ifá divination. Our presentation was entitled "Secrecy and Objectivity

in the Methodology and Literature of Ifá Divination," later published in 1993 as a coauthored chapter in a book entitled *Secrecy: African Art that Conceals and Reveals* (Abímbọ́lá and Hallen 1993). My concern is to bring your attention to the following excerpt from that paper:

> *Awo* [secrecy] is the collective term for various classes of secret information in Yoruba culture. . . .
>
> That *awo* is important in Ifá is clear from a number of key terms that incorporate the word. Most obvious is babalawo: the Yoruba word for an Ifá priest [diviner] is babalawo, which can roughly be translated into English as father of secrets (Abímbọ́lá 1975: 5). The babalawo *Olódù* "are full Ifá priests who have been initiated into the secrets of *odù*, the mythical wife of Ifá" (Abímbọ́lá 1976: 13). In addition there are *Ọmọ Awo*, "an Ifá apprentice . . . known as a child of secrets" (Bascom 1969: 83); *awo egan:* "The lowest grade of practicing Ifá diviners are known as . . . 'secret of *egan*' [a special type of medicines]" (Bascom 1969: 81); and *Olúwo,* a word meaning "master of secrets" or "chief of secrets" (*olú awo*), and referring to any of the three highest grades of diviners (Bascom 1969: 83).
>
> Secrecy [therefore] is a safeguard against the indiscriminate use of power. The *awo* of which one is said to be a child, father, or master is knowledge peculiar to the Ifá system, and is arranged in a hierarchy of grades of increasing complexity and power. Entry into each grade (as well as into the Ifá cult itself) is rigorously selective, and is controlled by a series of initiation ceremonies. To advance a grade (which one may do both at one's superiors' invitation and by personal application), one must have demonstrated one's professional competence on the preceding level, and have proven that one can exercise power responsibly and with discretion. *Awo,* then, both prevents the uninitiated layman from acquiring and misusing the power of Ifá, and acts within the profession to situate the Ifá priest at the level of expertise for which his own personal talents and abilities equip him. (Abímbọ́lá and Hallen 1993: 217–218)

My concern and question is, If Ifá is becoming as dispersed and possibly internationally diverse as might seem to be the case, is there an infrastructure in place to maintain the same level of quality control among babalawo, as was the case in the Yorùbá heartland when Professor Abímbọ́lá and I wrote about this positive sanction provided by secrecy in 1977? Or is the role of secrecy as a positive methodological element being significantly eroded?

Recently, a Google search using the terms "Ifa + divination," generated 123,000 hits. One website that attracted my interest concerns a very substantial volume (591 pages) selling for $50 entitled *Practical Ifá Divination: Ifá Reference Manual for the Beginner and Professional* (Popoola 1997). To be fair to the author (who himself seems to be a properly initiated babalawo), he makes it clear in the opening pages that "nothing in this book qualifies anyone to become a Babaláwo," that "[n]o one can become a Babaláwo unless he is initiated according to Ifa injunction," and so on. But for me this substantially detailed text, entitled "Practical *Ifá Divination*" and explicitly said to be for the "beginner," evokes memories of books such as Rowlands's *Teach Yourself Yoruba* (1969). Its purpose is to serve as a guide that is sufficiently detailed to enable one to literally *practice* Ifa divination. As the blurbs on the back cover indicate: "the message of Ifá is clearly given [i.e., discursive interpretations of various *ese* taken from the first of the 16 principal *odù*, the *Èjì Ogbè*], the sacrifice materials are stated while how to perform the necessary rituals and sacrifices are explained." Furthermore, a reviewer of this volume on Amazon.com says the following: "Though this volume is labeled Volume 3, it is the first published of a proposed eighteen volume series."[1]

My further concern is that if the infrastructure of Ifá as an international phenomenon is not adequate, who knows what varieties of unqualified babalawo may be out there, claiming to be initiates without really being so, and in turn furthering their own interests by falsely initiating other babalawo who will also not be legitimate representatives of Ifá?

At another website indicative of a possibly analogous troubling phenomenon, we find a presumably authentic "babalawo" (identifying information redacted) telling his potential clients that:

> It is highly recommended that one be present to sit on the mat with the diviner during the divination. Baring [*sic*] that possibility a person may send their contribution and a hand written letter, including their name, date of birth, questions, phone number, mailing address or email address to XXXXXXX. The priest will respond by collect telephone call, mail or email, whichever is your preference. Email your request to XXXXXXX or mail it to XXXXXXX.

That is followed by the phrase: "$50 Contribution (all services are tax deductible)."

Why do I draw your attention to this? Well, it is a pretty clear indication that among other things, Ifá divination has come to the Internet. And it seems to me there is a further question here: Is it a legitimate alternative for a client to consult a babalawo whom he or she never meets in person and whose professional qualifications may be total fabrications, on the basis of an Internet advertisement and email correspondence? In essence, I am asking two questions here: (1) Whether Ifá divination can make the transition to the Internet and still be regarded as genuine, and (2) How does one control unscrupulous fraudulent individuals who claim to be babalawo via Internet websites, but who simply see this as a way to line their own pockets by telling people what they want to hear?

12. One eminent Yorùbá academic, babalawo, and official emissary of Ifá to the world who has expressed his concerns about many of the points I have raised is Professor Wándé Abímbólá, the *Àwíṣẹ Awo Àgbáyé*, a title that indicates that his domain encompasses the entire planet. In his book, *Ifá Will Mend Our Broken World* (1997), he states explicitly that one of his missions is to stop Ifá from being prostituted in the diaspora via false initiations, babalawo who are not really

babalawo, and so on. As a further step toward "regularizing" Ifá, he has organized several World Òrìṣà Conferences in countries such as Brazil, Trinidad, and
Nigeria. But I wonder whether these measures are enough to bring the situation
under control. For one thing, he is only one man and the diaspora with which
he is trying to come to terms is vast. And, although the World Òrìṣà Conferences may bring together certain strata of Ifá professionals, I wonder whether
they are of consequence for diviners considered to be uncertified. In other words,
if many Ifá practitioners who are in fact unqualified would make a point of avoid-
ing such venues, how do we come to terms with them, shut them down, or shut
them up? Could a faction of apostates (a term used with apologies to both Ifá and
Christianity) result that might eventually have the audacity to declare itself as legitimate, regardless of what a truly legitimate authority like Professor Abímbọ́lá
might have to say?

13. Earlier, I referred to the possible importance of formal initiation into Ifá
as a prerequisite to a more profound understanding of the *odù Ifá* or literary corpus. But if a part of the initiation into Ifá also involves a vow of or commitment
to a degree of secrecy (*awo*) about divulging what one has learned, then I wonder
whether a catch-22 arises. In other words, would such a vow of secrecy about
certain information fundamental to understanding Ifá not interfere with the exegesis of the corpus by an Ifá initiate or priest, because he might be prohibited
from passing on his understanding of Ifá in a publication meant for a popular
(including academic) but uninitiated audience?

14. There is a virtually endless stream of second-order publications discussing how the *odù Ifá* and their constituent *ẹsẹ* might be interpolated and rendered
into discursive form, so that the knowledge contained by the Ifá system might
be made more explicit. Henry Louis Gates Jr. has drawn interesting parallels
between the paradoxes and ambiguities found in Ifá and in African American
literature, which he is convinced are not coincidental (Gates 1988). But to my
knowledge, no one has yet claimed to have identified a "key" of some sort that
will solve this "puzzle." My question, then, is whether this is a puzzle that is in
fact insoluble, or at least a convincing indication that the knowledge expressed
by the Ifá corpus cannot be rendered in a discursive format. If so, would we have
to conclude that this is a new or at least relatively rare form of discourse by which
knowledge can be expressed?

Many of these second-order publications make reference to some form of
hermeneutics as a promising interpretive instrument or tool. But was it not Martin Heidegger (pardon the intrusion of Western philosophy), one of the Western "fathers" of hermeneutics, who ultimately gave up on any form of discursive
writing as adequate to expressing new forms of knowledge and new insights into
the nature of existence, and as a result turned to poetry or verse as the most overlooked but richest source of such insights? The point would be not to relegate the

Ifá corpus to some lesser form of literary expression, but to elevate the poetic to a higher form of epistemic expression.

Or can we solve the puzzle by simply inverting the entire process of interpolation and exegesis, suggesting that there has always been a deliberately hermeneutic intent on the part of the creators of the ẹsẹ Ifá? In other words, it is the creators of the odù who are themselves deliberately concerned to fashion a rhetorical format that will withstand the ages and yet still provide a substantive basis for the corpus to produce relevant and meaningful interpretations or renderings, in principle, for the indefinite future. In which case it can be said that the ẹsẹ Ifá have been hermeneutic in character since the time of their composition, which is the most responsible generalization that can be made regarding a "key" to their interpretation. Even if this is another question that cannot be answered due to vows of secrecy, it would be interesting to know what a babalawo is taught about how to create and compose new ẹsẹ Ifá.

15. When I Googled "Ifa + divination + philosophy," I got over 29,900 hits, but apart from repetitive references to William Bascom's well-known study, I found nothing distinctly "philosophical" about the web sites to which I was referred. And as far as Bascom's book is concerned, apart from one chapter entitled "Professional Ethics" (of the babalawo) and another that discusses Ifá as a "system of beliefs," I could not identify a single passage in which he explicitly introduces the word "philosophy" with reference to Ifá. I had more success with the Widener Library catalogue at Harvard University, where I located a 1999 publication entitled *Yoruba Ethics and Metaphysics: Being Basic Philosophy Underlying the Ifá System of Thought of the Yoruba* (Akintola 1999). Note that this title refers to Ifá only as "a system of thought" rather than as "philosophy" per se.

I do not mean to appear as if I am an employee of Abímbọ́lá, Inc., but the volume I did finally turn to for a philosophical exploration of the whole of Ifá divination is Kola Abímbọ́lá's 2006 text, *Yoruba Culture: A Philosophical Account*. I was attracted to this book by statements such as the following, which occur in the opening pages of the preface:

a) "The book. . . . is simply a theoretical account of the philosophical ideas that underlie the world-view of traditional Yorùbá societies" (xv; note the plural).
b) "The Odù Ifá are (relatively) fixed and given, but there is considerable room for different critical reflective appraisal of them when Ifá priests and priestesses make use of the Odù Ifá as heuristic action-guiding principles on the basis of which they counsel and advise people" (xix).
c) "If you are interested in Western philosophy disguised as Yorùbá philosophy, this book is not for you" (xvi).

Discussions of the philosophical significance of Ifá constitute a substantial portion of Kola Abímbọ́lá's book, but I was most attracted and intrigued by his analyses of the relationship between religion and ethics in Yorùbá culture (87) and his discussions of ethics as it relates to an individual's *ìwà* or character (85). Those of us who have labored in the area of African philosophy are more than familiar with the tendency to treat Western viewpoints on ethics as paradigms or models that are then conventionally used as a basis for the exposition of non-Western value systems. In Yorùbá studies this has led, for example, to a fundamental disagreement as to whether the system of moral values enunciated by Yorùbá culture, as Kola Abímbọ́lá puts it, "derives its validity from religion" (87). Or whether "morality is primarily a this-worldly affair in which [the primary] focus [is] on issues of [correct and incorrect] co-operation, actions, emotions, character, etc. vis-à-vis relationships with [other human] beings" (88). In other words, the issue is whether morality in Yorùbá culture is most importantly divinely inspired or most fundamentally human in origin, in that it enunciates values created by human beings (rather than a god or gods) who were anxious to establish communities that would promote human welfare. Currently, the balance of opinion, at least among philosophers of Africa, seems to favor this latter possibility of human or naturalistic origin. I am thinking here of people like Kwasi Wiredu, Kwame Gyekye, Segun Gbadegesin and unfortunately, at least to some degree myself.

Kola Abímbọ́lá trumps this disjunctive conundrum by in effect embracing both alternatives, and I believe he successfully argues that his position does not involve a contradiction. There are, however, two questions I would like to pose at this point: (1) Is this a situation in which Western philosophical naturalism, which favors dispensing with the spiritual altogether and insisting that systems of values must be justified purely on reasonable (this-worldly) grounds, is having a negative influence on the exposition of a non-Western culture and thereby causing unnecessary confusion and complications in communicating both its meanings and significance? and (2) What philosophical approach has Kola Abímbọ́lá, himself a PhD in philosophy, found most useful for interpreting the Ifá corpus so that he does arrive at such unconventional conclusions in Western terms?

16. This question also arises from a statement in Kola Abímbọ́lá's book: "the Yoruba person who explicitly claims to be a Christian, a Muslim, or an atheist, but who consults the *oníṣẹgùn* [traditional healer] for medical treatment (and who uses/takes the herbal prescriptions in conjunction with the spiritual prescriptions) is *implicitly* subscribing to the Yoruba spiritual view of the world" (2005, 91, my emphasis). What intrigues me about this sentence is the use of the word "implicitly." I suppose the scenario I am about to outline could take place in Yorùbáland, but I would prefer to relate it to other non-Yorùbá geographical venues where Ifá is also in vogue—places in the Western hemisphere, for instance. Rather than speaking of the *oníṣẹgùn* let us speak of the babalawo and of Ifá divination. What exactly would be the status of an Ifá divination session in which the client was so committed as a Christian, Muslim, or even an atheist that he or she

could never explicitly agree to the spiritual reality of the Yorùbá divinities? I suspect that such situations do arise, where consulting Ifá is sometimes regarded as equivalent to going to a fortune teller, and I wonder what the status of the divination prescription becomes in such situations. Are we saying that, in effect, unless one undergoes an explicit process of religious conversion to the Yorùbá deities, Ifá can have no effective relationship to a person's life? On the other hand, is it possible that a person who was not initially spiritually committed to Ifá, perhaps even outspokenly skeptical about its status as a system of knowledge, would be so impressed by the positive results of a divination session that that experience itself became an instrument for spiritual conversion to the Yorùbá divinities? Finally, is there any form of obligation upon the babalawo to introduce the spiritual beliefs and values that Ifá takes as foundational to the non-Yorùbá Western client who comes to consult Ifá?

Notes

1. Peter G, Dunbar, "Coherent Treatment of Ancient Africanized Wisdom." 30 July 2001. Review of S. Solagbade Popoola, *Practical Ifa Divination*, vol. 3 (1997). Available at http://www .amazon.com/Practical-Ifa-Professional-Solagbade-Popoola/dp/1890157023/ref=sr_1_1?ie= UTF8&qid=1427591999&sr=8–1&keywords=practical+ifa+divination.

References

Abímbọ́lá, Kola. 2005. *Yoruba Culture: A Philosophical Account*. Birmingham, UK: Iroko Academic Publishers.

Abímbọ́lá, Wándé. 1975. *Sixteen Great Poems of Ifa*. Paris: UNESCO.

———. 1976. *Ifá: An Exposition of Ifá Literary Corpus*. Ibadan: Oxford University Press.

———. 1977. *Ifa Divination Poetry*. New York: Nok Publishers.

———. 1997. *Ifa Will Mend Our Broken World: Thoughts on Yoruba Religion and Culture in Africa and the Diaspora*. Roxbury, MA: Aim Books.

———. 2000. "Continuity and Change in the Verbal, Artistic, Ritualistic, and Performance Traditions of Ifa Divination." In *Insight and Artistry in African Divination*, edited by John Pemberton III, 175–181. Washington, DC: Smithsonian Institution Press.

Abímbọ́lá, Wándé, and Barry Hallen. 1993. "Secrecy ('Awo') and Objectivity in the Methodology and Literature of Ifa Divination." In *Secrecy: African Art That Conceals and Reveals*, edited by M. Nooter, 212–221. New York: Museum for African Art; Munich: Prestel.

Akintola, Akinbowale. 1999. *Yoruba Ethics and Metaphysics: Being Basic Philosophy Underlying the Ifa System of Thought of the Yoruba*. Ibadan: Valour Publishing Ventures.

Bascom, William. 1969. *Ifá Divination: Communicaiton between Gods and Men in West Africa*. Bloomington: Indiana University Press.

Gates, Henry Louis, Jr. 1988. *The Signifying Monkey: A Theory of African-American Literary Theory*. Oxford: Oxford University Press.

Hallen, Barry. 2000a. "Variations on a Theme: Ritual, Performance, Intellect." In *Secrecy: African Art That Conceals and Reveals,* edited by M. Nooter, 212–221. New York: Museum for African Art; Munich: Prestel.

———. 2000b. *The Good, the Bad, and the Beautiful: Discourse About Values in Yoruba Culture.* Bloomington: Indiana University Press.

———. 2002. *A Short History of African Philosophy.* Bloomington: Indiana University Press.

———. 2006. *African Philosophy: The Analytic Approach.* Trenton, NJ: Africa World Press.

Hallen, Barry, and J. Olubi Sodipo. 1986. *Knowledge, Belief and Witchcraft: Analytic Experiments in African Philosophy.* London: Ethnographica.

Olupona, Jacob K., and Terry Rey, eds. 2008. *Orisa Devotion as World Religion: The Globalization of Yoruba Religious Culture.* Madison: University of Wisconsin Press.

Popoola, S. Solagbade. 1997. *Practical Ifa Divination, vol. 3: Ifa Reference Manual for the Beginner and Professional.* New York: Athelia Henrietta Press.

Rowlands, E. C. 1969. *Teach Yourself Yoruba.* London: English Universities Press.

7   Kín N'Ifá Wí?

Philosophical Issues in Ifá Divination

Olúfẹ́mi Táíwò

Ifá, THE SYSTEM of divination that is prevalent among Yorùbá and related peoples of West Africa and the huge diaspora that they comprise in the Americas, has engaged the attention of scholars working from various disciplines. For the most part, its study has been dominated by anthropologists, foremost among whom is William Bascom. As such, Ifá is treated as a dominant aspect of Yorùbá religion, as this divination system was realized before the advent of alien religions and as it continues to be practiced wherever Yorùbá practitioners are. J. A. Adedeji (1970) has tried to use Ifá as a source of historical evidence. In his work, he traced the origin of the Yorùbá masque theatre to Ifá. He was concerned with identifying the "origin of the Egúngún," with the "development of a class of Egúngún known as the Òjẹ̀," and finally with the "role of the Òjẹ̀ in society" as articulated in the *odù Ifá* (1970, 70–71). Anyone who is familiar with the place of the Egúngún in the metaphysics native to Yorùbá life and thought will realize that being able to trace Egúngún to Ifá would point to a deep integration of the various elements of the Yorùbá lifeworld that continues to typify that world until now.

Olatunde Olatunji (1973), on the other hand, has worked on Ifá as poetry and he remains the preeminent scholar of the language of Ifá poetry. Rowland Abiodun (1983, 2014) has for years now been exploring the aesthetic dimensions of Ifá with a view to extracting some Yorùbá aesthetics that are inspired by Ifá. Akínsọlá Akìwọwọ (1983a) has gone further than anyone else in his exploration of Ifá for theoretical and philosophical insights. His interests, though, are in the creation of sociological paradigms inspired by African realities best suited to analyzing those realities while offering the world original theories that are capable of answering some perennial questions in both sociology and philosophy. For this purpose, he has mined the *Àyájọ Aláṣùwàdà* derived from *odù Ifá* and has come up with a distinct theory of society anchored on the concepts of *Àjọbí* and

Àjọgbé elicited from Yorùbá language, life, and thought. In further development of the same core concepts, he has brought us to an awareness of the theoretical possibilities contained in the *odù Ifá* for our understanding of human nature and the nature of society, through the concept of *aṣùwàdà* and how we might dedicate knowledge to the improvement of the world, *ifọgbọntáyéṣe,* as he has called it.[1]

But by far the preeminent scholar of Ifá in our time is Wándé Abímbọ́lá, who has chronicled Ifá in both Yorùbá and English and is himself a practitioner of it. He has followed in the footsteps of earlier scholar-practitioners as well as popularizers of Ifá, such as D. Ọnadele Ẹpẹga (1931), J. Olumide Lucas (1948), E. M. Lijadu (2010), and others. Much of the discussion to follow in this essay will build on materials collected by these illustrious predecessors. As important as the work of chronicling the corpus is, I am trying in this discussion to make a distinction between these analysts or glossators and practitioners, and interlopers like me who wish to mine Ifá for insights or explore its philosophical implications. No doxastic attitude is required to take part in this discussion, beyond the belief that Ifá is comprehensible and can be comprehended as a philosophical system.

Given what I just said, it might appear that Ifá has been well served by scholars. But, such an impression would be mistaken. For in spite of widespread attention of the sort identified above, there has been very little study of the strictly philosophical elements of Ifá. That is, very little has been done to explore Ifá for philosophical possibilities, especially regarding the epistemological, metaphysical, and ethical insights that are to be found therein. Of the little that has been done—outside of cursory references to Ifá in more general discussions of Yorùbá philosophy in the works of Moses Makinde (1988), Segun Gbadegesin (1991), and others—Wándé Abímbọ́lá's "Ìwàpẹ̀lẹ̀: The Concept of Good Character in Ifá Literary Corpus" (1975) represents a limited attempt by a nonphilosopher to extract some guide to right conduct from Ifá. Maulana Karenga (1999) has written an essay to distill the ethical teachings from *odù Ifá.* Attempts to trace the philosophical implications of Ifá for Yorùbá culture include those of J. A. I. Bewaji (1992), Kọ́lá Abímbọ́lá (2006), and Ọmọtade Adegbindin (2014).

At the risk of being immodest, I would like to suggest that (1) the philosophical possibilities inherent in Ifá are yet to be captured, much less explored, by philosophers, and that (2) the philosophical issues raised by Ifá, its theory and practice, have not been identified by anyone. In fact, I have been somewhat surprised that hardly anyone has seen fit to ask more narrowly circumscribed philosophical questions of Ifá, both of its theory and its practice.[2] Of course, I assume that this results more from oversight than from a belief that the theory and practice of Ifá do not raise any problems of interest in relation to philosophy. Quite the contrary, Ifá in its theoretical and practical manifestations is full of philosophical possibilities. For example, the epistemological issues within Ifá will include exploring how one learns and teaches Ifá. Given that it is only recently that a fair amount of its texts has been recorded in writing or in other media, Ifá tradition-ally has been learned and taught as orature. There are legitimate epistemological questions that are usually asked of similar genres in other traditions. We can ask about the criteria of certification for its practitioners,[3] and about how the practice identifies and differentiates among differing levels of competence in its performance.

A different set of questions pertains to the yardstick for identifying Ifá's con-stituent texts. If we are paying attention, nonpractitioners like me who work on the materials that have been gathered by scholar-practitioners must notice that the verses of the different odù Ifá are not always uniformly recorded or reported even by the same chronicler. For example, in conducting my research I noticed that there were different verses reported by Abímbọ́lá for Èjìogbè in different edi-tions of some of his collections. And his were different from those recorded by Bascom. When I first confronted this problem, I consulted more knowledgeable scholars who had worked in this sphere for several years, and they all assured me that a babálawo, depending on his competence, does know and can identify the relevant members of each odù once he hears any appropriate part of it. Needless to say, their assurance calmed my anxiety but did not resolve my conundrum. How might a scholar who is not a practitioner and who is merely interested in the philosophical dimensions of Ifá do the same?[4] The whole issue of what makes Ifá a system may turn on the resolution of this conundrum.[5] Then there are the questions of the standards of correctness for Ifá divination practice, of cogency for explanations derived from it, of the reliability of its mnemonic devices for its transmission, and so on.

Ifá is summoned on occasions as a diagnostic instrument for everything from personal failures to illnesses that are impervious to treatment regimens to the fate of whole communities. What are the criteria for determining that its diagnosis in any particular instance is correct? And when Ifá recommends a course of action for the amelioration, perhaps even cure, of a particular condi-tion, what are the criteria for determining that the recommendation is correct? That is to say, in the aftermath of performing the action recommended by Ifá, what grounds have we for believing that other factors might not equally explain the successful outcome? This is a question that is not often raised in the literature on Ifá, which shows how philosophers have been remiss in our relation to this discourse. In yet other circumstances, Ifá assumes a prophetic stance, and for this reason we are right to ask: how good a predictive mechanism is Ifá? In such situations, the babálawo announces what will happen, according to Ifá, unless certain specified steps are taken to avert the predicted outcome. I shall presently show how it is wrong to think of Ifá as an exercise in fortune telling.[6] Given that it is markedly different from the likes of palmistry, tarot card reading, and other attempts at foretelling the future, we are left with the task of inquiring into the nature of Ifá's predictions and their epistemic status. Is Ifá a system of probability, an explanatory model, or does it represent a philosophy of fatalism? These are but a few of the fecund epistemological questions pertaining to Ifá.

Furthermore, Ifá has often been construed as a religion. Regardless of one's attitude to that characterization, there is no doubt that there are some fundamental questions of metaphysics within Ifá. In the first place, Ifá is regarded as more than a mere manual of wisdom distilled from lived experience. Although its practitioners will easily concede its historical nature, there is a fundamental assumption that Ifá reaches out to a reality that is beyond the grasp of our cognitive capacities. There is an indication here of an ontological commitment to a form of dualism in its account of reality. Hence, it is no surprise that Ifá is regarded as timeless and its reach without limits.

Second, Ifá requires a commitment to a suprasensible and suprahistorical reality on the part of its adherents, a requirement that grounds their belief in its ability to see into the infinite past as well as divine the infinite future. Thus, one can raise questions about the ontology of time and space with which Ifá works; what is the nature of reality presupposed by Ifá? By the same token, one can raise questions respecting Ifá's positions on human nature, the nature of animals, of society, of things in general, and of the relationships among all instances of Being.

The philosophy of personal identity presupposed by Ifá has been much more explored by philosophers. Thus, there are serious discussions in the literature of the nature of the person, the role of *orí* in the constitution of personal identity, the nature and role of destiny in human affairs, and so on.[7] The implications of such analyses for ethics, social and political philosophy, and aesthetics cannot be overemphasized. For instance, in the perennial philosophical issue of free will and determinism, Ifá does not speak in one voice. Various *odù* suggest different leads from strict determinism to variants of compatibilism. We find here some tantalizing prospects for autochthonous philosophizing in an indigenous idiom with implications for a global audience, like those of insights from Asian philosophies for discussions of the perennial problems of philosophy in areas external to them.

In the limited context of the current discussion, I cannot even begin to delve into some of the issues that I have so far identified. It is important to identify them, though, just so that they can serve as a roadmap for professional philosophers who wish to explore them further. I perform a much more limited task here, one that is designed to explore a few strands of a philosophically fecund phenomenon. I hope thereby to convey a glimpse of what riches await those who would take seriously the indigenous philosophical traditions to be found in Yorùbá culture and life.

Ifá Defined

What is Ifá? This way of posing the question leaves out the concepts that are usually associated with Ifá in the literature, namely "divination" and "system." In the first place, Ifá does have divination as a huge component, but it is by no means limited to or synonymous with divination. One can trace the affirmation of a necessary connection between Ifá and divination to the fact that we are trying to talk about Ifá in English without an adequate translation manual. When we speak of Ifá in its original language, in the current case Yorùbá, it is easy to see that *Ifá dídá* (casting, creating, divining Ifá) is only one among the many manifestations that Ifá involves. There is *Ifá kíkì* (singing in praise of, chanting, exulting, invoking Ifá),[8] where babálawo as individuals or in groups perform Ifá by chanting verses and singing Ifá's praise. On such occasions there is hardly any divination activity. And for some time now we have had the Ìjo Òrúnmìlà, which is modeled after the liturgies of Christian worship, complete with original hymns and a whole hymnody traceable to Ifá if not wholly derived from it.[9] Thus divining, performing or praising, and worshipping Ifá all represent different though integrated elements of Ifá, and it is only an impoverished rendering traceable to translation difficulties that will reduce it to divination alone. My focus in the rest of this essay on the philosophical issues generated by Ifá divination should not obscure the fact that I am highlighting only one aspect of a complex reality.[10]

I propose to proceed as follows. First, I will describe what divination in Ifá entails, how it is done, what types there are, and what goals it sets out to achieve. I shall then identify various philosophical issues arising from the many ideas, practices, orientations, injunctions, and so on that are germane to Ifá divination. This essay has two distinct tracks. One track is programmatic, devoted to identifying as many philosophical questions as can fit into the discussion without particularly trying to answer most of them. As suggested above, my hope is that others might be moved to engage the questions I propose, and in so doing push back the frontiers of philosophical discourse and knowledge pertaining to Ifá. In my estimation, it is a road map for future work.

In the second track, I investigate some epistemological themes that I extract from Ifá divination. The ultimate aim is to provide some way of grasping the philosophy of Ifá and the philosophical puzzles that it elicits. One problem is that of how meaning is established and knowledge produced as well as certified in Ifá. Establishing meaning is one issue; creating knowledge and imparting it is another. The issues that I have raised and will raise in the rest of this chapter may not resonate with practitioners, who are familiar with internal criteria to which only Awo can have access.[11] They are members of Ifá's hermeneutic circle. I am not Awo, nor am I an empirical scientist seeking to record what happens in Ifá and how what happens is procured. Meaning may be taken to be simple. That

would be mistaken. We are not talking of meaning in the sense of the signification of ordinary language.

I wish instead to ask whether the procedures of Ifá yield knowledge and if
so, how good or adequate this knowledge is. Even a practitioner who decides to
look at the foundations and criteria of knowledge claims in Ifá will have to follow
a similar path: locate himself or herself outside the parameters of the practice
and inquire how well the criteria he or she embraces as a practitioner actually do
under critical scrutiny.[12] This is what a philosophical look requires. Of course, a
practitioner who elects to provide an exposition of Ifá epistemology and metaphysics will be no less philosophical. But if he is to persuade others of the coherence of his practice without converting his interlocutors into Awo, he must
discharge functions similar to those that we are articulating in this essay. To this
task we now proceed.

Ifá Divination

According to Wándé Abímbọ́lá,

> *Ifá jẹ́ òrìṣà kan pàtàkì láàrin àwọn Yorùbá. Àwọn Yorùbá gbàgbọ́ wí pé Olódù-*
> *marè ló rán Ifá wá láti òde ọ̀run láti wáá fi ọgbọ́ọn rẹ̀ tún ilé ayé ṣe. Ọgbọ́n,*
> *ìmọ̀, àti òye tí Olódùmarè fi fún Ifá ló fún Ifá ní ipò ńlá láàrín àwọn ibọ ní ilẹ̀*
> *Yorùbá. 'A-kéré-finú-ṣọgbọ́n' ni oríkì Ifá.*

> Ifá is a special divinity among the Yorùbá. The Yorùbá believe that it was
> Olódùmarè who sent Ifá forth from the heavens and who charged him to use
> his wisdom to repair the world. The wisdom, knowledge, and luminosity with
> which Olódùmarè endowed Ifá account for Ifá's preeminence among divini-
> ties in Yorùbáland. "The-young-but-immensely-wise one" is Ifá's cognomen.
> (W. Abímbọ́lá 1968, 6, my translation)

William Bascom described it thus:

> Ifà is a system of divination based on sixteen basic and 256 derivative figures
> (odù) obtained either by the manipulation of sixteen palm nuts (ikin) or by the
> toss of a chain (ọ̀pẹ̀lẹ̀) of eight half seed shells. The worship of Ifá as the God of
> divination entails ceremonies, sacrifices, tabus, paraphernalia, drums, songs,
> praises, initiation and other ritual elements comparable to those of other Yor-
> ùbá cults; these are not treated fully here, since the primary subject of this
> study is Ifá as a system of divination. (1991, 3)

I have cited the above passages because they come from two of the preeminent scholars of Ifá. Each proceeds to describe the mechanics of divination.
Abímbọ́lá's account identifies Ifá as one of the most important of the Yorùbá
gods, as one sent by the Supreme Being from on High, Olódùmarè, and charged
with the responsibility of using his incomparable wisdom and capacity for om-

niscience, which the Supreme Being had given to Ifá, to order the world aright and to ensure that both it and its inhabitants do not spin out of their proper orbit. Hence, Ifá's nickname, "A-kéré-finú-ṣọgbọ́n," is apt because Ifá is reputed to be among the youngest gods, yet is endowed with unsurpassable knowledge[13] and unfathomable wisdom.[14]

Ifá is omniscient; it is a repository of unsurpassable knowledge and wisdom. This means that Ifá transcends the limits of human cognitive capacities, has the capacity to know from several perspectives at the same time, and is not bound by the time-space constraints of human knowing. Now, if one proceeds from the religious standpoint and identifies Ifá as a god, the capacity that we have just mentioned follows as a matter of course. But we do not have to do so. Even if we do it still will not free us from dealing with the perennial problems of epistemology, especially as they relate to what Ifá and its practitioners—babálawo and supplicant alike—know, how they know it, and how we might go about establishing how and whether they really know what they claim to know. I suggest therefore that regardless of one's stand on the matter of whether or not Ifá is a religion, one can analyze it purely as a system of divination and seek to lay bare its presuppositions, its criteria of correctness and adequacy, and its philosophical assumptions. We shall now proceed to this task.

Making Meaning/Creating Knowledge in Ifá Divination

There are at least four different types of divination, namely, (1) *Ifá eni*, divining for a specific individual; (2) *Ifá ẹgbẹ́, ọgbà* or *ìlú*, divining for a group—say a club, an association, a city, a nation, or a country; (3) *Ifá ipò*, divining for a holder or occupier of a specific office or position; and (4) *Ifá ọdún*, divining for a ceremony or festival or rite of passage at regular intervals.[15] In every case, the babálawo is the one who is at once each of the following: the priest; the diviner, the one who can decipher Ifá's hieroglyphics;[16] the celebrant, whose concern is to praise or worship Ifá; and the guardian of Ifá's most abstruse wisdom. Hence, the appellation "babálawo" is usually misleadingly translated as "father of secrets." A more appropriate translation is "master of mystery."[17] In divination, there are the babálawo, the client or a relevant surrogate, and Ifá.[18]

Our focus here is on divining for the individual, *Ifá ẹni*. There are some subtle variations here on the epistemological questions raised by Ifá. The first deals with the agency of the person or persons who go to Ifá. One of the crucial elements of the process of *Ifá ẹni* is that the Ifá in that case must be made specific to and for that particular individual who seeks Ifá's wisdom. The divination must be separate, distinct, and uncrossed with any other's situation. One cannot overemphasize the importance of this factor in the cogency and accuracy of the outcome of any particular consultation. There are times that the babálawo assumes a surrogate position to *dá* Ifá. In *Ifá ẹni* instances, however, a client must come to the babálawo to have the latter *dá* Ifá for him or her. This is how Abímbólá describes the process:

> When the client enters the house of the Ifá priest, he salutes him and expresses a wish to "talk with the divinity." The Ifá priest then takes out his divining chain and lays it on a mat or a raffia tray in front of the client. The client whispers his problem to a coin or a cowry shell and drops it on the Ifá instruments. Alternatively, the client could pick up the divining chain or the ìbò and whisper his problem to it directly. In either case, it is believed that the wishes of the client's orí (God of predestination who knows what is good for every person) have been communicated to Ifá who will then produce the appropriate answer through the first *odù* which the Ifá priest will cast when he manipulates his divining chain. (W. Abímbólá 1977, 9)

There are many ways in which this personalization takes place; the singularity of the client needs to be established. An attempt is made to establish a direct connection between *this* client and Ifá; this is made to remove or at least minimize the possibilities of distortion (no crossed wires here). And there is a need to not interpose anyone between Ifá and client. But Ifá does not speak with the client, except through the babálawo. Here we find an asymmetry between the client/Ifá relationship and that of Ifá, babálawo, and client. Of course, the babálawo must "tell" Ifá of the need to speak; Ifá is not self-activating. Thus, it is obvious that the possibilities of interposition can only be reduced, not completely eliminated.

In the first place, the client does not talk with the babálawo; he or she expresses a wish to "talk with the divinity."[19] This is a critical element in Ifá's epistemology. In not talking directly with the babálawo, the client underscores the intermediary role of the babálawo, and the process simultaneously denies the babálawo any opportunity to play god or seer. The insight that is sought is Ifá's, not the babálawo's. The first element of Ifá as an interactive process is to personalize the divination for *this* client and none other. There are at least three parties to the process just inaugurated: the babálawo, the client, and Ifá.[20]

Second, the process is interactive in ways that are significant for the kinds of knowledge claims that are made in Ifá. After the initial steps we have described, the babálawo "throws the divining chain in front of himself and quickly reads and pronounces the name of the *Odù* whose signature he has seen. The answer to the client's problem will be found only in this *Odù*" (W. Abímbólá 1977, 9–10). There is meaning involved here, though in this case it is limited to the babaláwo's apprehension of the *odù*. But he is not alone, for he presupposes a universe of discourse shared by other babálawo who as fellow Awo can apprehend the same thing with him.

This is where the notion of a hermeneutic circle is relevant. The pattern formed by the chain when it lands on the receptacle is neither random nor without significance. How its different components are distributed is an inscription or a form of writing, the meaning of which is immediately apprehended by speakers of Ifá language. At one level, the *odù* represents a form of communication—a speaking, a signing, a writing—by Ifá. Ifá already has started communicating. There may be controversy among them concerning competence, correctness, or adequacy of the meaning involved here. Any number of things can go awry.

But once an *odù* appears, the babálawo does not exercise choice. He has to chant the *odù* whose signature is presented by the divining chain's pattern. He "then begins to chant verses from the *odù* which he has seen while the client watches and listens. The priest chants as many poems as he knows from that *odù* until he chants a poem which tells a story containing a problem similar to the client's own problem. At that stage, the client stops him and asks for further explanation of that particular poem. The Ifá priest will interpret that particular poem and mention the sacrifice which the client must perform" (Abímbọ́lá 1977, 9–10).

Here is a sample piece of an *odù*, of the kind that a babálawo would chant once it emerges from deploying the divination instrument. I have chosen this at random, because it matters less in the current discussion which *odù* is chosen than the role that *odù* play

Òwónrín Méjì, Ese Èkejì

Aparún ṣẹgi l'ókè ìhín;
Aparún ṣẹgi l'ókè ọhún
A díá fún Ọ̀wọ̀n,
Tí ń rogun Tẹ̀ntẹ̀sín.
Ogun tí òun lọ yìí,
Òun le ja àjàlà níbẹ̀?
Ni Ọ̀wọ̀n dá Ifá sí.
Won ní yóò ṣẹgun,
Ṣùgbọ̀n kí ó rúbọ.
Kín ni òun ó ha rú báyìí?
Wọn ní kí ó rú ẹwù ọrùn araa rẹ̀,
Kí ó sì rú ẹgbàaàjọ owó.
Ó rúbọ tán,
Wọn ṣe Ifá fún un.
Ó sì ja ogun náà ní àjàlà,
Ó ja ogun náà ní àjàmẹrú.
Ó mú ọkùnrin,
Ó sì mú obìnrin.
Ó ṣẹgun síwájú,
Ó ṣẹgun séyìn,
Ó bi ọtá lulẹ̀ láàrin.
Ó wàá n yin àwon awoo rẹ̀,
Àwon awoo rẹ̀ ń yin Ifá.

Ó ní, 'Ta ní ó ò mú méjì o,
Ọ̀wọ̀n l'ó mú méjì o.

Aparún cleared brush here;
Aparún cleared brush yonder
Ifá was cast for Ọ̀wọ̀n,
Who was going to war at Tẹ̀ntẹ̀sín.
This war he was about to fight
Would he overcome there?
Was why Ọ̀wọ̀n went to Ifá.
It was said that he would be victorious,
But he was asked to offer sacrifice.
What sacrifice would it be?
He was instructed to offer the garment off his back,
And offer 16,000 cowries.
He offered sacrifice,
Ifá was cast for him.
He was victorious in the war,
He came back with captives.
He captured males,
He captured females.
He won on advance,
He won at the rear,
He demolished his enemies in the middle.
He praised his diviners,
His diviners praised Ifá.
He asked, "who was it who captured both sexes?
Ọ̀wọ̀n it was who captured both sexes."
(W. Abímbọ́lá 2006: 32–33, my translation)

The main character in the *odù*, Ọ̀wọ̀n, was a warrior who was about to go to war. He was desirous of finding out how the venture would turn out for him. I would like to suggest that it is not too difficult to see the epistemic impulse inherent in the above passage. It reflects very clearly the kind of central epistemological concern that will provoke some serious reflection in other contexts. In the first place, when Ọ̀wọ̀n consulted Ifá, he did so because he either assumed, was convinced, or had reason to believe—all doxastic attitudes—that Ifá had answers that would enable him to solve or at least make sense of the problem or the circumstance that led him to the babaláwo's door. In other words, Ọ̀wọ̀n believes, explicitly or implicitly, that Ifá, as what Moses Makinde calls "an omniscient intelligence" (1988, 5–10), is plausible and possibly convincing, and that with all things being equal Ifá's house held a solution to his problem. One need not go into the grounds of this belief or how good they are. It is sufficient for our purposes to affirm that such is the minimum requirement for anyone to go to Ifá in this particular instance of divination.

The context for Ọ̀wọ̀n's consultation is relevant. He is about to embark on a venture marked by lack of knowledge of what would happen. We do not need to assume that he was not a good warrior, strategist and so on, or that he was not knowledgeable about war and what winning a war might involve. Yet there is always the unknown, which presumably is known to Ifá. This condition of uncertainty, which is always present in the human experience, is what invites the visit to Ifá to take care of all possibilities. The question is, to what extent are we justified in attributing knowledge of these possibilities, which are otherwise unknown to us, to Ifá? The assumption that Ifá is privy to such knowledge is fundamental in Ifá divination.

However often divination is performed, the outcome is always a central concern. This is best captured in that ubiquitous locution with which the client asks for the outcome of the divination: *Kín n'Ifá wí*? Simply translated: What says Ifá? The simple translation does not even begin to acquaint the reader with the many philosophical possibilities with which the verb *wí* is redolent. It means to say, state, elocutionize, enunciate, pronounce, assert, articulate, or affirm. In the first place, there is the assumption that Ifá does "say something" and that what it says is easy to ascertain by those qualified in its register. Here is the catch: the entire process, especially in *Ifá eni,* is interactive. Because each *odù* has six hundred *ẹsẹ* (roughly, "verses"), the process of chanting the *ẹsẹ* of a single *odù* can take several days. However, in spite of this time-consuming dimension, the babaláwo may not stop, save for fatigue, to tell the client that he as the babaláwo has decided that this is the appropriate *odù* for the client's problem. On the contrary, the client is the *only* person in this instance of *Ifá ẹni* who may stop the babaláwo, ask him to explain some *ẹsẹ* or another, seek clarification, and then *decide* that the problem spoken of in the text is the same as or akin to his or her problem.[21]

This is a very important requirement that bears significantly on the veracity of Ifá's prediction and on the inability of the babaláwo to insinuate himself in an inappropriate way into the process of communication between the client and the divinity. As such, it takes Ifá out of the orbit of fortune telling, with which Bascom (wrongly in my opinion) sometimes equated Ifá. It requires the client to be an active participant in the process of finding an efficacious remedy for whatever problem has led him or her to Ifá's door. It is a corollary that only an individual who is capable of exercising agency can participate in this instance of *Ifá dídá.*[22] Bascom reports:

> Actually it is the client himself who selects the verse. The diviner simply recites the verses that he has memorized for the initial figure, while the client listens for one that bears on the problem with which he is concerned. He may either

stop the diviner as soon as it has been recited or wait until the end of the verses before deciding which is most appropriate. . . . The client finds his own "answer," i.e. the prediction and the required sacrifice, when he chooses the verse most directly related to his own problem. (1991, 69)

But it is not the case that the client merely chooses the verses most directly related to his or her own problem. After all, as we have pointed out, the stories told in the *odù* concerned other figures who lived at times and in places vastly different and very distant from that of the client who has come to Ifá on this particular occasion. Additionally, given the multiplicity and variety of clients who might recognize themselves in the same *odù* at different times, it must be that the client is not a mere recipient of Ifá's message coming through the *odù*. He or she must also assume the role of a decoder or an interpreter who is capable of mapping Ifá's often cryptic message onto his or her own life's grid. As Bascom puts it, "the client, depending on his own problem, selects the verse that provides his 'answer,' and he also interprets the problems of the mythological characters in the verses in terms of his own needs and anxieties" (1991, 69).

A transposition occurs here. That is, the client becomes a coauthor of Ifá's meaning and a participant in its hermeneutic circle. There is respect for the integrity of the client, and by the same token the client is expected to be invested in the gravity and integrity of the divination process. No doubt here we have some assumptions about human nature that might offer another opportunity for philosophical analysis, in a different context. Although one may not discount the threat posed by a client motivated to mislead Ifá—*èjá* is what it is called—it does not seem as if this is considered a serious matter.

If what we say is plausible, then it follows that when the babaláwo announces what Ifá says in this particular instance, it is really a composite of *what-the-babaláwo-and-the supplicant-working-with-the-relevant*-odù Ifá *say*. As it turns out, the simple locution regularly deployed to announce the outcome of a divination—"Thus says Ifá"—hides a complex of philosophical questions such as we have highlighted above. Notice that I am limiting myself to one single instance of *Ifá dídá*. What Ifá says might actually vary from one divination context to another depending on whether it is *Ifá ẹni* or *Ifá ipò* or *Ifá ẹgbẹ́* or *Ifá ọdún*. Whereas any of the first three instances might impose constraints on the outcome because of the interposition of agency in each of them, in other contexts such as *Ifá odún, ìlú*, or even *egbê* where there is no individual embodiment present, the criteria of meaning that determine the boundaries of what Ifá says might be differently configured. Finally, *Ifá ọrọọrún*, the regular, mandatory weekly divination performances, are dependent entirely on the babaláwo, unless of course an *odù* shows up respecting the prospects of an individual, a group, an office holder, a state of affairs, future events, and so on. In such a situation, I must confess that I am at a loss to distinguish between Ifá and futurology. Maybe here the principles of probability ought to kick in, and what is at stake is less about meaning than about the adequacy or correctness of predictions.[23]

So far we have focused on the role of the client in the making of meaning and the generation of knowledge in Ifá divination. The emphasis is necessitated by the fact that this is not a theme that is often, if at all, apprehended in discussions of the practice. But the babaláwo's own role is no less complicated; indeed, his responsibility is much graver. We have seen that Ifá does not speak directly, if at all, to the client. Neither does it speak to the babaláwo. The babaláwo must correctly identify the *odù* whose signature results from his casting the divining instruments and from his proceeding to chant the appropriate *ẹsẹ*. Many things could go wrong at this stage.

To ensure that nothing goes wrong, the babaláwo must be a master of, or at least proficient in, the language of Ifá. He must also possess a superb memory from which the *ẹsẹ* are chanted. This is not to recommend rote learning. It is simply to acknowledge that orality and commitment to memory remain the primary forms of transmission of Ifá to date.[24] The babaláwo must resist the temptation to use his knowledge of his client's biography to rig the process to preselect an outcome.[25] He has to resist the temptation of hurrying the client into making a choice when the client is "taking too long" to find his or her story in the *odù* that the babaláwo has identified, because the babaláwo is about to exhaust his repertoire of *ẹsẹ* or is simply fatigued. Finally, one may not discount the possibility that the babaláwo is incompetent or that his power of recall may be inadequate or that his interpretive light does not shine brightly. In any of these cases, the reliability of the most basic elements of *Ifá dídá* is suspect. Thus, successful *Ifá dídá* is always premised in part on significant but seldom-stated assumptions that the babaláwo is honest, competent, has mastery of or proficiency in the language of Ifá, and overall can be relied upon to do right.

As we have argued so far, if the meaning that is yielded in divination is a composite that requires contributions from both the babaláwo and the client, it cannot be the case that what Ifá *wí* (says) has the simplicity, solidity, and integrity that is usually supposed when the question, *Kín n'Ifá wí?* (What is Ifá saying?), is asked and answered. Needless to say, I may be mistaken here. But it is the kind of mistake that is often instructive in terms of pointing us in the direction of problems that we may not have known existed.

Given that our focus in this essay has been on knowledge production in divination and the structure of meaning it presupposes, one final relevant aspect will round off this discussion. When the babaláwo has cast Ifá, the supplicant has discharged his or her role in deciphering what Ifá has said on a specific occasion, and the error detection mechanism of the *ìbò* (objects used to cast lots) has been deployed, it remains for the client or an appropriate surrogate to act upon the recommendation contained in the *odù*, while respecting what is to be done either to procure the fortune predicted or to avert the misfortune foretold. The *odù* always contains reference to *ẹbọ* (sacrifice) and its performance as parts of the outcome of divination. There is literature on the meaning of sacrifice as ritual. But I do not know of any inquiry into the role of *ẹbọ* in the structure of meaning relevant to divination or to the knowledge produced by it. Is it a part of the divination? If it is, then the meaning of the performance is actually never really complete until *ẹbọ* has been made. If it is not, then is it merely a corroborative mechanism that ex post facto validates the meaning already settled when the initial question was resolved?

What are the implications of *ẹbọ* for knowledge claims in divination? If the outcome is as predicted, we say that the *ẹbọ* worked. Might there be situations in which the outcome is at variance with what was predicted even though the *ẹbọ* was duly and properly enacted? In that case, do we say that Ifá failed or its knowledge was null? What does the babaláwo do in this respect? Of course, our judgment cannot rest on occasional failures. In fact, there are auxiliary explanations in the system to account for failures. Does this mean that we can retrodict from an outcome to the explanation on which it is based? If there are occasional failures that are otherwise inexplicable, does it mean that Ifá is at best a probabilistic system? These are all tantalizing questions for an epistemology based on Ifá divination. They present us with an opportunity and a challenge for sophisticated theorizing in an original African culture.

Notes

1. See Akiwowo (1983b, 1990).

2. I say this in spite of the fact that chapters 4, 5, and 6 of Adegbindin (2014) are titled "Ontology in Ifá Corpus," "Epistemology in Ifá Corpus," and "Ethics in Ifá Corpus," respectively. For example, the chapter on epistemology does not raise the kinds of questions that we do here respecting the epistemic status of Ifá's practice and knowledge claims within the system. Rather the author is concerned to show that "the Yorùbá" [his locution], do have a theory of truth and uses Ifá verses to show that this is supported by the system. The idea of a singular theory of truth that can be ascribed to an advanced civilization such as Yorùbá is an idea that I think is best retired if we are really interested in developing, rather than merely asserting Yorùbá philosophy, all under the pressure of refuting pedigree arguments from racist deniers of African intellectual achievements. This is sure to limit the appeal of Adegbindin's book for people like me who are eager to enter into debates respecting specific claims and traditions in various African-inflected philosophies. For what I consider to be better philosophical explorations of epistemology in Ifá divination, see Eze (1993), Bewaji (1994), and Uyanne (1994).

3. Although I do not know of any regulatory bodies charged with this responsibility, I am well aware that there are standards and hierarchies built on competence among its practitioners.

4. This is not an idle question. In fact, the relative absence of philosophical engagement with Ifá by scholars may stem, in part, from their fear that they do not have a fair enough knowledge of the lay of the relevant land to enable them to ask questions of it.

5. This is not unusual. It is a problem encountered by scholars of traditions in which what was originally oral text has been codified in writing. Questions arise regarding what rightly belongs to the corpus and what does not. Perhaps in acknowledging this problem Ifá scholarship might begin to explore these other traditions for what it might learn from what their scholars have done to resolve this issue.

6. I find that Bascom is erroneous in this interpretation.

7. See Hallen (1989) and W. Abímbọ́lá (1973).

8. I would like to acknowledge here Professor Olasope Oyelaran's caution regarding the danger of translating "*kì*" as "to praise." I hope that in suggesting the many construals of the verb above, the reader is not so misled.

9. For a discussion of this music, see S. Adedeji (1991).

10. For a richer account of Ifá, see K. Abímbọ́lá (2006, 47).

11. Awo is the proper name for those who are practitioners of Ifá and are privy to its most abstruse formulae. As such, they often exhibit the point of view *internal* to the practice whereby the justifications for outcomes rest on shared criteria and accumulated knowledge of how the system works. Nothing prevents Awo from simultaneously being scholars of their practice (a role that requires that they detach themselves from the practice) and scholars who function from a standpoint *external* to the practice by putting the practice and its claims under critical scrutiny.

12. What does it mean to say that Ifá knows? What does Ifá know? The past? The present? The future? Does Ifá only know what has happened or does it also know what will happen? If the latter, does this subject Ifá's knowledge to all the epistemic strictures regarding knowledge of future events?

13. Is this the kind of knowledge that is at issue in Ifá? In philosophy, much of the attention in epistemology is focused on what is called "propositional knowledge." Does Ifá ever know that X will happen? Can it be wrong? Who really knows: Ifá or the client or the babaláwo?

14. What has wisdom to do with knowledge? The wisdom may come from the dialectical nature of the *ẹsẹ Ifá*, the experiences and injunctions that abound there and the fact that one can glean guidelines for conducting oneself from the narratives of *ẹsẹ Ifá*. This will proceed more by analogy and indirection than by command and direct instruction.

15. There are serious metaphysical issues here. For example, the idea of *orí* and how each type of Ifá presupposes a different type of *orí*, and that this introduces the possibility of serious inquiries into *essence* and its connotations. I have also deferred until another discussion the many complexities of the categories I have just identified. Each one of them can be the subject of extended philosophical analysis.

16. "The person in charge of the cult of Örúnmìlà is both a hierophant and a priest, although he is known more by the former function of declaring and expounding the mysteries of Ifa" (Idowu 1995, 138).

17. The phrase is Professor Oyèláràn's. The exigencies of space will not permit any serious discussions of the intricacies of translation and meaning that bedevil the existing scholarship on Ifá.

18. I am leaving out the question of the ontological status of Èṣù in this picture. It is sometimes suggested that Èṣù is another party present in divination.

19. This is a critical moment in any epistemological discussion of Ifá. There is no guarantee that the babaláwo will not try to insert himself into the subject position in the process.

20. I shall resist the temptation to multiply entities in the discourse. I shall ignore the role of Èṣù and whatever other denizens of the Yorùbá supernatural universe are supposed to be present in this encounter. They are not germane to our task.

21. There are other circumstances where the issue is not so straightforward. There are situations in which the person concerned is not physically present. Different methods are deployed

and these come with their corresponding complexities that are not relevant in the present discussion.

22. Other conditions seem to be necessary in this respect. It is difficult to imagine one who is not proficient in the original language in which the *odù* are articulated being able to exercise the requisite agency, nor can this be done from a distance. No doubt, there are new ways in which the stringency of these requirements is being reduced in the contemporary situation as Ifá operates in our world.

23. There are control mechanisms designed to ensure that the *odù* is the correct one. Other questions arise concerning the cognitive capacities of the client, especially say, when the client is a newborn; this is a situation that arises when the *àkosëjayé* of newborns is divined.

24. I do not think that this method precludes the possibility of Awo adding to the corpus of Ifá *as they* interpret its texts. But I am alert to the dangers posed here for creativity and expansion of Ifá. No method is impervious to these dangers.

25. See Bascom's account for several checks on this temptation (1991, 77).

References

Abímbọ́lá, Kọ́lá. 2006. *Yorùbá Culture: A Philosophical Account.* Birmingham, UK: Iroko Academic Publishers.

Abímbọ́lá, Wande. 1968. *Ìjìnlẹ̀ Ohùn Ẹnu Ifá, Apá Kìíní.* Glasgow: Collins.

———. 1971. "The Yoruba Concept of Human Personality." *La notion de Personne en Afrique Noire Colloques Internationales de Centre National de la Recherche Scientifique* 544: 69–85.

———. 1973. *The Literature of the Ifa Cult.* Oxford: Clarendon Press.

———. 1975. "Ìwàpẹ̀lẹ̀: The Concept of Good Character in Ifá Literary Corpus." In *Yorùbá Oral Tradition,* edited by Wande Abímbọ́lá, 388–420. Ile-Ife: Department of African Languages and Literatures, University of Ife.

———. 1976. *Ifá: An Exposition of Ifá Literary Corpus.* Ibadan: Oxford University Press.

———. 1977. *Ifá Divination Poetry.* New York: Nok Publishers.

———. 2006. *Àwon Ojú Odù Mẹ̀rẹ̀ẹ̀rìndínlógún.* Ibadan: University Press.

Abiodun, Rowland. 1983. "Identity and the Artistic Process in Yorùbá Aesthetic Concept of Ìwà." *Journal of Cultures and Ideas* 1, no. 1: 13–30.

Adedeji, J. A. 1970. "The Origin of the Yorùbá Masque Theatre: The Use of Ifá Divination Corpus as Historical Evidence." *African Notes* 6, no. 1: 70–86.

Adedeji, Samuel Olufemi. "Ifa Music in 'Ìjọ Ọrúnmìlà.'" MA thesis, University of Ibadan, 1991.

Adegbindin, Omotade. 2014. *Ifá in Yorùbá Thought System.* Durham: Carolina Academic Press.

Akiwowo, Akinsola. 1983a. *Àjobi and Àjogbe: Variations on the Theme of Sociation.* Ile-Ife: University of Ife Press.

———. 1983b. "Understanding Interpretative Sociology in the Light of the *oríkì* of Ọrúnmìlà." *Journal of Cultures and Ideas* 1, no. 1: 139–157.

———. 1990. "Contributions to the Sociology of Knowledge from an African Oral Poetry." In *Globalization, Knowledge and Society: Readings from International Sociology,* edited by Martin Albrow and Elizabeth King, 103–117. London: Sage Publications.

Bascom, William. 1991. *Ifa Divination: Communication Between Gods and Men in West Africa.* Bloomington: Indiana University Press.

Bewaji, J. A. I. 1992. "A Critical Analysis of the Philosophical Status of Yoruba Ifa Literary Corpus." *Wiener Reihe* 6: 140–155.

———. 1994. "Truth and ethics in African philosophy—a reply to Emmanuel Eze." *Quest: Philosophical Discussions* 8, no. 1: 76–89.

Epega, D. Onadele. 1931. *The Mystery of Yorùbá Gods*. Ode Remo, Nigeria: Ìmọ́lẹ̀ Olúwa Institute.

Eze, Emmanuel. 1993. "Truth and ethics in African thought." *Quest: Philosophical Discussions* 7, no. 1: 4–18.

Gbadegesin, Segun. 1991. *African Philosophy: Traditional Yorùbá Philosophy and Contemporary African Realities*. New York: Peter Lang.

Hallen, Barry. 1989. "'Ènìyàn': A Critical Analysis of the Yorùbá Concepts of Person." In *The Substance of African Philosophy*, edited by C. S. Momoh, 328–354. Auchi, Nigeria: African Philosophy Projects.

Idowu, E. Bọlaji. 1995. *Olódùmarè: God in Yoruba Belief*. Plainview, NY: Original Publications.

Karenga, Maulana. 1999. *Odù Ifá: The Ethical Teachings*. Los Angeles: University of Sankore Press.

Lijadu, E. M. 2010. *Ifá (As Literature)*. Translated by Abosede Emanuel. Lagos: West African Book Publishers.

Lucas, J. Olumide. 1948. *The Religion of the Yorùbás*. Lagos: C. M. S. Bookshop.

Makinde, Moses. 1988. *African Philosophy, Culture, and Traditional Medicine*. Athens, OH: Ohio University Center for International Studies.

Olatunji, Olatunde. 1984. *Features of Yorùbá Oral Poetry*. Ibadan: Oxford University Press.

———. 1973. "Ìyẹ̀rẹ̀ Ifá: Yorùbá Oracle Chant." *African Notes* 7, no. 2: 69–86.

Uyanne, Frank. 1994. "Truth, Ethics and Divination in Igbo and Yoruba Traditions: (A Reply to Emmanuel Eze)," *Quest: Philosophical Discussions* 8, no. 1(1994): 91–96.

8 Diviner as Explorer

The Afuwape Paradigm

Rowland O. Abiodun

THE ACCOUNT OF Afuwape in the Ifá literary corpus, which we will call the Afuwape paradigm, seems like an appropriate place to start the discussion about Journeys and Lots. This paradigm helps to situate my discourse within the Ifá intellectual traditions, where—hopefully—most practitioners called babalawo, scholars of the Yorùbá Ifá divination system, and indeed anyone interested in enlarging their understanding of the Yorùbá concept of destiny (ori) can engage in a debate that promises to throw more light on the still relatively unacknowledged up-to-date nature of the Ifá divination system and practice. To proceed, Claude Levi-Strauss's observation is instructive. He writes, "As theories go, the Yoruba seem to have been able to throw more light than ethnologists on the spirits of institutions and rules which in their society, as in many others, are of intellectual and deliberate character" (Levi-Strauss 1966, 133).

To date, many writings on Ifá divination and practice have unwittingly given the impression that the system is so archaic it is no longer relevant to contemporary life, reality, and society—that is, Ifá is enshrined in the past and is therefore doomed to extinction with time. However, a close examination and diligent study of the Ifá divination system and practice will lead us to the opposite conclusion. We have good evidence to support the fact that Ifá babalawo are not only constantly searching for new materials, but also incorporating them into the Ifá literary corpus and charting new intellectual paths.

Afuwape, the son of Orunmila (the patron deity of the Ifá divination system), exemplifies this quality best. As narrated in the Ifá literary corpus, which Professor Wándé Abímbólá published in his influential book *Sixteen Great Poems of Ifá*, Afuwape and his two friends—Oriseeku, the son of Ogun, and Orileemere, the son of Ija—set out on an important journey to the house of Ajala, Alamo-tii-mori (Ajala is the molder of *ori*, the inner spiritual heads, that is to say the prenatal lots rather than the so-called destinies) to select their *ori* before leaving *orun* (the other world) for *aye* (this world) (Abímbọ́lá 1975, 178–207).[1] In Yoruba belief this *ori* or *ori-inu* is graphically symbolized by a conical form, *Kotopo-kelebe* (the nickname for the primordial Ori, Ori-Isese or Ori-Akoko in the otherworld). Also, many a babalawo often referred to it as *Akata-gbiri-gbiri-gbiri* (literally, "the umbrellalike form-that-rolls-from-side- to side") (Abiodun 1987, 263).

For this singularly important journey, we assume that the three friends consulted Ifá among their many preparations to ensure the allotment of a successful or good *ori*. We learn from the Ifá literary corpus that the three friends were warned in the strictest terms not to stop or break their journey to Ajala's house. This meant that they could not under any circumstance stop at a relative's or friend's house. Afuwape's two friends obeyed the injunction given them and headed straight to Ajala's house. Afuwape stopped at Orunmila's (his father's) house, where he got an update on their Ifá divination prediction from his father's Ifá priests, who prescribed certain crucial sacrifices—namely salt and cowries, both of which would prove indispensable to Afuwape's ability to receive a good *ori* and lead to a successful life in *aye* (this world).

On his journey to Ajala's house, Afuwape met an old woman who needed salt badly to flavor the stew she was preparing, but did not have any because salt was extremely scarce and prohibitively expensive. Afuwape gave her salt, and in return the old woman apprised Afuwape of the most important information that he needed to secure a good *ori*. Ajala, who alone could tell a bad *ori* from a good one, was a chronic debtor, always hiding from his creditors and those who came to choose their *ori* at his house. In short, Ajala was almost never present to help anyone who came to choose their *ori*. The only way to get Ajala to come down from the rafter, his hiding place, was to assure him that someone would pay off his debt. That was exactly what Afuwape did, because he was already loaded with a large amount of cowries, which were local currency. Thus, Afuwape, with the help of Ajala, was able to choose a good *ori* while both Oriseeku and Orilemere, who had followed the instructions given them at the outset of their journey, ended up with ill-formed *ori*—that is, *ori* that brought them nothing but failure and misery in *aye* (this world).

This story leads one to ask questions such as: Why were Orilemere and Oriseeku so unfairly rewarded with bad *ori* for fully obeying the instructions given them, whereas Afuwape, who knowingly disobeyed, was blessed with a well-formed and accomplished *ori*? Where is justice? These are questions that have fascinated scholars and Ifá priests alike. The story has even prompted a Yorùbá refrain; on one side there was supposedly an exchange between Orileemere and Oriseeku, who failed to choose a good *ori*, and on the other side there was Afuwape, whose *ori* turned out to be very good. Thus, Orileemere and Oriseeku sought an answer to their predicament:

Awa o mo'bi olori gbe yan'ri o
A ba lo yan tawa
Awa o mo'bi Afuwape gbe yan'ri o
A ba lo yan tawa.

If only we knew where people chose their good *ori*,
We would have gone there to pick ours.
If only we knew where Afuwape got his good *ori*,
We would have gone there to choose ours too.[2]

And Afuwape responded:

Eyin o mo'bi olori gbe yan ori o
E ba lo yan te'yin
Ibikan naa la gbe yan'ri o
Ayanmo o paapo ni

You do not know where one with a good *ori* got theirs
You would have gone there to choose yours.
We all got our *ori* from the same location
But they were all different
(Gbadegesin 1997)[3]

While scholars have offered many compelling explanations for this seemingly unfair deal, they have yet to take full advantage of the rich materials in the Ifá literary corpus and its potential for a satisfactory answer.[4] First and foremost, the Afuwape paradigm takes us to the fundamentally dynamic nature of the Ifá divination system—a fact with which Afuwape, the son of Orunmila—and indeed most babalawo—are abundantly familiar, unlike Orilemere and Oriseeku. Like meteorologists, whose predictions change on the basis of new developments even though they are based on hard scientific facts, babalawo revise their divination predictions quite frequently and update them for accuracy. This is the reasoning behind the following saying:

Bi oni tiri
Ola le ma ribee
Ni i mu ki Babalawo
O da'Fa oroorun

Today's divination
May not be valid tomorrow [that is, in the future]
This is the reason Babalawo
Must divine repeatedly every five days[5]

Thus, it is clear that Ifá rewards the systematic quest for knowledge and empha-sizes the dynamism of its own predictions. A perusal of Orunmila's *oriki* shows how perfectly true and natural these qualities are to the character of Ifá. Orunmi-la is praised as *Obiritii, A-p'ijo-iku-da,* "Nullifier-in-chief, who-alone-is-capable-of-changing-the-date-of-a-persons's-death," *Odudu ti i du ori emere; o tun ori ti ko suan se,* "Great-rescuer who alone is capable of saving the lives of born-to-die children and who reverses the *ori* of the less fortunate," and *Ogege a-gb'aiyegun,* "Primeval-order, Regulator-of-the universe." Ifá implicitly acknowledges the chaos and imbalance in life, but has a mission to correct them, especially for those who actively seek the counsel of Ifá priests.

The Ifá divination system also takes unforeseen and unpredictable develop-ments into account; these make Ifá divination predictions heuristic and therefore always subject to revision. Unlike the Holy Bible and the Qur'an, whose books or chapters are held to be immutable, the *odu* of the Ifá literary corpus are not closed: they continue to grow and incorporate new developments and events into the Yoruba world, such as the arrival of foreign faiths like Islam and Christianity, as well as new transportation systems like the Victorian rickshaw, the motorcar, and the railway. Ifá's tradition of orality is no doubt a most important factor in facilitating the expansion of the Ifá literary corpus. Thus, neither the Ifá divina-tion system nor the predictions of its priests are ever static or frozen in time.

To remain the guardians and curators of the Ifá divination system, a veri-table intellectual powerhouse of Yoruba thought and culture, Ifá diviners travel frequently and extensively outside their home territories to meet with other Ifá priests, sharing and learning new passages, updating and enriching one another's repertoire of Ifá knowledge. In the Ifá literary corpus, we learn that Orunmila, the patron deity and the preeminent priest of the Ifá divination system, man-dated three of his foremost disciples—*opon* (divination tray), *agere* (divination bowl), and *ibo* (divination instrument cast for binary choice)—to explore foreign lands before they could qualify as learned priests of Ifá divination. The following relevant passage is cited by Olabiyi Yai:

> *A difa fun Orunmila*
> *Ifá o te omo awo re nifa*
> *Ifá lo topon nifa*
> *Opon sawo lo siko Awusi*
> *Oba lo je nibe*
> *Ifá lo te Ajere (Agere) nifa*
> *Ajere sawo lo s'Odoromu Awuse*
> *Oba lo je nibe*
> *Ifá lo tebo nifa*
> *Ibo sawo lo s'Iworan ibi Ojumoore e tii mo*
> *Nibe ni o gbe di oba*

Ifá divination was performed for Orunmila
Who initiated his three disciples.
He initiated Opon
Opon traveled to Iko Awusi [the Americas] to seek knowledge
He became a king there
He initiated Ajere
Ajere traveled to Idoromu Iwase [Africa]
There he became a king
Ifá initiated Ibo
Ibo traveled to Iwonran in the Orient [Australasia] to seek knowledge
There he became a king.
(Yai 1994,110)

This citation metaphorically confirms Orunmila's implementation of an outward looking, progressive agenda that recognizes the relevance of acquiring knowledge in and beyond Yorùbáland. Olabiyi Yai, a prominent scholar of the Yorùbá language and philosophy, also remarks that polyglotism was a common feature among Yorùbá intellectuals. Ifá priests, who are indisputably among those at the top of this category, are therefore actively encouraged to be proficient not only in Yorùbá dialects but also in other non-Yorùbá languages, which explains why Orunmila himself is often greeted as *Afedefeyo*, one who communicates in all languages.

So important is the concept of making journeys, long or short, in search of knowledge, and of choosing one's prenatal destiny, *ori*, in the otherworld—as Afuwape and his two friends had to do—that the limbs and especially legs (the primordial means of locomotion) have acquired the status of orisa in Yorùbá religious thought. We notice that in Yorùbá visual arts, limbs are often singled out for considerable artistic and aesthetic attention, while the following Ifá passage underscores their indispensability to the pursuit and achievement of any goal on earth, and most importantly the liberation of self and mind:

Opebe awo Ese
Lo dia fun fese
Nijo ti n ti kole orun bo waye
Gbogbo awon orisa sa ara won jo
Won o pe ese si i.
Esu ni: E o pe ese si i.
Bi o ti se gun na nu un
Ija ni won fi tuka nibe
Ni won to wa ranse si Ese
Nigba na ni imoran ti won ngba to wa a gun
Won ni be gege
Ni awon awo won wi

Opebe, awo Ese
Lo dia f'Ese
Nijo ti won tikole orun bo waye
Opebe ma ma de o
Awo Ese
Enikan ki i gbimoran
Ko yo t'Ese e le
Opebe ma ma de o
Awo ese

Opebe, the priest of the Feet
Performed Ifá divination for the Feet
On the day he was coming from the otherworld to earth
All the orisa convened to deliberate over an important matter
But they did not invite the Feet
Esu remarked: You have left out the Feet
How do you expect to implement your decisions?
Their meeting ended in a discord
They then sent for the Feet
Whose participation enabled them to deliberate productively and accomplish their mission.
They said that was exactly what their Ifá priests had predicted
Opebe has surely come
Ifá priest of Feet
No one deliberates without reckoning with Feet
Opebe has surely come,
Ifá priest of the Feet.
(Abímbọ́lá 1976, 148–149)

When clients of Ifá are confronted with life-threatening situations, it is not un-usual to hear friends or neighbors utter supporting statements such as, "For the eyes not to behold evil, the feet are the antidote," and idiomatically, "in order to be wholesome, one needs to have the capacity for motion."

Not all images related to journey, exploration, and discovery give promi-nence to legs in Yorùbá art. Allusions to journey may be implied and not explic-itly stated, and therefore known only to initiates. For example, symbolic journeys between this world and the other world, transformations of states of conscious-ness, or initiations into the different stages of Ifá priesthood may be alluded to by means of dress and color-coded bead adornments worn on one's person. In such cases, recognition, significance, and understanding have to be deliberately learned.

The theme of intellectual exploration by Ifá diviners seems to be the inspi-ration for *agere-Ifá*, especially those with the horse-and-rider motif in the Ifá sculptural repertoire. The *agere-Ifá* is a container or bowl normally used to store or hold *ikin*, the sixteen sacred palm nuts used by Ifá diviners in the process of divination. However, the significance of the *agere-Ifá* is dramatically heightened when we recognize that it is what "houses" the *ikin*—the symbol of Orunmila's presence at all divination sessions. *Agere-Ifá*, rightly regarded as the "temple" of Ifá on earth, deserves the richness of design and the high quality of workmanship and artistic creativity lavished on it—justifying the high price of 3,200 cowries paid for an *agere-Ifá* in the age of cowrie currency (Abímbọlá 1968, 26). For these reasons and more, the *agere-Ifá* would and should be regarded as a visual *oriki* to Ifá. And like its verbal counterpart that empowers, affirms, and energizes its subject through citation, song, and recitation, *agere-Ifá*—as visual *oriki*—achieves similar results through sculptural form, design, color, and iconography.

Caryatid in structure, most *agere* (a short form of *agere-Ifá*), consist of a bowl and a pedestal that usually represents humans in jubilation and animals. They are carved from a single piece of ivory, wood, or metal and vary in size and design; on average, they measure between four and fourteen inches (ten to thirty-five centimeters) in height. Ifá priests and their clients contribute to the iconographic and aesthetic content of *agere* sculpture—a fact that often leads to a wide range of personalized motifs or icons that carry deeper meanings for the client and priests who commission them. However, of special interest to us is the horse-rider motif, because it is specifically referenced in *Ijinle Ohun Ifá, Apa Kiini*, which reads:

> *Mo ni esin la o ma a gun sawo*
> *Esin la o ma a gun sawo o*
> *Esin la o ma a gun sawo*

> I (Orunmila) hereby declare that henceforth Ifá priests will ride on horseback to perform divination
> We will ride on horseback as diviners
> We will ride on horseback to perform divination.
> (Abímbọlá 1968, 22)

Even though we cannot be certain of the exact time that the horse-rider motif first appeared in Ifá divination sculpture, a reasonable assumption would be that it coincided with the introduction of the horse into Yorùbáland. The horse's dramatic impact on the military prowess that established the Yorùbá imperial adventure and carried it as far west as Togo must undergird its use as a figure of speech for elevation and empowerment and its equivalent representation in Yorùbá sculpture. It is equally instructive to view Yorùbá equine history in the broader context of the African continent. For example, we know that from about the eleventh century CE horses were already in use in western Sudan. They also featured prominently in the military campaigns of the Ghana, Mali, and Songhai empires.

Herbert Cole rightly notes that "it was the horse, not the camel that opened trans-Saharan trade/travel . . . horses were for several centuries carriers of foreign products and thus important agents of change" (1989, 119). The situation was different, however, on the Guinea coast, where the excessive humidity of the tropical rainforests combined with the menace of the tsetse fly (the horse's deadliest enemy) discouraged the early adoption and use of the horse. Thus, it was probably not until about the seventeenth century that in the Yorùbá kingdom of Oyo, located in the more hospitable savannah, horses could be kept and used in wars to expand and consolidate the empire.

Yorùbá artists could also have used the horse motif in their sculpture prior to the horse's introduction, given the fact that there was an equestrian figure on a bronze fly whisk handle, dated to the ninth or tenth century CE and from Igbo-Ukwu, a location that although not Yorùbá is still within the southern Nigerian rainforest (Eyo and Willett 1980, plate 36). The mounted warrior and certainly the invading cavalry from the north were long preceded in Yorùbáland by graphically told stories of their impressive performance. In other words, both real and imagined images of horses left indelible impressions on the minds of Yorùbá rulers, warriors, and Ifá priests—all of whose influences have been unmistakable in the iconography of the horse-rider motif and especially its frequent appearance in Yorùbá sculpture.

There are interesting parallels and differences in the meaning of equestrian images: for example, between *Epa* masks and *agere-Ifá*. Although both appear to be similar because they portray horsemen in traditional military uniforms brandishing weapons of war and ready for battle, the *Epa* mounted warrior is often a simple, easy-to-read visual metaphor (J. R. O. Ojo 1981). While the horse rider in *agere-Ifá* is a more complex metaphor, the mounted warrior on the *Epa* mask is always a direct reference to one who engages in a real war on the battlefield, captures slaves, brings home plunder, and is honored as a result. The horse rider in *agere-Ifá*, on the other hand, represents the Ifá priest, who is not literally a warrior because he does not go to the battlefield. Ifá priests' "battles" are not enacted in physical locations, but occur intellectually in people's thoughts and in Yorùbá philosophical traditions. The Yorùbá intellectual who goes in search of knowledge is a diviner and custodian of mysteries, wisdom, and understanding; this is the reason he is respected and honored by his clients and the community at large.

The priests of Ifá have a demonstrably insatiable appetite for knowledge and have always searched for it wherever it could be found. The German scholar Leo Frobenius confirms this observation in his book *Voice of Africa*, where he writes that "Ifá is nothing but the expression of the need of searching for a final cause, of the endeavor to find a concrete idea of a universe which transcends native intellectual capacity. And this world of thought is incredibly full of wonders" (Frobenius 1968, 229). There is no reason to believe that the search for and the identification of an appropriate artistic motif to represent Ifá and his priest would have been different. Ifá priests and artists utilized their characteristic intellectual insight to adopt and keep the horse-rider motif on the *agere-Ifá*.

Olabiyi Yai's observation on Yorùbá art hints at some useful aesthetic considerations that can help us understand the choice of an artistic motif, such as the horse rider for *agere-Ifá* as a visual *oriki* to Ifá. He writes: "The Yoruba mode of artistically engaging reality and their way of relating to one another, to the *orisa*, and other cultures is more metonymic than metaphoric. To *ki* (that is, to perform *oriki* verbally) and *gbe*, or *ya*, (carve) is to provoke and be provoked. Art is an invitation to infinite metonymic difference and departure, and not a summation for sameness and imitation." Here Yai points to the "Yoruba mode of artistically engaging reality and their way of relating to one another, to the *orisa*," which might have been an important factor in the Ifá priests' inclusion and subsequent adoption of the horse-rider as one of their favored artistic motifs in *agere-Ifá* (Yai 1994, 113).

While the depiction of an Ifá priest seated on a mat performing divination for his client might be easily recognized as such, it does not go further than the stage of associative reaction. The horse-rider motif on the *agere* is undoubtedly more provocative and departs from the "imitation" and "sameness" syndrome. As already noted, the priest does not go to war and never engages in physical combat. He does not have a political constituency, strictly speaking, even though he enjoys most of the rights and privileges associated with the highest political office of the *oba* (Yorùbá rulers). Clearly, the Ifá priest's importance is in the sphere of Yorùbá intellectual/philosophical discourse, where the horse becomes a powerful metaphor to capture and convey his role as the communicator and elucidator of Yorùbá wisdom and knowledge. The following saying throws more light on this suggestion:

Owe l'esin oro
Bi oro ba sonu
Owe la a fi i wa a

Owe is the horse of discourse
When the explanatory account is elusive
Owe is the one we employ to find it.

The search for the connections between *owe* (figures of speech) and Ifá is even more intriguing when we consider another Yorùbá saying, which characterizes Ifá's utterances: "*Bi owe, bi owe ni'Fa nsoro*" ("Like *owe* are the pronouncements of Ifá") (Owomoyela 2005, 112). As if to prevent a reckless and inappropriate use of *owe*, Yoruba then adds the axiom, "*Bi owe ko ba jo owe, a kii paa*" ("If *owe* does not apply to a situation, we do not use it") (159).

As we acknowledge sculptures like those on *agere-Ifá* as "visual" salutes—or *oriki* "made visible," to borrow Sarah Brett-Smith's (1984) phrase—we will come to appreciate more fully the essential identity, character, and role of the Ifá priest in Yorùbá society. We also need to embrace *oju-inu*, a special kind of creative and imaginative endowment that Yorùbá artists must possess in order to express these qualities in their work. *Oju-Inu* (literally, "inner eye") refers to insight, an aesthetic sensibility, and a special kind of understanding that is not usually derived from an obvious source such as direct or preliminary studies of nature or life models. Perception is learned and developed through traditionally approved sources such as chants, songs, references to Ifá divination poetry, and extant examples of works of art on the chosen subject. It is through this intellectual gift of *oju-inu* that artists may discern the appropriate artistic vehicle, individualized forms, colors, outline, rhythm, and harmony applicable to their subject.

The carver of the Zollman example of *agere-Ifá* has chosen to use ivory as his medium, even though most *agere* are carved from wood. Since elephant ivory is not only costly but a highly valued artistic medium whose use is reserved for the *oba*, traditional Yorùbá rulers and high-ranking chiefs, we must assume that this *agere* was commissioned by someone who was highly placed and possessed the financial resources to order the material and act as the carver's patron.

The Zollman *agere-Ifá* was probably carved in Owo, which was hospitable to the development of the finest skills in traditional carving in ivory. Affluent clients from Oyo competed with the more usual Benin patrons for the services of Owo artists. Moreover, given the unusually large size of the tusk from which the Zollman piece was carved, it must have been taken from a very large elephant. Such an elephant was most likely to have been found in the Owo area of Yorùbáland, which according to G. J. A. Ojo had a "dense distribution of elephants" (G. Ojo 1971, 247–249).

Measuring about eight and a half inches in height, the Zollman *agere* shows the horse rider carrying a divination bowl, used in storing the sacred *ikin*, on his head. The rider's feet rest partially in the stirrups, suspended from what appears to be an interlocking chain fashioned from metal instead of leather. In the right hand the rider holds a horsetail fly whisk, which hangs over his right shoulder and falls diagonally across his back: it is just long enough for its tip to rest on the back of the saddle. The left hand rests lightly on the reins. He wears an *abe-tiaja* cap made of finely woven textured material, a string of tubular neck beads (probably coral), ivory wristlets, and a pair of traditional, loose, patterned pants. On his right hip he wears a wide war blade tucked in an elaborately designed sheath, and on his left a long sword also concealed in a simpler but still impressive sheath. The horse, though rendered smaller than life size, appears strong and stands firmly on its four feet. It is fitted with a complete headstall—an attractively designed crown piece, browband, noseband and throat latch. A saddle blanket with a zigzag border design covers the back and rump of the horse, and extends beyond the saddle on which the rider sits.

Viewed from the back, the Zollman *agere* appears to be composed along a vertical axis that runs from the inverted V shape of the rider's *abetiaja* cap into the tail of the horse. It seems that the carver has built his design on the basic vertical thrust of a large elephant tusk, the bottom part of which now forms the base of this sculpture. Thus, when viewed in the round, the *agere* starts with a circular base on which the horse stands and ends at the top with a slightly smaller circular bowl that tilts a bit backward from the sides. Though geometrically structured to achieve a sense of balance in its overall design, the human and animal forms in the carving have been softened to give them life and warmth and to create tactile interest. For example, when viewed from the rider's right, the horsetail fly whisk forms a soft-angled triangle in which the arm bends at just less than ninety degrees. And from the back the same horsetail fly whisk falls very softly, following the contour of the rider's back to create diagonal movement that provides relief from the dominant vertical thrust of the inverted V of the *abetiaja* cap. This diagonal movement is carried through the tail of the horse.

Similarly, decorative devices and surface patterning have been generously used to create areas of interesting visual activity. In fact, so successful is this artistic device that one may sometimes forget that the horse is perfectly still, with no suggestion of motion, and that the rider is calmer than a person standing on his feet would be. Particularly from the sides, the artist has exploited the decorative potential of the *abetiaja* cap, the handle of the horsetail fly whisk, the ivory wristlets, the neck beads, the sword and blade sheaths, the rider's pants, the stirrups and connecting chain, the reins, the bridle parts, and the saddle blanket to the fullest compositional advantage. All of these design components are used strategically in different parts of the sculpture to create horizontals, verticals, diagonals, and circles, which enliven and counteract any sense of boredom that may arise from the absence of explicitly suggested motion.

At the center of all this is the celebrant, the horse rider. His head is balanced on the neck at approximately a forty-five-degree angle, and has an arresting frontal presence and a composure that seems to underscore the importance of *Ifarabale*—which means "calming or controlling the body," "letting reason, not emotion control man," and "not losing one's composure" (Abiodun 1990, 77–78). The representation of the rider's look is youthful but not immature. His eyes are wide open, looking ahead but apparently undisturbed and undistracted by persons, events, or surroundings. For it is unbecoming of the Ifá priest to become or appear as excited as his client. These attributes imbue the rider with an aura of intellect, dignity, and reassurance—all of which the Yoruba greatly admire in their rulers, diviners, artists, and elders. With this kind of high regard, people in these categories become the focus of attention and deference in the community and are expected to behave in a manner befitting their status. Hence the Yoruba saying, "*Eni a n wo kii woran*" ("The person people have gathered to watch should not him- or herself be a spectator") (Owomoyela 2005, 116). In this case, the Ifá priest is clearly the "one we have gathered to watch" and should not behave like his client, "the spectator."

Although the horse-rider in the Zollman *agere* is dressed as a warrior, he also carries a horsetail fly whisk in his right hand. Other than the Yoruba traditional rulers, only Ifá priests ceremonially use the horsetail fly whisk as a symbol of their status. A verse from an Ayajo incantation confirms this:

> *Bi babalawo meji ba pade*
> *Won a se irukere won yeturu yeturu*

> Whenever two Ifá priests meet
> They wave their horsetail fly whisk in salutation
> (Fabunmi 1972, 67)

The exceptionally long horsetail fly whisk in this *agere-Ifá* makes a strong visual statement and compels us to recite its verbal corollary from another Yoruba *ofo* (incantation):

> *O da ko kukunduku tii soloja isu*
> *Oun irukere tii somo Olokun Seniade*
> *Won ni bo ba ye'rukere tan, to de'rukere lorun*
> *O deni a-gbe-ye-jo, o deni a-gbe-ye-wo*
> *A-gbe-jo laa gbe'ru esin*
> *A-gba-ye-wo ni ti'rukere*

> It was divined for Kukunduku (Sweet Potato) who is the king of yams
> And the Horsetail who was the child of Olokun Seniade
>   (The Custodian/Dispenser of prosperity and opulence)
> It was predicted that by the time the Horsetail had become famous and
>   prosperous
> He would become the focus of attention
> We dance carrying the Horsetail
> We carry the Horsetail in admiration
> (Ibid., 7)

Besides the use of the horsetail fly whisk to identify the professional class of Ifá priests, there is a subtle and indirect reference to a celebration of the elevation in status of the Ifá priesthood in Yorùbá society. This assumption is especially reasonable in light of Orunmila's declaration that "henceforth, Ifá diviners would ride on horseback to perform divination." This scenario is not difficult to imagine, given the indispensability of Ifá priests' services to society and the social, economic, and political gains accruing from them. The dress of the horse rider is further confirmation of this successful class of Ifá priests.

Apart from the *abetiaja* cap and a string of highly valued tubular neck beads, the horse rider wears nothing on his upper body. He is bare-chested, but considered well dressed in Yorùbá culture where the wearing of chiefly beads surpasses any garment in importance and more than compensates for the absence of any conventional fabric. A Yorùbá proverb says, *"Eniti o so ileke pari aso"* ("The person who adorns himself with beads has done the ultimate in self-beautifying [that is, dressing]") (Owomoyela 2005, 258).

Ifá indeed holds the chiefly title *ajiki* (he who must be greeted and acknowledged by the break of day) (Lijadu 1972, 71). Perhaps the greatest aesthetic appeal that the Yorùbá derive from these powerful verbal and visual *oriki* for the Ifá priest is that they are endless (*akiikitan*) (Yai 1994, 107). Ifá's *oriki* continue to challenge Yorùbá scholars in religion, art, literature, and philosophy; they do this even as the scholars seek to decode the horse rider motif in the *agere-Ifá* sculpture—a deliberate and indispensable metaphor in the Yorùbá concept of journey (Barber 1994). It is also now clearly evident that the *agere-Ifá* sculpture is not only an *oriki* made visible, but also a "horse of communication," which is mutually beneficial to both Orunmila/Ifá on the spiritual plane of existence and to his priests, clients, and admirers who are here on the material plane. The metaphorical horse provides valuable insights into the Yorùbá metaphysical systems, myths, and lore as well as how all of these affect and relate to the physical realm.

Like Afuwape, every being must select an *ori*, the prenatal lot assigner and the ultimate determinant of a person's social, economic, and physical well-being on earth. The visual symbol of the most successful *ori* in the human realm is the *ade* or *are* (in Ile-Ife); they, like *ori* itself, are also imbued with spiritual *ase*, authority, and life force that are transferred to the wearer, which would include Yorùbá divine rulers. This is the reason that Yorùbá rulers are greeted:

Kabiyesi
Oba alase
Ekeji Orisa
Iku
Baba-Yeye

One whose authority we dare not challenge
The custodian of *ase*
Who is a peer only to the Orisa
Personification of Death itself
Ultimate Father-Mother

However, no individual can know the content of his or her prenatal *ori* until he or she consults an Ifá divination priest after his or her arrival in this world.

Thus the long and complex spiritual exploration, which began before birth in the otherworld, continues here on earth. Ifá's clientele cuts across gender, social, and economic classes. It includes paramount rulers, artists, warriors, farmers, traders, and so on; all consult the Ifá priest to know the content of their *ori*. The indispensability of Ifá priests in the world is reflected in the following:

> *Ogboju o tera re ni'Fa*
> *Omoran o fara re joye*
> *Obe to mu o gbe eku ara re*

> The intrepid does not consult Ifá on his own behalf:
> The sagacious person does not enthrone himself
> The sharpest knife does not carve its hilt
> (Owomoyela 2005, 378)

Put simply, no person, *orisa*, or anything in existence can ignore the role of Ifá priests as he or she embarks on the complex intellectual journey to know the contents of their *ori*—their prenatal allotments.

In the end, it does seem that the diviner's search and the artist's search share a powerful commonality of purpose in the way they explore and discover the world. Wọlé Ṣóyinká sums up the artist's journey of self-discovery thus:

> The artist discovers a proto world in gestation; it's almost like discovering another world in the galaxy. The artist's view of reality creates an entirely new world. Into that world, he leads a raid; he rifles its resources and returns to normal existence . . . and when he returns from that experience he is imbued with new wisdoms, new perspectives, a new way of looking at phenomena. (1992, 17)

The aesthetic choices and visions of famous Yorùbá artists like Lagbayi, native of Ojowon, Olowe of Ise, and Lamidi Olonade Fakeye shaped the artistic traditions of Yorùbá society. These artists were sensitive to the needs of the society and changed it without being told to do so. By the same token, the Ifá system is most supportive of the Ifá priest's search for something new, an intellectual transformation of the priest and his role as an agent of continuity and change in the society. In Yorùbá art, this spiritually dynamic impulse is called *imoju-imora*, "sensitivity to the need of the moment," "ability to change without being formally told to do so" (Abiodun 1990, 80–81). Besides being an important factor in the adoption of new styles, techniques, and materials, *imoju-imora* is the quality that has enabled Yorùbá descendants in the diaspora, especially Ifá diviners and artists, to survive one of the most arduous and devastating journeys in human history—that of the transatlantic slave trade.

Notes

From an early age, I witnessed many private and public ritual practices led by priests and priestesses of Ifá, Erindinlogun (sixteen-cowrie) divination, Ogun, Orisa-Nla, Esu, and Oro among others. In addition to helping to avert sickness, epidemics, and natural disasters, healing physical problems and difficult personal, social, and political relationships, and offering a glimpse of the history and future of the community, these rituals were also occasions to learn about Yorùbá culture. My paternal grandaunt, Yeye Deke, was an Erindinlogun practitioner. My paternal grandmother, Olakoli, was a traditional midwife and derived her extensive knowledge and use of medicinal herbs from a combination of the divination systems mentioned above. A hunter, farmer, and devotee of Ogun, my grandfather knew much about the fauna and flora in and around the ancient Yoruba city of Owo. Occasionally, he cast the four-lobed kola-nut—a simple form of divination—to get answers to difficult and urgent questions. In this essay, however, my focus is Ifá, one of the most enduring intellectual powerhouses of Yoruba thought and culture.

At the University of Ife, I was fortunate to meet and interact with eminent scholars of Yoruba religion, literature, language, linguistics, history and philosophy. Among them were Professors Wándé Abímbọ́lá, Isaac Delano, Afolabi Ojo, Fatunmbi Verger, Adeagbo Akinjogbin, Sope Oyelaran, Akin Isola, Olabiyi Yai, Bade Ajuwon, Akinsola Akiwowo, Moses Makinde, and Barry Hallen—all of whom have contributed in various ways to my interest in and pursuit of Ifá studies. I am also indebted to the scores of babalawo in Owo, Ile-Ife, Ondo, Okitipupa, Ede, Oshogbo, Oyo, Abeokuta, Ijebu, and Opin-Ekiti for welcoming me into their homes and deepening my knowledge and appreciation of the Ifá divination system.

1. Advisedly, I have translated *ori* here as one's lot instead of "destiny" because "destiny" is in principle immutable, whereas in Yoruba tradition one may ameliorate one's lot through industry and sacrifice.

2. All translations are mine unless otherwise noted.

3. For a slightly different wording but essentially the same meaning, see Gbadegesin (1997).

4. See, for example, Ali (1995); Gbadegesin (1984, 1991); Makinde (1985); Oduwole (1996); Oladipo (1992); and Balogun (2007).

5. Collected in Ile-Ife (1974).

References

Abímbọ́lá, Wándé. 1968. *Ijinle Ohun Enu Ifá, Apa Kiini*. Glasgow: Collins.

———. 1975. *Sixteen Great Poems of Ifá*. Paris: UNESCO.

———. 1976. *Ifá: An Exposition of the Ifá Literary Corpus*. Oxford: Oxford University Press.

Abiodun, Rowland. 1987. "Verbal and Visual Metaphors: Mythical Allusions in the Yoruba Ritualistic Art of *ori*." *Word and Image: A Journal of Verbal/Visual Enquiry* 3, no. 3: 252–270.

———. 1990. "The Future of African Art Studies: An African Perspective." In *African Art Studies: The State of the Discipline*, edited by Rowland Abiodun, 63–89. Washington, DC: National Museum of African Art.

Ali, Samuel A. 1995. "The Yoruba Conception of Destiny: A Critical Analysis." *Journal of Philosophy and Development* 1 & 2, no. 1: 100–106.

Balogun, Oladele Abiodun. 2007. "The Concepts of Ori and Human Destiny in Traditional Yoruba Thought: A Soft-Deterministic Interpretation." *Nordic Journal of African Studies* 16, no. 1: 116–130.

Barber, Karin. 1994. "Polyvocality and the Individual Talent: Three Women Oriki Singers in Okuku." In *The Yoruba Artist*, edited by Rowland Abiodun, Henry J. Drewal and John Pemberton III, 151–160. Washington, DC: Smithsonian Institution Press.

Brett-Smith, Sarah. 1984. "Speech Made Visible: The Irregular as a System of Meaning." *Empirical Study of the Arts* 2, no. 2: 127–147.

Cole, Herbert M. 1989. *Icons, Ideals and Power in the Art of Africa*. Washington, DC: Smithsonian Institution Press.

Eyo, Ekpo, and Frank Willett. 1980. *Treasures of Ancient Nigeria*. New York: Alfred A. Knopf.

Fabunmi, Michael Ajayi. 1972. Ayajo: Ijinle Ohun Ife. Ibadan: Onibon-Oje Press.

Frobenius, Leo. 1968. *Voice of Africa*. New York: Benjamin Bloom.

Gbadegesin, Olusegun. 1984. "Destiny, Personality and the Ultimate Reality of Human Existence." *Ultimate Reality and Meaning* 7, no. 3LC: 173–188.

———. 1991. *African Philosophy: Traditional Yoruba Philosophy and Contemporary African Realities*. New York: Lang.

———. 1997. "For Kudirat, an Assured Immortality." *Isokan Yoruba Magazine* 3, no. 2.

Levi-Strauss, Claude. 1966. *The Savage Mind*. Chicago: University of Chicago Press.

Lijadu, E. M. 1972. *Orunmila*. Ado-Ekiti, NG: Standard Press.

Makinde, Moses. 1985. "A Philosophical Analysis of the Yoruba Concept of 'Ori' and Human Destiny." *International Studies in Philosophy* 17, no. 1: 50–66.

Oduwole, E. O. 1996. "The Yoruba Concepts of 'Ori' and Human Destiny: A Fatalistic Interpretation." *Journal of Philosophy and Development* 2, no. 1&2: 40–52.

Ojo, G. J. Afolabi. 1971. *Yoruba Culture*. London: University of London Press.

Ojo, J. R. O. 1981. "Headdress: Warrior (Epa Ologun)." In *For Spirits and Kings, African Art from the Paul and Ruth Tisman Collection*, edited by Susan Vogel, 117–118. New York: Metropolitan Museum of Art.

Oladipo, Olusegun. 1992. "Predestination in Yoruba Thought: Philosopher's Interpretations." *Orita: Journal of Religion* 24, no. 1&2: 34–51.

Owomoyela, Oyekan. 2005. *Yoruba Proverbs*. Lincoln: University of Nebraska Press.

Ṣóyinká, Wọlé. 1992. *Orisha Liberates the Mind: Wole Soyinka in Conversation with Ulli Beier on Yoruba Religion*. Bayreuth, DE: Iwalewa Haus.

Yai, Olabiyi. 1994. "In Praise of Metonymy: The Concepts of 'Tradition and Creativity' in the Transmission of Yoruba Artistry over Time and Space." In *The Yoruba Artist*, edited by Rowland Abiodun, Henry J. Drewal, and John Pemberton III, 107–115. Washington, DC: Smithsonian Institution Press.

9 "The Hunter Thinks the Monkey Is Not Wise. The Monkey Is Wise, But Has Its Own Logic"

Multiple Divination Systems and Multiple Knowledge Systems in Yorùbá Religious Life

Mei-Mei Sanford

YORÙBÁ KNOWLEDGE IS profoundly multiple. In the Western philosopher Isaiah Berlin's comparison of the hedgehog who knows one big thing to the fox who knows many things, there is a multiplicity of knowers, but also a totalizing tendency: both work, but the hedgehog's knowledge is a "big" thing (Berlin 1957). The following Yorùbá proverb makes a different point: "The hunter thinks the monkey is not wise; the monkey is wise, but has its own logic."[1] Both have their own knowledge; neither the hunter nor the monkey is totality. Akinsola Akiwowo relayed to me another proverb related to this point: "*Omode gbon, agba gbon; ni a fi da otu Ife*" ("Children's wisdom and elders' wisdom are what we used to create Ile-Ife"). Multiple knowledges are necessary to create Yorùbá common life.

This decentering runs deep. The potency of each *ori* (human, spirit or animal destiny, or deep being) creates a landscape of various decentered authoritative powers. Orisa are many and so are their "roads" (communally experienced aspects); their number is not fixed. Other beings of *orun* (the other or "unseen" world)—such as ancestors and *emere* (otherworldly companions),[2]—also possess their own potencies and knowledge. In this world, associations, lineages, work groups, and worship groups each have their own character and knowledge.

Divinatory systems are a subset of a larger category of knowledge modes concerning this and the other world (*aye* and *orun*), which include trance, dreams, visitations, and the interpretation of significant events. Yorùbá divination systems include water scrying, *obi* (kola), *orogbo* (bitter kola), Ifá (divination with palm nuts or a chain called *opele*), and *owo merindinlogun* (sixteen cowries). A practitioner may employ several of these, but rarely all, and may or may not confirm and extend the knowledge gained with that of other practitioners. If we center our attention on the lived religion of individuals, what emerges is not a fixed hierarchy of efficacy and appeal, but as the proverbs suggest, what emerges is a constellation of distinct and sometimes overlapping sites of divinatory knowledge and effectiveness.

Modes of Knowledge

The following are some of the modes of knowledge of the other world used by *alase* (people of power) in Iragbiji town and in nearby towns in Osun state.[3] It is necessarily a partial list—that is, a small but significant sampling of Iragbiji *alase*. The *alase* are adept at both knowledge and its practice by the nature of their *ase* as the power and authority to make things happen. In introducing each *alase* I shall briefly describe and situate them in the area's spiritual economy.

Obi (kola nut)

The Iyalaase Osun is the most senior of Osun priestesses in Iragbiji and the most senior of all the priestesses at the city shrine. She was one of the circle of *olosun* (priestesses and priests of the deity Osun) who installed the Aragbiji (Iragbiji's *oba* or sovereign). As her title indicates, she prepares the first yam to be eaten at the Ori Oke new yam festival. She is also one of the two priestesses who paint the city shrine. Her lineage also has the orisa Esu and Soponna, and she took charge of the main Soponna shrine when the senior priestess died and the successor had not been found. The Iyalaase divines exclusively with *obi*.

The former Iya Osun of Osogbo, most senior titleholder of the Osun priesthood of Osogbo, and an Oloya (priestess of the orisa Oya), also routinely divined with *obi*. She sometimes referred people to the palace shrine Osun priest Owolabi for sixteen-cowrie divination, if they asked for such a reading.

Adeleke Sangoyoyin—a priest of the orisa Sango and Ogun, with orisa Oko and Osun in his lineages, a herbalist, hunter, and artist—began to teach me the daily practice of divining with *obi* before my initiation to Osun in 1992, and he continued this instruction for many years. Sango, as he is generally called, reads the *obi* not only as up/down, on top of each other or distinct, pointing to the shrine or the questioner, and tightly grouped or diffuse, but as a single unified message. I learned from him by making my own readings and listening to his, rarely by explicit analysis. When I asked him if he sees the message first rather than the parts, he said, "Exactly, and you too; it is only that you have been doing it daily for so many years that you can do it."

Owo Merindinlogun (Sixteen Cowries)

Sango divines with *owo merindinlogun*. He learned cowrie divination through multiple extended apprenticeships, some in distant towns. He divines, creates *oogun* (medicines or efficacious substances), and makes *ebo* (offerings to the orisa) for clients locally and in Germany and the United States. He taught me *owo merindinlogun* only after he had prepared me and himself with protective substances. Cowries are his divination method of choice. He sometimes has checked my divinations (kola or cowries) by casting the cowries, but I believe that this is because I am his student and because he prefers cowries for his own use, rather than from a belief that cowries supersede *obi*.

Other Iragbiji diviners of *owo merindinlogun* include the current Oloya, who is the principal Oya priestess, the Iyalode of Iragbiji, and the head of the town association of *onisegun* (herbalist healers), as well as the former Iya Sonponna of blessed memory, head of Sonponna's principal shrine.

Orogbo (Bitter Kola)

Sangoyoyin Ajani, father of Adeleke Sangoyoyin, was Olode (chief of the hunters' society), senior Ogun and Sango priest, advisor to the sovereign, and a herbalist. At well over one hundred, he was the one priest in the city who was able to make the required offering to Ogun by severing of the head of a dog or goat with a single stroke. He divined with *obi* for Ogun and Esu and *orogbo* for Sango.

Ifá

There was one and only one occasion when I knew the above Iragbiji *alase* to consult Ifá (other than Sango's use of it for clients described below). I, an adopted member of Sangoyoyin Ajani's family, was summoned to a divination concerning a legal matter by a babalawo in another family. Not liking the verdict, my family—principally Sangoyoyin Ajani, Sango, and I—responded by consulting a babalawo in our own compound. Outside Ifá was met with family Ifá. It is common and unremarkable for Yorùbá clients of divination to consult multiple successive diviners until they find a reading that is satisfying to them.

Dreams

Extradivinatory sources of knowledge often take everyday precedence over divination. When I asked Sango why he did not divine with *obi* every morning as he had taught me, he said, "What I need to know now comes to me in dreams." Dreams are often used as a diagnostic tool to see how an initiation or the absorption of an *oogun* has progressed. I have received crucial information in a dream about an imminent offering I was to make. I learned that the goat was female and pregnant, which no one had noticed; so I added her to the family herd and bought *ogufe* (a male goat) in her place.

Dreams often contain important messages for the dreamer or for other people. Oakland *olosun* Luisah Teish once said, "If you dream about me, tell me. After that, you can interpret it any way you like" (pers. comm.). Messages from the dead are one important kind of dream information. *Olorisa* (priestesses and priests of the orisa) teach their children through dreams, which are often the most efficient means over long distances. The Iragbiji Iyalaase Osun once sent me a message in a letter that said, "If you talk about your dreams too much, we won't send them anymore."

Visions

Visions are another means of receiving knowledge. One night, on his farm, in the round conical roofed farmhouse built on great granite outcroppings, Sango sat teaching me. At one point, he broke off saying: "This room is filled with beings; it's only that you can't see or hear them."

Qualities of Yorùbá Knowledge

Yorùbá knowledge is progressive rather than static. In 1992, I watched the Iyalaase and her *ekeji* (associate priestess) paint the front of the city shrine. It was a task they had previously done every year, but were finding physically more and more difficult. As I recorded the designs in my notebook of the standard Nigerian school children's type, I asked her if they changed the designs from year to year. She gave me that long, wondering look that ethnographers receive so often, and said, "We progress, just as you progress in your studies."

Several years ago, Sango apprenticed himself to a local babalawo and friend to learn Ifá. He did so, I think, to expand his own knowledge and in response to interest in Ifá by clients he encountered on his visits to the United States. He continues to use the other modes mentioned above.

Yorùbá knowledge is also partial, in part because it is progressive and therefore unending, and in part because knowledge is tied to one's particularity and one's ability to control *ase* (the authority and power to make things happen). I asked Sango once, "Does everything have *ase*?" He responded, "I don't know; only God knows. But I know some things that have *ase*" (Sanford 1997, 228). One acquires knowledge to use it; therefore knowledge, like the *ase* that it concerns, must be matched to our capacities to control it and use it responsibly. Sangoyoyin Ajani, Baba Sango, said, "There are 201 leaves [for Ogun] in the bush. We must not use all 201 leaves. If we use them all, [the shrine] will talk like a human being. So we use twenty-one out of the 201. If we can get 21, we will use 11. That is how we do it" (Sanford 1997, 163). The number 201 (like the number 401, often used to describe the orisa) is a number connoting profusion and multitude rather than a fixed or even a known set.

Finally, Yorùbá knowledge is personal, transmitted through lineages both biological and nonbiological. Once, in conversation Sango referred to an *oogun*, which he said "my father taught you." I corrected him, saying "No, you taught me." Sango said "My father taught me and I taught you. So my father taught you." Knowledge is not separate from the effectuating power transmitted with it by the teacher, nor from the constraints that bind student and teacher in a relationship. It is embedded in and affected by the interactions and relationships that people have with each other and the uses to which it is put.

My description of knowledge systems of Iragbiji *alase* is clearly and necessarily progressive, incomplete, and informed by my experience, relationships, and responsibilities. My perspective is that of an *"omo Iragbiji"* (a child or citizen of the town), the adopted daughter of two Iragbiji lineages—maternal and paternal, an *olosun* and the Iyalode Osun of Iragbiji (an Osun priestly title referring to the senior priestess in charge of external affairs). Knowledge systems are embedded in the particularity of the knowers, in the contexts in which they appear and in which they are learned and developed, and in the systems' relationships with each other.

Perceptions of the Place of Ifá

There have been two notable external factors that have contributed to representations of Ifá in isolation from its embedded context in the varied knowledge systems of Yorùbá communities: the early missionaries and the (initially British) academy. These factors were linked, because most early Yorùbá scholars were also clergy.

Missionaries, unlike the Yorùbá *alase* described above, were involved in a totalizing endeavor. They understood religious knowledge as unitary, complete, and undifferentiated, in the sense of separate spheres and centers of knowledge, by the individuality of the knowers. At the same time, the clergy was organized hierarchically and limited to men.

As Robert Baum (1990) reminds us, the missionaries had expectations of what religious authorities were like, and this filtered their perceptions of Yorùbá *alase*. One of the most important of these was gender. Another was class. Brian Pennington's study of missionaries in India, a contemporaneous British colony, tells us that anxieties about class in Britain also dominated British missionaries' perceptions of the colonized there, specifically the poor who conducted most of their lives, religion included, outside of the church and beyond the reach of the clergy (Pennington 2005).

In "The Pastor and the Babalawo" (1990), J. D. Y. Peel lays out ways in which David Hinderer, S. A. Crowther, James Johnson, and other missionaries, British and indigenous, may have found babalawo recognizable as religious authorities; these were qualities they did not perceive in other female or male *alase*. The missionaries perceived the babalawo as forming an exclusively male professional group, possessing large bodies of verbal knowledge, undergoing long and often multiple apprenticeships, often traveling to practice, and apparently distanced from the messy and quotidian aspects of Yorùbá religious life in which female and male *olorisa* and other devotees participated. For example, Peel quotes from S. A. Crowther's description of a young Idagbe priest "crawling" into a shrine and "mumbling some words and passing out consecrated kola and rum—but rarely do the priests emerge as known individuals (in the missionaries' accounts). How undignified it seemed, the people scrambling for the consecrated food, their levity as the priest spurts water in blessing!" (Peel 1990, 346). Of course, we hear Peel's distaste, and quite likely behind it that of the missionaries as well. And behind that, we find a scene of invocation and divination of another kind—that of *obi*, food consumed by people, orisa, blessing conferred with the gift of *omi orisa* (water containing the potency of the deities), joy, and celebration.

Some of the elements of this composite missionary picture of the babalawo are arguably false. We can expect that the babalawo of the time did present *ebo* (offering) to the orisa, since divination verses specify the offerings to be made; by present-day evidence, the diviner often makes the *ebo* on behalf of the client. Other elements are accurate, but constructed to suggest that non-babalawo did not do them; learning by long apprenticeships, and traveling to apprentice and divine for clients. We can reasonably argue from present-day evidence, such as that of Sango's apprenticeships, that nineteenth-century *eleerindinlogun* (cowrie diviners) traveled and undertook multiple and substantial apprenticeships. There is definitely a gender bias at work here in the lack of understanding that nineteenth-century Yorùbá women did travel in large economic and religious networks.

Similarly, we know that other *alase* in addition to babalawo today possess great stores of verbal knowledge: proverbs, stories, and histories, *oriki* (praise poetry), *oriki orile* (praise poetry of the lineage and its origin), songs, incantations, *odu eerindinlogun* (sixteen-cowrie divination verses)—which Professor Wándé Abímbọ́lá argues predates Ifá—recipes of herbs and other *oogun*, and many other forms and categories of knowledge. We can reasonably expect that their counterparts in the nineteenth century possessed them as well. Yet the early missionaries did not engage with and record the women *alase*—the priestesses of the orisa, the *onisegun* (herbalists), the singers of *oriki* and *Sango pipe* (the particular *oriki* chanted by devotees of the orisa Sango)—and their male counterparts, as they did the male Ifá priests. Rather, the missionaries assumed that there was a singular elite and located it in the babalawo.

The second influential external factor was the British and larger Western academy during the colonial period and early independence. In discussions of religion and society, the question of what constitutes "real religion" as well as notions of the advanced and the primitive were very much in evidence. In addition, many intra-Christian, intra-Anglican debates were engaged and argued by scholars through their interpretations of other societies. As Yorùbá scholars

J. Olumide Lucas, E. Bolaji Idowu, and others demanded entry into the academy, they were forced to speak within these discourses and to contend with these presuppositions. With the strongest strategies they knew, they defended Yorùbá religion as real, authentic, and advanced.

As Anglican clergy, Lucas and Idowu were also defending the orthodoxy of Yorùbá Christians and their rightful place in the church communion. Chinua Achebe writes tellingly of the longstanding unease of the British church regarding the authority of indigenous bishops (Achebe 2010). When the discovery of quinine as a medicine against malaria made it safer for British to live in the Nigerian colony, the British church ousted Anglican bishop Ajayi Crowther in favor of a white bishop (Chametzky 1989, 10).

Lucas (1948) argued against the presumption that the Yorùbá were a local, small scale, ahistorical people—that is, primitive. He contended in their defense that the Yorùbá were descended from ancient Egypt, a society that England admired politically and philosophically if not for its religion. Egypt's written language was the root of the Yorùbá language, Lucas wrote, and its religious ideas, including monotheism, preceded and informed Yorùbá religion. Idowu (1962) argued for the traditional centrality of a Yorùbá high god constructed as omniscient, omnipotent, and omnipresent. Okot P'bitek was living in another former British colony, Kenya, when his book *African Religions in Western Scholarship* (1971) was published. In this book, P'bitek deconstructs the monotheistic model of religion as Western and as not appropriate in describing African religious systems.

The preoccupations of the early British academy are with us today: for example, privileging a single elite and a totalized single body of knowledge; verbal over ritual knowledge; discrete, direct teaching over indirect, kinesthetic, and relational knowledge; men over women; and narrowly identified professionals over the continuum of lived religion. I suggest to you that these preoccupations warp and limit our understanding of Ifá and of the larger landscape of interacting Yorùbá *alase* and knowledge systems. As Ajapa (the tortoise hero of many Yorùbá tales) learned, wisdom cannot be contained in one bag. As scholars and students of Yorùbá tradition, we have many people from whom to learn, with their knowledges forming and building on each other. To paraphrase the Iyalaase Osun of Iragbiji, "May we progress in our studies!"

Notes

1. See Beier (2001).
2. *Emere* are companions from the other world who sometimes venture into this world as playmates, friends, or spouses. As a group, they may be referred to as one's *egbe* or association.

3. The information in this section is based on research I completed in Nigeria in 1989, 1991–1992, 1997, 1998, 2001, 2003, and 2006. It is also informed by my interviews with Yorùbá visitors and expatriates to the United States from 1989 to the present. Some of the information is taken from my unpublished dissertation (Sanford 1997).

References

Achebe, Chinua. 2010. *Arrow of God*. Mississauga, CA: Anchor Canada.

Baum, Robert. 1990. "Graven Images: Scholarly Representations of African Religions." *Religion* 20, no. 4: 355–360.

Beier, Ulli. 2001. *The Hunter Thinks the Monkey is Not Wise*. Bayreuth, DE: Bayreuth African Studies.

Berlin, Isaiah. 1957. *The Hedgehog and the Fox: An Essay on Tolstoy's View of History*. New York: New American Library.

Chametzky, Jules, ed. 1989. *A Tribute to James Baldwin: Black Writers Redefine the Struggle*. Amherst: Institute for Advanced Study in the Humanities / University of Massachusetts Press.

Idowu, E. Bolaji. 1962. *Olodumare: God in Yoruba Belief*. London: Longmans.

Lucas, J. Olumide. 1948. *The Religion of the Yoruba*. Lagos: C. M. S. Bookshop.

P'Bitek, Okot. 1971. *African Religions in Western Scholarship*. Kampala, Uganda: East African Literature Bureau.

Peel, J. D. Y. 1990. "The Pastor and the Babalawo: The Interaction of Religions in Nineteenth Century Yorubaland." *Africa* 60, no. 3: 338–369.

Pennington, Brian K. 2005. *Was Hinduism Invented? Britons, Indians and the Colonial Construction of Religion*. Oxford: Oxford University Press.

Sanford, Mei Mei. "Powerful Water, Living Wood: The Agency of Art and Nature in Yoruba Ritual." PhD diss., Drew University, 1997.

10 Dagbon, Oyo, Kongo

Critical and Comparative Reflections on Sacrifice

Wyatt MacGaffey

In 1975, I attended a conference in Jos. To make the most of my first and so far only visit to Nigeria, I spent an extra fortnight as a tourist visiting Kano, Zaria, Ibadan, Ife, and Onitsha. In Ile-Ife, I visited the Ore Grove and a building in the style of an East Anglican church that I was told was the temple of Ifá. At least one local mosque was built in the same style. I attended Friday prayers at the Grand Mosque of Ibadan and services in churches of the Cherubim and Seraphim, as well as others more obscure. That is the extent of my personal contact with Yorùbá religion. Although in northern Nigeria I felt myself a total stranger, in the south, particularly in Yorùbáland, I felt relatively at home.

Much later, moved perhaps by this intuition, I wrote a piece at the invitation of John Pemberton, in which I revived Melville Herskovits' idea that Central Africa and the forested regions of West Africa belonged together in a single cultural zone. But whereas Herskovits based this unity on an unconvincing trait list, including presence of wooden sculpture and absence of cattle, I demonstrated a common cosmology and a common ritual structure related to it (MacGaffey 2000a).

For the past ten years, I have been visiting the kingdom of Dagbon in northern Ghana, which at first was as strange to me as northern Nigeria. One of the features new to me was the prevalence of animal sacrifice, which is also basic to Yorùbá ritual; but it is at best marginal in Kongo and Central Africa, which is a difference I am still trying to understand. The cosmology and ritual structure found in Dagbon, and in northern Ghana generally, are entirely different from the others. This is the origin of the title of this paper, in which I seek the common denominator of the practices ethnographically called "sacrifice" in three very different societies. I call the use of "religion" as a descriptive and analytical framework into question at the same time, while I point to the distortions imposed by its associated vocabulary. I offer an alternative perspective, based on work by Jean Bazin, which sets aside some of the favorite dichotomies of social science.[1]

Distortions

A number of scholars over the years have directed our attention to the distortions imposed on anthropological representations of African culture by careless ethnocentric use of the vocabulary of religion. Jean-Pierre Olivier de Sardan, complaining about exoticism in anthropology, explains: "Spontaneous western concepts of magic, of possession and sorcery, in contrast to African concepts, are linked with the supernatural, the extraordinary, the mysterious and the fantastic. These phenomena are beyond comprehension, whilst in Africa they form one of the pillars of the most elementary understanding" (1992, 14).

In the nineteenth century, anthropologists asserted that Africans and other people about to be subjugated by Europeans lacked religion and had only fetishism; this assessment was the product of the anthropologists' inability to assess African values correctly. African scholars still feel under pressure to defend Africa from the reproach that it lacks its own profound spiritual dimension worthy of the name "religion." Curiously, this defense usually takes the form of insisting that Africans do acknowledge a Supreme Being, the central feature of Middle Eastern (that is, Abrahamic) religions; thus the defense accepts the critique it purports to refute (Messana 2002; Shaw 1990; Nwoga 1984). Far Eastern religions have entirely different preoccupations, and there is no good reason to suppose a priori that the Middle Eastern model would fit in Africa. The anthropologist Benson Saler, after an extended and thoughtful effort to transform the folk category "religion" into an analytical category that would free transcultural research and understanding of prejudice, is forced to conclude with a definition that confirms the concept as inescapably ethnocentric. "Religion," he says, is simply "the Western monotheisms, our most prototypical cases of religion," together with whatever else scholars believe resembles the Western monotheisms in significant respects (Saler 2000, 225).

As support declines in the West for traditional Christianity, such thoughtful and erudite scholars as Wilfred Cantwell Smith (1964) and Karen Armstrong (1993) have shifted the discussion away from the questionable rationality of belief in gods towards a humanistic common denominator, either a putatively universal quest for some ultimate Reality or perhaps the diffuse "spirituality" that is often attributed to Africans.[2] Yet it is doubtful whether many people anywhere, except professional intellectuals, spend much time speculating about transcendence and Ultimate Reality. Speaking about the Akan, and Africans in general, the Ghanaian philosopher Kwasi Wiredu says that in the absence of such linguistic categories as the spiritual, mystical, and supernatural there is no conceptual cleavage between the natural and the supernatural, or the physical and the spiritual. The nonhuman beings in whom the Akan believe are, he says, "an integral part of this world" (Wiredu 1992, 325).

Not only should we challenge the place of Christianity or modern Western "spirituality" as a standard of international cultural respectability, we should go further and ask why one assumes that everybody has religion and that our task is merely to describe it. We cannot suppose that any community we would recognize as such, even a criminal gang or a refugee camp, lacks a regulatory structure (a government) and some system for supplying its material needs (an economy); these are necessary functions, but "religion" is supported by no such axiomatic assurance. It has no clearly identifiable function, unless we assume from within religious belief that there are gods whose presence and actions must necessarily be recognized by human beings in one way or another.[3] Without any result other than suggestions that are often absurd, in recent years evolutionary biologists have desperately tried to identify a function or functions that would explain the persistence of religion in Darwinian terms (Fuller 2008).

A large part of evolutionary biologists' difficulty comes from their assumption that religion is a clearly identifiable and universal object, although in fact no reliable definition of it is available; in practice, they equate "religion" with acceptance of certain false propositions, with obdurate error. Thus both terms of the relationship, biological cause and irrational effect, remain indeterminate. The "definition" of "religion" usually taken for granted is "belief in spiritual beings," or "the supernatural," but it is difficult to establish verifiable truth conditions for these entities.

Realistically, even without a definition we cannot expect to abandon religion entirely as long as we are speaking European languages, in which many activities cannot conveniently be described except with the vocabulary of religion. English is of course a Nigerian language, but we should be aware of the likely distortions it entails and should try to use its terms in ways that do not make invidious distinctions.[4] As an example of such misuse, consider how techniques used by experts to identify invisible forces acting upon a client and likely to affect his or her fortunes in the future are called "divination" when they occur in Africa but "economic forecasting" when they emanate from Wall Street. These two kinds of investigations of the occult present precisely the same intellectual problems, but only divination has given rise to conferences convened to discuss and explain the apparent irrationality of the natives.

The Dead in Kongo and Yorùbá

Among the troublesome words in the vocabulary of religion are certainly "belief," "supernatural," "spiritual," "worship," and "sacrifice." To illustrate the problem, I turn to Kongo and Yorùbá ideas about the dead and the proper way to address them. Kongo have no such category as the supernatural; their approach to experience is not a matter of belief, but as Igor Kopytoff says of the neighboring Suku, it is positivistic as a matter of evidence derived from experience and rational inquiry (Kopytoff 1981, 713). They are often wrong, in my opinion, but error is not religion nor is it disgraceful. The "spirits" BaKongo believe in are not spiritual; they are the names of natural forces, which can be mobilized by those with the necessary knowledge in the material form of *minkisi* (ritual devices) in the interest of clients. Misuse of the forces of nature, as by witches, is to be expected; but witches are simply neighbors up to no good and thus a fact of life, not a "belief" (Olivier de Sardan 1992, 11). A witch is not a spiritual being, he or she is your neighbor; he or she possesses exceptional powers, which to BaKongo are not supernatural but technical; to me witches are not supernatural but imaginary.

In Kongo the dead are not dead; they are thought to have moved to another place across some boundary from which they may return. I speak on this topic with the authority of experience, since when I lived in Kongo I was said to have returned from the dead.[5] The important point in this is that though I was an object of curiosity, at no time was I anything other than a human being; I was not a ghost or a spirit, I was simply a *mwisi Kongo* who had been changed by a journey. Something of the kind was also at least a possibility in Yorùbá, with respect to which Henry Drewal and John Pemberton are careful to speak of as "the Departed" rather than "the dead"; Ọmọṣade Awolalu heard that deceased persons occasionally visited the living "in human form, not in the form of spirits at all!" When he asserts that the idea of the survival of souls is universal, he is eliding very different senses of "survival" (Drewal and Pemberton 1989, 14; Awolalu 1996, 53, 58; Peel 1990, 345; 1995, 594n52). The African dead, as Kopytoff put it, are like elders whose descendants seek their goodwill as much as they did before the elders moved house (Kopytoff 1971). To list dealings with ancestors as a feature of religion seems justifiable only in terms of European concepts. It is not correct, as Karin Barber asserts, that Kopytoff says ancestors are simply elders (Barber 1981, 742n15). He says that when the mode of interaction with a father changes after his death, "we westerners express this difference as 'worship' and 'sacrifice' because we find such terms more appropriate to express our own dealing with the dead" (Kopytoff 1971, 139).[6]

Both E. Bolaji Idowu and Awolalu insist on the affinity between Christian and Yorùbá senses of the sacred, but have difficulty reconciling this alleged affinity with the details of Yorùbá practice. "When confronted with life's problems, a Yoruba wants to act in a practical way. And one way he acts is to find out from the oracle the source of any trouble and how it can be removed" (Awolalu 1996, 195). This scarcely sounds like worship of the sacred. Unlike Awolalu, Idowu rejects "worship" as the right term for dealings with ancestors, on the Kopytovian ground that they remain members of the family (Idowu 1963). John Peel, citing Kopytoff with approval, nevertheless counters that he fails to capture the heightened quality of dealing with the Yorùbá dead (Peel 2000, 95). The difference between Peel and Kopytoff is partly a function of the difference between an elaborately hierarchical, wealthy, and predominantly urban society and those such as Kongo or Suku where small villages were the norm and there was simply less of everything.

Spirits and Big Men

Whether "worship" is the appropriate term for these practices is not likely to be settled by further research. The problem recurs in the relationship between orisa and Big Men. According to Barber, awareness that men make gods is not only a sociological commonplace but "a central impulse to devotion" among Yorùbá; the orisa are thought to be "maintained and kept in existence by the action of humans." Yorùbá think this way, she says, because in their society, unlike more rigidly ascriptive ones, a human individual's power also depends on the attention of fellow men and women. Orisa reflect a magnified image of the Big Man; both offer protection, help, and guidance in return for praise and gifts, and are made bigger or smaller by the attentions of followers. If blessings in return for praise and expenditure are not forthcoming, clients, whom she calls "devotees," may threaten to transfer their allegiance (Barber 1981). People also make gods of other humans. Peel says, "Great chiefs, in fear of witchcraft, equipped themselves with all kinds of protection. But they themselves were regarded as in some ways more than human. To go beyond the norm for ordinary men in wives, slaves and wealth was to behave more like an orisa than a man." Again, "The parallels between behavior directed at orisa and at chiefs and important figures in the community are very close" (Peel 2000, 82, 101). Even town and village heads are regarded as sacred and are given the sort of reverence usually accorded to orisa (Idowu 1963, 132; Pemberton and Afolayan 1996). In short, as Kopytoff says, if there be a cult here, it is a cult of the living as well as the dead, a continuum rather than a dichotomy (Kopytoff 1971, 133).[7]

Although gifts to the orisa often carry symbolic significance—for example, fish and snails are associated with peace, pigeons emphasize good luck and longevity, and other foods are required by the dietary preferences of the recipient (Awolalu 1996, 165–169; Abímbọ́lá 1976, 196–226)—the characters of the gifts prescribed by diviners are markedly economic. Multiples and large quantities are often prescribed, allowing for division among the recipients and for bargaining with the diviner and with Ifá. Most of the items are things in daily use, foodstuffs above all, since according to Abímbọ́lá feeding a person or an orisa is a means of serving and respecting the recipients, who can be expected to provide support in return and "even serve as our 'errand boys' in carrying messages from us to their own spiritual, unseen world" (Abímbọ́lá 2000, 178). A particularly important element in sacrifices is the quantity of cowrie shells, a former currency intimately linked with the concept of high status. The cowries point directly to the function of prestations (honorific gifts due to a superior) conversions of value upwards from the utilitarian to the social sphere. J. Lorand Matory comments on the economics of sacred power, pointing out that the production of animal blood in and for sacrifice "is a capital intensive commercial project" (Matory 2005, 218). Toyin Falola and Olatunde Lawuyi remark that "the entire religious ritual is tinged with an economic tone," but it is at least as appropriate to describe the economic relations of clients with their patrons, both visible and invisible, and as "tinged with ritual" (Falola and Lawuyi 1990, 32).

Sacrifice: Theory

If the gift to orisa is an animal, killing is the most effective way to transfer it, because if you just left the goat at a crossroads it would run away. There is thus a difference between gods and men that is not just a matter of scale and cannot be ignored, in the practice of sacrifice. Unfortunately, this term is itself the source of a great deal of confusion. Ethnographers so take it for granted as a routine item of religious behavior that they rarely bother to describe in any detail what happens, what the materials are, how they are used, or why. Etymologically "sacrifice" means "to make sacred," but "sacred" is another word whose meaning and applicability are assumed rather than demonstrated. In the classic work of Henri Hubert and Marcel Mauss, Emile Durkheim's assertion of a universal distinction between the sacred and the profane is taken for granted, and it is argued that in sacrificing something, usually an animal, it is "made sacred," first by being subject to ritual preparation and then by being killed and thus "separated definitively from the profane world." The sacrifice creates a bridge that provides access to the deities with whom its soul now resides; its body remains behind as an instrument of the useful effects of the sacrifice. The authors treat procedural differences in sacrifice as insignificant variations (Hubert and Mauss 1964, 35).

Claude Lévi-Strauss regards efforts at continuity and communication between man and god as marks of intellectual weakness, unlike totemism, which is based on contrast and analogy. For him, sacrifice is a form of extortion in which the killing of the intermediary obliges the deity to restore continuity by making a gift to the sacrificer (Lévi-Strauss 1962, 298). Luc de Heusch looks closely at procedural variations, including the choice of animal, and submits them to structural analysis; but his chief interest is the Frazerian thesis that the paradigmatic sacrifice is that of the god himself. Along the way, he classes all examples of killing in a ritual context as sacrifice (de Heusch 1985). All of these ambitious studies have been subjected to severe critique.

In his apologetics for Yorùbá religion Idowu asserts that sacrifice is the essence of every religion the world has ever known, but such generalizations would be foolhardy even if we could confidently define sacrifice (Idowu 1963, 118). Nancy Jay has convincingly shown the association of animal sacrifice with male hierarchies, including both patrilineal descent groups and the priesthood of the Catholic Church. Sacrifice enacts corporate integration, communion, or continuity, but also separation, exclusion, or disjunction, as when only members may participate; it thus defines boundaries and produces social order. Since it denies and substitutes for the role of women in reproducing social order, it should be absent or rare in societies with matrilineal descent.[8] Jay remarks on its absence in several Central African matrilineal societies and shows that in matrilineal Asante, sacrifice occurs only in connection with patrilateral relations (*ntoro, sunsum*) and succession to royal stools, not in connection with matrilineal descent groups (Jay 1992, 63, 68–76).

Kongo Sacrifice

Data from matrilineal Kongo, where the social structure is essentially the same as in Asante though on a smaller scale, confirm Jay's analysis. Kongo today is almost uniformly Christian, whether Catholic or Protestant, with the result that indigenous beliefs and practices are muted, though still vital. For the pre-Christian past we can rely on the testimony of a large number of detailed indigenous manuscripts dating from 1915. They describe three kinds of events that ethnographers have called sacrifices: gifts to the dead, sacrifices to violent *minkisi*, and killings by chiefs (MacGaffey 2000b).

As in the past, gifts, *nkailu* (from "*kaila*," meaning "to give"), are offered today at the graves of fathers, not mothers or mothers' brothers. They take the forms of food, drink, tobacco, money, and things such as cloth or bracelets that will please the deceased and induce him to confer a blessing. The form of address is exactly what one says to living elders whose goodwill one seeks. Fathers, alive and dead, are the primary source of support and good fortune for their children and grandchildren and must therefore be shown respect. The only difference, according to one text, is that one does not give cooked food to living fathers. Good fortune characteristically takes the form of successful hunting, and it is only in response to bad hunting luck that blood sacrifices are offered to paternal ancestors, blood being poured on the graves.[9] As in Asante, matrilineal descent groups are crosscut by descending patrifilial kindreds some three generations deep, which often, in combination with patrilateral cross-cousin marriage among the elite, create de facto father-son succession to political titles (Jay 1992, 74–75; MacGaffey 1986, 94–95). In Asante this patriarchal recruitment is sealed by sacrifice, but in Kongo the equivalent link is effected by smearing grave dirt on the children and grandchildren of the deceased.

Blood sacrifice, *kimenga* (from "*menga*," meaning "blood"), occurs in the rituals of certain kinds of *minkisi*, (singular: *nkisi*) those that are expected to inflict violence on witches and thieves. The manuscripts consistently use not *kaila* but the verb *zenga*, "to cut," in this connection. The function of such killing is mimetic, a dramatic demonstration of the punishment the *nkisi* is expected to mete out. A text concerning Nkisi Mayiza specifies that no chicken is cut because this *nkisi* is used for healing only, not to pursue witches. Another text says that if there is no chicken available, it will suffice to explode gunpowder to arouse the *nkisi*. Some texts also say that blood should be rubbed on the *nkisi* to give it strength and vigor. The attitude of clients of *minkisi* was entirely pragmatic, like that of clients of *orisa*, a matter of obtaining a solution to a problem; a *nkisi* was treated with respect as long as it delivered. A disappointed client might insult the *nkisi,* or in extreme cases throw its embodiment into the bush.

There are also reports of human beings killed in ritual contexts, but these events should not be called sacrifices. Some violent *minkisi* were said to be empowered by the souls of victims imprisoned within them, but such imprisonment was a purely magical operation said to take place "at night"—real enough to Ba-Kongo but not to an outsider (MacGaffey 2000c). De Heusch treats the killing of a girl reported to occur in connection with a particular Kongo chieftaincy as sacrifice, and says that it is a perversion of Bantu morality—a transgression that gave the chief access to superhuman power (de Heusch 1985, 216). In fact this killing should be grouped with other examples of the requirement that a candidate for a title demonstrate the power to kill, for example by waging a successful war (MacGaffey 2000b, 136–140). Dramatic executions of criminals would take place, but were also no more than demonstrations of the chief's power; they were not addressed to any deity or spirit, and they were not supposed to induce good fortune or avert misfortune.

Nancy Jay never quite explains just how and why sacrifices, particularly blood sacrifices, should be the means whereby patrilineal hierarchies are maintained, but contributory factors can be identified. The killing of four-legged animals seems to be regarded universally as a specifically male activity contrasted with, and incompatible with, female childbearing and menstruation (MacGaffey 1986, 49; Matory 2005, 201). Blood sacrifices can therefore substitute for childbirth in creating consanguinity, negating matrifiliation, and incorporating new members in a masculine hierarchy. The initiation of recruits to the cult of Sango as a form of artificial kinship exemplifies this logic with multiple and markedly bloody sacrifices, even though the cult is not a patrilineage; Matory describes its rituals as instruments for social extraction and reinvestment of essential reproductive resources (Matory 2005, 191–194, 203). Peel says, "the relative exploitability of wives and slaves was a function of their degree of strangerhood. The use of slaves in sacrifice was merely the sharpest expression of the principle that the young and the stranger were there to be used to ensure the survival and reproduction of the social order" (2000, 63).

Since social order is always an imposition by some on others, Jay sees ritual action as always political, a matter of struggles for power (Jay 1992, xxvi), which it undoubtedly is—but is social order in matrilineal societies solely a product of matrifiliation and not dependent on sacrifice? The question remains unanswered. Continuity is an essential feature of corporate organization and hierarchy; sacrifice is therefore related to time, although Jay does not quite show why. Michael Lambek, without any reference to Jay, helps us to understand why blood sacrifice in particular should have this significance. It is one of the most literal acts possible, "univocal, exact, unmediated and unambiguous"; therefore, "no explanation that draws upon forces external to the act itself is necessary." Killing is one of the clearest acts of beginning, a way to mark time, parting the stream into a past, present, and future. After a blood sacrifice, there is no going back for the victim or the beneficiary; unlike birth, it cannot be undone (this effect is often enhanced by deliberate dramatization) (Lambek 2007, 27).[10] Whereas in matrifiliation membership results from birth, patrifiliation requires an even more decisive incorporation. It is interesting in this context that the KiKongo *zenga* means both "to cut" and "to decide."

Men and Gods in the Savanna

With the assistance of the late Jean Bazin, an anthropologist who wrote about Bamana shrines in Mali, I would like to adopt an entirely different approach to sacrifice and show how men make gods in the West African savanna, beginning with the kingdom of Dagbon in northern Ghana.

At dynastic shrines associated with the ancient history of Dagbon, the king must cause sacrifices to be offered to the royal ancestors from time to time, especially at his installation. It is said that on these occasions sounds of festivity can be heard, emanating from the village of the dead. Princes eager for political advancement may also present personal sacrifices, although no royal may ever visit one of these shrines himself lest the dead invite him to join them. These are basically gifts in return for favors or in expectation of them, but at the same time they celebrate the exclusive claims of a dominant group that traces them to an original conquest.

Other sacrifices related to the chiefs are those that must be performed by drummers, who are the praise singers and historians of Dagbon; these sacrifices appear to be motivated by quite other concerns.[11] Drummers begin studying at an early age and must be capable, like Yorùbá babalawo, of remarkable feats of memory. The history they recite, parts of which are considered to be dangerous, is that of the successive kings and chiefs of Dagbon. On special occasions before large gatherings, the recitation is preceded by the sacrifice of a ram; these gatherings are called *sambanlunga* and may go on all night. The principal singer holds the animal's tail while it is killed; he may not eat any of the meat, which is shared by the other drummers present, and he must make the personal sacrifice of a white chicken before reentering his own compound. Lesser sacrifices are required to avert the wrath of the royal dead when shorter but still dangerous stories are to be told. The most dangerous seem to be those which refer to the first holders of certain titles, to bloody events, to the dangerous magical powers that chiefs deploy in contest with one another, and to anything that could be considered derogatory. In 1958, when there was a move to remove the then king on the ground of physical defects, the chief drummer-historian of Dagbon, who was asked to say whether any previous king had been defective, would only answer after being provided with and sacrificing a white cow, a white ram, a white goat, a white cock, two white doves, honey cakes, and milk.

These rituals are related to history and thus in a sense to time, but their manifest function is to separate the praise singer from possible danger—an insurance policy, as it were. The ritual exemplifies one of the classic functions of sacrifice, expiation by substitution. A drummer says that the ancestors, meaning both past chiefs and past drummers, will have his blood if he does not provide that of an animal; but it is not clear what provokes the ancestors' anger. It is said that they do not like to be talked about—but why not, since their praises are being sung and since in any case the history, which is performed in public, is generally known? The sacrifice is straightforwardly a killing, substituting for the drummer's own death; it does not take place at a shrine or altar, nor does it make use of blood to feed or strengthen anybody except fellow drummers, who get to eat the animal.[12] It may not be far-fetched to think of drummers as the priesthood of the dynasty and of their sacrifices and those of the princes as typical of the correlation in patriarchal orders between blood sacrifice, as a form of begetting that excludes women, and ideological insistence on the alleged origins and genealogy of the hierarchy (Jay 1992, 94–111, 113). In Dagbon, only the ruling dynasty represents itself as a patrilineage.

Although a town may have one shrine particularly associated with its well-being, commoners offer sacrifices annually, or on the advice of a diviner, at family shrines and also at local shrines that are said to be "for everybody" and are emphatically not related to social hierarchy or group membership. The family itself, though commonly described in Dagbon as a patrilineage, is in fact a bilateral descending kindred focused on a founding grandfather or great-grandfather; the affiliation of individual members may be a matter of adoption, matrifiliation, or clientage rather than birth. Family shrines are a means of contacting one or more of the household gods of Dagbon, a fairly short list; the form and placement of the shrine are appropriate to the particular god. The offerings are not made to the family ancestors as such; both the dead and the living have an interest in keeping the family god or gods happy by gifts. Household shrines in general are called *bag'yuli*, which is also the word for rituals, although one can also say *njem*, "to pacify." One particular family known to me has four shrines, two for men and two for wives; the latter are kept in the grandmother's house but brought out when necessary for the men to perform libations and sacrifices. At the annual "washing," a family festival, all these shrines are renewed at once.

At local shrines the annual festival is meant to "wash" or renew the shrine, which consists of stones or broken clay pots (*bugudugu*); the sacrifices are usually small animals and birds, which are roasted and eaten on the spot by whoever has brought them, after blood has been dripped on the shrine itself (*bugli*).[13] An appellation of several shrines is "the deaf god," *Bugtikpura*; at the end of the annual revival those present thump on the ground with sticks to awaken it. Each shrine is associated but not identified with a particular animal, usually of a threatening kind such as a python, a monitor lizard, or a swarm of bees. Such shrines and festivals, found all over the north, vary greatly in importance. Some of them attract people from all parts of the country. Sacrifices may also be offered, on the advice of a diviner, for help with personal problems. Blessing a white fowl is required, and a red or a black one is blessed to clear oneself from bad things. If the bird dies on its back, the sacrifice has been accepted; if the sacrifice is intended to avert misfortune the client should eat some of the meat. All of these are explained as gifts to the deities; milk and millet are also appropriate gifts. If prayers are answered, a further sacrifice is expected as thanks.

The Dagbani term for a local shrine, *bugli*, is cognate with the Bamana word *boli*, although the latter designates a broad range of portable and even pocket-sized devices as well as fixed shrines, for example those marked by clay pots. In this respect, *boli* resemble Kongo *minkisi*, a point to which we will return.

Jean Bazin offers a provocative interpretation of *boli*. He says it is a shrine, a material thing, but one that acquires its aura of apparent power by its singularity, as its history of contingent events; it is the product of individuation, not representation (Bazin 1986). Killing at a shrine is not, as European intellectual habits would dictate, an offering by the faithful to some hidden, quasi-anthropomorphic entity able to respond to entreaties. Instead it is one of an ongoing series of acts by which the body of the god is built and thereby renewed. Bazin strongly opposes other ethnographers of the Bamana who assume that sacrifice to a *boli* is an act of worship at the altar of a god. One can always find an informant, accustomed to European questions, who will confirm such assumptions. But in ritual practice no one mentions a god. What exactly is going on when blood is sprinkled on the shrine? Is the offering made to the thing itself, or do the adepts mistake an object for a god? Our problem starts with our idea that in true religion one approaches a hidden person by way of an object that is no more than a mediating means. We distinguish matter from spirit; since the *boli* is matter, its spirituality must lie somewhere else. If we reject the easy condescension of nineteenth-century assumptions about fetishism, what is it about an object that could make it a deity and not a symbol for or representation of something else?[14]

Instead of a division of the world into material and immaterial things, which the Bamana do not recognize, Bazin suggests we think of a scale of entities from the unique to the commonplace, which are both material and immaterial. The more unusual an entity, the more it stands out from the commonplace, attracting attention and speculation as to what special power makes it so, such as the inexplicable mounds that appear here and there in the savanna and that are often chosen as shrine places. Stories gather around it or him or her, pilgrims and tourists arrive, contact is sought, offerings and praises submitted. The accumulation of verses about the orisa in Ifá divination is an example; other examples of celebrity include striking features of landscape, great works of art, charismatic or notorious individuals, Big Men, shrines, and famous *minkisi*. The fame of singularity organizes the space around it, and the most singular entities are divine.

An altar or other object mediating access to a divinity can be destroyed and the god lives on, but a *boli* is the "god" itself, by virtue of its singularity and its contingency. *Boli* have been taken apart and their contents inventoried, but the report provides no recipe for a new one. A *boli* is unique by virtue of the particular history of its composition: not just the "hair of a black horse" but hair of a particular, known black horse; earth from the grave of a particular man, known for named qualities; and the leaf of a fig tree, the one that grows by the parting of the ways at the edge of the village. A *boli* has a name, and is unique also in the history of singular events imputed to it: the death of so-and-so, catastrophe avoided, enemies defeated. Besides adding one more act of devotion to enhance the reputation of the shrine, the man "sacrificing" by pouring blood on a *boli* is literally continuing the work of making and renewing the divine body, much of whose substance may be a mass of congealed blood.

Unlike most *minkisi*, a Bamana *boli* is enigmatic, offering little to intrigue the eye and provoke astonishment; instead, its ambiguous form implies the secret history within, which only initiates are supposed to know. A Dagomba shrine is nothing much to look at, but each sacrifice animates it and each visit by a devotee enhances its reputation, which may extend all over Ghana. Contrariwise, as times change, villagers move to town and Islamic orthodoxy advances, and small local shrines are neglected and forgotten. A great *nkisi*, especially of the kind formerly known as nail fetishes, was constituted over time, beginning with an approach by a *simbi*, a "nature spirit," to a named man or woman. The medicines originally inserted in it only established its potential. In the course of use, complaints were aired, curses uttered, nails driven in, and personalized bundles attached, creating a visible record of increasing distinction. Small *minkisi* cost less, take less time and trouble to assemble, and may be known only to their owner.

The biography of a European work of art likewise adds to its singularity and its reputation; it was created by a certain artist at a particular time and subsequently was owned, exhibited, stolen, and recovered. Its fame distinguishes it, makes it an object of pilgrimage even for those who know nothing about art; a work lacking attribution and provenance has little value, whatever its looks.

The blood poured over some *minkisi* to animate and strengthen them is the equivalent of the souls of supposed victims magically incorporated in other *minkisi* to energize an otherwise inanimate body. Powerful and long-lived men were likewise supposed to have accumulated souls by witchcraft, in addition to the one with which they were born. Clearly there is a metaphorical element here in addition to the mime of vengeance: blood is as much life as the shedding of it is death. This idea is conspicuous in the rituals of Sango initiation, in which the initiate is "bathed in blood" to strengthen him or her. In Yorùbá ritual language "'blood' is a prominent trope of vitality, kinship, and reproduction" (Matory 2005, 200). In certain East African societies, animals are suffocated, not cut, and a different life substance, chyme, is used to transfer vitality from one entity to another (Ruel 1990).

The Yorùbá word *ebo*, usually translated "sacrifice," is based on the verb *bo*, which Yorùbá-speaking friends tell me means "to worship or honor something more powerful than oneself." This sense closely corresponds to the medieval meaning of "worship" in English, given in the *Oxford English Dictionary* as "to regard or treat with honor or respect."[15] In that sense, the word has been obsolete since 1600; its semantic evolution tracks the progressive differentiation of the religious from the secular in the course of the Renaissance. Although the conflict engendered by the distinction continues to this day, by the end of the seventeenth century the idea that there are two kinds of truth, religious and scientific, was well established in Europe. The coupled verbs "worship" and "honor" are at the heart of our problem. In our present way of thinking, living elders are honored, but dead ones are worshipped, a distinction we would not have needed to make in the sixteenth century.

The word *ebo* is accurately translated "prestation," a word that entered anthropology through the work of Marcel Mauss; meaning an honorific gift due to a superior, it was an archaic term even in the French of his day, and no longer appears in modern English dictionaries. He needed it, as we need it, to describe what he called "total" relations—those that combine religious and economic elements that seem disparate to us in a form of social relationship (Mauss 1954).

Kongo gifts offered to dead fathers are explicitly similar in content and intent to those offered to living elders. In Dagbon, though the intent of gifts to shrines is similar—to seek good fortune and avert bad—the content is different from offerings made to chiefs, which are always kola nut, money, and praise. Gifts to elders, patrilateral ancestors, chiefs, shrines, and orisa all function as prestations addressed to a patron to induce him or it to confer favors. As long as the perception continues that the desired results are forthcoming, the buildup of the patron's reputation increases; thus gods and Big Men are created and destroyed. This is a universal phenomenon (Graeber 2001, 34).

Most African "sacrifices" consist of food. Abímbọ́lá says, "nourishment is at the very center of Yoruba religion. Feeding a person or an orisa, or even an ordinary object of nature, is a means of serving that being or thing, nourishing it, saluting and respecting it, and proclaiming its right to exist" (Abímbọ́lá 2000, 178). In Africa, politics is often "of the belly" and corpulence is a sign of importance and well-being (Bayart 1993).[16] In this connection, it is interesting that in the three languages with which we are dealing, all members of the Niger-Congo family, the cognate terms for "to eat" (*di, je* and *dia*) in combination with an object idiomatically describe socially significant states of being, such as to feel jealousy ("to eat jealousy"), to be punished, to curse, to accept a fee, and to accede to an office. The sharing of food is eminently social; an analysis of Ifá verses shows that the acceptability or otherwise of sacrifices corresponds to ethical rules about proper or improper behavior. To cause harm to another, one may sacrifice an unacceptable item to an orisa in the name of the other, thereby provoking its anger (Sachnine 1996, 127, 131n62).

There is no clearly defined entity to be called sacrifice, in form or function. In both Kongo and Dagbon, the people distinguish between prestations, among which there may be slaughtered animals, and blood used by itself. In Kongo blood marks time: the end of misfortune, the removal of harm, and the beginning of new luck. Killing also dramatically represents a power of death exercised either by chiefs or by certain *minkisi.*

We are hampered in cross-cultural studies by our Enlightenment heritage, which has naturalized distinctions between sacred and profane truth, between social and economic transactions, and between the material and the immaterial for us. What is now the usual sense of religion imposes distortions on African cultures, in which religion is not a matter of conversion, orthodoxy, or spirituality; nor is it distinguished from other practices of daily life.

Notes

1. The kingdoms of Kongo and Dagbon and a Yorùbá kingdom such as Oyo have little in common besides monarchy. Kongo, founded perhaps in the thirteenth century, was subject to European influence in the sixteenth and seventeenth centuries, particularly by Catholic missionaries and the transatlantic slave trade. In this period the social structure and political organization of the kingdom were complex enough, but not on a scale approaching that of Oyo. By the mid-nineteenth century Christianity survived only in occasional traces, and the kingdom had been reduced to minor importance. Dagbon, a kingdom reputedly founded

in the fifteenth century, was an association of warlords who reorganized it on the model of a Hausa emirate in the early eighteenth century.

2. See Idowu (1973) for a perceptive review of this literature and its application to Africa.

3. For E. B. Idowu, religion is not only universal but a function of human awareness, not of *a* Supreme Being but of *the* Supreme Being (1973, 92).

4. On problems about translating "Yoruba traditional religion," see Matory (2005, 231).

5. In 1970, in Matadi, which was by no means a bush village but the principal port of Kongo, it was said of me "*ndombe kena; fwa kafwa, tekwa katekwa*" ("He is black; he died and was sold.") (MacGaffey 1983, 132). Other white people in Central Africa who were thought to be unusually close to Africans and their culture have been similarly regarded, but the fact has usually been relegated to footnotes.

6. One of the differences between Kongo and Yorùbá cosmology is that the Kongo universe is predominantly spiral rather than reciprocal (MacGaffey 1986). That is, the dead in *nsi a bafwa*, literally "the land of the dead," are not reincarnated. After living for some time in the land of the dead they "die the second death" and eventually a third or even in some accounts a sixth death, becoming increasingly remote from the living and merging with the landscape as termite hills and rocks. At some stage in this process they become *bisimbi*, forces of nature, and as such they may choose to make themselves more useful to the living by having themselves incorporated in *minkisi*, which correspond closely to Yorùbá *orisa*. Each one deals with some limited range of afflictions, problems, or possibilities of concern to a particular congregation, ranging in number from a few individuals to whole districts.

7. See David Graeber's account (2001, 235) of *hasina* in Madagascar, where people are quite conscious that they make their gods.

8. Anthropology is still inclined to fetishize matrilineal and patrilineal organization as essentially different and as characterizing different kinds of society.

9. A text from Mayombe (western Kongo) describes a surprising reason for killing a pig: "If a man falls ill, the priest puts him in a ritual shed and they throw a huge party, killing two or three pigs so that the witches [malicious neighbors] will have enough meat and not be inclined to eat the sick man."

10. Lambek bases his argument in part on the self-sacrifice of a legendary Malagasy queen who thereby, in effect, turned herself into a patriarch, the founder of a dynasty restricted to her own children and excluding any other descendants of her husband. In this instance there was no third-party deity to whom the act was addressed or who benefited from it.

11. Drummers are referred to as the chief's "wives," because he has to "woo" them to join his entourage, but they do not demonstrate any sign of "wifeliness" in dress or comportment (cf. Matory 2005, 12).

12. In most traditions, expiatory sacrifices are not eaten (Jay 1992, 95).

13. Most Dagomba are at least nominally Muslims, but few see any contradiction between their faith and shrine sacrifices, which are usually preceded by Koranic prayers.

14. In fact the problem of distinguishing between a representation from a power in its own right has long vexed the Christian Church (Freedberg 1989, 161–191).

15. *Oxford English Dictionary*, s.v. "worship."

16. Jacob Olupona has given me the Yorùbá saying, "*Orisa bi ifun ko si, ojoojumo ni i gb'onje lowoeni*" ("there is no more powerful deity than one's belly, it consumes food daily").

References

Abímbọ́lá, Wándé. 1976. *Ifá: An Exposition of Ifá Literary Corpus.* Ibadan: Oxford University Press Nigeria.

———. 2000. "Continuity and Change in the Verbal, Artistic, Ritualistic, and Performance Traditions of Ifá Divination." In *Insight and Artistry in African Divination,* edited by John Pemberton III, 175–181. Washington, DC: Smithsonian Institution Press.

Armstrong, Karen. 1993. *A History of God.* New York: Ballantine.

Awolalu, J. Ọmọṣade. 1996. *Yoruba Beliefs and Sacrificial Rites.* New York: Athelia Henrietta Press.

Barber, Karin. 1981. "How Man Makes God in West Africa: Yoruba Attitudes towards Orisa." *Africa* 51, no. 3: 724–745.

Bayart, Jean-François. 1993. *The State in Africa: The Politics of the Belly.* London: Longman.

Bazin, Jean. 1986. "Retour aux choses-dieux." In *Corps des Dieux,* edited by Charles Malamoud and Jean-Pierre. Vernant, 253–273. Paris: Gallimard.

de Heusch, Luc. 1985. *Sacrifice in Africa.* Bloomington: Indiana University Press.

Drewal, Henry John, and John Pemberton III, 1989. *Yoruba: Nine Centuries of African Art and Thought.* New York: Center for African Art.

Ejizu, Christopher. "Emergent Key Issues in the Study of African Traditional Religions." Available at http://www.afrikaworld.net/afrel/ejizu.htm. Accessed April 23, 2012.

Falola, Toyin, and Olatunde Bayo. Lawuyi, 1990. "Not Just a Currency: The Cowrie in Nigerian Culture." In *West African Economic and Social History,* edited by David P. Henige and T. C. McCaskie, 29–36. Madison: African Studies Center, University of Wisconsin Press.

Freedberg, David. 1989. *The Power of Images.* Chicago: University of Chicago Press.

Fuller, Robert C. 2008. *Spirituality in the Flesh: Bodily, Sources of Religious Experience.* New York: Oxford University Press.

Graeber, David. 2001. *Toward an Anthropological Theory of Value.* New York: Palgrave.

Hubert, Henri, and Marcel Mauss. 1964. *Sacrifice: Its Nature and Function.* Chicago: University of Chicago Press.

Idowu, E. Bolaji. 1963. *Olodumare: God in Yoruba Belief.* New York: Praeger.

———. 1973. *African Traditional Religion.* Maryknoll, NY: Orbis.

Jay, Nancy. 1992. *Throughout Your Generations Forever: Sacrifice, Religion and Paternity.* Chicago: University of Chicago Press.

Kopytoff, Igor. 1971. "Ancestors as Elders in Africa." *Africa* 41, no. 2: 129–142.

———. 1981. "Knowledge and Belief in Suku Thought." *Africa* 51, no. 3: 709–723.

Lambek, Michael. 2007. "Sacrifice and the Problem of Beginning." *Journal of the Royal Anthropological Institute* 13: 19–38.

Lévi-Strauss, Claude. 1962. *La Pensée Sauvage.* Paris: Plon.

MacGaffey, Wyatt. 1983. *Modern Kongo Prophets.* Bloomington: Indiana University Press.

———. 1986. *Religion and Society in Central Africa.* Chicago: University of Chicago Press.

———. 2000a. "The Cultural Tradition of the African Rainforests." In *Insight and Artistry in African Divination,* edited by John Pemberton III, 13–22. Washington, DC: Smithsonian Institution Press.

———. 2000b. *Kongo Political Culture.* Bloomington: Indiana University Press.

———. 2000c. "Aesthetics and Politics of Violence in Central Africa." *Journal of African Cultural Studies* 13, no. 1: 63–75.

Matory, James Lorand. 2005. *Sex and the Empire that is No More.* New York: Berghahn Books.

Mauss, Marcel. 1954. *The Gift: Forms and Functions of Exchange in Archaic Societies.* London: Cohen and West.

Messana, Daniele. 2002. "African Traditional Religions and Modernity: The End of a Stigma." Available at http://www.afrikaworld.net/afrel/religionitrad.htm.

Nwoga, Donatus Ibe. 1984. *The Supreme God as Stranger in Igbo Religious Thought.* Ahiazu Mbaise, Nigeria: Hawk Press.

Olivier de Sardan, Jean-Pierre 1992. "Occultism and the ethnographic 'I': The Exoticizing Of Magic from Durkheim to Postmodern Anthropology." *Critique of Anthropology* 12, no. 1: 5–25.

Peel, J. D. Y. 1990. "The Pastor and the Babalawo: The Interaction of Religions in Nineteenth-Century Yorubaland." *Africa* 60, no. 3: 338–369.

———. 1995. "For Who Hath Despised the Day of Small Things? Missionary Narratives and Historical Anthropology." *Comparative Studies in Society and History,* 37, no. 3: 581–607.

———. 2000. *Religious Encounter and the Making of the Yoruba.* Bloomington: Indiana University Press.

Pemberton, John, III, and Funso S. Afolayan, 1996. *Yoruba Sacred Kingship: "A Power Like that of the Gods."* Washington, DC: Smithsonian Institution Press.

Ruel, Malcolm. 1990. "Non-Sacrificial Ritual Killing." *Man* 25: 323–335.

Saler, Benson. 2000. *Conceptualizing Religion: Immanent Anthropologists, Transcendent Natives, and Unbounded Categories.* Leiden: Brill.

Sachnine, Michka. 1996."Nourir les dieux." *Journal des Africanistes* 66, no. 1–2: 105–135.

Shaw, Rosalind. 1990. "The Invention of African Traditional Religion." *Religion* 20: 339–353.

Smith, Wilfred Cantwell. 1964. *The Faith of Other Men.* New York: Harper & Row.

Wiredu, Kwasi. 1992. "Formulating Modern Thought in African Languages: Some Theoretical Considerations." In *The Surreptitious Speech: Présence Africaine and the Politics of Otherness 1947–1987,* edited by V. Y. Mudimbe, 301–332. Chicago: University of Chicago Press.

11 Ifá

The Quintessential Builder of Our Bank of Images

Akínwùmí Ìṣọlá

At THIS DISTANCE in time, it is crucial to stop and discuss our priorities in terms of academic research directions and sociopolitical proactive initiatives in African studies. For the purpose of this chapter, we must consider what has been said about culture in general. Culture has been defined as "the set of distinctive spiritual, material, intellectual and emotional features of a society or social group, encompassing, in addition to art and literature, lifestyles, ways of living together, value systems, traditions and beliefs" (UNESCO 2002).

For groups and societies all over the world, culture is simply each group's ways of living together. However, the most important fact about culture is its diversity, as expressed in Article 1 of the United Nations Educational, Scientific, and Cultural Organization (UNESCO) Universal Declaration of Cultural Diversity (2001):

> Cultural Diversity: the common heritage of humanity. Culture takes diverse forms across time and space. This diversity is embodied in the uniqueness and plurality of the identities of the groups and societies making up humankind. As a source of exchange, innovation and creativity, cultural diversity is as necessary for humankind as biodiversity is for nature. In this sense, it is the common heritage of humanity and should be recognized and affirmed for the benefit of present and future generations. (UNESCO 2001)

The point being made here is that the world is a world of diversity: biodiversity and cultural diversity. "The earth is one but the world is not. We all depend on one biosphere for sustaining our lives," but each group or society of humankind creates its own elaborate, culturally rooted ways of living together (de Cuellar

1995, 37). African traditions and belief systems variously posit that transcendent spiritual entities have demonstrated a preference for diversity in human, social, and cultural spheres of life and in particular in the ecosystem. Cultures and societies have also created unique languages for communities to ensure effective and independent operation. In this regard, language is the heart of a culture. When a language dies, the culture atrophies and dies. Language is the hub of the wheel of culture, while other aspects are the spokes operating a robustly effective feedback system. The great mystery of the origin of language can never be solved. The general assumption is that because language is so intrinsically linked to human survival and innately linked to human existence, it is a coveted gift and therefore must be protected, nurtured, and preserved for posterity. This is why many research foundations are committed to restoring and preserving endangered languages in Africa, Asia, and Latin America. With adequate language the people in a community possess the tools for creating and recording knowledge in a memorable fashion and for laying the groundwork for acceptable standards in all aspects of life, in order to ensure sustainable development and authentic continuity. Therefore, every culture has rules that lay down what is allowable in particular circumstances. The greatest emphasis is always placed on the careful education of the child.

It is important to note that every culture has its own myths of the origin of humans and of language. There are almost seven thousand languages in the world. No one myth can attain the status of historical fact. And in this regard, no one myth is superior to another. However, some cultures have been able to popularize their own myths of origin, mainly through their aggressive religious evangelism, thereby transforming mere myths to virtual facts of history in the minds of adherents who now close their minds to edifying lessons from other cultures. Ideally a good citizen of any society or culture should have an open mind, and should protect his or her own God-given culture. As Mahatma Gandhi observed, "I do not want my house to be walled in on all sides and my windows to be stuffed. I want the cultures of all the lands to be blown about my house as freely as possible. But I refuse to be blown off my feet by any" (quoted in de Cuellar 1965, 20). Cultural diversity is indeed the common heritage of humanity; however, it is this humanistic potential of culture that has engaged the active attention of UNESCO for over three decades now. This is often couched in development paradigms: "Development, in UNESCO's view, is a means of enhancing the relationship between material and spiritual well being of men and women, and only culture can negotiate that" (UNESCO 2002, 12).

The record of development, especially in Africa, has not been so positive, mainly because development has been so wrongheadedly defined in material terms such as dams, factories, houses, food, and water. Development in humane qualities, which includes issues that can ensure sustainability such as participation, empowerment, transparency, and accountability, has been absent. It is clear that development needs cultural content to make it sustainable. In this regard, literature is our most potent component of culture. So what is literature?

What Does Literature Do?

In creative oral or written compositions, using materials from the local environment, literature teaches men and women how to understand the world. However, the most important component of the material used is the local language. It is the local language that can communicate directly with the local environment and make meaningful comments. Literature teaches the mother to calm her crying child. It sings the praise names of the staple diet. It retells tender tales told by trees. It teaches the farmer the best methods of tending tendrils. It warns about the weather and documents the behavior of rain and sunshine. Information about plant and animal life, insightful remarks about the nature of the language, mnemonics for counting, ways of identifying medicinal plants, and a lot of moral instruction are woven into memorable poems and stories. Literature is also used to play a cleansing role for the community when artists compose special songs to expose erring members of the community for castigation. Folktales are used to introduce children to the sociopolitical problems of the society, because the folktales of a society tend to reflect the fears and aspirations of the people.

In traditional African society, the whole fabric of living was beautifully patterned with the threads and colors of literature. The process of socialization from the cradle to the grave was eased and made effective through the use of literature. The conditioning of life by patterns of belief was achieved by the use of literature (Ìṣọlá 1996).

Literature is therefore a most important component of cultural heritage. Our cultural heritage has tangible and intangible components. Tangible heritage refers to those things that have physical form, such as carved wood and calabashes, statues, drums, costume, historical landscapes and sites, buildings, monuments, and so on. Intangible components are those aspects that have no physical form, such as our language and literature, oral traditions, customs, music, rituals, festivals, and other special skills. The important fact is that it is the intangible component of cultural heritage, where literature is dominant, that sustains the tangible aspect. This is because the intangible is the source of valuable ideas such as dignity, hope, sense of duty, acceptable standards of right and wrong, hard work, faithfulness, accountability, honor, fraternity, and other humane qualities.

It is the duty of literature in the local language to craft those humane qualities into valuable genres, the nuggets and souvenirs of language that will produce the memorable images that are stored in a bank at the front and back of the minds of the owners of the culture. Some people have wondered why literature in a foreign language cannot perform the same function. The reason is simply that language and literature are predominantly culture bound. The culture-in-language and environment-in-language aspects of a literature bind it tightly to particular minds. "But literature can be exported." Sure! Colonialism brought the literature of European languages to Africa. It is the receivers who must be on their guard; otherwise fraud will be introduced into their bank of images in the form of blurred, meaningless, irrelevant, and misleading images. For example, African children were being taught English lullabies like "Baa, baa, black sheep / Have you any wool? / Yes, sir, Yes, sir / Three bags full" (Kipling 1890). For goodness' sake, three bags full of wool from a single black sheep in a country like Nigeria where sheep have barely enough hair to cover their backs? There are many other examples, especially in foreign proverbs like "Carrying coal to Newcastle" where a local proverb would provide a clearer image that can be easily stored in our bank of images (Whiting 1977).

The Link with Development

This function of literature, including scriptures—as an important part of our intangible cultural heritage in providing a bank of images as a guide for acceptable behavior—is of crucial importance to a people's development in any community or country. Without intangible development, there can be no sustainable development. Otherwise, as a Yorùbá proverb says, "a child not built up morally will sell the house built by the parents."

This is why many African countries cannot yet attain sustainable development. The roads are bad. The money is stolen. Schools, factories, and hospitals cannot be maintained, because the leaders and the elite in charge lack the humane qualities they ought to have acquired from our intangible cultural heritage mediated by literature. The material aspects of development imported to or dumped on Africa from abroad are not accompanied by the intangible aspects. Many African leaders erroneously believe that they can import globalized ideas about the legal monitoring of behavior from the World Bank or the International Monetary Fund while forgetting that ideas about dignity, hope, honesty, and so on do not appear in generic universal forms. Different peoples articulate them in terms of highly specific idioms of value, meaning, and belief (UNESCO 2002, 10). This is what the young generation of every culture must learn and imbibe through the intangible aspects of cultural heritage. Specific images of beauty, harmony, chivalry, and justice that usually come from inspiring episodes of literature and group history always guide people in determining what they want to be in life and how to attain it. Those images are culturally framed and experienced, so that there is always a bank of images to chose from.

Although the preference for variety—as clearly demonstrated in cultural diversity among humankind and in biodiversity in ecology—has long been recognized, the similarities in the earthly fates of both cultural and biological ecosystems have not been given adequate attention as far as Africa is concerned. Major threats to the biological ecosystem include long droughts, forest fires, desertification, ozone depletion, poachers, and loggers. Similarly the major threats to the cultural ecosystem include foreign invasions, wars, the slave trade, colonization, foreign religions, and globalization.

If the supreme power behind nature prefers variety, we can say that defending our own cultural heritage and respecting those of others should be a religious or at least an ethical duty. Here at least the goals of religious practitioners, cultural nationalists, and environmentalists should have coincided. But everywhere you turn they seem to be talking at cross purposes. Why? The answer may be found in the pernicious alliance among religion, trade, and politics. The three are always in constant and calculated cahoots to suppress and suffocate the cultures of the militarily weaker peoples of the world; this involves using all kinds of weapons, from the slave trade, religion, and colonialism to the glamour of entertainment through the Internet and globalization.

Biodiversity, the lucky twin sister of cultural diversity, has a lot of committed defenders and supporters. Whenever any species in the ecosystem is endangered, many organizations take sustained measures to help it struggle back to a more vigorous position. By contrast, few organizations marshal the endangered aspects of cultural heritage in Africa. While defenders and supporters are few indeed, traducers and redoubtable enemies are many.

But that is not the whole story. One of the most enduring attributes of African culture, which should have been its strongest and most admired quality, has turned out to be its fatal flaw—its suicidal hospitality of tolerance. African hospitality has become proverbial. For example, African traditional religion threw its doors wide open to foreign religions. The foreigners entered, destroyed Africans' property, promptly threw them out of their own houses, and have since then continued to pursue the offspring of Africans relentlessly. Why are we so tolerant?

> When noise perpetuates,
> It becomes inaudible
> "When evil accumulates,
> It becomes invisible!"[1]

Phenomena have the amazingly confounding power to become so completely familiar over time that we really do not hear, see, or notice them any more. People who live near motor parks, or near certain churches and mosques in Nigeria, or whose neighbors use howling generators grow so accustomed to the noise that they stop hearing it. Our perception of the world can wither that away completely, leaving us with only hazy recognition (Chomsky 1972, 24). The power of familiar phenomena to benumb our perception and compromise our reactions can lead to a careless or criminal tolerance that allows atrophy, decay, and stagnation to set in. Perhaps this is why most otherwise intelligent and patriotic Africans do not feel disturbed in the least today that all aspects of our cultural heritage continue to suffer neglect and corruption to such an extent that they are now in danger of disappearing.

It appears that what we, Africans, need now is to earnestly search and acquire faith in the developmental capacities of African culture. Ifá provides a passable way back to the culture because it establishes a holistic way of life, and the very first step in this direction is to ensure that it does not disappear. *Ese Ifá,* composed by gifted creative and collective minds in the culture through divine inspiration, provide suitable parables that can create humane images for sustainable development in our mind banks. A thorough study of the ramifications of Ifá by Odeyemi (2008) shows that it comprises eight basic essences: the spiritual essence, "which relates to the place of man . . . in the cosmos, the powers of matter and all aspects of ontological evolution and development" (13); the religious essence, "which relates to faith, catechism and preaching" (ibid.); the divine essence, "which relates to the methods of Divination and accessing of esoteric information. The mechanics of Divinaiton and the systematics of Divine Message collection, processing, and interpretation" (ibid.); the worship and sacrificial essence, "which relates to the basis and meaning of worship and sacrifice" (ibid.); the medicinal essence, "which deals with both magical and materialist medicine" (ibid.); the historical essence, "which deals with the history of all creation, including the creation of materialist, non-materialist and spirit worlds" (ibid.); the scientific essence, "which deals with the power of observation, axiomatics, astronomy, cosmology, cognitive and precognitive experience, astral science, physical and biological sciences, logic, philosophy, mathematics, statistics and computer science" (ibid.); and the cultural essence, "which relates to rites, rituals, politics, socio-economics, languages (and literature), dress, and normative value systems" (ibid.).

All these essences provide a template for understanding the Yorùbá religious quest and worldview in which cultural, social, sacred environmental, and technological spheres all dovetail. It is clear from Yorùbá studies that the disciplines of history, arts, literature, and religion are very connected, because these essences are all related to each disciplinary angle. The essences have been copiously illustrated in Wándé Abímbọ́lá's and William Bascom's works, especially in their seminal books, respectively *Ifá* (1976) and *Ifá Divination* (1969).

Among the Yorùbá, as elsewhere, Ifá and its babalawo have been tested and trusted by the clients who consult divination. The babalawo threads and knits together all aspects of socioreligious life, culture, and tradition. So, according to Peel:

Uncommon qualities were required in a babaláwo. A memory, intelligence, and self-discipline were necessary for him to acquire the knowledge of *ese* which was fundamental to his practice, as well as the psychological insight and worldly experience needed for dealing with clients. . . . They often added medical practice to their divination. Babaláwo were thus the intellectuals of Yoruba society, the people most able to take a long term and supra-local view of things, adept at the analysis of novel situations in terms of precedents, and prone to the rationalization of the cultural materials—myths, proverbs, oriki, maxims, fables, historical fragments—which were built into the *ese Ifá*. If there was a keynote to the Ifá cult, it was control: control of circumstances through knowledge of the relevant precedents for action, a control which itself depended on the babaláwo's own self control. (Peel 2000: 114)

In Ifá we therefore have a system at the center stage of our intangible cultural heritage that will ensure that reliably positive images are stored in the mind banks of the younger generations as they are socialized into African societies. It is hard to find anything better in the systems and scriptures of other world religions.

We all know what happened to African societies in the past, but sadly, worse things are happening to us today. The big question is whether there is anything we can do. The answer is yes. UNESCO elevated Ifá to the status of a Masterpiece of the Oral and Intangible Heritage of Humanity in 2005. The Ifa Heritage Institute in Nigeria has started running courses in Ọ̀yọ́, under Professor Wándé Abímbọ́lá as founder and president. We should all support this safeguarding project in every way. Moreover, the impact of the new initiative is clearly seen in the popularity of the Osun Osogbo Festival that was a part of the UNESCO initiative under the then governor of Osun State, Prince Olagunsoye Oyinlola.

But we should do more. We should improve upon our attitude to African culture in general, especially African religion. We should ensure that our children and grandchildren do not remain alienated. Most of the other things can wait, but the education of our children cannot. Above all, we should think of establishing projects with the sole aim of prizing our minds out of the gridlock of Western culture. If we do not act now, African culture will be lost in a forest of world cultures. It is like the well-known Yoruba folktale about the goat and the monkey:

The goat and the monkey engaged in a hot argument in front of the King's palace. Each one claimed to have a greater number of children. Their noise disturbed the king, and he ordered them to be brought before him. When they stated their cases, the king laughed and told them how foolish they were to be arguing over what could be easily verified. He therefore asked each of them to bring her children to the palace the following morning. The goat arrived first bringing all her children. Actually she had only four children, but her husband also came along. When the monkey arrived with a family of about twenty-five, all the spectators believed that the goat had lost the contest.

The king came out of the palace, sat on a high chair, and asked the contestants to bring their children forward to be counted. The goat promptly stepped forward and saluted the king. She asked permission to first introduce herself and her husband. The king agreed.

"This is my husband, Mr. Òbúko." Òbúko saluted the king smartly and the spectators clapped.

"This is me, Madam Aké, the mother of these children." She saluted the king elegantly and received applause.

By the way, let me remind you that Aké is the name given to the biggest goats, the type preferred by reputable Ifá priests for sacrifice. Such a babalawo would have many such goats in his backyard tied to pegs or trees. He would then cut the rope to release an Aké for sacrifice as the need arose. Babalawo in that category were given the nickname "ojakenide fisebo" ("He who cuts the rope to release an ake for sacrifice") or simply Jakenide, from which the name Jakannde arose.

The goat went ahead to introduce her children.

"This is my first child, Mr. Layewu." Layewu, the hairy one, bowed obediently and was cheered.

"This is the second child, Miss Ideregbe." She bowed and received cheers.

"This is my third child, Miss Asinrin." Asinrin received applause as she bowed.

"And lastly, for now, before the others join us, may I introduce my little Láróndó"? Láróndó bounced three times, bowed smartly, and received a loud ovation.

The goat then said that she would like to give the floor to Mrs. Monkey to introduce some of her own children too. The king agreed.

The Monkey saluted the king and said, "I am Mrs. Monkey and this is my husband Mr. Monkey." The audience clapped.

Then she went on: "And this is my first child Mr. Monkey, and the second one, Mr. Monkey, and the third one, Miss Monkey, and the fourth one Mr. Monkey. . . ."

The king started laughing at her, saying, "But you have only one name! You are all the same! Where is the difference? Even if you had one hundred children, there is only one Mr. Monkey! All of you will be lost in a forest of monkeys, whereas each member of the goat family has an identity." The goat won the contest for her originality in the art of naming in the spirit of cultural diversity. (My rendition)

So we should know what to do. We know where the problems lie. It is with us, the so-called African elite, the school-educated elite. Again, it is like another well-known Yoruba folktale: the story of Mother Rabbit:

Ehoro, she just had a new baby, and all the other animals in the bush came to rejoice with her at the naming ceremony on the fifth day. There was plenty to eat and drink and the animals were really enjoying themselves. But Mother Rabbit was not happy. Each animal prayed as they came in, but Mother Rabbit was not saying Amen! There was a petulant expression around her mouth, like a sneer. Some animals became rather uncomfortable. So, at a point Mr. Bushpig suggested that they all pray together and he offered to lead them. So they all rose. Mr. Bushpig said "Oh God, powerful OLÓDÙMARÈ, please protect this baby from all danger! Spare his life." And all animals were saying Amen! Except of course, Mother Rabbit! You know, when animals pray, they don't close their eyes! It would be too risky! They would need to see if any danger was approaching. *Tojú tìyé làparò fi í ríran.* So they all noticed that Mother Rabbit was still not saying Amen. Mr. Bushpig then stopped praying and demanded to know why Mother Rabbit was not saying Amen.

Mother Rabbit angrily said "How can I say Amen to hypocritical prayers? You are all hypocrites! You know the truth, but you are never bold enough to face true realities!"

The animals were shocked! And Mr. Bushpig wanted to know what was wrong with their prayers.

Then Mother Rabbit said, "Well, may I ask all of you a few questions?"

They all said, "Yes, of course!"

Mother Rabbit then asked them, "Who gives us children?"

They all said, "God, of course! Who else?"

"Thank you," said Mother Rabbit, "but may I ask you another question?"

"Yes, of course!" they all shouted again.

"Well now, does the merciful God, Olódùmarè who gives us those beautiful children also wantonly kill the children?"

The animals hesitated. But some of them said, "Well, no of course, God does not kill people's children."

"There you are!" shouted Mother Rabbit. "You know who kills our children, don't you? It is Mr. Ògúndélé the hunter from that big village. It's him you should go and beg, not God; we must all find a way of protecting our ecosystem."

All the animals instantly dropped their heads and started thinking of a way out of the problem. (My rendition)

In this chapter, I have provided both a personal reflection and an interpretation of Ifá and oral narratives to argue that traditional religions matter. I have also argued that Ifá, as a genuine tradition, is central to contemporary discourse on religion in modernity. This is what Wándé Abímblá had in mind when he gave his very influential inaugural speech, "Ifá Will Mend Our Broken World," at Boston University some years ago (1997). The increasing marginalization of Ifá in modern Nigeria will ultimately create cultural inertia if it is not addressed in a timely fashion.

Notes

1. This is a composite poem. The last two lines evoke Bertolt Brecht, and the first two lines are original material.

References

Abímbọ́lá, Wándé. 1976. *Ifá: An Exposition of Ifá Literary Corpus*. Ibadan: Oxford University Press.
———. 1997. *Ifaʼ Will Mend Our Broken World*. Roxbury, MA: Aims Books.
Bascom, William. 1969. *Ifá Divination: Communication Between Gods and Men in West Africa*. Bloomington: Indiana University Press.
Chomsky, Noam. 1972. *Language and Mind*. New York: Harcourt Brace Jovanovich.
de Cuellar, J. P. 1965. *Our Creative Diversity*. Paris: UNESCO.
Ìsọlá, Akinwumi. 1996. "Uses of Literature Among the Yoruba: The Survival of the Cultural Eco-System." *Research in Yoruba and Literature* 6: 57–64.
Kipling, Rudyard. 1890. "Baa Baa Black Sheep." In *Wee Willie Winkie, and Other Stories*. Allahabad: Wheeler; London: Sampson Low, Marston, Searle & Rivington.
Nieć, Halina. 1998. *Cultural Rights and Wrongs: a Collection of Essays in Commemoration of the 50th Anniversary of the Universal Declaration of Human Rights*. Paris: UNESCO.
Odeyemi, I. 2008. *Ogundarosun Festival 2008*. Ilawe Ekiti.
Peel, J. D. Y. 2000. *Religious Encounter and the Making of the Yoruba*. Bloomington: Indiana University Press.
United Nations Educational, Scientific and Cultural Organization (UNESCO). 2001. *Proclamation of Masterpieces of the Oral and Intangible Heritage of Humanity: Guide for the Presentation of Candidature Files*. Paris: UNESCO.
———. 2002. *Universal Declaration on Cultural Diversity*, series 1. Paris: UNESCO.
———. 2003. *International Convention for the Safeguarding of the Intangible Cultural Heritage*. Paris: UNESCO.
———. UNESCO. 2004. *Museum International*. Paris: UNESCO.
Whiting, Bartlett Jere. 1977. "Carrying Coals to New Castle." In *Early American Proverbs and Proverbial Sayings*. Cambridge, MA: Belknap Press of Harvard University Press.

12 Odù Imole

Islamic Tradition in Ifá and the Yorùbá Religious Imagination

Jacob K. Olupona

THIS CHAPTER ASSUMES that popular Islam and Ifá share similar worldviews and that historically their interactions predated modern Yorùbá society. One is also not surprised that Ifá makes copious references to Islam. The chapter will provide an analysis of sets of *ese Ifá* in a verse of an Ifá poem that speaks to this relationship and interaction between Islam and Yorùbá traditional religion. By analyzing these texts, I will show the historical, political, social, and ritual relationship between two apparently diverse traditions.

Scholars of the Yorùbá tradition have always marveled at the body of knowledge that is *ese Ifá*. One *ese Ifá* reads, "*Aye l'aba Ifá, Aye l'aba 'Mole; Osan gangan n'lgbagbo de*" ("We met Ifá on Earth, we met Islam on Earth, Christianity arrived in the midafternoon/at noon time").[1] This text has been debated and discussed by many scholars. Historically, Islam arrived in Yorùbáland around the fifteenth century, and some have argued that it came from the Mali Empire, the land of Mansa Musa, the legendary African king whose famous pilgrimage to Mecca led to the collapse of gold in the world market because he squandered so much gold on his trip. The Mali Empire is also a central place in the western Sudanese state where African Islamic intellectuals and architectural traditions are still celebrated today, in the form of the Timbuktu manuscripts and the ancient mud mosques, currently endangered by the Tuareg insurgency, that have drawn the attention of UNESCO and the whole world. Many Yorùbá Muslims themselves in the postmodern era say that the true exegesis of *Imole*, the Yorùbá term for Muslims, is "hard knowledge"; this is apparently a reference to the tough practice of Islam that involves mandatory prayers five times daily, compulsory training in the acquisition of the Arabic language, and the difficulties involved in the pilgrimage to Mecca. But more importantly, the above-quoted *ese Ifá* privileges the significant relationship between Ifá, Islam, and Yorùbá religion as equals and coterminous while Christianity is portrayed in the context of its missionary zeal and its regular attacks on indigenous religion, which is seen as damaging to Ifá. One is not therefore surprised that Ifá orature makes copious references to historical, cultural, religious, and ritualistic events and practices in Islam. Can we assume that Ifá and Islam have similar cosmologies?

I would like to propose the following aims: (1) to examine certain genres of Ifá and their metaphors in their references to beliefs and practices in orthodox Islam; (2) to examine Ifá's critique of Islamic beliefs and practices, particularly those that are considered inimical to Yorùbá religious practices; and (3) to provide a deep comparative analysis of religious beliefs and practices such as pilgrimage, prayers, sacrifices, jihad, and pietism. My central thesis is that Ifá and Islam maintain a highly ambiguous relationship. I will portray this analysis in specific historical and cultural contexts, drawing from a few of the several *odu* in Ifá that speak extensively on *Imole* (Islam or Muslims). The following *odu* have been identified:

- *Otuurupon 'fun*
- *Ika 'bara*
- *Okanransode*
- *Otura Meji*
- *Otuurupon Lawori*
- *Owonrin Elejigbo*
- *Ejiogbe*
- *Ika 'wonrin*
- *Oyeku Palaba/Obara*
- *Owonrindagbon*
- *Osa Oloyan/Ogunda*

In Ifá divination practice, the babalawo recites a few verses of the *odu* and gives an extensive prose narrative followed by a full explanation of the meaning of the verses. In pursuing our thesis, we shall adopt this method before our hermeneutical exercises.

Odu Ika'bara and the Ka'aba Narrative

Ika'bara
Ika ka 'bara
Ka-di-'bara
A dia fun won lode Ikaba
Ni jo gbogbo ohun buruku buruku n ka won mole birikiti.

Ika ka 'bara
Let us fold it properly
Let us tie it properly
Performed Ifá divination for them at Ikaba street
When they had barrages of evil and pestilence.

The explanation of this *odu* given by the babalawo Fatogun runs thus:

> The people of *Iraba* (Ka'aba) were very dedicated to Èṣù. They offered regular rituals to him, and as a result, they were prosperous, happy and peaceful. At a certain point they became lethargic at offering required sacrifices and all kinds of evil started to befall them. They called Orunmila to perform a divination so as to unravel the cause of their predicament. When Orunmila cast the *opele*, the Ifá that appeared was *Ika'bara*. It was revealed that the reason for their predicament was principally that they had abandoned their age-long-cherished worship of Èṣù. They were instructed to annually go to Èṣù at Ka'aba to worship him and to be initiated into Ifá, an indispensable prerequisite to their peace and prosperity. (pers. comm., 1986)

The babalawo further remarked that the processes involved in the pilgrimage to Mecca, including the scraping of hairs and tying of white clothes around their bodies by the pilgrims, are initiation rituals reminiscent of Yorùbá indigenous practices. He also indicated that the idea of stoning Èṣù at Ka'aba was a pretense by Muslims, whereas the real intention is the worship of Èṣù during pilgrimage. In fact, their recognition of the person and activities of Èṣù led to Muslims building a magnificent shrine with gold for him.

From here on, I will refer to this fascinating story as the Ka'aba narrative. The narrative provides us with an exposition of the status of the Ka'aba as an important center of Islam, a pivotal shrine, the holy place of Islam, and the space for the millions of Muslim pilgrims during the annual hajj. In *odu Ika'bara*, Ifá attempts to accomplish two things. First, in line with the Yorùbá cultural response to the global religious traditions, it domesticates this new religion and in the process expands its own horizons to encompass Islamic rituals and beliefs. One is therefore not surprised that virtually all the key ritual processes in the hajj are replicated, reimagined, and reinterpreted in Ifá. Undoubtedly, this is a subjective explanation of the complex narrative that indicates many references to Islamic symbols, especially the Ka'aba, the holy place of worship in the Islamic pilgrimage tradition.

I will now examine the Ka'aba as an Èṣù shrine, as narrated in the above Ifá text. In this narrative about Èṣù, the Yorùbá god of destiny is interestingly presented as a key figure in the Ka'aba. This bears on an unresolved knotty issue in Islam, the Ka'aba as a shrine formerly harboring the polytheistic gods and goddesses of Arabs in the pre-Islamic period. Muhammad's reform of the area involved destroying this citadel of polytheism and reclaiming it for the worship of Allah. Though Islam argues that the Ka'aba was originally built by Adam as a shrine for the worship of God, the rites of the hajj make a lasting impression on Ifá devotees who see similarity between initiation into the Ifá priesthood and the hajj religious rites of passage.

One of the rituals of Islam in the pilgrimage is the stoning of the devil, which I addressed in the discussion of the *ese Ifá* cited above. It fascinates babalawo that Èṣù is given such a significant place in Mecca. Islam's ritual practice is familiar to them, because it is comparable to the Ifá initiation ceremonies where the devotees wear seamless white clothes and men shave their heads. Ifá projects a different interpretation upon the stoning of Èṣù, however. As one babalawo said, "The idea of stoning Èṣù at the Ka'aba is a gimmick and pretense that the Muslims have devised to cover their actual propitiation and worship of Èṣù during the annual pilgrimage" (Babalawo Bolu Fatunmise, pers. comm., April 15, 1996). The babalawo cannot imagine that it is the same Èṣù in the Ifá thought system that the Muslims said they were stoning. In reality, he claims, Islam at its beginning recognized the importance of Èṣù and built his shrine in gold. This text raises a number of questions in Yorùbá comparative religion, specifically the meaning and status of Èṣù in Yorùbá religion and his reappropriation as a symbol of the devil in Christianity and Islam. The latter tradition denies the central place of Èṣù as a quintessential deity in Yorùbá religion, and in the former missionaries relegated that powerful divinity to being a symbol of evil.

In this ritual of stoning the devil at the Ka'aba, which is regarded as an expulsion of Satan, Muslims are enjoined to purify their inner souls. The Yorùbá Muslims interpret this act of pilgrimage as a reference to the Èṣù in their own cosmology. Ifá quickly reacts to this misunderstanding of the role of Èṣù in the Yorùbá religious discourse. The Ifá priests propose that Muslims who abandon Èṣù at home to travel thousands of miles to Mecca cannot escape the Èṣù that they have abandoned in their own backyards. But unlike the Ifá's Èṣù—regarded by Muslims as evil and abandoned for its love of sacrifice and its insistence that all humans perform regular sacrifice—it is the ambiguous figure that the Muslim pilgrim confronts in Mecca. Èṣù as a liminal figure appears in ritual contexts as belonging to two opposing sides at the same time. As the Yorùbá would say *"as'otun, s'osi, bi alaini itiju"* (someone who plays both sides of an issue or speaks from both sides of the mouth). One *ese Ifá* on Yorùbá sacrifice says that Èṣù's cardinal role is to ensure that Ifá devotees perform sacrifices, because the act of performing sacrifices is the central obligation of worshippers: *"t'alo ru ebo, tani koru ebo"* ("who has or has not performed sacrifices"). Ifá claims there is no escaping this issue. The text explains that Èṣù at home is neglected, because Muslims abhor the incessant sacrifice that he requires. The Èṣù of Ifá takes sacrifices daily. As a messenger of the gods, he is offered his own food first, before sacrifices are offered to other deities. Ifá cautions that this is not the same thing as the Muslim devil. We can assume that the text is a critique of the mistranslation of this cultural archetype, caused by Christian missionaries who translated the Bible. The Ifá text attempts to rescue the Yorùbá's Èṣù from this mistranslation and to place him in the proper context. The refusal to give the sacrifice that Èṣù requires led to loss and pestilence in the *odu* citation. But on the other hand, Ifá sees the Muslims' encounter with the Ka'aba's Èṣù as a form of sacrifice that they abandoned and refused to perform at home.

In the Yorùbá imagination, the Muslim pilgrims' participation in the stoning of Èṣù is indirectly a propitiation of and sacrifice to the Èṣù at home. But beyond this apparent connection, also supported by biblical narratives, lies a deep hermeneutical problem. The stoning of Èṣù, which in the Muslim pilgrimage tradition takes place outside the Ka'aba, is very similar to the way that the Èṣù at home is always placed outside the house or gateway to the city. The pilgrimage ritual of hajj must have made a significant impression on the Yorùbá people's inquisitive imaginations. In another Ifá narrative, Oduduwa the great ancestor and primogenitor once had a conversation about the possibility of performing *hajj* himself. When Oduduwa was asked how he would cope with the hazardous journey to Mecca, he explained in *odù Ifá* that he would fortify himself ritually to ward off all evils that would disrupt his hajj.

In another instance, the Yorùbá vividly capture the most pivotal experience and essence of the *hajj*, which is the climbing of Mount Arafat (*Oke Arafa*). The significance of this ritual is reflected in the Muslim popular lyrics that devotees sing whenever the newly arrived pilgrims step down from a plane, to the joy of their relatives:

> Barika re o,
> Barika re o,
> oke Arafat to gun,
> Barike re!

> Congratulations,
> Congratulations,
> For successfully climbing Mount Arafat,
> Congratulations!

At the center of the jubilation expressed in song is the ritual of the climbing of the holy mountain of Arafat, the success of which makes one a true pilgrim. After the Mount Arafat experience, the sacrifice of the lamb is performed—reminiscent of Abraham's sacrifice.

Also, in the performance of *Ifá odun* (casting the year's divination) in Ile-Ife, one of the key rituals is the climbing of the hill that leads to the Ifá temple on Oke Itase. In this ritual, just as in the Arafat case, the Ifá priest and devotees will gather at the base of the hill and begin the short journey and pilgrimage to the holy temple. While they are doing this, they sing songs that remind devotees that they are on their way to the mountain of prosperity, such as "We're going to the mountain of glory and affluence. Let those who are in possession of witchcraft depart." The songs also contain a warning that those in possession of witchcraft should disappear.

When I interviewed the devotees during this festival fifteen years ago, I was surprised that without prompting, they informed me this was their own Arafat, *"Oke Arafat tiwa niyan."* Oke Itase, the primordial mountain in Ile-Ife, is regarded as a mountain of purity where those in possession of witchcraft must not enter. I asked a devotee in 1990 how they would know those who had witchcraft. He responded that if the witches disobey their warning and come to Oke Itase with evil purposes, they will be killed by the deity Ifá. He said that climbing Oke Itase and performing rituals and sacrifice there require clear thought and a good heart and spirit; and that since another purpose of the rituals was to perform the *Ifá odun*, it was important to maintain a pure mind and heart so that all the problems and issues of the coming year would be addressed.

Thus, *odu Ika'bara* plays on the word "Ka'aba." But it is in the study of this *odu* that we understand the minds of ancient Yorùbá about the significance of Ka'aba in Islam and the role of the vociferous deity Èṣù in Ifá divination rituals. This shows the misunderstanding featured in the translation of the Bible where the Yorùbá Èṣù is presented as the equivalent of the Christian devil by the missionaries.

Odu Otuurupon'fun and the Aalu Narrative

Pandoro,
Oke lo wa lo ta eyi tan
Ki ba wa nilee le, a ta, aju'su lo
A dIfá fun Orunmila ti n lo ree ra Aalu leru.

Pandoro [a type of African breadfruit],
You grow up above the ground up and you have as many seeds
If you were to grow under the ground as in tubers, you would have been
    fruitier than yam tubers.
Performed Ifá divination for Orunmila who was going to buy Aalu as slave.

According to this Ifá narrative, Orunmila bought Aalu as a slave. He loved him dearly, and he opened up to him because he was very dedicated and hardworking. As a result, Ifá taught Aalu the secret of ritual administration, herbal preparation, and the use of incantation. Ifá was an apt teacher. Hence, Aalu was able to master all that Ifá wanted him to know. Ifá graduated him, knowing full well he could practice on his own. However, Aalu became very proud and arrogant. He refused to give Orunmila his deserved respect and honors. He felt he knew more than Orunmila and that Orunmila should henceforth no longer claim mastery over him. When Orunmila observed this, he put a curse on Aalu: he would do a lot of work, but with little gain. Furthermore, he would have to do a lot of praying, fasting, and shouting for a long time before Olódùmarè would hearken to his smallest request. This explains the reason for the saying:

Eyi o t'ofo
Eyi o t'ofo
Fila imole ku peeki.

This is not a loss (IS THIS LOSS NOT TOO MUCH)
That is not a loss (IS THIS LOSS NOT TOO MUCH)
The Muslims keep losing, and their caps remain very small.

The babalawo claimed further that this is the reason why the cap of a Muslim is always very small and his trousers just a little above his knees.

In this *odu*, Ifá places Islam and Muslims in context regarding the origin of their tradition. In another portion of this *odu*, it euphemistically refers to Muslims as the slaves of God (*eru Olorun*) and their descendants as the benefactors of Orunmila. This undoubtedly is a response to the Muslim believers themselves, who refer to adherents of their faith tradition as those who submit to the will of God. Ifá in this text also defines the relationship between Aalu and Ifá himself. Aalu is an apprentice and trusted servant of Ifá. Ifá predates Islam as a body of knowledge and as an autonomous faith tradition worth teaching to others. Both Islam and Ifá predate the coming of Christianity to Yorùbáland by centuries, of course, but as Aalu (the Muslim) got his independence, he began to express signs of strength and a lack of submission to Ifá, a metaphor for the demand that Muslim converts abhor all forms of "pagan" Ifá practices. Thus, a disagreement began between Aalu and his master, so much that Ifá cursed him, which is not an unusual response to conflicts in the indigenous sense. The open antagonism between Islam and indigenous Yorùbá religion is very clear here. The text also refers to Islam as the breadfruit, which is abundant and shows signs of rapid growth. The text then places yam tubers, which grow under the earth, as its opposite. The curse Orunmila places on his disobedient servant and mentee is that he will labor and stress before gaining converts, an apparent reference to Islam's rigorous faith practice (five daily prayers, fasting, alms, and recitation of the Qur'an in a loud voice) as what it takes for the supplicant to reach God. In a parody, Ifá refers to Muslim proselytes as those whose prayer skullcaps are continuously shrinking and whose pants are a little bit above the knee. This is apparently a metaphorical reference to Muslim clerics' dress and prayer habits.

The poetic narrative again defines the relationship between Ifá and Islam. Aalu, who personifies Islam, is referenced as Ifá's slave, an apparent expression of the Yorùbá Muslims' description of themselves as the "slave of God (*eru Olorun*)."

As an autochthonous faith, Ifá sees Islam in the subordinate relationship of a slave to his master. It is assumed that Islam learned the secret of the practice of medicine, healing, and divination from indigenous Yorùbá tradition. The competitiveness of the two systems for clients is clearly alluded to in the text and in the claim of superiority that Islam, being a proselytizing faith, makes over Ifá as a nonconversion ethnic tradition. This is again a reflection of the tense relationship between them. The climax of this tense relationship and the subsequent quarrels is the curse invoked by Ifá on Aalu, the former slave-cum-rival. Ifá's curse on Aalu tends to explain why Muslim devotional practices and prayers are strange to the Yorùbá perception and mind. Those shouting and rigorous prayers and supplications are what Ifá interprets as bizarre practices. If Aalu did not literally yell, Olódùmarè would not hear his prayer. But perhaps the most fascinating part of this narrative is the comparison of the Islamic expansionism and conversion model to breadfruit (*Artocarpus altilis*) and to the yam tuber that grows underneath the earth. While Ifá as an autochthonous faith tradition is linked to the yam tuber, Islam is represented as the breadfruit; both are sources of the Yorùbá delicacy, pounded yam. While Ifá would like to claim the superiority of the autochthonous yam, like the breadfruit Islam is above ground and flowers exceedingly well. As a universal faith tradition, Islam produces more fruitful results in its large conversion of souls, compared to Ifá as an autochthonous nonproselytizing faith tradition. Both traditions have different contextual concerns and different growth rates.

Odu Otura Meji and Asungangan dina Olote Orature

Opo'le
Awo Igbare odede
A dIfá fun Olomo a-sun-gangan-dina-olote
Ni jo ti yoo maa jagun k'aye.

Opo'le
The diviner of *Igbare odede*
Performed Ifá divination for *Olomo a-sun-gangan-dina-olote*
When he was to be waging war round the world.

According to this babalawo's narrative,

Olomo a-sun-gangan-dina-olote was a belligerent warrior. He would wage war towards the end of seas and lagoon. He waged war and even fought his own people. For this reason, everyone started to run away from him. He then ran away and escaped to an isolated place. He was abandoned and became very lonely. He therefore needed people around him. He invited people to visit, but they refused. He then went to Orunmila and inquired about the solution to attract people to him so that he could be happy. He was asked to offer sacrifice. Although he made the sacrifice, he still continued to wage war. Yet he needed people around him. However since he had offered the required sacrifice, the people remained around him.

Babalawo Fatogun further explains this narrative as follows:

> According to this *odu, Olomo a-sun-gangan-dina-olote* was the first Muslim and a warrior. He was always restless, wanting to fight war. But because the first Muslim offered sacrifice, Islam will keep fighting war, and despite that will keep having followers through wars. This is the reason for the saying:
>
> *Idena ko nii dena*
> *Ki olusona o sona*
> *K'omo Eriwo-Osin o mo lo.*
>
> Though the gatekeeper will shut the gate
> The gate-watcher will block the road
> The children of Eriwo-Osin would always find their ways.

Ifá's response in this context to Islam is understandable. The Prophet Muhammad, as we all know, founded his community (*ummah*) in Medina after the hegira from Mecca. It was in Mecca that he found strong opposition to his new-found religion. Christian monks and Jews, to a great extent, made him change his point of orientation from Jerusalem to Mecca. He persecuted Jews who, according to him, plotted against the success of his new faith. Yorùbá encounters with Islam were similarly construed in the text in the context of a jihad designed to convert the Yorùbá to Islam. However, Ifa will prevail against the jihadists.

The narrative is a story of the early jihadists waging wars on their neighbors, and certainly a reflection of the Yorùbás' encounter with Islam, especially at the zenith of Yorùbá history before the demise of the old Oyo Empire. Even though Asungangan waged jihad, Ifá's sacrificial offerings saved him from total isolation and ostracism. This narrative, however, undermines Islam's own narrative suggesting that it triumphs because of the favor of Ifá. Asungangan's sacrifice provides the answer to why he continued to wage war and still succeeds in having people around him.

War and civil strife are reflected in the verses of *odu Otura Meji* about Islam. The narratives above point to a strong warrior called Asungangan dina-Olote, who waged incessant war and was a nightmare to his neighbors and friends, who all parted company with him. In spite of the sacrifices of atonement he offered, he never ceased to wage war against his own people. Ifá's description of this first Muslim cleric is that of a jihadist who wages war against his own, a reference to the jihad of those of a puritanical faith against those perceived as lax. It is also interesting that sacrifice enabled him to draw more people to him in spite of his jihadist tendencies. This was made possible because sacrifice rarely fails. This story is a presentation of the complex circumstances surrounding the growth of Islam in Yorùbáland and the efficacy and superiority of Ifá's sacrifice. But Ifá also points to another interesting response: *Idena koni dena* (that no obstacles can obstruct the one whom Orunmila protects).

Baba Imole *Story (The Father of Islam Story)*

Otura meji
A bi laa bi
Kawu mon gaani
A gi laari
Huku huku bon ni
Edo ba lau lau lau lau
Alaafia lau edobo.

Ifá divination was performed for the progenitor of Islamic religion
That has turban cloth thickly weaved around his neck
After he covenanted with Ifá, he started to insult Ifá
He said if Ifá send him on an errand that should normally take 20 years to
   complete
He said he would go for it in just one year.

The narrative is as follows:

The progenitor of Islam was very eager to learn the mastery of divination, ritual administration, and other medicinal and spiritual powers of Orunmila. So he stooped low under him. Orunmila loved him so much that he revealed all the secrets of his practice to him. There was so much affinity that no one would see the difference between the two of them. They used to go for outings together and whenever they were outside *Baba Imole* always wanted to show off and bring down Orunmila. He refused to accept Orunmila as his master openly, as he was always very forward. He did all to glorify himself above Orunmila who was his master. He would go for outings most of the time without Orunmila. In other words, he used every opportunity to showcase his self-proclaimed "superiority." However, he became more popular than Orunmila. Hence, he had many followers and clients.

When Orunmila realized that *Baba Imole* was becoming insubordinate, he challenged him. Instead of stooping low, *Baba Imole* became arrogant. He started to devise a secret method, different from the one he had learned from Orunmila. Many times, he would do the opposite of what Orunmila would do. For example, instead of using Ifá powder, he would use sand, and instead of *opele,* he would use a Muslim rosary (*tasbih*). He also began to use Arabic instead of the Yorùbá language; instead of using an Ifá tray, he would use his own kind of tray called *opon walaa.* However, he would always come to Orunmila in secret to seek authority for the potency of his medicine.

In the *Baba Imole* narrative, Islam is presented as a tradition in competition with Ifá. It betrays Ifá's generosity and kindness, having agreed metaphorically to fly under Ifá's wings. That Islam and Ifá existed in harmony for a period in

Yorùbáland is acknowledged. But in the end, Islam sets itself up as coequal to Ifá in order to generate more clients. One could surmise that it was the economy that was at the root of their conflicts. The text also describes the different divinatory mechanisms involved in the two traditions, which at times are esoteric and opposite to one another. There is a suggestion of a deeper relationship between the two that might not be obvious on the surface.

Yorùbá words and vocabularies borrow heavily from Arabic, though less so than the Kiswahili language of East and Central Africa. For example, the words "peace," "onion," and "priest" all have Arabic derivations, not to mention the Islamic concepts and ideas that have flowered in the Yorùbá thought system. In spite of this, Ifá speaks disparagingly of Islam and Muslim clerics. For example, in *odu Otura Meji* above, Ifá describes a Muslim cleric as "*Baba Imole* who was always in conflict with Ifá."

I have cited the entire narratives collected during my interviews because of their fascinating details about the relationship between Orunmila and Islam. Undoubtedly these references indicate conversion to Islam and how two religious traditions with two different divination systems competed for the same clients. The narratives also point to similarities between Christianity and Islam in their material sense: divining chain/rosary, divining powder/sand, and Yorùbá/Arabic. They acknowledge that Islam gained the upper hand, but not without telling us the common message we hear from Ifá about the agents of converted religions—Islam and Christianity are always seeking their secret knowledge, while publicly denying their relationship.

The above narratives and the limited interpretation I have given indicate the interaction between Islam and Ifá divination tradition in the southwestern part of Nigeria. We can assume that these stories came about as a result of Islam's encounter with the primary indigenous Yorùbá religion, during which Yorùbá not only reacted to this new monotheistic religion but indeed provided a critique of its standards and practices, and ultimately absorbed some of these practices and beliefs into its own worldview. This is consonant with the Yorùbá penchant for elasticity and Yorùbá's ability to domesticate other traditions that may be said to be in competition with its own thought system. It is interesting that a sizable number of Ifá diviners today are Muslim converts who revere both traditions, and serve as guides in the symbiotic relationship between the two cultures. These texts also point at the stereotypes that Ifá devotees and early Yorùbá Muslims had about each other.

Notes

1. All translations are mine.

PART III.
IFÁ IN THE AFRO-ATLANTIC

13 Ifá Divination as Sacred Compass for Reading Self and World

Velma Love

My GRANDFATHER WAS a diviner of sorts. He used an ordinary deck of cards to investigate the mysteries surrounding the meaning of life. Someone taught him. I don't know who, so I begin this paper with an *oriki* to my diviner ancestors, known and unknown.

> The ancestral grounds on which I stand are scattered with debris: fragmented bones and broken shells, beads of glass and beads of stone. But these grounds are not a desolate wasteland, nor a distant island, for they may be found in the midst of the hustle and bustle of New York City and in the tranquillity of the quiet countryside. Memories of the African ancestors saturate this landscape, extending to the other side of the waters where in a previous life the ancestors communicated with the divine and consulted the Oracle for answers to life's perplexing questions. As enslaved Africans in a strange New World, these ancestors turned to the memories embedded deep in the soul and they called forth the wisdom of the gods to make meaning of life. Their descendants have done no less.

Generations removed from West Africa, and from the ancient spiritual technology of Ifá divination, how is it that African Americans came to know, understand, embrace, and appropriate the odu literary corpus and its accompanying ceremonial and ritual practices? How and why have they engaged these traditions? In search of answers to these questions, I conducted a field study in New York City and Oyotuniji Village, South Carolina. Without exception, the nineteen individuals with whom I conducted formal interviews and many others with whom I had casual conversations said that the accuracy of their first reading was one of the compelling factors that ultimately led to their embrace of the tradition. For them the divination narrative was an uncanny, near-magical construction of sacred knowledge, a sacred compass that helped them get their bearings in life.

According to an initiated priest of thirty-five years in the Orisha tradition, any client or practitioner "comes to the fullness of the religion with a story to tell. . . . It is the role of the priest to understand this story and help the client re-write it" (Scott and Torres 2002, 53). Commonly referred to as a "reading," divination is the means through which the client's story is revealed and interpreted. A young African American woman tells her story:

> I was living in Manhattan at the time, on the Upper West Side, at the edge of Harlem. I had always known that I had a keenly sensitive spiritual self. I dreamed a lot and had visions, sometimes even when I was not asleep. I didn't know what to do with this, and I was looking for help. I was on an ordination track with the AME Zion Church, but still I felt that something was missing. So when my friend called and told me that a Yorùbá priest was going to be at her house on Saturday evening and suggested that maybe I would want to come and get a reading, I was a little bit leery, but I jumped at the chance. As soon as I saw the priest he said, "You know spirits." I was puzzled and I didn't say anything. He continued, "There are lots of spirits around you. You have lots of dreams. You can't be getting anything out of all that." Then he cast the divining chain and he said, "Oh, we can't go any further. We have to stop here because it says you are at war with the mothers. You will need a head feeding."
>
> I had absolutely no idea what he was talking about. He was from out of town and referred me to a local priest for follow-up work. A few weeks later when I walked into that Bronx apartment, I felt this powerful energy in the room. It was an energy that I had not felt before. I sat on the mat across from the priest and he did some prayers in a language I didn't understand and he threw the shells, made some marks on a paper, and began to tell me things about myself. I couldn't believe he could tell me all these things. He told me to go to the doctor, that I had a problem that needed medical attention. I already had a medical appointment, but there was no way he could have known this. There were other things too, and all that he said just made me more curious. Just in that moment, that moment when I sat down on the mat, a whole new world opened up to me.
>
> During the reading he started talking about orisha, which I wasn't even sure if he meant spirits or entities, or energies or what that were speaking to him. I just knew that I wanted to know about whoever or whatever was giving him this information. Afterwards, I did go to the doctor, and I learned that I had several fibroid tumors that needed to be removed. Before scheduling the surgery I went back to the priest for another reading, secretly hoping that he would tell me that the surgery would not be necessary. But I didn't even have a chance to ask my question, for as soon as I sat on the mat and he threw the shells, he said, "So when are you going to have your surgery?" That's the first thing he said. . . . I don't recall what else. Then he began to give me my prescriptions. I was so amazed by the process I didn't even think to ask questions.
>
> One of my prescriptions was to set up an altar to the ancestors and to three of the orisha (Oshun, Yemonya, and Oya) whom he said were guiding me. After I set up the altars with the different symbols and colors, I slowly be-

gan to understand on a different level what this was all about. I felt connected or reconnected in some way that I still can't fully explain. I really felt like I was recapturing something that was lost ages ago. It seems like a whirlwind of changes happened after those first readings. I had a sense of peace before and after the surgery, such that people were saying there was something different about me, a kind of lightness and brightness.

I felt an internal shift, but I wasn't quite sure what the changes were. I felt stronger and I felt a new sense of possibility. I guess I felt like this was the closest I had come to knowing my life's purpose and destiny. So this gave me a new sense of resolve, to live life fully. But the journey has been difficult. I've participated in two other rituals. I received the elekes and the warriors and at the time did not know what this meant. I've learned more and I've become more familiar with those energies. But the past few months have been difficult. I've experienced a lot of spiritual unrest. I felt like I was wrestling, struggling to break through some resistance, but I knew it was not going to last forever.

Now, it feels like this difficult period is past and I'm ready for the next thing, the initiation into the religion, if I can get the money. I'm excited about it and I think it will help usher me into getting those answers I was seeking about my visions and dreams and what to do with all of that. My life has changed. I'm more connected to myself because I'm connected to the ancestors. I think this is providing an avenue for me to use my spiritual expression in new ways. My whole sense of self as a black person living in this country has been fragmented. I was adopted as an infant. I never knew my biological mother, so having the ancestral connection is really a big thing. It's like glue that allows me to put myself together and to be whole. (Anonymous graduate student, pers. comm., New York City, June 2002)

This is an abbreviated version of one person's—whom I will call "Beverly"—story about the reconstruction of self. A closer look at this story reveals a mythological paradigm—a hero/heroine's journey. Phase 1, departure, starts with Beverly's self-assessment: "I was drawn to it [the Yorùbá religion] because I was feeling like I needed some other spiritual avenues through which to express myself" (Anonymous graduate student, pers. comm., New York City, June 2002). Beverly, as the heroine, was called forth from the familiar to the unknown into an "ontological journey" of self. She speaks of the challenges: "The journey has been difficult. . . . I've experienced a lot of spiritual unrest. I felt like I was wrestling, struggling to break through some resistance, but I knew it was not going to last forever" (Anonymous graduate student, pers. comm., New York City, June 2002). She speaks of the fulfillment—phase 2: "Now it feels like this difficult period is past. . . . My life is changed. I'm more connected to myself because I'm connected to the ancestors. . . . My whole sense of self as a black person in this country has been fragmented. . . . so having this ancestral connection is really a big thing. It's like glue that allows me to put myself together, to be whole." In this scenario, Beverly speaks of change and a sense of "connectedness" heretofore missing in her life. The story suggests that she has experienced the "dark night of the soul" followed by a breakthrough, and is about to enter phase 3, one of reintegration, reformulation, return. She comments that she is looking forward to the next step, initiation into the religion, because she believes she will find more answers to her quest for understanding herself and her life's purpose. This conscious quest for self-understanding started with her divination session and the ensuing prescriptions. Though she did not elaborate in this account of her experiences, Beverly mentions setting up altars and participating in ceremonies, activities that in the Orisha tradition are essential to the reconstruction of self. A more detailed discussion follows.

Ceremony and Ritual

According to Scott and Torres, both longtime priests of the tradition, "the Orisha tradition is a psycho-social-spiritual healing, evolutionary system [that] can bring about changes in body, mind and spirit at the individual as well as the communal level" (Scott and Torres 2002, 14). They suggest that in Orisha ceremonies, certain distinguishing drum rhythms and *oriki* chants are used to attract particular energies, create certain moods, and evoke certain responses. John Mason, a priest of Obatala and an accomplished musician, confirms the "indispensable role music plays" in the Yorùbá religion. Amazed by the fact that Cubans, African Americans, and Puerto Ricans were so moved by the sonic and spiritual power of song and dance that they memorized hundreds of songs in a language they did not know or understand, Mason collected, translated, and published *Orin Orisha: Songs for Selected Heads.* The volume includes songs and chants for each of the major orisha. Of the task of the master drummer and lead singer, Mason says they use tratado, a played or sung discourse or narrative that speaks of historically important places, persons, or events (J. Mason 1992, 7). He further notes that through the medium of sound, the drummer or singer is able to evoke and direct tremendously potent psychic forces.

This could explain why many of the participants in this study said they were first involved in the music and dance before they began to embrace the religion. Of the nineteen persons who participated in the study, eight of them mentioned music, drumming, and dance as major factors that drew them to the religion. One person commented that growing up in the Catholic Church she learned that "one song is worth seven prayers," and she firmly believes in the power of song. She sings nearly every weekend for a bembe in New York.[1]

There could be no bembe without song. Why? Because the lyric voice, as Frederick Ruf explains, reflects the self at the deepest, most intimate level. In other words, a moan tells us something that a story does not (Ruf 1997).[2] Note the following example:

It was midday on a Sunday morning in Sheldon, South Carolina. My friend, my brother and I were at the Best Western hotel waiting for one of the senior priests of Oyotunji Village to return for a scheduled meeting with us. The temperature was mild and though the skies were gray and overcast, it was no longer raining. Tiring of waiting, we decided to drive over to the village, a short ways—perhaps about a mile—down the road, and walk around the grounds. We drove through the trees, down a bumpy, winding dirt road, parked the car, and entered just as the tour guide was telling two visitors that if they hurried they would be able to watch part of a ceremony. He motioned for us to come quickly and follow him. He led us toward an enclosed ritual space with an open entrance area where we could stand and peer in. Several men and women were singing and chanting to the music of the drums and other traditional instruments. They were dressed in traditional African attire in white and wore red stoles draped across their shoulders. They were speaking in Yorùbá and for the most part I did not understand what they were saying. I was, however, able to decipher one phrase and it was uttered with such reverence and emotion that I knew a prayer had been spoken. The words were "Adupe, baba, adupe." I whispered to Beverly, "I think she is praying. She just said, 'thank you, father, thank you.'" Even though I did not understand the language, I understood the presence created by the words spoken. In the witnessing of this ceremony, I had recognized the power of the lyric voice. However, the power was not in the words alone, but in the context, in the embodiment, and in the performance. (Anonymous graduate student, pers. comm., New York City, June 2002)

The above ethnographic scene is an account of a ceremony that I caught a glimpse of at Oyotunji Village, a South Carolina community of African American Yorùbá practitioners. It is an example of the lyric voice that creates a presence in Yorùbá ceremony. Attendance at such ceremonies is generally a part of the re-creation and establishment of the self in the religious tradition. Ceremony is one of the ways through which practitioners develop a rapport with Orisha energy. Experienced musicians know how to pace the music, and they know which rhythms and which tones are used to evoke each orisha. When an orisha possesses a devotee and speaks to the guests, the speaking voice is not always the same, but movement and gesture are universal. It is through the characteristic movements that one recognizes the Orisha energy communicating. It is thus the embodied voice that makes a difference. Scott and Torres remind us that even though "it may appear that one is building a rapport with something outside yourself, you are really building an inner rapport. It is by tapping the Orisha energy within that one can better understand the information" (Scott and Torres 2002, 57).

This rapport with Orisha energy starts with a ceremony that marks one's formal entrance into the religion. In the *Lucumi* tradition, this initial ceremony, one that Beverly alluded to in her story, is referred to as "receiving the elekes" or the "beads." She received five strands of beads, each a different color configuration, one for each of five major deities. Just as important as the beads themselves and what they represent, however, is the ritual process by which they are received. The term "receive" is significant and seems to place the recipient in a passive role, but this is only partly true. In the "receiving" of the beads, things are done to the initiate, but the initiate is also an active participant and the ritual process represents a kind of self-transformation.

The first phase of this process is a form of "departure" from the old self. The initiate is "washed" with a special herbal mixture, and the old clothes are cut off and discarded. The initiate is dressed in white, and after participating in a ritual behind closed doors, shares a meal with her new ritual family. But she is considered a "baby" now and as such must sit on the floor and eat her food with a spoon. The plate, the floor, the spoon, and the white dress are ordinary objects without special meaning, but here in the ritual context special meanings are given. As studies of cultural performance have pointed out, "meaning is not latent in ritual signs and awaiting discovery; instead, people involved in ritual performances engage signs and activate them" (M. Mason 1994, 25).[3]

This ritual marks the beginning of a new understanding of self, and it establishes a new set of social relationships. The priest from whom the initiate received her "elekes" becomes her "godfather," a kind of teacher, mentor, and role model; the priest is responsible, to a great extent, for Beverly's growth and development in the religion, for much of the learning is not "cognitive" but experiential, relational, and communal. Beverly's godfather trains her the way his godmother trained him: "564 Amsterdam Avenue, New York City, New York . . . Mercedes Nobles, Obanjoko, sits in her apartment delegating, instructing, and commanding, attracting, creating and recreating her 'Pueblo,' an enriching community . . . a culture in raw creation . . . each individual representing a thread in the fabric of her ever-evolving community" (Scott and Torres 2002, 39). Beverly will have subsequent divination readings from her godfather, and will consult him for guidance in interpreting and understanding dreams and other vectors of spiritual knowledge. The godfather and godmother will play significant roles in helping Beverly to develop proficiency in reading self and re-storying life. Beverly contacts her godfather on a weekly basis to find out if he has information or prescriptions for her. Generally, he tells her the result of her energy reading for the week, but does not discuss the *odu* that came forth in divination—which again supports the point that it is not the text so much as the person that is significant.

Altars: Art, Icons, and Symbols

In the above case study, Beverly mentions setting up altars and establishing connection with her ancestors as very significant aspects of her life. What problematic cultural or psychological situation has been addressed? For Beverly, it was a feeling of alienation, fragmentation, and disconnection. Perhaps for this reason, establishing an altar for one's ancestors is considered very important in the Orisha traditions. Such rituals of remembrance are integral to the African cosmology and indicate the cultural value placed on the "birth, death, rebirth" life cycle. Death is considered a moment of transition from one form to another, material to spirit, from embodied to disembodied existence. Orisha traditions teach that ancestral spirits can be accessed and engaged as support in the vicissitudes of life. Beverly established a basic ancestral altar, which included one or more glasses of water, a white candle, pictures of her deceased mother and father, a Bible, and sometimes fresh-cut flowers, all attractively arranged on a shelf covered with a white cloth. She prays in front of the altar and seeks guidance from the spirits of her ancestors. One of her deceased relatives often appears in her dreams. Her godfather has told her not to be afraid of shadows or feeling a presence in her room, for accepting and understanding this phenomenon is a part of her spiritual development. Thus the ancestral altar is a critical part of Beverly's reconstruction of self.

In addition to ancestral altars, Orisha practitioners also establish altars for their most important deities, particularly their guardian orisha, the one who is said to rule the head, the center of spiritual life. In one of her readings, Beverly's godfather told her that she was a child of Oshun and should find ways to engage the energy of Oshun. After several informal conversations, Beverly learned that "Oshun is creativity, sensuality, sexuality, joy, and love. Her number is five; her symbols include the peacock, the catfish, the pineapple, as well as combs, mirrors, and brass bangles; her colors are yellow and orange."[4] Using items from this list, Beverly erected an altar to Oshun and included more "Oshun colors" in her wardrobe as well as her home decor. In these ways she began to embody the Orisha traditions, reflecting not only a new understanding of self but also a new expression of the energy matrix called Oshun. Thus not only has Beverly changed, but so has the Oshun text. And what we see here is an integration of myth and ritual, signs and symbols in aspects of personal development as well as in the transmission of culture and the expansion of social knowledge.

In explaining this phenomenon, Clyde Ford suggests that the orisha should be viewed as "personifications of those archetypal energies that manifest in nature and within human life. . . . The individual, through ritual address, possesses the gods and goddesses as a way of repossessing those essential, divine aspects of one's self" (1999, 145). Soyinka refers to these archetypal energies of the Yorùbá pantheon as "essence-ideals," reflecting the self. Drawing examples from the Yorùbá pantheon of deities to illustrate his point, Soyinka focuses on Ogun, who in Yorùbá mythology is considered the "lord of the road" (1976, 1).

In the ontological journey of self, Ogun is the one who clears the road of inner and outer obstacles standing in the way of personal and social change. As

Soyinka tells the story, there was once only one "godhead" in Yorùbá mythology. This primogenitor God was attended by a servant, Atunde, who became angry one day and decided to seek revenge by smashing God into many pieces by rolling a boulder down the mountain. Thus, the one God became many gods, known today as orisha. In time, the orisha began to long for oneness and realized that the experience of oneness could be achieved only by uniting with humans, with whom they shared a common ancestry. In order to accomplish this goal, there had to be a risky journey through cosmic winds of dissolution to a final reintegration of self. Only the orisha Ogun was equal to the task (Soyinka 1976, 29–30).

The journey and its direction are at the heart of the divine/human relationship in Yorùbá cosmology. The pantheon of deities represents archetypal energies engaged in the ontological journey of self and the quest for wholeness. The guerreros' ritual or "receiving of the warriors," one of the ceremonies Beverly referred to in her story, is an important part of the Orisha tradition. In her case the "warriors" included symbolic objects representing Elegba (a small cement head-shaped figure), Ochoosi (the archer's bow and arrow), and Ogun (metal tools—knife, rake, shovel, and so on). Every morning she prays that Elegba will open her roads, that Ochoosi will point her in the right direction, and that Ogun will clear away any obstacles. As Beverly engages the sacred in this way, she could be viewed as an actor in the play of what Carl Jung (1969) calls "ritual archetypes," involved in a journey of self, experiencing challenges and hardships, and receiving new information for reflection and integration.[5]

"The journey (*irin ajo,* or simply *ajo*) is an important metaphor in organizing Yorùbá thought," and in the Orisha tradition it is expressed in a variety of ways (Drewal 1992, 33). Noticing how often she recognized the journey motif in the stories narrated by ancient diviners, Margaret Drewal posed the following question, "Are all rituals journeys?" Her diviner friend answers the question by telling another story and then pointing out that she (Drewal) is one of the actors in the journey; so he wonders how she could even ask if they are all journeys. Drewal posits that wherever Yorùbá religion thrives throughout the diaspora, the journey motif is expressed in a myriad of ways; the motif is expressed in narratives, in ritual performances, and in possession trances, always illuminating the experiences of day-to-day living (ibid.). The journey always represents some kind of change, some kind of progression.

As an example of such, Drewal points to her work with Oshitola, a Nigerian diviner and ritual specialist who shared with her the following explanation of an important sacred ritual:

> All people who go to the sacred bush [igbodu] benefit from it. They may be observers; they may be priests; they may be initiates. Only we concentrate on the initiate most. Yet everybody is involved, particularly the priests, for there is a belief—and it's an agreement between ourselves and Odu [the deity]

within the sacred bush—that we are reborning ourselves. Even we priests, we are getting another rebirth. At every ritual, we are becoming new because we have something to reflect upon. We have something to contemplate during the journey, at the journey, after the journey. Our brain becomes sharper. We become new to the world. We do there and we see there. And even more simply we pray for everybody. (1992, 37–38)

This is but one example of ritual performance embodying the characteristics of a journey, its tripartite movements of separation, liminality, and reaggregation.[6] The priest defines it as a "reborning" of self, with every participant coming away different, emerging with new ways of seeing the world.

Beverly's story embodies these same movements and it is not atypical. In fact, the well-known African American priestess, scholar, and spiritual activist Luisha Teish calls to the Beverlys of the world, teaching them to understand what it means to evolve at the level of individual consciousness. She urges women to accept the responsibility of transforming self and environment. "Come sisters," she says, "take this journey with me, share this responsibility with me . . . Are you willing to serve in the house of the Mother?" (Teish 1988, 47–48). To "serve in the house of the Mother" means cultivating one's intuitive faculties, embracing one's power, defining one's self.

Serving in the house of the Mother is equivalent to what Patricia Hill Collins refers to as rejecting theories of power based on domination and "embracing an alternative vision of power based on a humanist vision of self-actualization, self-definition, and self-determination" (Collins 2000, 224).[7] Collins also argues that "offering subordinate groups new knowledge about their own experiences can be empowering. But revealing new ways of knowing that allow subordinate groups to define their own reality has far greater implications" (222).

In effect, this is what the Ifá tradition is all about for African Americans, embracing a new/old way of knowing. This alternative way draws its knowledge from "women's ways of knowing," from intuitive thought, from dreams, from nature, from the deep recesses of the human psyche. This way of knowing is performative in nature, rich in symbol, ritual, and metaphor, evoking responses that lie deep within the human psyche. For many, it all started with divination as a sacred compass locating self. For others it started with the rhythm of the drums, the lure of the dance, the transforming experience of symbolic interaction with an unseen, unknown, other dimension of power, the ritualistic replenishing of the primal life force ashe, or the awesome realization that "Words uttered in a particular sequence, rhythm, and tone can bring a rock to 'action,' cause rain to fall, or heal a sick person a hundred miles away" (Teish 1988, 62).

For African American practitioners, the Ifá tradition represents an opportunity to reclaim a cultural memory, as well as providing an inner and outer sacred space for the healing of cultural trauma. Divination has served as a sacred compass pointing the way for renewing self and culture at the level of conscious awareness. Those who engage it are seeking to engage in what bell hooks refers to as a strategy for self-recovery, recovery from the forces of domination that have wounded the "hearts, minds, bodies, and spirits" of black people. According to her prescription, knowing one's self and where one comes from is the first step to recovery and it necessitates finding "a space within and without," where one can "sustain the will to be well and create affirmative habits of being" (hooks 1993, 14). In discussing her awareness of and sensitivity to the "psychic wounding that takes place in the daily lives of black folk in this society," hooks (1989, 30) refers to a passage in Toni Cade Bambara's novel *The Salt Eaters,* where the black women ancestors come together to talk about healing the character who has attempted suicide. One of them poses the question, "What is wrong, Old Wife? What is happening to the daughters of the yam? Seem like they just don't know how to draw up the powers from the deep like before" (Bambara 1992, 44).

hooks suggests that one of the strategies for well-being is knowing how to "draw up the powers from the deep" (1989, 156). Knowing how to "draw up the powers from the deep" is a central theme in the Ifá tradition as practiced by African Americans. It is the "powers of the deep" that the diviner relies on when interpreting the *odu* and providing a narrative that applies to the client's life. When practitioners said that the tradition gave them a feeling of finally "coming home," they were connecting with the "powers of the deep." This is what we glean from Beverly's story. For her, Ifá divination served as a sacred compass helping her locate herself in a web of energy called life. It opened up a new world to her, new modes of knowing that she continues to explore. What does this ancient tradition offer contemporary society? My study leads me to suggest several things, of which I think two are most important:

1. It directs the attention of the scholar of religion to the performative, embodied, and relational nature of scripture and scripturalizing practices, suggesting that not only the odu but all scriptures are both text and performance, and as such call for research methodologies, such as the narrative inquiry I have showcased, that allow for the examination of the range of human engagements involved in the construction and production of sacred knowledges.

2. It directs those interested in the study of spirituality and human potentiality to an ancient, indigenous spiritual technology consistent with the idea of a field of oneness in which all life is connected. More extensive research into the diviner's ability and techniques of tapping into this field of oneness, and more research into the individual's capacity to act from any one of the multiple personas embedded deep in the human psyche as represented by orisha archetypes, may shed new light on how to make greater use of human potentialities in creating "a world that works for everyone."

Both these ideas have epistemological and pedagogical implications, potentially expanding our understanding of what counts as knowledge, as well as our understanding of how knowledge is developed and how teaching/learning communities can operate most effectively in creating optimal learning environments with space for alternative modes of knowing. Perhaps, then, Ifá divination can be a sacred compass for all those who wish to advance new ways of knowing relevant for the challenges and complexities of life in contemporary times.

Notes

1. From an interview with a priestess of Yemonja in Brooklyn, August 2003.
2. Ruf, drawing on Don Ihde's concept of the "phenomenology of voice," discusses contextuality, sociality, and embodiment as aspects of the presence created by voice.
3. Mason's discussion of this concept is influenced by Edward Schieffelin (1985).
4. Notes from Yorùbá Religion/Culture Study Group Ile (House) of Shango of the Nine Winds in Brooklyn, 2002. I attended this group as a participant observer.
5. See Margaret Thompson Drewal's discussion of the initiate's establishment of self in the traditional Itefa rituals observed in southwestern Nigeria (1992: 63–87).
6. In this discussion, Drewal cites Victor Turner's explanation of the tripartite movement found in ritual process as a heuristic tool for understanding the rites of passage ritual as a journey that evokes personal transformation (Turner 1977, 94).
7. Collins also acknowledges the presence of these concepts in the scholarly work of other black feminists, including Lorde (1984), Steady (1981), Davis (1989), and hooks (1989).

References

Bambara, Toni Cade. 1992. *The Salt Eaters*. New York: Vintage Books.

Collins, Patricia Hill. 2000. *Black Feminist Thought: Knowledge, Consciousness, and the Politics of Empowerment*. New York: Routledge.

Davis, Angela Y. 1989. *Women, Culture & Politics*. New York: Random House.

Drewal, Margaret Thompson. 1992. *Yorùbá Ritual: Performers, Play, Agency*. Bloomington: Indiana University Press.

Ford, Clyde W. 1999. *The Hero with an African Face: Mythic Wisdom of Traditional Africa*. New York: Bantam Books.

hooks, bell. 1989. *Talking Back: Thinking Feminist, Thinking Black*. Boston: South End Press.

———. 1993. *Sisters of the Yam: Black Women and Self Recovery*. Boston: South End Press.

Jung, Carl G. 1969. *The Archetypes and the Collective Unconscious*. 2nd ed. Translated by R.F.C. Hull. Vol. 9, part 1, *The Collected Works of C. G. Jung*. Princeton, NJ: Princeton University Press.

Lorde, Audre. 1984. *Sister Outsider: Essays and Speeches*. Trumansburg, NY: Crossing Press.

Mason, John. 1992. *Orin Orisa: Songs for Selected Heads*. Brooklyn: Yorùbá Theological Archministry.

Mason, Michael Atwood. 1994. "'I Bow My Head to the Ground': The Creation of Bodily Experience in a Cuban American Santeria Initiation." *Journal of American Folklore* 107, no. 423: 23–39.

Ruf, Frederick J. 1997. *Entangled Voices: Genre and the Religious Construction of the Self.* London: Oxford University Press.

Schieffelin, Edward. 1985. "Performance and the Cultural Construction of Reality." *American Ethnologist* 12: 707–724.

Scott, Lionel F. (Odufora) and Hermes Torres (Ifaraba). 2002. *The Amber Talisman: Orisa In the New Millennium.* New York: Xlibris.

Ṣóyinká, Wọlé. 1976. *Myth, Literature and the African World.* London: Cambridge University Press.

Steady, Filomina Chioma. 1981. *The Black Woman Cross-Culturally.* Cambridge, MA: Schenkman.

Teish, Luisah. 1988. *Jambalaya: The Natural Woman's Book of Personal Charms and Practical Rituals.* New York: HarperOne.

Turner, Victor. 1977. *The Ritual Process: Structure and Anti Structure.* Ithaca, NY: Cornell University Press.

14   Ìtan Odù Òní

Tales of Strivers Today

John Mason

WHEN CUSTODIANS OF the memories of important, distilled, traditional wisdom are asked to provide an empowering story about successful striving, it must be a tale that will provide the tools to affect today's evils when retold. It must answer the petitioners' query, what does that story have to do with solving my problem? The telling of important tales is like the administering of transformative medicine, which, if properly applied, will be as efficacious today as it was two thousand years ago and will be two thousand years hence. For those of us in the diaspora who are trained storytellers but are not native Yorùbá speakers, these strongly medicinal tales must be able to transcend national language, and speak when told truly to the inner spirit that connects and moves all things. The tale becomes a song that can be adapted in order to touch all hearts. This was true in the West African diaspora and is true in the American diaspora.

We will retell three *ìtan* (tales) associated with specific *odù Ifá*, and then examine what particular past events they depict and how best to profit from the story of their practical solutions when applied in today's world.

What ingredients of a story compel you to pay attention to its telling and then supply you with the much-sought-after remedy to the problems that the *ajogun* (death, disease, loss, wicked people, and the like) have presented? *Awo* (women and men versed in mysteries) must always consider this when remembering the words that show our relationship to prevalent tales of past history. Those epic contests must be restaged and their solutions properly retried so that we can rejoice in reciting the success formula taken from a tale of the *odù Ifá*, Ògúndá Méjì: "Ìbọ rú. Ìbọ yẹ. Ìbọ ṣiṣẹ" ("The sacrifice is given. The sacrifice is suitable. The sacrifice is making it come to pass").

Destiny must first be experienced and then reflected upon as meaningful tales. As *asọtàn* (storytellers), it is of primary importance that we are able to connect the petitioner, virtually, both to the actors and to the time period of the tale. They must see and hear the tale as being their story and therefore as the way to their eventual victory. It is our understanding of how they fit into the tale that helps us to prescribe the proper medicine to help solve their problem.

Like improvisational musicians, storytellers favor telling certain stories over other stories. Maybe they see themselves or their friends or family members in the story. Whatever the case, the story speaks to them and they assuredly wear it much like an old comfortable pair of shoes that is easily put on and that recalls reliable past service, taking us to goodness and warm memories.

An *ìtàn* from the *odù Ifá Òdí Èjìogbè*, is such a story:

> There was a time when the *Lùkùmí*/Yorùbá went to war with the Arará/Daho-means, and *Enigbè* ["person favored"] was given command of the army. Be-cause the *Lùkùmí* were greatly outnumbered, Enigbè consulted Òrúnmìla and was told to sacrifice to Ògún and Òṣóòsì and to present them with three *àgèrè* drums, which are sacred to them, and three bottles of liquor. After complet-ing the sacrifice, Enigbè ordered all of the young women to assemble along with all the drummers and palm-wine sellers. When they were all gathered, the women were ordered to disrobe and to oil their bodies and the drummers were told to begin playing a lively tune. The drummers played and the women danced and the whole assembly moved out onto the battlefield with the palm-wine sellers and their wares bringing up the rear. On seeing the joyful proces-sion, the Arará, thinking it a religious celebration of some sort, wasted no time in joining the festivities. Western observers had noted that the Yorùbá and their neighbors would not put off a celebratory opportunity that would keep them from having to fight and spilling blood. Wine, women, singing, and dancing were enjoyed fully by all. Nightfall found the Arará army exhausted and in a drunken state. Enigbè gave the signal for the women, drummers, and palm-wine sellers to leave the field; his army came and either slew or cap-tured the sottish Arará army. This is how Enigbè defeated the Arará and won the war.

This *ìtàn* speaks of an actual event in Òyó history that took place in 1726 during the reign of Aláàfin Ojìgí. Baṣòrun Yau Yamba, reputed to be one of the most capable warriors produced in Òyó, and the fearless *Èṣó* (captain of the guard) Gbònká Latoyò were the two whose job it was to prosecute the war (Johnson 1969, 174). Agaja was the king of Dahomey. Johnson reported the incident: "An Òyó cavalry force invading Dahomey was baited with French brandy and then attacked while they slept off their drunkenness" (1921, 260–261).[1] In the *ìtàn*, the names have been changed to save the face of Òyó; yet the message about the tac-tics one should employ when trying to defeat a powerful adversary is quite clear. Òyó lost the battle, won the war, and used the story to instruct future strivers. Sometimes the best strategy is to invite those of the opposite camp, who strive against you, to eat, drink, and correspond with you. The Yorùbá word for this is *jọjẹ*. Similarly, the Yorùbá word for being a dance partner is *àjọjó*. I have found that it is hard to call a host-opponent a bad name with his or her good food and drink warming your stomach while you are stepping together, keeping time to exciting music. The *jọjẹ* can be used tactically to melt your opponents' anger and change or cloud their minds by displaying our shared, human commonality. Did I forget to mention that a certain number of beautiful women are always necessary to make any party a success? This type of strategic diplomacy is called *ìṣèlú* (intelligent politics) by the Yorùbá. Invoking Ifá is necessary research that provides us with annotated reviews of the historic record that will aid in finding past references and solutions to our present dilemmas.

In Cuba, most versions of this tale replace the Arará with the Kongo as the adversaries. This change may indicate a look back to the ancient, formative, competitive times of the Tiv, Jukun, and Igbo, "Plateau Nigerians," who are found within the Benue River Valley and credited as the progenitors of the Bantu peoples (Mabogunje 1976, 22). Or it may bespeak an update that reflects the competiton for meager resources and for dominance among ethnic *naciones* and *cabildos* (self-help associations comprised of freemen, women, and slaves) going on in Cuba at that time. The diviners' clients would more likely know what was entailed by the conflict being described when told in their real-world terms. In Cuba, *Lùkùmí* and Arará were seen as children of the same parents stuck in a bad situation. This attitude is understandable when we consider that from 1748 until the end of the eighteenth century, it was proper to treat Dahomey and Ọ̀yọ́ as two parts of the same empire whose citizens worshipped the same and similar divinities and created transnational extended families. There is evidence of this understanding in the town of Matanzas, where the *Lùkùmí* and Arará Savalu initiates could participate in each other's ceremonies and refer to the same Ifá corpus. The Yorùbá and related groups (that is, the Arará) arrived in Cuba later than other groups. Their numbers increased sixfold from the eighteenth century and became an outright majority in the nineteenth century. This coincided, in the early 1800s, with the legalization of African *naciones* or *cabildos*. The *Lùkùmí cabildos* outnumbered those of the Kongo, and were generally wealthier and more influential (Manfredi 1993, 559–560). To indicate the tension and distrust that existed between certain factions of the *Lùkùmí* and Kongo *cabildos* over informants who cooperated with white authorities, the saying "Squeeze a Kongo and Kongo talk" was related to me by Juana Manrique Claudio "Omi Yínká" (1899–2002), a priestess of Yẹmọja. J. Lorand Matory related similar betrayals in Brazil: "Indeed, many conspiracies to mass flight and rebellion were hatched among members of one single "nation" or another during the early 19th century. And although many conspiracies were multiethnic, rival "nations" often betrayed each other's rebellions" (2005, 161).

We should also note that the name Kongo happens to be the name of an Ìjẹ̀bú combatant who was reportedly captured by the forces of Ìbàdàn during the Ìjàyè War of 1860–1862 and executed on the grave of Kúkùlà, who had been killed in the battle that routed the Ìjẹbú forces. The Ìjàyè War was a civil war set off when Kúrumí, Ààrẹ of Ìjàyè, aided by the Ẹgbá and the Ìjẹbú of Ìjẹbú Òde and Ìjẹbú Igbó, defied the Aláàfin of Ọ̀yọ́, Adélù, son of Àtìbà (Johnson 1969, 340–342). This war helped to open the way for the British subjugation of the Yorùbá. By its conclusion, the importation of slaves into Cuba would have continued officially for another three years, until 1865, and unofficially until emancipation in 1886. It is very likely that Ẹgbá, Ìjẹbú, and Ìbàdàn Yorùbá slaves arrived in Cuba and modified this *itan odù* to act as a reminder to their countrymen and others of the terrible cost of not sticking and moving together (*kò jọjẹ, kò jọńjó*) in the face of a common enemy, spilling the blood of your relatives. This message needs to be shouted loudly today.

The name Kọ̀ngọ́ is the name of the drumstick that is used to beat *dùndún* and *bẹ̀mbẹ́* drums; these drums are played for chiefs and hunter-warriors such as Ògún and Ọ̀ṣọ́ọ̀sì. This fact adds another dimension when we consider that the drum (probably the *bàtá*, also a talking drum) is said to have been born in this *odù*, Òdí Èjìogbè. Enigbè is also credited as the first drummer of Ṣàngó, and therefore a devotee of Àyàn, the ultimate expression of God as sound. Àyàn's symbol is the drum, particularly the *bàtá* drum, which serves as both repository of divine power and the vehicle to give it voice. Àyàn is the motivator of humankind that spurs humankind to action (Mason 1992, 6–7). Being born implies ushering consciousness, *ìmọ̀*, into the Yorùbá world and being acknowledged. A new tool that could be used to manipulate mankind and the nature and outcome of conflict had been implemented with favorable results. The emblem of Ọ̀yọ́/Ṣàngó resurgence, victory, and cultural dominance is reestablished in Cuba. It should be noted that the first fully consecrated and universally recognized symbol of this cultural resurgence and resistance was fashioned by Ọ̀yọ́ loyalists who had been initiated as followers of the Ifẹ̀ based tradition of Ifá in order to give their construction ritual validity and priority in Cuba. Ṣàngó's *bàtá* drums became the prime representatives of Àyàn's power and authority and also became the top validator of the initiations of the other òrìṣàs' priests and priestesses.

What does that have to do with you and me? We are part of this continuing history. The drum, especially the *bàtá* drum, can unequivocally be considered one of the most important symbols of the African cultural resistance and reclamation movement in the Americas. The following group of men were prompted by the mandate contained in the foregoing *odù* tale to recreate the sacred vessels that would both embody and sound the call to cultural revolution. In 1830, Nõ Juan el Cojo/Àyànbí and Nõ Filomeno Garcia/Àtàndá Fálúbí, two manumitted Ẹgbádó slaves who were both initiated into Ifá, created the first set of fully consecrated *bàtá* drums in Cuba. Flashing forward to July of 1961, the babalawo Francisco "Pancho" Mora/Ifá Mọ̀rọ́ tì, who had been initiated into Ifá by Quintin Lecón Lombillo/Fálọlá, the grandson of Filomeno Garcia, held the first public *bèmbé* (religious drum feast) to be given in the United States. The revolution had come to New York. A few years later, in 1963, Cristobal Oliana/Qba Ìlú Mi (1924–1994), a priest of the òrìṣà Aganjú, compelled by the *odù Ifá, Òdí Èjìogbè* (cast during his 1959 initiation in a *Lùkùmí*-Arará Savalu *cabildo* in Matanzas, Cuba) led a group of fellow initiates in the construction of the first set of *bàtá* to be made in the United States (Mason 1992, 13–19). I began playing drums in 1963 at the age of fifteen years old. Cristobal Oliana initiated me as a priest of Obatala in 1970. It was the drum and *odù* that revealed the Enigbè and brought me to the revolution that is òrìṣà.

My godfather and teacher Cristobal Oliana would always speak of this *ìtan* as instructing us in the use of the powers of wine and intoxication (wanting to feel good), women and sex (needing intercourse), and song and theatrical performance (seeking to be seen, heard, and lauded) to put an opponent off balance in order to conquer and enslave the opponent; he spoke of how we should not be conquered and made slaves by those very same powers.

What story do Americans of West African descent tell when asked, how did your family get to the Americas? The *odù Ifá Ìròsùn-Òṣé* allows us to look at the track that leads back to that time and that provides medicine to protect us. We are warned that this *odù* speaks of War. Death is making the rounds, looking for someone to take. Be careful, they are making a noose to get you. When the *ibò* (lot) indicates that *ajogun fàkúrò* (the wager of war who abducts people) threatens, we are advised to put a burning piece of charcoal at the door at noon and to extinguish it with water while saying, *"Bá omi òjò pa iná, jé Ìròsùn-Òṣé ké ku ṣé àtí ṣégun òtá mi"* ("As rainwater [soft water] puts out fire, allow Ìròsùn-Òṣé to cut suddenly [evil] becoming fulfilled and to conquer my enemies").

As I. A. Akinjogbin explains, Òyó came under the rule of Aláàfin Abíódún, an astute trader and a clever and ruthless politician, who ascended the throne in about 1770. Imperial expansion was stopped and the exploitation of the resources of the empire developed. Slavery became big, state business. "It seems that the bulk of [the slaves] did not come from Yorùbáland," but were more probably taken from the Bàrìbà, the Nupê, and the Hausa (Akinjogbin 1976, 409). But who can be sure? The rapacious greed of the Òyó slavers and their European partners must have made a lot of Yorùbá nervous about their futures (Akinjogbin 1976, 407–412). Death and Ṣàngó both wear osùn-colored (camwood—that is, red) clothes and are both feared for their unpredictable, implacable, and violent natures. Why else would this fear have been encapsulated in the *Ifá odù* record? The burning coal at the door being extinguished by rainwater might have been a signal that the household worshipped Ṣàngó and as such was under the protection of the divine avenger.

In 1776—just in time for the birth of the United States, where slavery would become the biggest multinational business in building the wealth of the country and of slave owners—Porto Novo/Àjàṣẹ́ became the main port for dealing in slaves and European goods on the Bight of Benin. It was an Ọ̀yọ́-owned and operated port. This occurred after the treaty of 1730 between Ọ̀yọ́ and Dahomey, which was reconfirmed in 1748, and which brought stability until Abíọ́dún's murder in 1797. From 1748 until the end of the eighteenth century, it was proper to treat Dahomey and Ọ̀yọ́ as two parts of the same empire (Akinjogbin 1976, 409). They were partners in the crime of selling their people and neighbors into slavery. When there is lightning on the ocean, it is said to mean that Ọ̀run lọ̀ dà fún Ọsán (Heaven proclaimed favorably for the Pealer/Ṣàngó). This implies that Ṣàngó/Ọ̀yọ́ was born (again) and ruled at sea, and that rulership was sanctioned in the heavens as was their business of selling slaves. All rapacious nations seem to cite God as the sanctioner of their evil schemes of manifest destiny achieved through disfranchisement, marginalization, forced resettlement, murder, and subjugation of the primary owners of the land.

Our third story comes from the *odù Ifá, Ọ̀ṣẹ́-Èjìlá*. One of its *òwe* (proverbial refrains) tells us, "Heaven confirms what you do."

> Ọ̀ṣun arrived at the marketplace and she saw that there was great poverty. From her own coffers, Ìyálóòde began to give money to the people, but the merchants were afraid to accept the money. They thought the money was counterfeit and had no value. Ọ̀ṣun immediately went to heaven/Ilé Ọ̀ọ̀ni Ifẹ̀ (House of the ruler of Ifẹ̀) to complain to Olófì and to procure more money. By the time Ọ̀ṣun had returned to the marketplace, Olófì's order that his money would have value in the world had already been implemented. In this way money cowries (owó ẹyọ) and brass and other metal money gained value in the marketplace.

This tale points to the fact that by as early as 1400 when the Europeans had reached Benin, the cowrie shell (*Cypraea moneta*) already formed the common currency among the Yorùbá and Aja peoples (Mason 1996, 37; Saul 1974, 80–81). This emphasized their unity and distinguished them from their western neighbors, the Fanti and Ashanti, whose common currency was gold; it also distinguished them from their neighbors east of the Niger who used the *manilla* as the commonly accepted currency. Copper and brass *manillas* were probably cast or forged from copper deposits mined in the area around the town of Abakaliki, seventy-five miles east of Ìgbò-Ukwu, from as early as 900 AD. The Yorùbá would have most likely been familiar with copper and brass items and the method of their manufacture from at least those early times. By 1500, the Ìjọ́ people, who covered the Niger Delta between the Forcados and Bonny/Real Rivers, accepted metal objects (iron, copper, and brass bars) as money in their delta ports. Copper bars were made into arm rings, and brass bars or rods were converted into leg rings for girls. *Manillas* (made of copper or brass) and cowrie shells were the most widely used money objects in the delta states and their hinterlands, and they spread inland along the rivers. During the 1500s, *manillas* and cowrie shells were seen in Benin. They penetrated the subsistence sphere of the economy and largely eliminated barter. Bascom wrote, "Although tradition speaks of a time when goods were bartered, for centuries, at least, money in the form of cowrie shells was the basis of trade, and tradition also speaks of cowries (*cypraea stercoraria*) being found in the lagoon" (1969, 27). If the Yorùbá did not have cowries before the Portuguese explored the coast, or perhaps had them only in small numbers through trade from the Indian Ocean, one wonders what gave the Portuguese the idea that they were worth importing so quickly.[2]

We do not know the date when the cowrie became more than just *owó* (money), and the large tiger cowrie (*C. tigris*) became the emblem of the òrìṣà Ajéṣàlúgà, divinity of wealth. But we may surmise that being called a child of two powerful mothers did not hinder that upward move. Ajéṣàlúgà's first mother is Ifè-based Yémòwó (Mother enveloped in wealth), wife of Ọbàtálá, Ọba Ìgbò. She is called Ìyá Alájé (Mother who owns *ajé* (wealth)) and is represented by an eggshell cowrie (*Cypraea ovula ovum*).[3] Yémòwó is praised in Ifè as:

> Obìrin sègè sègè, obìrin pàtàkì
> Ó yẹ ọkọ rẹ ní (ọ) jó aré.
> Ó yẹ ọkọ rẹ ní (ọ) jó ẹbu.
> Ó rú ọ̀ọ́dun ẹbu tàn.
> A kó sẹẹrù-sẹẹrù níwájú ọkọ rẹ.

Dignified woman, important woman
She is suitable for her husband to have days of play.
She is suitable for her husband to have an assembly of kilns and dyeing pits.
She produced three hundred kilns and dye pits that spread.
We gathered folded load on folded load in front of her husband.
(Verger 1957, 470–471)

Ajéṣàlúgà's second mother is the archmatriarch, Yẹmọja. Yẹmọja tied Ajé's birth, in Yorùbá consciousness, to several factors: Nupê ancestry; North African trade and the time of the dynastic expansion of his other father, Ọrányàn; his sibling, Ṣàngó; and the market-building efforts of his relative Ọṣun. Ọṣun's "sisters," Ọya, and Ọbà, would join her in widening the commercial spheres of Ọ̀yọ́.[4]

Ọṣun, as Ìyálóòde, went to her royal benefactor, who may have been one of two rulers who would suit the needs of our tale. First, there is the historical Ọlọ́fin who is credited with repulsing the Biní attack of Èkó/Lagos sometime in the late 1400s. After his death, his ten eldest sons divided the island of Lagos and became the ancestors of the Idéjó (owners of the land). Arómirẹ, the oldest, with his brothers introduced the Ìdó custom of wearing white caps or hats and gave birth to the Adímún-òrìṣà. To represent its trade interests and to forward tribute there, Benin established its rule at Lagos in the late sixteenth century with the installment of Aṣípa as ruler. Along with trade in goods, Lagos was on its way to becoming a prominent slave port (Smith 1969, 105–107).

The second Olóòfi (Owner of Looms) or Olóòfin (Owner of Laws) mentioned in the story is most likely either Yémòwó, who was also a chief and was credited with ownership of the traditional looms and the invention of cloth weaving, or her husband Ọbàtálá as ruler of the òrìṣà and their home base Ilé-Ifẹ̀, who is credited in some legends with the introduction of cowrie shell divination among the Yorùbá divinities (Parrinder 1967, 19–22). In another legend, it is Ọṣun who gives them instruction in their use.[5] She is also credited with the birth of slavery. Her bracelets are said to have been used to fashion the first handcuffs and leg irons that captives wore. What is certain is that owó mẹ́rìndílógún (sixteen-cowrie) divination is intimately tied to ascertaining the ups and downs of the marketplace that is the world. Ọ̀run nílé; ayé lọjà (Heaven is home; the world is a market.) Sixteen cowries are used in critical sections of the ritual initiation of the priests of most of the major òrìṣà and as the oracular vehicle for accessing the wisdom of the Ifá corpus and plotting the right course.

The òrìṣà priests and their òrìṣà are adorned with rich cloths, bracelets of brass, copper, and nickel silver or white brass, as well as beads and red parrot feathers to display the wealth of the market. The iyàwó (bride) of the òrìṣà stands in state before the community, adorned with owó idẹ, owóo bàbà and owó irin (brass, copper, and iron or white metal money). The bride has become Ẹlẹ́ẹ̀gbà owó (owners of bangle money). In Brazil, the 'yàwó also wear crowns made of these metals. This not only alludes to market trade goods, but to the older traditions of Ṣbalùfọ̀n of Ifẹ̀ as patron of the asudẹ (brass casters) that migrated to the Ìjẹ̀bú. The Ìjẹ̀bú priests of Òrìṣà Ágẹmo (chameleon), considered female in Cuba and whose ceremonies are hidden from women, wear brass crowns when performing ceremonies. Brazilian Jeje/Fọ̀n 'yàwó, the majority of whom are women, co-opted the authority to wear similar crowns and waist pendants adorned with brass amulets (balangandans).[6] Ọṣun Ibú Yému owns the ẹdan idẹ-abẹ́rẹ́ (brass male and female figures united by a chain in the shape of two needles). This indicates her place as an honored member of Ògbóni/Òṣogbo, Olorì Erelú. Ọṣun's title in Ògbóni, reputed to be the highest, is Ìjókó (The Seated One). Metal crowns adorn the sacred vessels of the female òrìṣà Ọṣun, Yẹmọja, and Ọya.

Often the initiate has had to save money and buy the clothes for his or her initiation, little by little, over several years. Sometimes the institution where the funds are kept is made up of friends and family members who save together cooperatively. As head of the market women, Ọṣun is linked to the overseeing of the availability of credit through the èṣúsú. As Bascom reported, the èṣúsú was considered

an institution which has elements similar to installment buying, a credit union, and a savings club. The èṣúsú is a fund to which a group of individuals

make fixed contributions of money at fixed intervals; the total amount contributed each period is assigned to each of the members in rotation. . . . There
is neither gain nor loss; but the advantage to the members is that they have a
lump sum with which to purchase goods, pay for services, or repay debts. . . .
An attempt is made to make the fund available to members at times when they
have need for it, assigning it to a member who applies for it unless he has been
tardy in making his payments or has already received the fund during the
current cycle. (1969, 27)

Looking again at the *ìtàn*, it could be suggested that Ọ̀ṣun was using the
new forms of currency, giving advances on future *èsúsú* contributions and some
outright gifts, with the aim of stimulating the burgeoning currency-driven market economy and paving the way for the coming system of enlarged foreign exchange. The story could be applied to several transitional economic periods in
the history of the Yorùbá, both in West Africa and the Americas. The Ìyálóòde
would be pivotal in rallying her fellow vendors, female and male, who looked to
her for guidance in order to meet the challenges of the new era and to ensure that
the proper stimulus funds and economic packages were available.
Bascom noted that in Ifẹ̀

women traders deal largely in local produce. Some have been able to obtain
credit running into thousands of pounds sterling for imported goods, which
they retail through their associates. In the last century, however, they could
obtain merchandise produced outside of Ifẹ̀ only from a guild of importers
known as Ipanpa ["compact" or "conspiracy"], which is said to have had two
hundred members, most of whom were men. All European trade goods, merchandise from other towns, and slaves passed through the hands of the Ipanpa,
who resold them in town to women traders or directly to the consumers. . . .
    When traders came from Ijẹbu, Lagos, or other towns, they were not per-
mitted to retail their goods in Ifẹ̀. They sought out the Ipanpa representative
in charge of the ward in which they had found lodging, and were taken to the
Paakoyi. The Paakoyi bargained for the whole or a part of their merchandise,
and if no agreement was reached, they had to take their goods to another town.
Whatever the Paakoyi purchased he distributed to the Ipanpa members who
resold it in Ifẹ̀. Again half of the daily profits were turned over to the Paakoyi
the following morning, when the Ipanpa met at his house and ate together
[jọjẹ]. . . . The monopoly of the Ipanpa was broken about 1911 or 1912 when
European trading firms obtained permission from the Ọni and his chiefs to
establish stores selling directly to consumers, following which the guild disin-
tegrated. At about the same time, toll gates were abolished. (1969, 26–27)

Is it possible that the Ìyálóòde of that time, spurred by her patroness Ọ̀ṣun
and the interests of her sister businesswomen, whispered in the ears of the fram-
ers of the 1893 treaty to make sure that the words "to use every means in our
power to foster and promote trade" (Bascom 1969, 26) were included? I am sure
that this telling of the tale would resonate with my wife and two daughters and

any of my children and friends who look to be given a level playing field on which they might take full advantage of what the marketplace has to offer.

Notes

1. This is cited by Smith (1969), 128.

2. Bascom notes, "In 1515 the King of Portugal issued a license to import cowry shells from India to Sao Tome; by 1522 they were being imported into Nigeria from the Malabar Coast, and during the seventeenth century from the East Indies" (1969, 27).

3. In Cuba and the United States Yémòwó is represented by a snowy white alabaster egg. Visually, it is very similar to the tiger cowrie. It is easy to see how the exchange, if there was one, took place (Mason 1996, 245).

4. An *ìtàn* from the *odù* Ifá, Ọ̀ṣẹ́ Méjì tells how Ajé, the son of Òrìṣálá, trapped and caught death and took him to Òrìṣálá to be punished. But Death, even though the cause of all good and evil, could not be done away with. Ajé Ṣàlúgà is considered the òrìṣà of dyes. It may be that at some time in the distant past dyes were been obtained from the crushed shells of the various types of molluscs—common whelks (*Nucella lapillus*), river snails (*ìsawùrú*), Ghana tiger snails (*Ìgbín Ikarahùn*) that live in the sea and rivers and on the land of coastal Nigeria. Or the crushed shells may have been used as a mordant in the *aró* (blue indigo), *èlú* (red indigo), and *èse* (yellow dye) solutions.

5. In Cuba a "hand" of eighteen cowries forms the sacred oracle for each of the òrìṣà except Ọ̀rúnmìla, who uses sixteen palm-nuts. *Ẹgbẹ́ èjìdílógún* (the association of eighteen) is an association of wealthy women, formerly widespread among the Yorùbá.

6. Drewal (1999) provides thick description of this ornamentation:

> Soon after arrival in Brazil, Africans adapted or established sacred and secular associations for mutual help, solidarity, and liberation. One of these was the Catholic lay organization, or *irmandade*. Afro-Brazilians, whether they were Muslim, Christian, or followers of ancestral gods, managed to operate effectively within such Church groups, using them to their own advantage, and for their own purposes. Thus, the women of Boa Morte carry their Christian icons in procession on Church festival days, as well as their beads of devotion to Africa's gods (òrìṣà) for night ceremonies. In addition they wear on their bodies, silver, copper, and gold waist pendants known as balangandans. Seen as "jewelry" by Euro-Brazilian society, such regalia actually served as commemorative objects and protective amulets. Cylindrical pendants, representing containers for documents of manumission, were symbols of freedom and assertive action or *àṣẹ*. Other symbols (keys, fish, birds, animal teeth) were associated with a variety of faiths, both African and non-African.

References

Akinjogbin, I. A. 1976. "The Expansion of Ọ̀yọ́ and the Rise of Dahomey, 1600–1800." In *The History of West Africa*, vol 1, edited by J. F. A. Ajayi and Michael Crowder, 407–412. New York: Columbia University Press.

Bascom, William. 1969. *The Yorùbá of Southwestern Nigeria*. New York: Holt, Rinehart and Winston.

Drewal, Henry John. 1999. "Memory, Agency and the Arts: The African Diaspora in Brazil." Paper presented at "Global Diasporas" conference, University of Wisconsin—Madison, October 29.

Johnson, Rev. Samuel. 1969. *The History of the Yorùbás*. London: Routledge & Kegan Paul.

———. 1921. The History of the Yorùbás. London: G. Routledge & Sons.

Mabogunje, Akin. 1976. "The Land and Peoples of West Africa." In *The History of West Africa*, vol. 1. edited by by J. F. A. Ajayi and Michael Crowder, 1–32. New York: Columbia University Press.

Manfredi, Victor. 1997. "Sources of African English in North America (Corrected Republication)," review of *The African Heritage of American English* by Joseph E. Holloway and Winifred K. Vass. International Journal of African Historical Studies 29, no. 3: 557–582.

Mason, John. 1992. *Orin Òrìṣà: Songs for Selected Heads*. Brooklyn: Yorùbá Theological Archministry.

———. 1996. Olókun: *Owner of Rivers and Seas*. Brooklyn: Yorùbá Theological Archministry.

Matory, J. Lorand. 2005. *Black Atlantic Religion: Tradition, Transnationalism, and Matriarchy in the Afro-Brazilian Candomblé*. Princeton, NJ: Princeton University Press.

Parrinder, E. G. 1967. *The Story of Ketu: An Ancient Yorùbá Kingdom*. Ibadan: Ibadan University Press.

Saul, Mary. 1974. *Shells: An Illustrated Guide to a Timeless and Fascinating World*. Garden City, NY: Doubleday.

Smith, Robert S. 1969. *Kingdoms of the Yorùbá*. London: Methuen.

Verger, Pierre. 1957. *Notes sur le Culte des Orisa et Vodun á Bahia, la Baie de Tous les Saints, au Brésil et á l'ancienne Côte des Esclaves en Afrique*. Dakar: Ifan.

15 Orunmila's Faithful Dog

Transmitting Sacred Knowledge in a Lucumí Orisha Tradition

Joseph M. Murphy

IN THE LATE 1970s I was a graduate student researching what I called "ritual systems in Cuban Santería." I was led to one of the great Cuban-American babalawos, Pancho Mora (Ifá Moroté) who had accepted me as his godchild. He read Ifá for me several times and at the end of one session he told me this *pataki* story about Orunmila and his dog.

Orunmila had developed a shining reputation as the most proficient and penetrating diviner in all Africa, with the unsettling skill of always telling the truth. He traveled far and wide with his faithful dog, who aspired to be like him in every way. One day Orunmila divined for a great *oba* and guilelessly told the monarch that he was not the rightful ruler of the city. The king dismissed Orunmila in a rage, but later thought to send soldiers to his lodgings to deliver a royal beating. When the soldiers arrived, Orunmila quickly hid in the closet, but his faithful dog answered the door. "We have come with a present for Orunmila," said the sergeant. The dog happily led the soldiers to the closet so that his teacher might enjoy their gift. The soldiers, of course, beat Orunmila soundly, and as they escorted the bruised and limping diviner to the city limits, he carried only his divining tools and a cat.

It was literally months after I was told this story that I began to understand why it was told to me. Who is the senior diviner who tells the truth? What are the risks of telling the truth? What are the consequences of hearing the truth? Who is the little dog who endangers his master and loses his position through his naïveté? Who is the appropriate student of the diviner, and why? Nearly thirty years after hearing this *pataki,* the story remains with me, teaching me something of my responsibilities as a teacher. Each year, in the confines of a college classroom,

I tell this story on the first day of my classes in the religions of the African diaspora, because I have come to see in it a way to describe the limits of my role as a teacher of these traditions. The story raises issues about the initiatory context of sacred knowledge, the gap between the way that practitioners of Orisha religions pass on their traditions and the way that outsiders present it, and finally, the responsibilities of teachers and students.

Until very recently the texts of Ifá and Orisha traditions have been transmitted orally, in rather formalized ceremonial contexts.[1] These texts consist of narratives, like the one above, as well as songs, prayers, and instructions for the preparation of foods, herbal medicines, and the host of ingredients necessary for the construction of spaces, times, and objects energized by the power of the orisha. This information constitutes sacred knowledge in Orisha traditions; that is, it is privileged knowledge that has the power to manifest and direct the power of the orisha. This knowledge is privileged because traditionally it has been transmitted only to persons chosen and sanctioned by those who possess it. It has been transmitted through a fairly limited number of ceremonial relationships, which include divination, apprenticeship, initiation, and mediumship.

Fundamental sacred knowledge in these traditions is contained in the oracular "calabashes" widely referred to as the *odu* corpus, and it is dispensed to querents by a complex process of divinatory selection in Ifá—'*dilogun* with sixteen cowries—and other divinatory systems. Sacred knowledge may also be communicated in an apprenticeship relationship between *Lucumi* teachers and students, which is perhaps most applicable to the context of the story retold above. In this case the student would be a candidate for initiation under the direction of an initiated priest or priestess, and sacred knowledge would be dispensed in the course of his or her instruction. During actual ceremonies of initiation, novices are taught a great deal of concentrated information about the details of ceremonial construction, to which only other initiates are privy. Finally in the dramatic drum ceremonies called *guemilerés* or *bembés,* the orishas themselves may reveal sacred knowledge through spirit-filled priests or priestesses who act as mediums for their presence.

Through all these contexts of transmission, it is always understood that selections from the large memorized bodies of verbal and gestural material are related in a particular context: a face-to-face interaction between a querent and diviner, a student novice and an initiating teacher, or a medium and a community. Though this *pataki* of Orunmila belongs to a large corpus of memorized stories, it was told to me, then and there, for the particular purpose that I was so slow to grasp.

Ifá, all authorities from Bascom to Abímbọlá agree, is designed to answer problems (Clarke 1939; Bascom 1969; Abímbọlá 1977; McClelland 1983). Abímbọlá writes: "It is believed that the wishes of the client's *orí* . . . who knows what is good for every person . . . have been communicated to Ifá who will then produce the appropriate answer through the first Odù which the Ifa priest will cast when he manipulates his divining chain (Abímbólá 1977, 9).

The problem is brought to Ifá, the *odu* verses are selected, and through what Bascom calls "applied art in the field of literature," the querent takes one of the verses as the answer to his or her problem (1943, 127, 130). I am still not sure whether my *pataki* "came up" through the ritual selection of *odu* during my Ifá session, or whether the diviner merely chose it from his memorized corpus because of its relevance to his purpose.[2] For what it is worth Bascom writes of his babalawo teachers in the 1930s that it was "taboo" for them to tell folktales except as part of their divining (1943, 130).

In any event, I am convinced that during this "storytelling event" the intent of Ifá communication was fulfilled, if not to the letter (Georges 1969). A transmission of "sacred knowledge" took place and its source—whether Ifá or Ifá-adapted—lay in the role played by *odu* in *Lucumi* spirituality. Like the *odu* of Ifá, divination by *pataki* was intended to transmit sacred knowledge between teacher and student. The story was told in a particular context by and to a particular person. It took months of acclimation to the tradition before I began to understand a principle of African teaching that is sometimes called "indirection" (Obeng 1994; Young 1978).[3] While my babalawo godfather was speaking directly to me, he had veiled his definition of our relationship through the indirect narrative of a long-ago diviner and his dog. While his indirection may have been motivated by his reluctance to offend a sincere but naive outsider with his critical assessment of my acumen, the narrative also acted as an elementary lesson in developing an understanding of important issues of the tradition. By the time I was ready to understand why the story was told to me, I could be considered ready to progress in my instruction. I had to understand first that the story was being told to *me* indirectly but pointedly. From there, I had to realize that the story was establishing the rules of my relationship with my babalawo teacher. His relationship to me was like that of the diviner to his dog. I was to be a companion, a student—attentive, loyal, and quiet. Then, I had to see that the transmission of sacred knowledge—the truth—has powerful consequences, both for me and for my master. My indiscretion could result in dangerous repercussions for him and the loss of instruction for me.

The story is thus a primer on the importance of secrecy in Ifá and Orisha traditions. Sacred knowledge is secret, because if it is bandied about by naive outsiders it might have serious consequences for the revealer. The babalawo who told the story of Orunmila to me had good reason to fear that if I told others indiscriminately about his ceremonies of, say, animal sacrifice, he would be likely to be visited by real police or other forms of hostile civil authority. Or if word spread among his peers that he was revealing sacred knowledge to a white Anglophone academic outsider, they might be angry and hold him accountable. Might he be opening up something intimate, precious, or powerful to one unworthy to receive it? Finally, and we will return to this point, how is the secret to be expressed when it is the dog's turn to transmit knowledge?

Just as the story seeks to establish the conditions for the relationship of master and student, so too secrecy functions to maintain the initiatory hierarchy of orisha communities. Participation at ceremonies is limited to those who carry certain initiations, wherein they learn the details and meanings of the elements of the ceremonies. Status accrues to those who know the most and most appropriate songs, prayers, dances, rhythms, and narratives. Sacred knowledge is prized and scraps of information are avidly sought and parsimoniously parceled out.[4] Secrecy enforces the initiatory status of members of the community, and the uses of secret, sacred knowledge are the currency of power for those in authority.

Yet I wish to say something more than that Ifá narratives and the sacred knowledge that they comprise and convey are the means by which the community sanctions its social structure. The story of Orunmila and his dog, and of the diviner and me, as its direct and personal force has struck me, has persuaded me that secrecy and initiation are connected to the development of the initiate him- or herself. The meaning of the story is itself a kind of secret whose revelation depends on the hearer obtaining a basic grasp of the issues of transmitting an oral tradition. Again, perhaps because this and other stories were told directly to me not as interesting narratives but as direct evaluations of my competence in the tradition, I have come to see the role of secrecy and initiation from a view that I think might be more consonant with the intentions of Ifá practitioners. I believe that sacred knowledge in the Ifá and other Orisha traditions is not only power over others in the community, or even power over oneself in the self-knowledge that the images of the tradition afford, but mystical knowledge available only to those who have "eyes to see and ears to hear."[5]

From this point of view sacred knowledge might be more precisely understood as a mystery rather than a secret. I suspect that this meaning might be at the heart of the Yorùbá word for these phenomena, *awo*, which has so many resonances in initiatory contexts. A mystery, in a religious setting, is at once something that *ought not* be revealed to those unprepared for it and something that one is *incapable* of revealing to them because they are unready to understand it. In the first sense, the sacred knowledge of Ifá and the Orisha traditions is privileged information that, for all the social and moral reasons that we have discussed, ought not be revealed to those who are not sanctioned to hear it. This preserves the hierarchy and the group and protects what is intimate, beautiful, and perhaps controversial from the gaze of those who would profane it by misuse or attack. And in the second sense, the mystery of sacred knowledge in Ifá and the Orisha traditions is incapable of being revealed to such people, because its meaning is ineffable outside of initiatory contexts. The "meaning" of sacred knowledge is dependent on the state-specific cues of its ritual context. These may be obvious sensory and neural cues of drum rhythms during ceremonies or sense deprivation during initiatory seclusions. They may also obtain in the less obvious dynamics that control communication during Ifá consultation and the ritual relationships outlined above: querent-diviner, student-teacher, and novice-initiate.

I return to Victor Turner to see a powerful apparatus in ritual for the manipulation of consciousness. The oppositions of structure and antistructure bring the ritual "passenger" to fundamental new understandings of social roles, personal identity, and holistic interrelationships among all experiences, which religious traditions consider to be sacred. Turner writes: "The arcane knowledge or 'gnosis' obtained in the liminal period is felt to change the inmost nature of the neophyte, impressing him, as a seal impresses wax, with the characteristics of his new state. It is not a mere acquisition of knowledge, but a change in being" (1967, 102).

In Orisha traditions it is understood that this knowledge cannot be transmitted outside the experience of the ritual relationships that mark initiation into the traditions. Again, as sacred mysteries, they *ought* not be transmitted because information without experience is dangerous, and they are *incapable* of being transmitted because information without experience is not sacred knowledge. Sacred knowledge acquired in the altered, antistructured, or liminal state of ritual relationships becomes fundamental (*fundamento*), the basic pattern of experience upon which other experience can be built and through which other experience is integrated. The narratives and other elements of the *odu* become paradigms through which the ordinary experiences of love, health, and making a living are understood and developed.

I have spoken about the importance of the ritual context of the transmission of sacred knowledge in Orisha traditions and the crucial role that initiation plays in understanding and defining that knowledge. It remains to discuss the presentation of that knowledge outside the confines of those ritual relationships, as the gap that I referred to between the way that Orisha practitioners transmit the tradition and the way it is taught outside them. In my case and that of other academic students of Ifá and Orisha traditions, the representation of the tradition occurs in the college classroom and in the meeting rooms of scholarly conferences. I said that I tell the story of Orunmila and his dog on the first day of my courses in the religions of the African diaspora. I hope that I might make (perhaps all too) clear the limits of my understanding, but more importantly something of the responsibilities of teachers and students of African traditions. For now the little dog is the teacher; how is he to tell the truth?

For it is my story now. When I tell it, as at the beginning of this paper, I make decisions about how to edit and present it. Gone are the *ipsissima verba* and any attempt to reproduce all the modalities of the original storytelling event (Georges 1969). The context has now shifted to the academic environments of classroom or meeting room and the relationships are those of professor-student or researcher-colleague. The *pataki* is intended to be applicable in a new context where its meaning serves to chasten and guide the presentation of Orisha sacred knowledge. Sanctioned by my hearing the story in the initiatory context of my relationship with my diviner godfather, it is now mine to pass on its new meanings to students and colleagues. Yet it cautions me that I cannot pass on the mystery of Orisha sacred knowledge both because I *may not* and because I am *unable* to do so. As a matter of fieldwork ethics I may not pass on some of the details of ceremonies that were given to me under ritual conditions. And I am unable to pass on to students and colleagues the experience that initiation both marks and creates.[6]

Ifá is supposed to begin with a problem, a question that the querent brings to the oracle and may whisper to the offering or the divining tools (Bascom 1941, 49; Clarke 1939, 243). Back in my godfather's consulting room, I had not formulated a precise question or problem to bring to Ifá, but he or Ifá was quick to see one. After nearly thirty years of learning and teaching I am still formulating my question: Why do we come to the oracle? What do we hope to learn? The unsettling truth? What do we really want to know?

Thirty years ago, I believed that my problem was, "How can I learn things about Orisha traditions that can't be found in books?" Or even more desperately, "How can I get the babalawo to teach me his secrets?" The ultimate reason for these questions? "How can I get a PhD and a job as a teacher?" And the better question, "How can I be a good teacher?"

I speak personally, but I hope that my problem might have resonance with all of us engaged in the problem of teaching. What are the consequences when it is our turn to transmit sacred knowledge? Orunmila and his dog have set the paradigm for my role as student and professor of Orisha traditions. Every semester, as I knot my tie before the mirror before stepping into the classroom, I see a little dog eager to tell the truth about African traditions. Even as I write these words, I wonder if they would sound to Orunmila more like little barks.

Notes

Portions of this paper were delivered in a presentation at the Annual Meeting of the American Folklore Society, Jacksonville, Florida, October 1992.

1. While *santeros* in Cuba have kept private "libretos" or notebooks of instruction recorded during the days of initiation, there are many indications of the increasing importance of written texts to the traditions. More and more leaders have felt it necessary, in order to combat charlatanism and ignorance, to teach by means of written texts. It will be interesting to see if a canon and orthodoxy develop for Ifá and other Orisha texts. For an overview of the importance of this transition to written texts, see the preface of Murphy (1992).

2. My colleague Ysamur Flores-Peña has more than once at my request searched his long acquaintance with *Lucumí odu* and believes that my babalawo *padrino* may have taken a Cuban folktale and adapted it to the corpus, a process he has seen many times (pers. comm.). He commented further on the unusual nature of the story, "in all my years as a diviner I never heard of a Pataki where a figure of such stature as Orunmila or any other of the Santos for that matter is beaten up."

3. In the preface to a study of the role of secrecy in African art, Mary Nooter writes of the "indirect, allusive, and metaphoric means by which knowledge is often both restricted and transmitted in Africa" (1993, 19).

4. My colleague David Brown refers to the "secretification" of knowledge, which if I interpret him correctly refers to the shifting quality of what is considered secret among practitioners in the tradition. He argues that the designation of any information as secret is subject to something like laws of supply and demand, so that information becomes secret in direct proportion to a seeker's desire for it—thus spurring the seeker to offer further services to obtain it. See Johnson (2002).

5. Adapted from Mark 8:18, in which Jesus is exasperated when his disciples do not understand the esoteric knowledge that he is transmitting.

6. An interesting case in point occurs each time I show the film *Divine Horsemen* to my classes in comparative mythology to animate their reading of Maya Deren's classic text. In it there are at least four scenes of animals being killed and offered to the spirits. The film is grainy black and white, the voiced-over exegesis is sober, and there is no element of sensationalism in the presentation. Yet every time I show the film, these scenes evoke audible groans, gurglings, and even flights from the room. I have felt compelled to issue a kind of advisory at the beginning of the film and try to explain that it is only our urban alienation from the sources of our Chicken McNuggets that prompts us to be squeamish. Yet all is to no avail. I have begun to wonder if this film contains sacred knowledge and should not be shown to those without understanding. Undergraduates are not "mature enough" (as the old movie rating "M" tried to indicate) to see in explicit presentations of esoteric material the real issues involved. Are North American urban and suburban audiences not mature enough for Orisha sacred knowledge? Are white audiences insufficiently mature to appreciate the subtleties of black spirituality without black experiences? What is the "truth" of Haitian Vodou?

References

Abímbólá, Wándé. 1977. *Ifa Divination Poetry*. New York: Nok Publishers.

Bascom, William R. 1941. "The Sanctions of Ifa Divination." *Journal of the Royal Anthropological Institute of Great Britain and Ireland* 71, no. 1/2: 43–54.

———. 1943. "The Relationship of Yoruba Folklore to Divining." *Journal of American Folklore* 56: 127–131.

———. 1969. *Ifa Divination: Communication between Gods and Men in West Africa*. Bloomington: Indiana University Press.

Clarke, J. D. 1939. "Ifa Divination." *Journal of the Royal Anthropological Institute* 69: 235–256.

Georges, Robert A. 1969. "Toward an Understanding of Storytelling Events." *Journal of American Folklore* 82, no. 326: 313–328.

Johnson, Paul C. 2002. *Secrets, Gossip, and Gods: The Transformation of Brazilian Candomblé*. New York: Oxford University Press.

McClelland, E. M. 1983. *The Cult of Ifa Among the Yoruba*. New York: Ethnographica.

Murphy, Joseph. 1992. *Santería: African Spirits in America*. Boston: Beacon Press.

Nooter, Mary, ed. 1993. *Secrecy: African Art that Conceals and Reveals*. New York: Museum for African Art; Munich: Prestel.

Obeng, Samuel. 1994. "Verbal Indirection in Akan Informal Discourse." *Journal of Pragmatics* 21, no. 1: 37–65.

Turner, Victor. 1967. *Forest of Symbols: Aspects of Ndembu Ritual*. Ithaca, NY: Cornell University Press.

Young, Katherine. 1978. "Indirection in Storytelling." *Western Folklore* 37, no. 1: 46–55.

16 Mofá and the Oba

Translation of Ifá Epistemology in the Afro-Cuban Dilogún

Ysamur M. Flores-Peña

THIS CHAPTER FOCUSES on the use of *pataki* by *Lucumí* diviners (babalao and *oriaté*) to explain issues of authority and to assert rank.[1] Diviners transmit religious and cultural knowledge and assert authority through the telling of *pataki*, sacred narratives contained in the *odu* corpus. This corpus of sacred narratives originated among the Yorùbá of southwestern Nigeria. Originally, the sacred poetry and stories belonged to Ifá, the culture's paramount divination system, and to its specialized body of priests, the babalao. Other minor oracles exist, including one that uses sixteen cowries. But it is in the sacred stories of Ifá that practitioners of Oricha[2] worship find their place in society and learn how to relate to others. It is through *pataki* that diviners define matters of power, rank, and authority.

As the *Lucumí* community evolved during slavery and after the founding of the republic in Cuba, it became polarized. Priests of Ifá, the babalao, claim a divine right to religious supremacy, based on their close links to Africa and the court of old Oyo in Nigeria. By contrast the *obá oriaté*, a Creole institution, vigorously disputes such claims. The nature of the debate has become increasingly complex, as both sides have drawn on the same corpus of stories to validate their rights and traditions.[3]

Enslaved Yorùbá, along with members of other ethnic groups, were forced to live radically different lives in Cuba. Slavery did not diminish their need for social cohesion and a distinctive identity. Their native religion remained the basis for Yorùbá life in Cuba. *Odu* stories provided their foundation for reconstructing, redefining, and interpreting the new world.

Odu identifies two aspects of the religious culture. The first is the sacred account of events—historical and mythical—that the diviners use to instruct, diagnose, and solve problems. Second, the name refers to the way in which one diviner graphically writes divination figures. In the case of Ifá, the figures are created using lines and circles vertically from left to right. *Dilogún*, by contrast, uses Arabic numerals. Considered less influential by devotees on both sides of the Atlantic, *dilogún* or *awo merindinlogun* is a divination system that uses sixteen cowrie shells. Each one of the divinities of the pantheon has his or her own set of *dilogún*. The system is similar to Ifá, but is more limited in the scope of stories it possesses. Unlike Ifá, which is available only to initiated men, *dilogún* is accessible to both men and women. George Brandon points to the *cabildos* (religious associations created to group slaves of similar ethnic origin under the advocacy of a patron saint)[4] as responsible for the preservation of African traditions: "Yorùbá religion was preserved in the urban *cabildos*, possibly in the maroon communities, and among rural slaves" (1993, 74). In his scheme, Brandon allows a place for the diverse population of Yorùbá slaves to participate in the creation and preservation of the new faith. But rural *cabildos* had contact with other ethnic groups already in Cuba and benefited from their experiences in the new land. Religious manifestations emerged as a result of this multiethnic interaction, which predates those *cabildos*.

The form of worship known as *Santos Parados/Santos de Manigua* (Standing *Santos*/Bush *Santos*) provided basic elements in the formation of the new religion.[5] While interviewing Osvaldo Crdenas Villamil, the priest in charge of the *Cabildo Santa Teresa* in Matanzas, I heard him talk about *Santos Parados*. Defining the meaning of the term he said, "Standing *Santos* are the old *Santos*, those that they could not enthrone on the head (*Santos Parados son los Santos viejos, los que no se asentaban*)" (pers. comm. 1996).[6]

My research in Cuba, from Matanzas to Santiago de Cuba, always pointed to the lack of babalao as the main reason for this early development of *Lucumí* practices. My informants were very emphatic about this fact. On one end of the spectrum, the *oriaté* saw it as the reason why they came into existence. Babalao for their part justify the present state of affairs in the religious culture as a disjunction made permanent. Old practices developed without Ifá. Now that the cult of Ifá has been established, many advocate a return to a more "African practice." Researchers assume the existence of Ifá as a body of knowledge and the babalao as guardians of such knowledge. However, *Lucumí* created a new religion out of the parallel recollections of Congo and Yorùbá cults, which were later united by the Ifá epistemology.

The Divination Practices

Change did not develop in a vacuum. The lack of babalao, who traditionally had the authority to interpret the culture, required the use of a minor divination system for Ifá. *Awo merindilogun* or sixteen-cowries divination already possessed a corpus of stories, but it lacked the depth and authority of the Ifá corpus. Ifá as an oracle is very important in traditional Yorùbá culture. Practitioners will undertake no important enterprise without consulting the babalao, the priest in charge of the Ifá oracle. Thus, William Bascom characterizes the system of Ifá as follows: "Ifá is the most respected, in many ways the most interesting, system of divination of five to ten million Yorùbá in Nigeria" (1969, ix).[7]

The Ifá oracle and the information contained in the divination verses address problems in all areas of human life. The structure of these divination verses is very specific, and diviners have devised a mnemonic process to simplify the consultation. Many characters and situations became irrelevant in the New World. The new Cuban prose version of *Ese Ifá* lacked all the adornments and concentrated mostly on basic plots. *Lucumí* reduced the introductory section to a phrase or *refrán* that admonishes and sets the tone for the story or *pataki*, "*La Lengüa es el azote del cuerpo; el que mucho habla, mucho yerra*" ("The tongue is the whip of the body, he talks a lot, makes a lot of mistakes") (Cortés 1980, 218). Also, "Olokun was ordered to perform ebo, she did it and that is why she is the owner of the whole sea" (ibid., 351).

Lineages, places, and characters became condensed. A new character emerged in the Cuban Ifá stories, that of *Mofá*. The name *Mofá* is a contraction of *Omo Ifá* (the child of Ifá), the babalao. This character appears in most stories in place of *Orúmila* and represents the babalao as a group. He is always presented as being assigned or undertaking impossible tasks, but by using his knowledge of Ifá he can conquer everything. As a collective character *Mofá* encapsulates all the values and mores espoused by the babalao. There are many instances in which the appearance of *Mofá* coincides with his arrival in a new kingdom, and the struggles and tribulations he undergoes to establish himself and Ifá as a bonafide authority.

Arrival of Ifá in Cuba

Natalia Bolívar Aróstegui reports about the first babalao who came to Cuba:

> In the last century in *Calimete*, province of *Matanzas*, lived a black slave of exceptional religious intuition. [His name was] *Eulogio Gutíerrez*. In 1880, after the emancipation, he returned to Africa, his land of origin. Once in Nigeria he was recognized as a descendant of *Obbas*, kings by a tribe that we have not yet identified. We know that he visited *Ife* where he received Orula's message claiming him as his child . . . *Gutíerrez* had *Obatala* made and had to share his beloved *Orisha* with the babalao's secret order. They respected him, and he lived as a noble. It was then that he received a disturbing order from Orula: to return to Cuba, the land where he had been a slave, to instate the rule of Ifá, the sacred order of babalao. Gutíerrez returned to Cuba and to *Calimete*. (pers. comm. 1996).[8]

It is significant that the first reported babalao in Cuba appears in Calimete, an area in which the *Santo Parado* practices developed. This fact suggests the existence of a thriving religious community able to support the office of a babalao. If Ifá were absent in the religious life everywhere else in Cuba (as this information suggests), only an area (such as Calimete) where worship was uninterrupted could support the establishment of the first lineage of Ifá in Cuba.

If Yorùbá culture was to survive in Cuba, the Yorùbá had to recreate Ifá as a culture and religion. The absence of babalao presents an interesting puzzle. Some argue that they came but their number was few. Dr. Lázaro Vidal claims that "they did not reveal themselves to the rest of the slaves" (pers. comm. 1996). Some diviners themselves claim that the babalao remained aligned with the court, which prevented them from being sold as slaves. One can argue the hypothesis, but the history of Ifá in Cuba is too recent to accept Vidal's claim of the babalao as being present but incognito in Cuba.

By 1887, seven years after emancipation, two important individuals, an African woman named Latuán, a child of the oricha *Changó*, and Lorenzo Samá (Obadimeji) were also reforming and unifying Yorùbá traditions in Cuba. They revised the *dilogún* and created the new, improved version of cowrie shell divination.

Changes to the Dilogún

Changes in the *dilogún* were necessary to make the system a viable tool for worship and social identity. Cowrie shell divination is a minor oracle compared to the oracle of Ifá. Even those who worship other deities consult Ifá because they understand that the oracle is the mouthpiece for the whole religious pantheon. The *dilogún* system, like Ifá, uses the structure of *odu* and *ese* or poetry. *Dilogún* is the main tool for the separate cults of the Yorùbá religion on both sides of the Atlantic. The principal difference between the two is the manner in which each diviner obtains and writes the *odu*. Ifá's world view is dualistic: good and evil, male and female, and so on. But it also recognizes the gray area between these extremes. Because of its wisdom Ifá can define the areas of action for human and supernatural forces. The notion of *osi* (left) and *otun* (right) sums up this worldview. The concept of right and left is important because it serves to organize the world in the divining tray during divination. The circle of the divining tray is thus divided into left and right twice, that is, horizontally and vertically creating the crossroads in the center of which Eshu, the master of dichotomies, dwells. The dual pattern gives Ifá its paramount position. The Yorùbá view this duality as a reflection of the world, which enables the babalao to diagnose and assuage problems.

The *odu* in the cowrie system is single rather than dual. Therefore, it lacks the depth to handle the intricacies of life, death, society, and divine interaction.

But both systems share the names of *odu* (stories) and often strategies to handle life's complexities. It is true that the *dilogún* in Africa lacks the authority granted to Ifá, but the Afro-Cuban variant was upgraded to meet the demands of the religious community. Several steps led to the development of the *dilogún* as a system and practice. To repeat, the cowrie shell divination in Africa is a single *odu* system. In Cuba, due to the lack of babalao, a second *odu* was added; this equated the *dilogún* to Ifá. This step allowed *dilogún* diviners to draw from the Ifá corpus, which elevated their system to parallel heights.

An important aspect of this transformation is the way in which babalao and *oba oriaté* write the *odu*. In Cuba and Africa the babalao writes the *odu* using vertical lines and circles. The babalao writes from right to left and the *dilogún* writes from left to right. The *dilogún* differentiates itself by using Arabic numerals. By using foreign writing the *dilogún* identifies itself as a Creole creation. The *dilogún's* innovative approach separated the systems to the point of antagonism. The upgrading of the *dilogún* not only helped *santeros* to organize the religion and culture in the absence of Ifá and its priests, but also freed them to give the religious culture a unique personality that reflected Creole influences. This newly acquired relevance forced the second change, the creation of the office of the *oba oriaté* to handle the new, improved version of the divination system. The *Lucumí* religious community in Cuba gave the office of the *oba oriaté* to priests or priestesses in charge of learning and interpreting the corpus for the devotees. It is in the hands of the *oba oriaté* that the stories of the corpus became popularized and were transmitted prior to the arrival of Ifá in the nineteenth century.

The *oba oriaté* and the babalao engage in an exchange that defines the religion, usually from very strained opposite sides. The antagonistic nature of this discourse occurs during the events that both diviners share. The telling of *pataki* occurs mostly during initiations, opening-of the-year ceremonies, and private consultations. By dividing the religious community, these events create tension. Babalao and *oriaté* claim to speak from the text of Ifá,[9] but often the stories reflect their lack of communication and the way each practices the religion. This opposition divides practitioners between those who are guided by Ifá (the babalao) and those who use the *oba oriaté* to define matters of ritual practice. Both points of view are very fluid, and both sides interact constantly.

The structure of the *Lucumí* tradition now allows the *oba oriaté* to be absolute master of ceremonial space. The *oba oriaté* presides over the *Kari Ocha* or consecration ceremonies pertaining to orichas other than Ifá,[10] including the *itá* for newly initiated priests. Itá is a highly formalized divination session in which the deity speaks to the new initiate using the *dilogún* of the particular god or goddess. *Pataki* as art and culture plays a central role in these ceremonies.[11] The babalao performs other duties, but his role in storytelling is limited to individual consultations and the initiation ceremonies of Ifá proper.[12] Devotees often use the services of both the babalao and the *obá oriaté* according to their needs. Still, among practitioners in the religion there is a clear acknowledgment of the babalao's supremacy over the *oba oriaté*. Commonly babalao claim that the *Awo Merindilogún* is "an offspring of Ifá."

Pataki is a direct descendant of the Yorùbá *itan*. William Bascom's characterization of *itan* provides a useful framework: "The Yorùbá recognizes two classes of tales: folktales (*alo*) and myth-legends (*itan*). Myth-legends are spoken of as 'histories' and are regarded as historically true; they are quoted by the elders in serious discussions of ritual and political matters whenever they can help in setting a point of disagreement" (Bascom 1984, 18). It is not an accident that the most formal recounting of the stories from the corpus is the *itá* ceremony. *Pataki* is the main metaphor of the culture. Its topics are as varied as society itself. Topics range from the creation of the world (*Ejiogbe*) and the alliance with Muslims (*Iroso Meji*), to why men are required to ask women to marry them (*Odi-Bara*) and why women menstruate (*Ogunda-Che*). No area of the religion and the culture escapes the influence of *pataki*. It is only logical that the narrative itself became the political charter and the arena to settle differences within the ranks of the religion. When an elder wishes to probe an area of dispute, the usual question is, "In what *odu* or *pataki* is that born?" The question is not an idle one. If there is no *odu* or *pataki* to support an argument, there is nothing to argue. Everything is created by the narration of the *pataki* and its subsequent manifestation in a particular *odu* or oracle.

In *Mofá*'s case, the diviner is always a newcomer in town. His coming into town creates a crisis of power that only Ifá can resolve. However, his practice is always resented by the presiding authority, the *Oba* or king. With the newcomer apparently victorious, Ifá becomes the organizing authority in the kingdom. The following *pataki* is an example of this:

By God's order a babalao named Ollecu-Turá came to town disguised as St. Barbara [Changó]. He planted his red flag almost as high as that of the king. When the king found out, he ordered the babalao arrested and brought to his presence. He demanded an explanation from Ollecu-Turá. Ollecu-Turá said he was thankful for the invitation and because of that he placed his flag (as God commanded) to divine. The king ordered him to divine something and the babalao said that despite his riches and material goods there was a spiritual emptiness in the king's heart. That is why he (*Ollecu-Turá*) came to town. This emptiness felt by the king was like an evil shadow oppressing his soul. Also, he added, the king will cry bitter tears. Humiliated and offended the king responded that he was the one wearing the crown so he ordered the death of the babalao.

The king had a daughter who was very spoiled. She was always alone around town day or night. She went to prison, and saw the prisoner, and complimented him on his red cape. She asked for the cape and *Ollecu-Turá* gave it to her since he was not going to need it. The next day when he was to be killed he gave her the cape and requested clothes from her. The girl gave him the clothes and took the cape. That night she was walking in town wearing the cape and [the guards] seized her and killed her by mistake. When the king was looking for his daughter the whole town was astonished when they realized that the king's daughter was dead and the prisoner was alive. The king called [*Ollecu-Turá*] to his presence. Devastated, the king conceded the reality of divination and had no other option than to allow *Ollecu-Turá* to place his banner any place he wished. (Castillo 1976, 106–107)

In most cases *Mofá*'s tricks signal the collapse of the king's rule. The new order heralded by Ifá will always clash with the reign of the *oriaté*. With great subtlety the Cuban diaspora registered the absence of Ifá and the disruption it brought to the established order, in an effort to become reinstated. The total silence of the Creole texts about a peaceful coexistence of Ifá and *dilogún* demonstrates the preoccupation babalao have about their lack of participation in the development of *Lucumí* religious culture. In much of *Lucumí* narrative, *Mofá* (in some cases Orula) appears to set society in order when devastating events threaten social and religious order.

For example, in one *odu* story Orula enters the land of the Congos who were suffering a mysterious calamity that rendered their women barren and their fields unable to sustain them. Orula divines for the Congos and asserts the cause of the calamity to be the fact that they did not bury their dead. (This refers to the Bantu practice of using human remains to fabricate the *Ngangas*.) Orula advised the Congos to bury their dead and to worship *ocha*, the deities. After doing so the enigmatic curse disappeared and the Congos prospered. Could this *pataki* signal the entry of Ifá in Cuba with the effort to convert Bantu practices to Yorùbá-based practices? As I discussed earlier, the first documented *Lucumí* practices emerged in the slave quarters where Bantu and Yorùbá slaves lived. It is possible, since this is the only *odu* in the *Lucumí* divination system that advises the worship of Congo spirits. The political agenda of the babalao centered on the idea of a practice, which was (in their view) essentially African and peripherally Creole. Even when Ifá itself suffered the changes necessary for adapting to a new environment, it persistently drew from its remembered African matrix for its preservation in Cuba. In Angelina Pollak-Eltz's words: "In no other country have Ifá divination practices have been so well preserved as in Cuba. Babalao formed a secret confederation in which they kept the best of African traditions" (1977, 238). In that sense *Mofá* will always be a newcomer to the *Lucumí*.

For babalao the process of attaining control of the religion is encountering resistance every step of the way, and not only from the *oriaté* but from the culture at large. Rather than obtaining a central position, Ifá must allow for others to share the nucleus. The *obá oriaté* is appropriating many of the duties discharged by babalao, with the exception of the title and the paraphernalia. Referring to the way in which babalao lost power to the *oriaté*, Allan Tamayo explains: "There was a staggering amount of work [when babalao first arrived] and they delegated functions. For example, to sacrifice they used a child of *Ogún*. They washed a knife for him to use. It is from there that the famous *pinaldo* of the *Santo*, which doesn't exist [has no religious foundation] comes from. That is the origin of the *cuchillo* [ceremony]. That was in part their fault, because of the amount of work [babalao had] but also there was some lack of knowledge [on the part of the babalao]. But we [the babalao] are the ones responsible for all those changes by delegating [our] responsibility because of the pressure"[13] (pers. comm. 1996).

In the years since I became a priest, I have heard the same argument used to justify the babalao's loss of ceremonial authority. At present it is obvious that the dominant cult among *Lucumí* appears to be that of the *oriaté*. Most of the religious life is organized around the direction and ritual performance of the *oriaté*. In this, at least for the moment Ifá plays a secondary role. The pointed top of the *Lucumí* social pyramid must be flattened to accommodate two officials: the babalao and the *oriaté*.

The *oriaté* unifies all the cults of the orichas and in fact he can effectively work on his own to discharge his duties. The *oriaté* can and does eliminate the babalao from his ritual practice; yet the babalao cannot do the same. On the contrary, the scope of babalao is vastly limited, and aside from the worship of Orula they require the participation of the *oriaté* in every aspect of the religious life. Currently, there is more ritual responsibility vested in the *oriaté* than in the babalao. The adaptations and transformations the office is making go beyond merely ritual functions; they involve the role Ifá will play in the future of *Lucumí* religious culture. In the past the *oriaté* had to remain in the shadows, but with the phenomenal expansion of the religion in the United States after the Cuban Revolution the *oriaté* has become a cultural line of defense.

Cultural validation in the hands of scholars shaped a vision of *Lucumí* religious culture as the harbinger of African traditions. Most efforts focused on collecting data that could strengthen such views, and in the shadows the *oriaté* was carving a niche out of official patronage. Confronting social realities within the culture, the *oriaté* created a style that could only be followed by others like him or her. For the most part the office is created out of need, a need to perpetuate those elements that made *Lucumí* culture unique within the plethora of African practices in Cuba. While the ranks of the babalao increase because of the social prestige of the office, the *oriaté* keeps its ranks in close check.[14]

In order to fully understand *Lucumí* culture, the researcher must be aware not only of the African commonalities (which are many) but the treatment of those commonalities in Cuba. The mortar that unites the blocks of *Lucumí* culture—Ifá included—is the *obá oriaté*. Granted that the main building elements are African—elements every *Lucumí* is proud of—the ties that bind and keep them working are ordered in the Creole treatment of those elements.[15] The crowning glory of the culture (and perhaps its biggest secret) is what the late Ernesto Rivera Téllez characterized as "the one that goes alone," the *obá oriaté* (pers. comm. 1996). Sometime in his or her religious path, every *Lucumí* worshiper—even the babalao before he can be called such[16]—must say in front of the assembled community:[17] "*La bendición obá*" ("Give me your blessing, *obá*") to which the *obá oriaté* invariably answers: *Santo*.

Notes

1. In this chapter I use Creole orthography. In Spanish all the Yorùbá "sh" sounds became "ch." *Lucumí* modeled titles and designations after Spanish pronunciations, creating a distinct dialect in use to this day. The *pataki* quoted in the text, unless otherwise indicated, are references to specific *pataki* that come from my own training and knowledge of the repertoire.

2. "An Orisha is a spiritual being that possesses a divine power. Each Orisha in the pantheon is a patron of an idea or of occurrences in nature. For example, there are Orishas representing thunder, fresh water, or the sea. Others symbolize the hunt, death, or birth. In these aspects they are quite similar to angels or saints in other religions" (Flores-Peña and Evanchuk 1994: 7–8).

3. By *tradition* or *traditional*, I mean those customs, ideas, or practices generally accepted by individuals within the culture as being directly associated with a particular individual or office.

4. These associations evolved as mutual aid societies and keepers of ethnic traditions. Folklorist Lydia Cabrera characterizes the *cabildos* as: "congregations, always religious in character [composed] of older Negroes and their Creole descendants, slaves, ex-slaves who belonged to the same nation or tribe" (1983, 24, my translation).

5. I use the Spanish word *Santo* instead of the translation "saint." In Spanish popular speech, *Santo* does not refer only to the saints of the Catholic tradition. A *Santo* may or may not be of religious origin. What makes something a *Santo* is its ability to manifest divine power. On many occasions I have heard *Lucumí* elders speak about the Catholic *Santos* when they refer to the saints of the church and refer to the orichas as "*el Santo africano*" or African *Santo*. A *Santo* is both what it signifies or represents and more importantly, what it can do of its own volition. Statues and icons become *Santos*, because in many instances they act independently.

6. The head is the most important element in Yorùbá/*Lucumí* religious practice. People believe that the guardian oricha resides in the head. An elaborate consecration ceremony enthrones the oricha in the head. *Lucumí* call these ceremonies in Spanish *asentar*—to be seated, to enthrone. By this act the head becomes an icon, the visual representation of *Ori*, the Godhead. What Villamil characterizes is a practice that was unable to perform such rites on the head. According to him, they made those *Santos* rather than consecrated them. The only available information about this practice is an article by Rodriguez Herrera and Rodriguez Reyes: "In the aforementioned communities (Calimete, Manguito, and Amarillas) the Yorùbá cult of the Orichas had as a result a cultural variant called *Santo parado* or *Santo de manigua*" (1993, 29).

7. Bascom's monumental work on divination presents the oracular system of Ifá in such a comprehensive way that it has become an essential reference for scholars and priests who

are dealing with Yorùbá cosmology and culture. *Santeros* and babalao who also consult the book for comparisons and education have recognized the authority of this work. The book is an educational tool for non-Spanish-speaking babalao as well. On my recent trip to Cuba, I found that a babalao association in Cuba edits some books following Bascom's plan, and his Ifá *Divination* is considered an authoritative book.

8. According to Bolívar, this information came from an unpublished manuscript she owns that was written by Cuban scholar Teodora Díaz Fabelo. The title of the undated manuscript is *Adendad del Dilogún* (pers. comm. 1996).

9. Most *oriaté* acknowledge the supremacy of Ifá and the babalao, and do not differentiate between the stories and their sources. Many times one can find Ifá literature in the libraries of the *oriaté*.

10. Also those deities associated with Ifá, which only babalao can consecrate.

11. R. C. Abrahams defines the Yorùbá word *pàtàkì* as "[something] important" (Abrahams 1958, 546). In *Lucumí* speech, the word is synonymous with sacred account or story.

12. Duties includes performing ritual sacrifices in consecrations when they are called for, initiating his own godchildren into the cult of the warriors and Ifá, and performing ceremonies for those devotees initiated into the cult of Ifá.

13. Lucas mentions a ceremony among Yorùbá babalawos called *Pinodu*: "For the purpose of this test the candidate dips his hands into consecrated Ifá water. He then receives on the palm of his hands flaming oil from a new lamp and rubs it on his body. If he sustains no injury, he then becomes an Ifá priest who has given proof that he is secure against all ills and will thereby be able to safeguard others against them" (1948, 72).

The *cuchillo* is a ceremony that confers the elderhood status to *santeros* by allowing them to use the knife to sacrifice four-legged animals.

14. Many individuals may attempt to begin to work as *oriaté*, but the community may reject or isolate their practice. As stated before, it is the community's will that creates and maintains the *oriaté*. In *Lucumí* tradition, "vox populi" is "vox dei." Sometimes the *oriaté* may attempt to establish changes and practices that can be adopted as rulings. On occasions, changes can be rejected all together by the community. The success of the *oriaté* resides in his or her wisdom and the ability to guide and serve the interest of the population the office serves.

15. Yet as important as these African commonalities are, many *Lucumí* practitioners (me included) consider a return to the African mode of worship a historical impossibility. We are so far detached from the "old land" that in order to return, *Lucumí* culture must cease to exist. In my opinion there is nothing to go back to. At least for *Lucumí* culture.

16. Unless he made Ifá without making *ocha*.

17. Every priest or priestess at the end of their year of novitiate must be presented to the ceremonial room. This rite of passage authorizes the new *santero* or *santera* to begin his or her active practice. Since the *obá oriaté* is the presiding authority in the room, his or her blessing is required to give validity to whatever is done in the ceremony.

References

Abrahams, R. C. 1958. *Dictionary of Modern Yorùbá*. London: University of London Press.

Bascom, William. 1969. *Ifá Divination: Communication Between Gods and Men in West Africa.* Bloomington: Indiana University Press.

———. 1984. "The Forms of Folklore: Prose Narratives." In *Sacred Narrative: Readings in the Theory of Myth*, edited by Alan Dundes, 5–29. Berkeley: University of California Press.

Brandon, George. 1993. *Santeria From Africa to the New World: The Dead Sell Memories.* Bloomington: Indiana University Press.

Cabrera, Lydia. 1983. *El Monte: Igbo, Finda, Ewe Orisha, Vititi Nfinda.* Miami: Coleccion del Chichereku en el Exilo.

Castillo, J. M. 1976. *Ifá en Tierras de Ifá.* N.p.

Cortés, Enrique. 1980. *Secretos del Oriaté de la Religión Yoruba.* New York: Vilaragut, Artículos Religiosos.

Dundes, Alan. 1992. "Foreword." In *African Folktales in the New World,* edited by William Bascom, vii–xx. Bloomington: Indiana University Press.

Flores-Pena, Ysamur, and Roberta J. Evanchuk. 1994. *Santeria Garments and Altars.* Jackson: University Press of Mississippi.

Lucas, J. Olumide. 1948. *The Religion of the Yoruba.* Lagos: C. M. S. Bookshop.

Pollak-Eltz, Angelina. 1977. *Cultos afroamericanos (vudú y hechicería en las Américas).* Caracas: Universidad Católica Andrés Bello.

Rodriguez Herrera, Ilean, and Andres Rodriguez Reyes. 1993. "Los santos pardos o santos de manigua." *Del Caribe* 21: 28–34.

17 The *Pai-de-santo* and the Babaláwo

Religious Interaction and Ritual Rearrangements within Orisha Religion

Stefania Capone

ONE OF THE most significant developments in the field of Afro-American religions is the expansion across ethnic and national barriers. In the last decades, moving from secret and persecuted religions, they have become public and respectable, reaching people from different social backgrounds as well as foreigners who are importing these religions to their own countries. The spread of these religions has created networks of ritual kinships that now span national boundaries, giving rise to transnational communities of worshippers—for instance the Batuque and *Africanismo* in Argentina and in Uruguay, and the *Regla de Ocha* or *Lucumí* religion in Cuba and in the United States. Since the 1980s, the proliferation of these increasingly active networks of priests and their attempts to gain recognition as a real world religion from persons in established religious and secular institutions has become an important aspect of the array of Orisha traditions.

Afro-American religions are historically characterized by their extreme fragmentation and lack of a superior authority that could impose orthodox rules for its followers. Nevertheless, religious leaders aspire today to unify their practices, highlighting the existence of a common ground in all Afro-American religious modalities. Since the early eighties, there have been various attempts to standardize the different Afro-American religious practices on the American continent. The International Congress of Orisa Tradition and Culture (also called COMTOC or Orisa World Congress) has helped to create networks between the initiates of Brazilian Candomblé, Cuban Santería or *Regla de Ocha*, Haitian Vodu, North American Orisha-Voodoo and Yorùbá traditional religion.[1] These attempts generate new ways of religious Creolization, in which the syncretic work—the historical base of these types of religions—is resignified, giving preference to African or Afro-American endogenous variables instead of European or Catholic exogenous influences (Capone, 2007b). The ritual borrowings in the *Lucumí* religion of Cubans living in Miami of practices that originated in Brazilian Candomblé, as well as the ritual borrowings in Brazilian Candomblé of divination practices from Cuba and Nigeria, are telling examples of this founding tension between unification and fragmentation within these religious phenomena.

The International Congresses of Orisa Tradition and Culture have been the first to attempt to organize an international network of initiates of Africa-derived religions. Since their beginning, these congresses have set out to gather Yorùbá and diaspora religious leaders in order to unify the Orisha tradition.[2] The main discussion topics at these forums are tradition, religious practices standardization and the fight against syncretism; these are topics that are common to different regional modalities of the "Orisha religion."[3] The networks between practitioners facilitate the circulation of values, symbols, and practices between different modalities of Afro-American religions, helping to build the so-called Orisha religion.

This chapter will focus on the growing interconnectedness between different local traditions and on the influence that ritual and discursive practices, taking place in a tri-continental context, are having on local religious practices in the diaspora. In recent years, this interconnectedness has concerned two of the most important Afro-American religions: Candomblé and Santería or *Lucumí* religion. Brazilians initiate Cubans living in the United States into the worship of forgotten orisha and into the secrets of *orí* (head) cult (Capone 2007a), while Cubans and Nigerians initiate Brazilians in the secrets of Ifá. The analysis of the reintroduction of Ifá worship in Candomblé houses via Yorùbá language courses, and the subsequent structural changes in hierarchy and legitimacy will show how the transnational context in which Afro-Cuban and Afro-Brazilian religions are now evolving not only modifies the extent of local struggles for religious power but also exacerbates them. Mediumship then becomes the ritual pivot in the reassessment of religious hierarchy, opposing *pais-de-santo* (heads of the cult, *babalorisha*) and babalawo ("masters of the secret").

Going to Africa, or The Search for Tradition

Ifá, the most elaborate of African systems of divination, occupies a unique position in what is called "Yorùbá traditional religion." According to Peel, its saliency in Yorùbá religion is directly connected to "its capacity to 'ride' social change" (1990, 338). The current diffusion of the priesthood of babalawo, the specialist of Ifá divination, in several locations in the diaspora seems to confirm the babalawo's flexibility and capacity "to respond in its own terms to new experiences" (348).

Orisha religions in the New World were reshaped within a framework of forced and free migration, as well as mutual contact and exchange. The ties between Brazil and Africa, especially Nigeria and Benin, were never completely severed, even after the end of the slave trade during the middle of the nineteenth century. Several authors have shown the circulation of religious goods, specialists, and ideas among these diverse locations during the nineteenth century.[4] Recently J. Lorand Matory (2005, 50) has analyzed the two-way travel and commerce between Brazil and Africa, demonstrating how a class of literate and well-traveled Afro-Brazilians helped to shape Yorùbá culture and Yorùbá traditional religion, and to canonize them as the preeminent classical standard of African culture in the New World.

The first journeys by descendants of Africans between Brazil and Africa go back to the first half of the nineteenth century, when the movement of returning to the west coast of Africa intensified among freed slaves. This movement, which began with the failure of the 1835 rebellions in Bahia and the expulsion of the condemned rebels, soon took on the nature of a symbolic journey for members of Candomblé toward the land of their origins. Going to Africa, which signified making contact with the source of religious knowledge and tradition that had been broken up by slavery, was rapidly becoming a source of prestige for members of Candomblé.

Several stories remain about the most renowned characters of Bahian Candomblé's comings and goings between Brazil and Africa. The most celebrated example is undoubtedly that of Martiniano Eliseu do Bonfim. Nina Rodrigues's informant and collaborator and a legendary figure of Bahia Candomblé, Martiniano do Bonfim went to Nigeria for the first time with his father in 1875, and he stayed in Lagos until 1886. Roger Bastide justified his travels based on his desire "to learn the art of divination," and he later became "the most prestigious *babalaô* in Bahia" (1978, 165).[5] This first journey earned Martiniano do Bonfim great prestige among the members of Candomblé, and very soon he became a much-sought-after babalaô (diviner) (Verger 1981, 32). In 1910, Martiniano helped Aninha (Eugenia Ana dos Santos) to found the Axé Opô Afonjá *terreiro* (cult house), which is considered as representative of "African tradition" in Brazil today. Martiniano, who died in 1943 (Carneiro 1986, 120), is generally considered one of the last babalaôs in Brazil, along with Felisberto Sowzer who was part of a "dynasty of Brazilian-Lagosian travellers and priests that began with his diviner grandfather from Oyo, Manoel Rodolfo Bamgbose" (Matory 2005, 47).[6]

Other priests who were already active in Brazil made the trip back to their homeland not to learn but to display their ritual knowledge. According to Peel, José Filipe Meffre, who was a returnee from Brazil, practiced Ifá divination in Lagos in the 1850s with ritual objects he had brought back from Brazil; Meffre became "notable and unparalleled both here [in Badagry] and at Lagos" (1990, 352).[7]

The travels between Brazil and Yorùbáland required the knowledge of African languages. In the beginning of the twentieth century, Raymundo Nina Rodrigues (1988, 129) was already underlining that Yorùbá played the role of lingua franca among the slave population in Bahia. However, he recognized that depending totally upon the memory of slaves' descendants could sometimes lead to error:

> The importance of the Nagô [Yorùbá] language in Bahia is so well known that it is sometimes exaggerated. In 1899, when they arrived in this city [Salvador], the Catholic missionaries who traveled around Brazil in an attempt to collect donations for the catechesis in Africa were advised to address the city's colored population in Nagô. Father Coquard's sermon in the cathedral on January 4th was a complete fiasco. . . . it was a mistake to suppose that our Creole population has maintained such a pure Nagô language that it would be able to understand the missionaries; those who spoke the language used a patois, a debased mixture of Portuguese and various African languages. (Rodrigues 1988, 132, my translation)[8]

Nevertheless, this did not prevent Nina Rodrigues (who worked very closely with his key informant Martiniano do Bonfim) from emphasizing the superiority of the Yorùbá language: "It has, here, a certain literary quality which, it seems to me, no other African language in Brazil has ever had, except, perhaps, Hausa written in the Arabic alphabet by the black Muslims" (1988, 132). Thirty years later, the Bahian ethnologist Édison Carneiro reaffirmed the need to study the Nagô language, which is "the Latin of Sudanese languages" (Carneiro 1991, 110). In 1933, Carneiro began to learn Nagô with Martiniano do Bonfim as his teacher with the help of the *Practical Guide to Yoruba or Nagô* by the African Missions Society of Lyon (1991, 113).

Learning the original language is a dream that has persisted ever since. In 1959, the first professorship in Yorùbá was created at the Center of Afro-Oriental Studies (CEAO) of the Federal University of Bahia. This chair was filled by Ebenezer Latunde Lashebikan, a professor from Nigeria. Afro-Brazilian religious elites attended the course, which was taught regularly at the CEAO from 1965 onwards. In 1974, an agreement was signed between the Brazilian government, the Federal University of Bahia, and the city council of Salvador in order to launch a program of cultural cooperation between Brazil and African countries and develop Afro-Brazilian studies.

The agreement made it easier for many Nigerians to come to Brazil, either as students or professors. In 1976, this was so for Olabiyi Babalola Yai, "a lecturer in the Department of African Languages and Literatures, University of Ifé, who was in Brazil . . . as the Yoruba language teacher in Bahia" (Abímbọlá 1976b, 619). The importance given to Yorùbá language courses by Candomblé initiates was a reaction to what Abímbọlá defined as a "linguistic problem": "The situation is a painful one to many of the *Orisa* devotees who would pay any price to acquire the linguistic ability necessary for an understanding of their own repertoire" (1976b, 634). As a result, officials of the University of Ifé decided to send Yorùbá professors to the CEAO, with the aim of providing Candomblé adepts with linguistic competence so that they could understand the meaning of their sacred texts at last. However, according to Abímbọ́lá, the orisha worshippers in Brazil had been separated from their African counterparts for too long: the spatial distance exacerbated the "linguistic problem." He therefore suggested coordinating regular exchange visits, either through private or public means, to facilitate contact between initiates from America and Africa (1976b, 635).

In 1977, officials of the Center of African Studies at the University of São Paulo (USP) organized their first course in Yorùbá language and culture in the university's Social Science Department. For ten years, more than six hundred students, mostly Candomblé *pais-* and *mães-de-santo,* took this course.[9] The Nigerian students responsible for the course soon realized that their pupils were more interested in the "secrets" of the religion than in the language itself. Over time, learning the language took second place, superseded by teaching of the myths and rites of the Yorùbá divinities.[10]

At the same time as officially teaching Yorùbá, these Nigerian students began giving lessons on orisha rituals. To do so, they relied on the works of the Africanists; their knowledge of English enabled them to translate these works for their Brazilian public. Thus, oral transmission, which had been the basis of learning in Candomblé, was in part replaced by the study of a collection of "sacred" works, written mostly by anthropologists.

Vagner Gonçalves da Silva, who took part in the USP course, describes how the initiates, who were mostly attached to the Brazilian tradition, experienced consternation as a result of encountering this new source of knowledge:

> During the course, the discovery of the existence of books revealing information usually regarded as taboo in the *terreiros* was greeted with great enthusiasm. The lessons and contact with Africans, as well as providing rudimentary Yoruba (which can be used to translate chants and the names of the orixás), enable us to relativize questions which, up until now, were presented as dogma, or to reconsider knowledge reputed to be "certain." I saw disappointment among many of my friends, especially those who were initiated, when they realized the difference that existed between the Brazilian orixá worship (at least as it was practiced in their *terreiros,* mixed with other "nations" such as Angola, or subject to Catholic influence) and the religion practiced in Africa, as described by the Nigerians. Confronted with the impossibility of harmonizing the teaching received in the *terreiro* with that received on the course, these students then abandoned the course. However, the younger ones (in terms of initiation age), or those who were to a greater or lesser extent in disagreement with certain Brazilian practices such as syncretism, were able to redefine some

of their religious notions, and thus legitimate them "academically." (da Silva 1992, 237–238)

Despite these legitimate concerns, Yorùbá language and civilization courses, as well as parallel courses in the "secrets" of religion, became synonymous with culture and proficiency in a sacerdotal career. The old *pais-de-santo* were almost all illiterate and without education; today, the new initiates, especially in the big cities of southeastern Brazil, are cultured, study at universities, and can speak several languages. The classic division between researcher and initiate is gradually fading; instead it is now widely accepted that one has to conduct research to understand one's religion and to rediscover the "true" Africa through bibliographic sources.

Orisha courses were created and developed progressively in institutions especially for this purpose. The great demand from the religious market—this thirst for further knowledge about religion—made the courses a success.

Studying odù in Rio de Janeiro

The first course in Afro-Brazilian culture was organized in Rio de Janeiro in 1976 by Ornato José da Silva, a *babalorixá* and author of books on Candomblé. He worked closely with a young Nigerian, Benjamin Durojaiye Ainde Kayodé Komolafe (Benjy Kayodé), a medical student at the Rio de Janeiro State University. Kayodé presented himself as an *awó* who had just arrived from Nigeria.[11] This "first basic training course for seminaries in Afro-Brazilian religions" was held at the Umbandist Spiritual Congregation of Brazil. Among the first intake of pupils were two great figures who worked extremely hard to make this type of course widely available in Rio de Janeiro: Ruth Moreira da Silva and José Beniste. It was also in 1976 that the Yorùbá Theological Society of Afro-Brazilian Culture was founded; it was directed by Eduardo Fonseca, Jr. A journalist by trade, Fonseca organized the first Afro-Brazilian Culture Week in 1976, which took place in the presence of Nigeria's ambassador, Olajide Alo. In his closing speech, Alo emphasized the importance of such initiatives in developing ties between Africa and Brazil.

In 1977, the Yorùbá Theological Society of Afro-Brazilian Culture employed another young Nigerian, Joseph Olatundi Aridemi Osho, a student from the Polytechnic School of Rio de Janeiro State University, as a Yorùbá professor. This lasted until the beginning of 1979, when Osho started giving lessons at the Yorùbá Culture Research and Study Center founded in 1977 by Fernandes Portugal. The Center's goal was to bring together religious adepts and social sciences researchers who specialized in the study of Afro-Brazilian culture. To do this, conferences were given at *terreiros* and associations as well as at the Estácio de Sá, a private university in Rio de Janeiro; also, Yorùbá courses were held at the center itself. The public attending these courses consisted of religious adepts who were seeking to further their knowledge of Yorùbá culture. They complained of being held back by the fact that the "elders" had not passed down all the knowledge they possessed to the younger generations.

One of the ritual practices that had been forgotten in Brazil was divination by *odù* or the configurations (signs) that form the basis of the Ifá divinatory system.[12] From the sixteen principal *odù*, 256 combinations were possible, each linked to a story (*itan*) from the corpus of Ifá. The aim of divination is to reveal, via the identification of the *odù* and *itan* corresponding to each particular situation, the sacrifices men and women must make in order to restore harmony between the material world and the spiritual world.[13] The first divination courses included teaching the Ifá literature, which was then combined with studying the Yorùbá language.

On January 14, 1978, Benjy Kayodé and Richard Yinka Alabi Ajagunna, another Nigerian student from Rio de Janeiro's School of Medicine, conducted the closing ceremony of the first African divination course, granting the title of *omó Ifá* (son of Ifá) to their pupils. Becoming *omó Ifá* is equivalent to receiving the first confirmation of the "hand of Orunmilá" (*awó fakan*) or the first step in the initiation process of a new babalawo, as when a man discovers the *odù* that will direct his material and religious life.[14] At the end of the 1970s, another *babalorixá*, Torodê de Ogun, organized Yorùbá language and Orisha mythology courses in his cult house, the Ilé Axé Ogun Torodê in Rio de Janeiro. After being confirmed as *omó Ifá* in 1978, Torodê continued his initiation in order to become a babalawo and to carry out annual ceremonies with the Nigerians. After nine years of studies, Torodê received the title of babalawo from Kayodé. In 1984, Torodê began to teach Ifá divinatory practices as well as Yorùbá culture and ritual in his own *terreiro*. The emphasis was on the Ifá corpus, the divinatory method, and above all on the study of the *odù*. Every year he organized one or two study groups, consisting of forty to fifty people who were usually initiates interested in African tradition. But according to Torodê himself, being initiated into Candomblé was not a decisive factor for being accepted into the course, "for one can be a priest of Ifá without being initiated into the cult of the orixás."[15]

Yorùbá culture and language teaching was based on texts from Nigerian literature and anthropological studies, such as Bascom's *Sixteen Cowries* (1980) and *Ifa Divination* (1969a). As these works were not translated into Portuguese and were somewhat inaccessible to initiates, the young Nigerian students translated extracts; in this way, they were gradually divulged. Torodê talks here of the consequences that the courses had in Candomblé circles:

> They caused quite a stir because Brazilian customs were entwined with Catholic beliefs. What's more, when the Africans tried to separate the two, the most radical [people], who believed that Saint Barbara was Yansan and Ogun was Saint George, did not accept it. . . . Personally, I found it all absurd. I could

not understand why, for a Bahian, Ogun should be Saint Anthony, who was Portuguese, or Saint George, who was George of Cappadocia, a Syrian from the Roman army. This is why, when my *pai-de-santo* died in 1971, I wanted to return to the religion's roots in Africa.

The end of the 1970s saw a change in the nature of Yorùbá language courses. This was expressed by a growing demand for information about the *fundamentos* (foundational principles). In 1980, the radio host José Beniste launched the *Afro-Brazilian Cultural Program* on Radio Roquette Pinto. Beniste began to run courses with Richard Ajagunna in the North Zone of Rio de Janeiro. Beniste benefited from Ruth Moreira da Silva's collaboration; she also ran a course with him at the Brazil-Nigeria Institute.

Since 1990, another course in divinatory practice has been given by Adilson Antônio Martins (Adilson de Oxalá), who was initiated in 1968 in Jeje Candomblé. Adilson began to take an interest in the cult of Orunmilá (Ifá) when the African students arrived. He became friends with Benjy Kayodé and the other Nigerians, and together they worked on bibliographical research. Ultimately, he felt the need to delve deeper, and was initiated as *awó fakan* by Rafaél Zamora Dias (*Ifá Biyi*), a Cuban babalao living in Rio de Janeiro.

Zamora, a former journalist on Cuban TV, had arrived in Brazil in 1991 to make a documentary in which he planned to compare the "African" religions in Cuba and Brazil. The documentary was never completed. Zamora established himself in Rio, and organized the first Ifá ceremony of *Awó Fakan* and *Kofá Fun* according to the Cuban tradition in 1992. Among the members of this first group were Adilson Antônio Martins, his wife Lúcia Petrocelli Martins (who became the first Brazilian *apetebí* in the Cuban tradition), and Alberto Chamarelli Filho, *Omó Shangó*.

In August 1992, Rafaél Zamora, *Awó ni Orunmilá Ifá Biyi Omó Odù Ogunda Keté*, initiated his first Brazilian babalaô in Cuba, Alberto Chamarelli Filho. Filho was already *Awó Fakan Obara-Kana*, and he became *Babálawó Ifáladê Awó ni Orunmilá Omó Odù Odisá* after his Ifá initiation. Adilson Antônio Martins, who had received the ritual name of *Awó Fakan Ogbe-Bara* in 1992, was eventually initiated into Ifá by Adisa Arogundade Adekunle, a Nigerian babalawo; Martins received the title of *Babaláwo Ifáleke Awó ni Orúnmilá Omó Odu Ogbe-Bara*. Today, several Cuban babalaos are living in Rio de Janeiro, while many Nigerian babalawo have established themselves in São Paulo.

Ifá and Candomblé

The presence of Cuban babalaos in the city of Rio de Janeiro created new models for initiates in Candomblé. This religion, contrary to what is generally believed, has long been present in Brazil's old capital of Rio de Janeiro (Capone 1999). But what consequences can we expect from the introduction of new practices into a ritual system structured around a complex religious hierarchy, in which the main characters are *pais-* and *mães-de-santo* and where mediumship is highly valued? Ifá priesthood is restricted to heterosexual men, who do not fall into trance. In Candomblé, on the contrary, the highest positions in the ritual hierarchy are restricted to women and men, often homosexuals, who are possessed by their deities. Once they are chosen by the orixás, women or men who do not fall into trance can occupy religious functions (*ogan* and *ekedi*), but they will always remain inferior to their initiators: Candomblé *pais-* and *mães-de-santo.* Furthermore, mediumship, meaning one's capacity of falling into trance and incorporating the deities, is a necessary condition to the reproduction of religious lineages. It is said in Candomblé that if one has not experienced trance with the gods, one cannot initiate novices, because "one can not transmit what he has not received for himself."

The case of a Candomblé house situated in the suburbs of Rio de Janeiro seems to constitute a meaningful example of the tensions between these different priesthoods as well as of the effects of the superposition of different hierarchical systems. If the Ifá divinatory system and priesthood share their belonging to a Yorùbá cultural complex with Candomblé, its integration in Candomblé ritual practices is not irrelevant. In actuality, it can entail ritual dramas, which eventually lead to the splitting of the religious group.

The Ilê Axé Omo Alaketu is a *terreiro* of Ketu Candomblé.[16] It was created in 1975 by the *pai-de-santo* Carlinhos de Odé (Carlos Alberto Assef).[17] Pai Carlinhos's story is representative of the typical religious path of mediums in Candomblé houses of southeastern Brazil. An Umbanda member, well known for his capacities as a medium,[18] Carlinhos was inspired by his spirits to deepen his spiritual quest by getting initiated into Candomblé, a religion considered closer to African roots. He was initiated in São Paulo in 1975 and rapidly opened his own cult house in Imbarié, a popular suburb of Rio de Janeiro. The land on which the *terreiro* was built was bought by Carlinhos's brother, João, who had been initiated as an *ogan* by another *mãe-de-santo*, Edeuzuita de Oxoguian, a woman from Bahia initiated in the Ketu "nation." In fact, Carlinhos had already asked assistance from other religious specialists in order to compensate for the distance between him and his initiator. Another *mãe-de-santo*, Leticia, helped him during his first initiations, and Edeuzuita de Oxoguian, who was part of a prestigious *axé* (religious tradition) in Salvador, executed the initiation rituals for Carlinhos' wife Regina as well the confirmation rituals for his brother João. Regina became the *terreiro*'s *mãe pequena*, while João became one of the main *ogan* of the Ilê Axé Omo Alaketu.[19] One result of Edeuzuita's great influence was the "correcting" of Carlinhos's initiation. According to her, Carlinhos' initiation had been "partially done," since he also needed to be initiated into the worship of Oxalá, an orixá who shared his head with Odé.[20]

By doing this, Carlinhos "changed his waters," placing himself under the ritual supervision of a *mãe-de-santo,* a member of a prestigious nation of Candomblé. Changing the waters (*trocar as águas*), where water represents the religious tradition or nation, is one of the most efficient ways of renegotiating ritual ties. By placing himself under the protection of another *pai* or *mãe-de-santo,* the initiate severs the ties of submission with his original *terreiro.* The purpose of this practice, which is extremely widespread in Afro-Brazilian religions, is often to legitimate one's religious origins.

This quest for a high-valued religious origin closer to traditional roots is not a strategy restricted to the elites of Bahian Candomblé, but a key factor in most worshippers' daily lives. In fact, in Candomblé one can always change nation thanks to affiliations by *obrigação* (by ritual ceremony). After the initiation process called the *feitura do santo,* which is the moment of definite integration inside a Candomblé house, the new initiate has to perform a set of rituals that confirm his or her status within the religious group. After the *feitura,* an *obrigação* is made for the first, third, seventh, fourteenth, and twenty-first years of initiation. Each of these ritual ceremonies can provoke a "changing of the waters." One can be initiated in a *terreiro* of Angola nation, but perform one's first- or seventh-year ritual ceremony in another *terreiro* and with another *mãe-* or *pai-de-santo.* Such a modification can be the result of conflicts between the initiate and his initiator, as happens often in Candomblé houses. But often such a modification is performed as a political strategy in order to legitimate one's religious career. Therefore, the initiate can change his Candomblé "nation" as well as his *zelador de santo,*[21] thanks to ritual ceremonies allowing him or her to become a member of a more prestigious *terreiro.*

Edeuzuita de Oxoguian thus became Carlinhos' *zeladora de santo* in a time when his house was at its best, with a great number of initiates and clients. In 1983 João Velho, who eventually became an *ogan* of the Ilê Axé Omo Alaketu, began participating very actively in the *terreiro* when the cult house was in the middle of a process of re-Africanization. Regina, the *mãe pequena,* was teaching the religious foundational principles (*fundamentos*) to the *terreiro* classes; she was explaining the significance of Nagô (Yorùbá) words used in ritual practices and in searches for data in the traditional practices of Yorùbá religion.[22] João Velho describes this phenomenon in these terms:

> The ritualistic aspect was very strong, but in terms of ethics and philosophy there was a blank. I think this is the weak point of the Bahian model in Candomblé. I think everything comes with the lack of knowledge of the Yorùbá language. We are doing ceremonies without knowing what they really mean. ... The faith is big but it is based on an ideology of fear, ignorance and submission to pure ritualism. At that time, we did not have any other information. We did not have access to Cubans or Nigerians. Bahian leadership was the

only one who would impose its religious rules. (Pers. comm., Rio de Janeiro, 2005)

In 1988, the death of the *mãe pequena* created a crisis within the religious group, which deepened the quest for *fundamentos* even more. This "back to the roots" process led Pai Carlinhos and his brother João to organize a trip to Africa during that same year, in order "to restore African tradition." In Nigeria, João performed a divination with the Araba of Ifé and discovered that he needed to be initiated into Ifá worship. At first, this provoked incomprehension, because Ifá worship was no longer present in Candomblé houses. João Velho explains how complex this news was for the two brothers: "Their religion was Candomblé. But Candomblé had nothing to do with 'Ifá culture.' As in most Brazilian cult houses, we did not have any information on Ifá" (Pers. comm. Rio de Janeiro, 2005).

In 1995, the two brothers finally found an opportunity to rediscover the "Ifá culture." During that time, as stated above, Rafaél Zamora was the only Cuban babalao living in Rio de Janeiro, and he had started to introduce the Ifá divinatory system according to Cuban tradition. The first member of the Ilê Axé Omo Alaketu who participated in a ceremony directed by Zamora was Pai Carlinhos's brother, João. During this ritual, he received the "hand of Orunmilá," the first level of initiation in Ifá priesthood. Having become *awó fakan,* he opened up his own *terreiro* to the ritual influence of Cubans and their followers. Zamora had already initiated as babalaos a group of five Brazilians who had traveled to Cuba to complete their initiation. Indeed, in order to initiate a new babalao, one has to assemble eight other babalaos who will chair the initiation rituals. In the 1990s, because that was impossible in Rio, it made the trip to Cuba inevitable. In April 1996, João went to Cuba and was initiated as a babalao. When he returned, other members of the *terreiro* became interested in this ritual system imported from Cuba and supposedly closer to Yorùbá traditions and cultural roots.

Contrary to what happened with the divination classes taught by Nigerian students, Ifá worship did not attract the leader of the *terreiro,* but its *ogan.* Indeed, Cuban babalaos had insisted that an initiation in Ifá was not compatible with mediumship. Therefore, those who fell into trance were not allowed to become babalao. By definition, *ogan* are not possessed by the gods. After João, Marcos de Oxalá who was the main drummer (*alabé*) in the house, and Pai Carlinhos' right-hand man, was also initiated into Ifá worship. This initiation soon became the cause of a new drama: "They began to fight. Once initiated into Ifá, the *ogan* started to act as if he was more important than his own *pai-de-santo.* A lot of people left the house at that time. It was 1997" (Rafael Assef, pers. comm. Rio de Janeiro, 2005).

The crisis started when Marcos de Oxalá challenged a tacit rule in Candomblé: the head of the house is the only one who can practice divination in the *ter-*

reiro, using the *dilogun*.[23] In the case of Pai Carlinhos's *terreiro*, divination was not the *pai-de-santo*'s monopoly any more, since his brother João had become the babalaô of the shrine house. Marcos de Oxalá, once he was initiated into Ifá, tried to practice his own art and challenged the initiator and the elders' authority directly. According to João Velho, this was not the only effect of Cubans' strong influence in the house:

> Cuban culture deeply influenced the *terreiro*, managing to modify rituals. We were beginning to adopt *coco* [four parts of coconut, used for divination], *Lucumí* songs for the sacrifices of animals, *moyuba* . . . I remember that we often followed both rituals during the sacrifices. The *pai-de-santo* was telling us that, for orisha, it made no difference, that the same effect could be expected after a Ketu or a *Lucumí* ritual. He explained that they were two paths leading to the same goal: being in contact with the orisha. But most of the *filhos-de-santo* [initiates] did not understand. There was a lot of confusion between us. (Rafael Assef, pers. comm., Rio de Janeiro, 2005).[24]

Carlinhos and João, under the supervision of Zamora and his group, began to "Cubanize" Candomblé rituals. Divination with kola nuts (*obí*), generally used in Candomblé, was replaced by divination with four pieces of coconut—also called *obí* in Cuba. This was a paradox, since the absence of kola nuts in Cuba forced practitioners to replace the African fruit with coconuts. Therefore, instead of re-Africanizing the religion, Candomblé rituals were being Cubanized. Furthermore, when individual altars were consecrated, the number of stones (*otan*) contained in the ritual pots had been modified in order to suit Cuban tradition. By the same logic, Cuban rituals such as *lavatorio* and *paritorio*) were organized during the initiation and even the divination with the *dilogun* changed. After having performed the *awó fakan* ceremony and having positioned himself in a place of dependence towards his Cuban initiator therein, Carlinhos was confirmed as an *oriaté* (a Cuban specialist of divination with cowries and "master of ceremonies" during initiation rituals) by Zamora. He began using books or Ifá *tratados* (treatises), which were popular in Cuba, in order to "correct" the way in which one "reads" cowries in Candomblé. In the majority of Candomblé houses, cowries are traditionally considered "open" when the handmade opened side is up, whereas in Cuba it is the naturally open side (the fissure of the shell), that represents the "mouth" speaking for the orisha.

The repeated tensions inside the *terreiro* resulted in the splitting of the religious group. Soon, this led to the departure of some of its most important members who chose to follow Zamora. It was at that time that João Velho, *ogan* of Odé, the god of his *pai-de-santo*, and Dudu Assef, Pai Carlinhos's son, decided to be initiated into Ifá under the supervision of yet another Cuban, Wilfredo Nelson; Nelson acted as their own *ojugbona* (second ritual parent), as he had in Cuba during the initiation of Carlinhos's brother. Nelson was the master of ceremonies and João acted as the leading babalaô in the initiatory rites for Dudu and João Velho.

Until then and despite the crisis triggered by Marcos de Oxalá, ritual collaboration between the two brothers had always been peaceful. João participated in the initiation rituals as a babalaô, and he was in charge of animal sacrifices. While Carlinhos performed the *itá* divination (during the third day of initiation) following the Cuban tradition, João helped him with the interpretation of the *odù*.

When João Velho and Dudu Assef decided to be initiated into Ifá, Nelson traveled to Cuba in order to bring back Olofi's *fundamento*, without which, according to Cuban tradition, no babalao can be initiated. He considered that it was possible to initiate a novice in Brazil, since the number of babalaôs in the country was high enough. But he decided this without realizing that Zamora would be Nelson's main rival in the religious market.[25] Indeed, in order to counter this first initiation in Pai Carlinhos's *terreiro*, Zamora organized another initiation on the same day, preventing babalaôs from attending the ceremony. Nelson reacted by showing the candidates a treatise of Ifá, which stated that an initiation could be performed with only five babalaos.

The initiation took place in the *ronkó* (*igbodú*), the room dedicated to the initiation in the *terreiro*. The *ronkó* and access to this sacred space became the pivot of a new ritual drama. Only those who have already gone through the process of initiation can enter this space during rituals. The fact that Pai Carlinhos did not get a full initiation as a babalaô because of his mediumship—thus remaining an *awó fakan*—challenged his authority in the most sacred place of the Candomblé house. If he was in charge of all the ceremonies taking place in his *terreiro*, he was not welcome in an Ifá ritual, whereas his brother João was by his own right a legitimate participant. Religious hierarchy was then deeply challenged, since João's status was different in Candomblé and in Ifá. His position in Candomblé as an *ogan* made him inferior to his brother, while his role as a babalaô made him superior in the hierarchy of Ifá priesthood. This could only lead to new tensions in the religious house.

At the same time, João—along with Rafael, who was his son and Carlinhos' nephew—met some Nigerians with whom they discovered, in João and Rafael's words, "other information, pointing to the cultural distortions in Cuban tradition" (Velho and Assef, pers. comm. Rio de Janeiro, 2005). João Velho discovered Bascom and Abímbọ́lá's writings, began researching Ifá on the Internet, and registered to take a Yorùbá language class taught by a student from Nigeria. Slowly this confrontation between various models of the tradition led the religious group to emancipate itself from Cubans' authority. In João Velho's words, they began a process of "Africanization": "I started to bring information from Africa which challenged the Cuban tradition. They were not the masters of truth as we once thought. We began new research, which helped us re-evaluate what they had taught us" (Pers. comm., Rio de Janeiro, 2005).

In this search for the "real fundamentals" of Yorùbá religion, a new *terreiro* was founded: Ilé Asè Igba Asiko, in the suburb of Itaboraí, in the State of Rio de Janeiro. The main change in rituals that happened with this new connection was the installation of collective altars for the orixás, according to Nigerian tradition. This led to new divisions inside the *terreiro,* and some other initiates decided to leave the house because they were perturbed by the recent changes.

In August 2000, Rafael traveled to Nigeria to be initiated as a babaláwo in Ibadan. He was introduced to the Ogboni society and to the Gélédé female society. Back in Rio, he mixed Nigerian influences and Cuban traditions. Pai Carlinhos still used Cuban Ifá treatises in order to interpret the *odù* during divination, while he added Nigerian prayers to the rituals. Coconuts were no longer used in the house; it was decided that kola nuts should be used because they are used in Africa. Rafael's father, João, who had been initiated as a babalao in Cuba, founded an Ifá temple in Teresópolis in the state of Rio de Janeiro, where he performed *Kofá* and *Awó fakan* ceremonies. The creation of that temple underlined the new fracture that appeared between the two brothers. They were now rivals, in particular when it came to divination, prescription, and *ebós* as the ritual sacrifices. These tensions could only be solved by a strict separation of ritual spaces. In fact, the Candomblé *terreiro* would now only deal with rituals for the *filhos-de-santo,* whereas the temple would focus on the initiates into Ifá worship. Thus, the religious group became divided bewteen two centers, according to ritual needs. As Rafael explains, "When it came to Ifá, we worked under the supervision of João, but when we had to deal with the orixás, it was Pai Carlinhos who remained the absolute leader." Inside the ritual practice, the two priesthoods were then finally separated.

Hierarchy, Mediumship and Conflict

The encounter of two different traditions in the Orisha religion seems to enhance the structural characteristics of both. Orisha religion appears then as a "conflictive space," where tension acts as balance (Lefebvre 1976). For many Yorùbá scholars, Ifá is important as a vast cultural archive, a distillation of the Yorùbá philosophy of life that can support interpretations of Yorùbá practices and institutions. But as Peel rightly stated, this interpretation hardly focuses on "the role of divination in the micro-politics of social existence" (1990, 340). Peel explains further, "Ifá aspired to be a hegemonic cult. Whatever its origins, it succeeded in making itself the point of articulation of the cults of the other orişa, such that the babaláwo performed an analogous function to the king. In the community, the king stood at the head of all cults between his people and the orişa" (ibid., 342).

The ritual tensions highlighted in the story of Pai Carlinhos' Candomblé house are an outstanding example of this capacity of the Ifá system to occupy new spaces, deeply modifying the internal balance between power and prestige. When superimposed on a belief system such as Candomblé, where the highest positions are occupied by female or male homosexual leaders and in which mediumship plays a very important role, the Ifá priesthood, in which hegemonic aspirations are mainly expressed by male domination, entails a series of ritual dramas provoking an inversion in spiritual hierarchy.[26] The main arena of these dramas is the monopoly of divination as well as the exercise of mediumship.

This conundrum is not only characteristic of the encounter of Candomblé and Ifá. In Cuba, these same structural tensions inside the ritual practice exist in the relationship between the *oriaté* and the babalao, whose ritual roles are at the same time complementary and competing. For a long time, the term "Santería" has designated two different *Reglas* ("rules," ritual systems): the *Regla de Ocha* and the *Regla de Ifá*. The majority of the adepts are aware of the differences between these two *Reglas,* and they think of themselves as members of the *olochas* community (initiated into the Orisha worship) or babalaos community.[27] David Brown (1989) highlighted an important period of "professionalization" of the priesthood between Cuban independence (1898) and the 1950s, during which the *oriaté* emerged as an important new center of authority in religious practice.

The ritual role of the *oriaté* embodies the aspiration to establish a model of orthodoxy in the religion. According to Lydia Cabrera, the babalaos traditionally held certain ritual prerogatives over *olocha:* "But one must agree that the old babaláwos were so despotic and wanted to dominate the *santeros* and these were slipping out of their yoke" (1980, 184). The role of the *oriaté* emerged then as the new *Oba* (king) of the *Regla de Ocha,* taking on ritual tasks previously assigned to the babalao.[28] The presence of an *oriaté* or a babalao in a ritual is a matter of complex negotiations about legitimacy and ritual competences.[29]

Despite these controversies about the "orthodox" way to perform rituals, these two specialists assert the legitimacy of their ritual authority through the same narrative appealing to "African tradition." The multiplicity of the roots of this tradition entails the formation of many variants in the same religion.

In Cuba as well as in the United States, the organization of the ritual activities in the *Lucumí* religion follows two different models, which David Brown defines as two extreme camps that may be referred to as *"oriaté*-centered" and "Orula-centered" (1989, 214). In the houses directed by a babaláwo, or depending on his services, he will always occupy the highest place in the hierarchy, independent of when he was initiated. Hence, a young babaláwo with two years of initiation will be the "elder" of an *olocha,* with thirty years of initiation. According to the babaláwo, this is the logical consequence of the dominant position held by

Orula in relation to the other orisha, a dominant position that will be seriously questioned in the houses where *oriatés* are the higher ritual authority.

In "babaláwo-centered" houses, the devotee receives the sacred necklaces from the hands of his *padrino* (godfather) or *madrina* (godmother) in the *Ocha*. Then a babaláwo, who will become his *padrino* in Ifá, gives him the *guerreiros* (warriors), and during the initiation or *asiento* the novice will be also connected to a second *padrino* or *madrina* who plays the ritual role of *ojugbona*. After receiving the "warriors" (Ogun, Ochossi, Osun, accompanied by Eleguá), the devotee can perform the first initiation in Ifá worship by receiving the "hand of Orula" ("*Awó fakan*") for men and *Kofá* for women. The godchild is thus inscribed into a network of religious kin that connects him or her to different houses or *ramas* (religious lineages). The role played by the babaláwo in the godchild's religious life will then depend on the relations already established in his or her house or religious kin with Ifá worship. Nevertheless, in many houses or *ramas* of *Ocha*, the babaláwo is not essential to the accomplishment of rituals.

The initiation of an *olocha* in Ifá worship always entails the rearrangement of ritual relations between initiator and initiate. According to the Cuban tradition, regardless of the initiatory age, the babalao is always "higher" than the *olocha* (or *olorisha*, the initiate into the Orisha worship), as Orula is "higher" than all the other orisha. The new babalao will therefore occupy a higher position in the hierarchy then his own *padrino*, if the *padrino* has not been initiated into the Ifá worship himself. However, he ceases to show submission in front of his elder "brothers":

> Although that godchild is "younger" in *Ocha*, the new priest of Orula comes to supersede his *madrina* or *padrino* and all his *hermanos* in rank as far as the "house of Orula" is concerned. Thus upside-downing of status can provoke no small tremor in the personal relationship between the two parties. A rule of respect between the two *Reglas* recognizes the special place the *padrino* or *madrina* holds in the babaláwo's life, regardless of his new rank. (David Brown 1989, 188)

This same inversion of the hierarchical order is found in Pai Carlinhos's *terreiro*. During his Ifá initiation, João Velho was told that he had become a "king" (*Oba* being the title bestowed on a babaláwo) and that he could even ask his own *pai-de-santo* to prostrate himself in front of him as a mark of respect. He was also told that even the orixás would show this kind of consideration, prostrating themselves in front of the new babalaô. In fact, some of his "brothers in the religion" ("*irmãos-de-santo*"), once possessed by their orixás, began to act in that way, publicly showing their respect for the new initiate. Nevertheless, orixás only show this kind of respect in front of the *pai-de-santo* or the *mãe-de-santo* who initiated their "horses." Prostrating oneself in front of a new initiate who just performed his initiatory rites in Ifá is clearly a way to question the established hierarchical order inside the religious group.

The globalization of the Yorùbá religion has to take into account these ritual rearrangements and the tensions that they provoke.[30] The knowledge and corpus of the texts of the Ifá system can help to explain and deal with the new situations entailed by this type of encounter between distinct models of tradition. Thus, Rafael Zamora finds the ultimate reason for his "mission" in Brazil in the divination sign that governs his life. The *odù* Ogunda Keté explains how all the religions can live together harmoniously. One day, Orunmilá (Orula), the god of the Ifá oracle, was visited by a man who complained about the religious divisions among his people. They didn't understand each other, and everyone within the divisions believed he or she was the owner of the truth. After consulting with Ifá, Orunmilá declared that trouble would disappear when people understood that all religions converge toward the same goal; peace cannot be obtained without a real understanding of the Other.

Following the teachings of his divinatory sign, Zamora made an excellent device to foster exchanges between Ifá and Candomblé—two "sister religions" deeply connected in his vision—from his Society of Ifá and Afro-Cuban Culture in Brazil. According to Zamora, Ifá and Candomblé are not different or divergent religions, but two branches of the same tree, which worship the same divinities and have the same origin. This idea makes a clear reference to another *odù*, Ogbe Odi, which explains how knowledge has been distributed among all men on earth. Each of them possesses some fragments of this sacred knowledge. Religious cooperation is thus possible and suitable. As stated by Lázara Menéndez Vázquez, Olofi "shared knowledge between all the heads."

However, this partition did not bring harmony into the world, because it is not peace that governs the universe. As Abímbólá stated, "the most important issue in our own part of the cosmos is conflict. Conflict rather than peace is the order of the day" (1997, 3). Only sacrifice can rearrange the forces of the universe, recovering the balance and reintroducing peace into conflict. For that to be possible, it will be necessary to bring together the different fragments of an ancestral knowledge that has been dispersed throughout the world.

This tendency to preserve ancestral knowledge and to compensate for ritual loss is what fuels African American religions. Fragments of this tradition have been preserved in Cuba, Brazil, and Nigeria. Today, the process of strengthening the roots involves travel to these traditional centers of Orisha worship perceived as a temporal regression towards the "true" African tradition, and the search for re-Africanization via courses in Yorùbá language and civilization. The reconstitution of this lost unity is an attempt to find a common past and a shared tradition, both of which are indispensable to the creation of a community of practitioners of Orisha religion.

This kind of syncretism between sister religions is based on the idea of a common African cultural ground. Melville Herskovits (1941) was the first to declare the existence of a "cultural grammar" common to different people of western Africa that could allow for the formation of an Afro-American culture. This idea of the persistence of an African substrate, in which religion plays a fundamental role, can also be found in the "rapid early synthesis" or "Creolization" model developed by Mintz and Price (1976). In this model, we can find the same kind of tension between Africa and America as in Roger Bastide's work (1971, 1978): on one side was the African "cognitive orientations" that allowed the slave to adapt to his new land and that gave birth to Afro-American cultures; on the other side was the idea of a "rigid core of African culture" immune to external influences that allowed for the preservation of African traditions in the New World. The idea of a basic unity of African culture has inspired several unification projects of Afro-American religious practices.

In the quest for *fundamentos* or religious secrets lost in the Middle Passage, the syncretism between "sister religions"—Candomblé, *Regla de Ocha*, and Ifá— becomes a "good" syncretism, a "positive" approach that can open the way to "re-Africanization."[31] What is sought today in Brazil is a tradition compatible with modernity. To re-Africanize also means to acquire knowledge, and books are the sources of a lost tradition that can and must be reconstructed. Without a sacred book that determines religious dogma, work by anthropologists becomes one of the main bases on which practitioners rediscover the *fundamentos*, which can confirm the traditionalism of their practices. The irruption of Ifá into Candomblé provides new forms of legitimization of ritual practice. The Ifá corpus, with its *ese* (verses) and *itan* (stories), is the sacred book for which Candomblé initiates were longing.

The exchanges between "sister religions," such as Brazilian Candomblé and Cuban Santería or the *Lucumí* religion, aim to reestablish a common belief system in which elements of different Afro-American religions that all claim a Yorùbá origin are blended. Nevertheless, the attempts to regain this lost unity have to take into account the structural tensions that span this religious universe as well as the multiplicity of models of tradition that constitute what we call today the "Orisha religion."

Notes

1. The Yorùbá term òrìṣà (divinity) is spelled differently in Brazil (*orixá*) and in Cuba (*oricha*). It is spelled *orisha* in English; that term will be used in this chapter and in all references in the international context of Afro-American religious practitioners. The terms *orixá* and *oricha* will be kept when referring to regional belief systems, such as Candomblé, Santería, or *Lucumí* religion.

2. See Capone (2005, 279–297) for an analysis of COMTOC or *Orisa* World Congresses from 1981 to 2005.

3. At international forums, Afro-American religions, like Candomblé, Santería or Orisha-Voodoo, are considered different aspects of one whole: the "Orisha religion." They become thus regional variations of the same belief system, based on the worship of Yorùbá divinities.

4. See for example Turner (1975), Verger (1976), Cunha (1978), Cobley (1990), Capone (1998, 1999), Matory (1999, 2005), Guran (2000).

5. The Yorùbá term babalawo (*baba-ní-awo*, "father of secrets") is spelled differently in Brazil (babalaô) and in Cuba (babalao). These terms will be used in a Brazilian or Cuban context.

6. Felisberto Américo Souza has been one important figure in the founding of Candomblé in Rio de Janeiro (cf. Capone 1999). He anglicized his name to Sowzer and was one of the last diviners from Bahia, the direct rival of the famous Martiniano Eliseu do Bonfim (Verger 1981, 32; see also Carneiro 1986, 121). His grandfather, Bambôxé (Bamgbose) had been one of the founders of the first Candomblé house, the Casa Branca or Engenho Velho, in Salvador de Bahia.

7. According to Matory (2005, 53), by 1889 one in seven Lagosians had lived in Cuba or Brazil. The famous Adechina, who was enslaved in Cuba, is said to have returned to Africa for initiation as a babalawo, later returning to Cuba (Sarracino 1988).

8. All translations are mine unless otherwise indicated. The linguist Yeda Pessoa de Castro reveals an identical situation for Yorùbá as it is spoken today in *terreiros*: "This supposed 'Nagô language' used in Candomblé is nothing more than operational terminology, specific to ritual ceremonies . . . , which uses a lexical system composed of different African languages which were spoken in Brazil during [the period of] slavery" (1981, 65).

9. In Candomblé, the religious terminology refers to a ritual kinship: the initiator is the "father" (*pai*) or "mother" (*mãe*) of "sons" and "daughters-of-saint," initiates to the gods. The terms *pai-de-santo* and *mãe-de-santo* correspond to the Yorùbá *babalorisa* and *iyalorisa*, which are spelled *babalorixá* and *iyalorixá* in Brazil. See Costa Lima (1977).

10. Abimbola writes about the "contra-acculturative" experience to which Lashebikan was subjected in Salvador. He was the first Yorùbá professor in Bahia and a "well-known scholar of the Yorùbá language": "But Lashebikan was grossly ignorant of the ways of the *orisa*, since in Nigeria he regarded himself as a Christian. Therefore, when he first reached Brazil, he could not understand the people to whom he had been sent to educate. But he soon adjusted himself and learnt more about the *orisa* as he himself taught the Yorùbá language to his students who were mostly made up of *babalorisa* and *iyalorisa*" (Abímbólá 1976b, 634–635).

11. Initiated into the cult of Ifá. "The Ifá diviners are most commonly called babalawo or 'father has secrets' . . . or simply *awo*, secrets or mysteries" (Bascom 1969a, 81).

12. In Brazil, after the death of the last babalaôs, *mães* and *pais-de-santo* still practiced the *merindilogun* divinatory system, but the memory of *odù* was almost completely lost. The divination was performed through different techniques in which inspiration and medium skills were very important, most of the time without the utilization of *odù* or *ese Ifá*.

13. *Odù* are also known as the "paths" by which the orisha "come," thus influencing their actions on men in a positive or negative way. *Odù* are regarded as living, active entities, which must be fed and made propitious with sacrifices.

14. For a description of an initiation ritual in the Ifá divination held in São Paulo in 1987, see Prandi (2003, 151–163).

15. In reality, a babalawo should not go into a trance, while Candomblé initiates (unless they are *ogan* or *ekedi*, assistants of the *pai* or the *mãe-de-santo* who are not possessed by orisha) are all possessed by their divinities. Although women's initiation into the secrets of Ifá is

restricted, they are accepted as well as men into Torodê's course. In Cuba, where there is a great number of babalaos, mediumship is not an indispensable condition for initiation in the Orisha cult, women can receive the *Kofá*, and the first level of initiation to Ifá is the *apetebi* (assistant) of the babalao. I analyzed the gender issues in Ifá worship in a previous work (Capone 2005, 236–246).

16. Candomblé is divided into "nations": Nagô (Ketu, Efon, Ijexá, Nagô-Vodun), Jeje, Angola, Congo, Caboclo. The concept of *nation* lost its original ethnic meaning and now has more of a "political" and theological meaning. For an in-depth discussion of this concept, see Costa Lima (1976) and Parés (2006).

17. The story of this *terreiro* was collected in Rio in August 2005 during a long interview with João Velho and Rafael Assef, two members of this Candomblé house.

18. Brazilian religion was born from a combination of African rituals (above all of Bantu origin), indigenous cults, and the Spiritism of Allan Kardec. Umbanda was born in the 1930s in Rio de Janeiro (Diana Brown 1986), from which it spread to nearly all of Brazil.

19. The *mãe pequena* is the *pai-de-santo* or *mãe-de-santo*'s direct assistant. She is also known as *iyá kekeré*, "little mother" in Yorùbá. The *ogan* is a ritual position reserved for men who do not enter into trance and serve as protectors of the cult group, as well as drummers and animal sacrificers. In Candomblé, a *pai* or a *mãe-de-santo* cannot initiate his own partner or his own children. He needs to ask another priest or priestess to perform the initiation rituals for them.

20. In Candomblé, the expression *feitura do santo* ("making the saint") is used to describe initiation. During this period the initiator (the *pai-de-santo*) is supposed to give new life to the novice, who will be bound to his orixá forever.

21. The expression *zelador de santo*, an equivalent to the *pai-de-santo*, carries a lightly different meaning. Indeed, if the *pai-de-santo* is usually the initiator, the *zelador* is the one who takes care of the initiate's entities. This second expression does not involve any notions of religious kinship.

22. I dealt with the analysis of the process of re-Africanization in Candomblé in a previous work (Capone 1999, 2010).

23. The *dilogun*, also called *jogo de búzios*, is a divination method in which the god Exu speaks directly to the worshipper via the way the cowries fall. In Brazil it supplanted divination with the *opelé*, the divinatory chain to which eight halves of palm nuts are attached, and whose combinations refer to the *odù* (divinatory configurations) of the Ifá system.

24. *Moyuba* or *mojúbà* is the invocation preceding every *Lucumí* ritual. It honors the deceased in the priest's family as well as in his religious genealogy.

25. At the end of the 1990s, an initiation in Ifá could cost as much as 6,000 *reais*. At that time, *reais* and dollars were in parity. This cost was then seen as excessive to most Brazilians, including the middle class.

26. If in the *Ocha* sexual orientation is not a factor of exclusion, allowing homosexuals to enhance their spiritual career, the Ifá priesthood is only open to heterosexual men. Women can become *madrinas* and have a certain number of godchildren, while men can pursue their religious itinerary and get initiated into the Ifá worship or be confirmed as *oriatés*, the ritual specialists and diviners. This ritual position, once held exclusively by women (Ramos 2003), is today exclusively for men. A *santera* can always receive the *Kofá* and become *apetebí*, the babalao assistant, but she cannot complete his initiation into Ifá.

27. An *olocha* can be initiated into Ifá worship, becoming in Cuba an *oluwo*, which is a babalao who passed first through the initiatory rituals of the *Regla de Ocha*. Once initiated into Ifá, he will refer to himself as a *babalao* and no longer as an *olocha*.

28. In a recent work, Ramos (2003) defends the primacy of *oriatés* over *babalaos* by producing new historical evidence that questions the information given by *babalaos* to Lydia Cabrera.
29. In a previous work (Capone 2005), I analyzed the conflicts between *babalawo* and *oriatés* in the United States. These conflicts epitomize the tensions existing in the Afro-Cuban religious field.
30. On this topic, see Capone (2001–2002, 2004, 2005), Clarke (2004), and Olupona and Rey (2008).
31. See Capone 2007a.

References

Abímbólá, Wándé. 1976a. *Ifá: An Exposition of Ifá Literary Corpus,* Ibadan: Oxford University Press.
———. 1976b. "Yoruba Religion in Brazil: Problems and Prospects." *Actes du XLII Congrès international des américanistes* 6: 620–639.
———. 1997. *Ifà Will Mend Our Broken World.* Roxbury, MA: Aims Books.
Bascom, William R. 1969a. *Ifa Divination: Communication between Gods and Men in West Africa.* Bloomington: Indiana University Press.
———. 1969b. *The Yoruba of Southwestern Nigeria.* New York: Holt, Rinehart and Winston.
———. 1980. *Sixteen Cowries: Yoruba Divination from Africa to the New World.* Bloomington: Indiana University Press.
Bastide, Roger. 1958. *Le candomblé de Bahia (rite nagô).* Paris: Mouton.
———. 1971. *African Civilisations in the New World.* Translated by Peter Green. New York: Harper & Row.
———. 1978. *The African Religions of Brazil: Toward a Sociology of the Interpretation of Civilizations.* Baltimore: John Hopkins University Press.
Brandon, G. 1993. *Santería from Africa to the New World: The Dead Sell Memories.* Bloomington: Indiana University Press.
Brown, David H. "Garden in the Machine: Afro-Cuban Sacred Art and Performance in Urban New Jersey and New York." PhD diss., Yale University, 1989.
Brown, Diana. 1986. *Umbanda: Religion and Politics in Urban Brazil.* Ann Arbor, MI: UMI Research Press.
Cabrera, Lydia. 1980. *Koeko Iyawó: Aprende Novicia.* Miami: Colecion del Chichereku en el Exilio.
Capone, Stefania. 1998. "Le voyage initiatique: déplacement spatial et accumulation de prestige." *Cahiers du Brésil contemporain* 35–36: 137–156.
———. 1999. *La quête de l'Afriquedans le candomblé. Pouvoir et tradition au Brésil.* Paris: Karthala.
———. 2001–2002. "La diffusion des religions afro-américaines en Europe." In "Les pratiques européennes des religions afro-américaines," edited by Stefania Capone. Special issue, *Psychopathologie africaine* 31, no. 1: 3–16.
———. 2004. "A propos des notions de globalisation et transnationalisation." In "Religions transnationales," edited by Stefania Capone. Special issue, *Civilisations* 50, no. 1–2: 9–22.
———. 2005. *Les Yoruba du Nouveau Monde. Religion, ethnicité et nationalisme noir aux États-Unis.* Paris: Karthala.
———. 2007a. "The 'Orisha Religion' between Syncretism and Re-Africanization." In *Cultures of the Lusophone Black Atlantic,* edited by P. N. Naro, R. Sansi-Roca, and D. H.Treece, 219–232. New York: Palgrave Macmillan.

———. 2007b. "Transatlantic Dialogue: Roger Bastide and the African American Religions." *Journal of Religion in Africa* 37: 1–35.

———. 2010. *Searching for Africa in Brazil. Power and Tradition in Candomblé*. Durham, NC: Duke University Press.

Carneiro, Édison. 1986. *Candomblé da Bahia*. Rio de Janeiro: Civilização Brasileira.

———. 1991. *Religiões Negras/Negros Bantos*. Rio de Janeiro: Civilização Brasileira.

Clarke, Kamari Maxine. 2004. *Mapping Yorùbá Networks: Power and Agency in the Making of Transnational Communities*. Durham, NC: Duke University Press.

Cohen, Peter F. 2002. "Orisha Journeys: The Role of Travel in the Birth of Yoruba-Atlantic Religions." *Archives de Sciences Sociales des Religions* 117: 17–36.

Cobley, Alan G. 1990. "Migration and remigration between the Caribbean and Africa." In *The African Caribbean Connection: Historical and Cultural Perspectives*, edited by Alan G. Cobley and Alvin Thompson, 49–68. Barbados: University of the West Indies.

Costa Lima, Vivaldo da. 1976. "O conceito de 'nação' nos candomblés da Bahia." *Áfro-Ásia* 12: 65–90.

———. "A família-de-santo nos candomblés jeje-nagô da Bahia: um estudo de relações intra-grupais." Master's thesis, Universidade Federal da Bahia, Brazil, 1977.

Cunha, Manuela Carneiro da. 1978. *Negros, estrangeiros: os escravos libertos e sua volta à África*. São Paulo: Editora Brasiliense.

———. 1995. *Orixás da metrópole*. Petrópolis, BR: Vozes.

Guran, Milton. 2000. *Agudás, os brasileiros do Benim*. Rio de Janeiro: Nova Fronteira.

Herskovits, Melville. 1941. *The Myth of the Negro Past*. Boston: Beacon Press.

Lefebvre, Henri. 1976. *The Survival of Capitalism: Reproduction and the Relations of Production*. Translated by Frank Bryant. New York: St. Martin's Press.

Matory, J. Lorand. 1999. "The English professors of Brazil: On the Diasporic Roots of the Yorùbá Nation." *Comparative Studies in Society and History* 41 (1): 72–103.

———. 2005. *Black Atlantic Religion: Tradition, Transnationalism and Matriarchy in the Afro-Brazilian Candomblé*. Princeton, NJ: Princeton University Press.

Mintz, Sidney W., and Richard Price. (1976). *The Birth of African-American Culture: An Anthropological Perspective*. Boston: Beacon Press.

Nina Rodrigues, Raymundo. 1988. *Os Africanos no Brasil*. São Paulo: Editora Nacional.

Olupona, Jacob K., and Terry Rey, eds. 2008. *Orisha Devotion as World Religion: The Globalization of Yoruba Religious Culture*. Madison: University of Wisconsin Press.

Parés, Luis N. 2006. *A formação do candomblé: história e ritual da nação jeje na Bahia*. Campinas, BR: Editora da Unicamp.

Peel, J. D. Y. 1990. "The Pastor and the Babalawo: The Interaction of Religions in Nineteenth-Century Yorubaland." *Africa* 60, no. 3: 338–369.

———. 2000. *Religious Encounters and the Making of the Yoruba*. Bloomington: Indiana University Press.

Pessoa de Castro, Yeda. 1981. "Língua e nação de candomblé." *África* (Sao Pãulo) 4: 57–77.

Prandi, Reginaldo. 2003. "As artes da adivinhação: candomblé tecendo tradições no jogo de búzios." In *As Senhoras do Pássaro da Noite: Escritos sobre a Religião dos orixás*, edited by C. E. M. da Moura, 121–134. São Paulo: Editora da Universidade de São Paulo, Axis Mundi.

Ramos, Miguel "Willie." 2003. "La División de La Habana: Territorial Conflict and Cultural Hegemony in the Followers of Oyo Lukumi Religion, 1850s–1920s." *Cuban Studies* 34: 38–70.

Sarracino, Rodolfo. 1988. *Los que volvieron a Africa*. Havana: Editorial de Ciencias Sociales.

Silva, Vagner Gonçalves da. "O candomblé na cidade: tradição e renovação." Master's thesis, University of Sao Paulo, 1992.

Turner, J. Michael. "Les Brésiliens: The Impact of Former Brazilian Slaves on Dahomey." PhD. diss., Boston University, 1975.

Vázquez, Lázara Menéndez. 1995. "Un cake para Obatalá ?!" *Temas* 4: 38–51.

Verger, Pierre. 1976. *Trade Relations between the Bight of Benin and Bahia from the 17th Century to the 19th Century.* Translated by Evelyn Crawford. Ibadan, Nigeria: Ibadan University Press.

———. 1981. *Orixás.* Salvador, BR: Corrupio.

18 The Role of Women in the Ifá Priesthood

Inclusion versus Exclusion

M. Ajisebo McElwaine Abimbola

ALTHOUGH SOME MALE Ifá priests in the diaspora may argue the contrary, practices in Africa prove that women not only can but must be involved in the Ifá priesthood. Excluding women from Ifá would be tantamount to disobeying a direct instruction of Olódùmarè; yet conditions in the diaspora have led our male counterparts to reject women. My own exposure to the idea that women should be excluded from the Ifá priesthood began in the Afro-Latino diaspora. This sentiment is particularly strong among Spanish-speaking babalawos, many of whom I have worked with closely and hold in high regard. The hostility exhibited toward the inclusion of Ìyánífá among the ranks of Ifá priests is not indigenous to Africa; it may be a function of the brutal history and circumstances of the African diaspora or of the strong influence of Catholicism in those areas. Certainly the institutions of slavery and colonialism needed to subvert the respect for women that is paramount to Yorùbá culture in order to destroy identity and serve their inhuman capitalistic intentions. Therefore, I believe that the sexism that is found among Yorùbá practitioners in the diaspora is a function not of Africa, but of the white supremacy and imperialism that unsuccessfully continues to try to extinguish the fire of our religion from continuing to enlighten our minds with its wisdom. I have infinite respect for every manifestation of Yorùbá religion, and salute the traditions of *Lucumí*/Santería, Candomblé, Shango Baptist, and all other forms of our beautiful religion. With utmost humility and respect to diasporic Yorùbá religions, I would like to humbly examine the question of women's roles in the Ifá priesthood in Nigeria and as represented in my own limited knowledge of Ifá literature.

I became interested in the question of women's roles in Yorùbá religion generally, and women as Ifá priests in particular, as a result of my interactions with Ifá practitioners both in Oyo, Nigeria, and in the Yorùbá diaspora. I take careful note of the point made by Iya Oloye Aina Olomo Iyagan Ajidakin, who drew our attention to the fact that having experienced certain rituals and ceremonies does not necessarily a priest make.

In the context of this chapter, then, I use the phrase "Ifá priest" to refer to initiated persons of any gender who are practicing Ifá as their life's work and way of life. I noticed such a dichotomy between the expected place of women among Ifá practitioners in the diaspora and practitioners in Oyo that I wanted to investigate the subject further. Could I find any substantive proof within the Ifá literary corpus to show that women either should or should not be involved among the ranks of Ifá priests? Is the exclusion of women from the Ifá priesthood a natural phenomenon of Ifá or was it adopted during the course of the horrible history of enslavement of African people?

While doing Ifá work in various locales in the Spanish-speaking Yorùbá diaspora, I have encountered resistance on many occasions to the concept of female Ifá priests participating in certain sacred rituals, and often to the very existence of female Ifá priests at all. At a meeting of Ifá priests in Maracay, Venezuela, during the *Festival Internacional de Tradiciones Afroamericanas* in 2006, more than 100 babalawos gathered for two separate meetings to learn about their craft from master babalawos, the foremost of which was Àwíse Àgbáyé, Professor Wándé Abímbólá, in whose honor this project began. This group of Ifá priests, who gathered in Maracay from all over South America but predominantly from Cuba, was jarred by the presence of an Ìyánífá at the first session, and demanded to know why this was not a men's only meeting. These priests of Ifá in its multiplicity of manifestations fiercely believed that it is taboo for a woman to hear, learn, and see the secrets of Ifá. One babalawo told me in earnest, "There is no way that you can be an Ifá priest, since there is no such thing as a woman Ifá priest."

The intensity with which the babalawos protested women's participation bordered on anger and led me to want to examine the real role of women in the Ifá priesthood in Africa more closely. The officiating elders, however, emphasized that Ifá is not limited to any particular race or gender, and that anyone who wants to study seriously can learn about Ifá. Although certain topics discussed at that session were for initiates only, the elders insisted that the priesthood of Ifá was available to both men and women alike. The babalawos proceeded to use their entire time asking for more details on the roles that women play in the Ifá priesthood in Nigeria. Their questions were asked vehemently and intensely: How can a woman be a priest of Ifá? What can they do? Do they divine, and if so, with *ikin* or *opele*? Are they allowed to use the *opon Ifá* or divining board? Are there rules as to when a female priest can handle the instruments of Ifá and where they must be placed? Can she do sacrifices? Can she do initiations? What about when she is on her menstrual cycle? Can she do Ifá work on her own or must she always work with a babalawo? Can she learn to chant *odù Ifá*? What must be her relationship to Odù herself? What are the restrictions on what an Ìyánífá can do, if female Ifá priests exist at all?

This moment represented the culmination for me of an opinion that I had been hearing repeatedly in different forums for some time, and I decided to look more deeply into the idea and the practice of Ìyánífá. This inquiry into the role of women in the Ifá priesthood in West Africa confirmed that women are not at all excluded from the practice or the priesthood of Ifá. It seems that the exclusion of women from the Ifá priesthood is a factor of Yorùbá religion in the African diaspora, while on the African continent women are very much included. According to the Ifá literary corpus, Ìyánífá have been a crucial component of the Ifá priesthood since ancient times, and women have been a part of the Yorùbá priesthood since òrìsà first came to earth from heaven. Practices among Ifá devotees and initiates in West Africa illustrate that women's participation is as important today as it was then. Among the sacred literature of Ifá, we find female Ifá priests and female *odù*. We also find in traditional practice that no Ifá initiation can take place without the involvement of an Ìyánífá. Based on the Yorùbá concept of inclusion, let us consider that the idea of excluding women from the priesthood of Ifá runs contrary to the very nature of Ifá religion.

Using the notion of inclusion and exclusion, which is fundamental to Yorùbá religion and thought, I would like to examine the extent to which women are involved in the Ifá priesthood in Africa, based on my experience with Yorùbá religion in Nigeria, primarily in Oyo. In examining where women are included in the practice of Ifá and where they are excluded, it becomes apparent that it is imperative for women to be involved. Within each subgroup of the religion, among the multiplicity, depth, and magnitude of deities and practices, there is always a window of some size that allows for the participation of women. The very nature of Yorùbá religion is inclusive, leaving space for difference while not excluding anyone from participating in the group or groups of their choice and calling. This fact provides a model that illustrates one of the many ways in which Ifá, Elérìí Ìpín, witness of destiny, knows people's *orí* or inner heads and does not confuse *orí* with physical features nor with gender. As no one but Ifá himself knows the contents of another person's *orí* and destiny, I would like to defer to Ifá with regard to whether or not some women are destined to be part of the Ifá priesthood. To operate on the assumption that women should be excluded from the priesthood of Ifá runs counter to the very pillars of Ifá/Yorùbá religion, thought, and theology.

The theory put forth by Wándé Abímbọ́lá that Yorùbá religion in general is an inclusive religion is in contrast with Western approaches to religious traditions such as Christianity, Judaism, and Islam that self-identify as exclusive. This is why, for example, Christians, Jews, and Muslims all believe that anyone who is not ready to accept their dogma and who cannot meet certain prerequisites is not one of God's chosen ones. All three rely on the belief that there is a finite number of human beings who are a part of the group that makes up God's special or "chosen" people, and that all others are excluded from God's greatest blessing, eternal life. Yorùbá theology, however, insists that *every* human being is chosen by God. In fact, the Yorùbá word "*ènìyàn*," which translates literally into English as "human," has been translated by our Awise as "those chosen by God to do good [in the world]." Thus, based on this logic, everyone is a chosen one and nobody is excluded from being marked as divine. It is the responsibility of all humans to do good things in their lives, to maintain good character, and to fulfill the destinies that they chose in heaven before coming to earth as people.

Although Yorùbá religion in general and Ifá in particular was born out of a specific geographic, linguistic, and cultural setting, no person is excluded from participating in this way of life in which all humans are chosen people. In fact, the more people who practice Yorùbá religion, the greater the number of people in the world who do not follow a way of life based on exclusivity, and the closer we come as humans to reaching a critical mass of people who can effect change to the mindset taught by the mainstream power structures. The idea of Ifá as an inclusive religion is central to its belief system. One could even assert that the inclusive nature of Yorùbá religion demands that no person, regardless of race, gender, class, location, or other facets of identity, be excluded from the practice of Ifá religion. We see that according to the Ìyánífá tradition in West Africa, women have never been excluded from the study of Ifá, and have been included in the priesthood of Ifá since ancient times. In Nigeria, they continue to be included today. Within the framework of Ìyánífá tradition, though it is true that there are certain restrictions that an Ìyánífá must observe, they are not arbitrarily derived from a mindset of machismo or misogyny. They are rooted in the literature of Ifá itself and speak to the high regard for women that is embedded in Yorùbá life.

As it has been from ancient times until today, Ifá is a vast body of knowledge, virtually incomprehensible in its magnitude. The Ifá literary corpus contains 256 *odù* or separately catalogued conclaves of sacred verses or stories. Each one of these 256 *odù* is believed to contain eight hundred verses in total, out of which elder Ifá priests would learn at least sixteen by heart during more than twenty years of study. Therefore, Ifá is not for the weak-minded, and it is only serious students who can access even a small piece of the knowledge contained therein. In learning to chant and understand *odù Ifá*, one must also be able to understand the extent of it. Because the material to be mastered is so vast, women have always participated in the study of Ifá, but they have admittedly been a minority among those students who enlist in the consuming, long-term training of an Ifá priest. Women who wish to marry and have children or work in another capacity, as is becoming less uncommon, may find a conflict of interest with the depth of commitment required to be a proficient Ifá priest. There has been and still is, however, a core group of female Ifá priests known as Ìyánífá. Learning to be a proficient Ifá priest is by itself a consuming task, practice, and profession. But it is also a deep calling and a fulfilling commitment for those who are involved, the Awo (knowledgeable ones) and Iyawo (new initiates) alike.

Please note that I have chosen to use the English word "priest" to refer to both male and female initiated persons who do work in their capacities as Ifá devotees. Although many English speakers are fond of using the term "priestess," I believe that it is laden with western connotations of gender that do not apply as far as Ifá is concerned. For the most part, men and women who are initiated to Ifá serve in the same ritual capacities and provide the same services to the community. The distinguished scholar Oyèronké Oyewùmí has extensively discussed the importance of the fact that the Yorùbá language does not contain any gender-specific pronouns. She recommends the use of the terms "anamale" and "anafemale" to illustrate the fact that in the Yorùbá context western gender constructions are not relevant, and that men and women were generally able to serve in the same social capacities although their anatomical features were obviously distinct. Although the Yorùbá language does have two different terms for male and female Ifá priests, the connotations of those words do not refer to western gender constructs at all. I would like to emphasize the conundrum of discussing Ifá through the medium of the English language, with apologies for the fact, as Adrienne Rich once noted, that "This is the oppressor's language / yet I need it to talk to you" (1971, 16).

The word Ìyánífá is the Yorùbá name for a female priest of Ifá. There are two possible translations of the morphemes of this word—"Iya ni Ifá": (1) "Mother Who Has Ifá," or (2) "Mother in the Work (Practice, Profession) of Ifá." This is the female counterpart in the Yorùbá lexicon to "babalawo," the word for a male Ifá priest. It is generally agreed that the word "babalawo" can be translated into "father who has Awo" or "father of secrets." I appreciate that some advocate the parallel construction "iyalawo" alongside babalawo, but I do not see an advantage in adopting a new term that historically has not been in use. "Iyalawo" is not a more advanced Ìyánífá, but rather an invented term. Ìyánífá and babalawo both rely upon the *odù Ifá*, or the sacred oral literature, as the foundation of their knowledge and *àsé*, or sacred potentiality. Ìyánífá and babalawo both undergo a long period of intense training, apprenticeship, and an initiation ceremony before they can practice as priests of Ifá. Although some practitioners in the diaspora like the parallel structure of the word "iyalawo," I have not seen it used in traditional settings and do not object to the term Ìyánífá.

There is some evidence to contend that Òsun, the only female òrìsà who was among the first seventeen òrìsà to come to earth from heaven and who was the first wife of Ifá, held the àsé of an Ìyánífá. It is a commonly held belief in West Africa that the tradition of divining with sixteen cowries began with Òsun. In fact, Awise Agbaye Wándé Abímbólá contended in *Òsun Across the Waters* (2001) that the binary tradition of Ifá itself may have grown out of *Eerindilogun*, the system of divination that uses sixteen cowries. If these are true statements, then Òsun would have been an Ìyánífá, since she was in charge of the divination system out of which the Ifá system was born. Òsun was an Ìyálórìsà with the power to be Ìyánífá as well, especially during the time when she was holding Olódùmarè's bag of wisdom. Today, most women who are initiated into the priesthood of Yorùbá religion are known as Ìyálórìsà or Iyalòòsà, and they divine with sixteen cowries, which is also known as Òòsà. There are plenty of men who divine with *Eerindilogun* as well, called "Babalorisa" or "Babaòòsà." Despite the number of Yorùbá priests who use sixteen cowries, there are many Ìyánífá who divine with *ikin* and *opele*. An Ìyánífá is not to be confused with Apetebi, the wife of a babalawo who takes care of her husband, his shrine, his work, and most importantly his Ifá. Yeye Òsun would have been both Ìyánífá and Apetebi, and she set the first example of the critical role of women in Yorùbá religion and in Ifá.

Evidence of female Ifá priests can be found in the Ifá literary corpus; this is proof that from ancient times until today, it is expected that women will be involved in the priesthood of Ifá. We will cite a verse of Ifá here from Wándé Abímbólá's research in Òtúúrúpòn Méjì, in which it is Ato, a female *Egúngún* priestess among a priesthood that in fact is reserved primarily for men, who divined for Alapini. Ato is always a woman who was born holding the umbilical cord in her hand. Women born in this way are the only women permitted to participate in the *Egúngún* priesthood where the Ancestor Masquerade is situated. A relevant point is that Ato is a good example of the fact that even when men would like to establish secret societies for themselves, they must always somehow allow the participation of women. Because the diviner here is named Ato, in this *ese Ifá* the diviner was certainly a woman. Also note that the inquirer here is the Alapini or chief priest of *Egúngún*. In this *ese Ifá*, the Oluwo (Ifá priest) is a woman and is both a priest of *Egúngún* and an Ìyánífá, illustrating the removal of any perceived limitation of a woman's capacity to function in the Yorùbá religion. Not only is she an embodiment of the àsé of *Egúngún* (the ancestral divinity) and the àsé of Ifá, she is casting Ifá for her senior in the *Egúngún* tradition, as Alapini must be. The fact that she is called Ato kékeé might also indicate that she was still in her youth. She must have been quite proficient as an Ifá priest and diviner for her superiors to summon her to divine for them. This *ese Ifá* illustrates that women are not excluded from functioning as Ifá priests, nor are they completely excluded from serving as *Egúngún* priests in special cases. It also confirms that priests of one òrìṣà are not excluded from learning and becoming priests of another.

> *Olúògbògbò ló dífá fún Aátàgbórí*
> *Mokélùúgbè, ato kékeé,*
> *Abenu jége jége*
> *A dífá fún Alápìíni,*
> *Òfòríípáà okùn,*
> *Níjó tí n ménuú sèráhùn omo.*
> *Rírú ebo ní í gbe 'ni.*
> *Àìrú kì í gbèèyàn.*
> *E wáá bá ni ní màrínrín omo.*

Olúògbògbò[1] was the person who cast Ifá for Aátàgbórí[2]
Mokélùúgbè,[3] diminutive female *Egúngún* priestess (either young or small in stature)
Who could chant *Egúngún* literature ceaselessly
Was the person who performed Ifá divination for Alápìíni,[4]
Whose praise name is Òfòríípáà okùn[5]
On the day he, Alápìíni, was crying because of a lack of children
Performance of sacrifice brings blessings
Refusal to perform sacrifice does not bless any person
Come and find us amidst many children.[6]

In Owònrín Méjì we see evidence of Òsùmàrè, a female òrìṣà who reveals herself from the heavens above as the Rainbow, practicing as an Iyanifá. Òsùmàrè was the wife of Olofin, who took her own life while she was on her way to receive a great honor and chieftancy title. She has revealed herself through divination as an òrìsà who would agree to remove death (*iku*) from a devotee of Ifá. We see further evidence of òrìsà who also practice as Ifá priests. In the *ese Ifá* below, Òsùmàrè, the great Rainbow, is the Oluwo who divines for Ìrókò, another òrìsà who is represented on earth as a strong, huge tree. Òsùmàrè casts Ifá in order for the Ìrókò tree to conquer his enemies in the city of Ìgbò. Ìrókò performs his sacrifice and becomes recognized. He praises the great Rainbow, the female Ifá priest who divined for him when Èṣù commanded the farmers never to cut down Ìrókò Tree.

> *. . . Agada-ngba Òsùmàrè;*
> *A díá fún Ìrókò Ìgbò,*
> *Nbà tì nje nírògbun òtá.*
> *Igbó kìí dí gángán,*
> *Kíó dí gàngàn,*
> *Kéni mó mòrókò.*
> *Mo yagada-ngba Òsùmàrè,*
> *Òsùmàrè náà.*

. . . The great Rainbow,
Performed Ifá divination for the Ìrókò tree in the
city of Ìgbò
When he was living in the midst of enemies.
The forest cannot be so full of trees,
The forest cannot be so crowded with trees,
As to make impossible the recognition of Ìrókò tree.
I have become a great Rainbow.
(Abímbọ́lá 1977, 76)

There is also evidence in the Ifá literary corpus that some of the *odù* themselves were female. Each of the 256 *odù* is not only a body of sacred oral literature, but also a divinity in its own right. Not all can be identified according to their gender, but some are quite obviously male or female entities. A verse of Ogbètómopòn (Ogbè Òtúúrúpòn), which was taught to me by the Awise, demonstrates that *odù Ifá* can be female as well as male. That which reveals that this *odù* is female are the morphemes in the name of the *odù* and several verses in which the Oluwo's or diviner's name is Ogbètómopòn herself. Ogbe *Tomopon* or Ogbe *tún omo pon* may mean "Ogbe adjust the baby on your back" or "Ogbe mount a baby on your back once again." (The morphemes can be broken down as follows: *Tún*-again; *Omo*-child; *Pòn*-the back.) The phrase Ogbetomopon may refer to putting another, different baby on your back or adjusting the one that is already on your back. It also can be interpreted as an instruction to bear another child.

Ogbè tómo pòn,
Ogbè súnmo sí.
Àgbàpòn ò lérè,
Bómo bá wù ó,
O lòó bí tìe.
A díá fún Rìnkínkí
Èyí tí í sobìnrin Àpáta.
Àwon méjèèjì ni wón ní kí won ó rúbo araa won sáìkú.
Wón wáà n rayéè láì níí kú.
Njé rírú ebo,
Èrù àtùkèsù.
Kèè pé,
Kèè jìnà,
E bá ni láìkú kangiri,
Àìkú kangiri
Là á bá ni lésè obarìsà.

Ogbè, mount a child on your back once again.
Ogbè, move up (adjust) the child on your back.
Mounting other people's children on the back brings no profit.
If you love children,
Go and produce your own.

Ifá divination was performed for Rìnkìnkí
Who was a wife of Bare Rock.
Both of them were told to perform sacrifice to avert death
When they were going to the earth to become immortal.
When we perform sacrifice,
When we sacrifice to Èsù,
Before long,
At no distant date,
Come and meet us living long and in perfect health.
Living long and in perfect health,
That is how we always are at the feet of the king of divinities.

Now, if *odù* are sacred components of the vastness of Ifá, and if *odù* themselves are deities, how can *odù* be female but Ifá priests cannot? In West African Ifá tradition, women are practitioners and priests, and are as integral to the practice of Ifá as is the sacred literature of Ifá in its entirety.

It should be recognized that there are two types of *odù*: *odù* the literature and Odù the woman, the great wife of Orunmila, who is in essence Ifá himself. *Odù* the literature is discussed above, wherein references are made to female *odù* or sub-bodies of this literary corpus. Odù the woman cannot be seen by women, nor can she be seen by men who have not undergone a specific ritual to clean and prepare their eyes. Under penalty of death or blindness, every Yorùbá person must honor the sanctity of Odù regardless of initiation. The reasons for this taboo are clearly laid out in the Ifá literary corpus. Odù herself is an *àkúdàáyá*, someone who has died and yet is still living on earth; therefore she must be kept secret and her privacy respected. Orunmila brought her back to earth to serve as his wife, but she only agreed to do so on the condition that he would keep her secret and nobody should see her or enter the room where she was kept. Today, while some babalawos receive the icons of Odù in tangible form, many do not. Odù is the secret of many great babalawos, but it is not required to have her to be a great babalawo. I believe that the ill-evidenced idea held by so many male babalawos in the diaspora that women cannot be priests of Ifá is due to confusion around the subject of Odù. The fact that women cannot see Odù does not mean that women cannot be priests of Ifá.

Based on this principle of Odù, there are two types of babalawos, Babalawo Elégán and Babalawo Olódù. Both serve as effective priests, diviners, counselors, and healers for their communities. Both cast Ifá and do *ebo* or sacrifice, while chanting the sacred prayers of Ifá. Both can perform any function that Ifá priests generally perform. The difference is that one has Odù (Babalawo Olódù) and one does not (Babalawo Elégán). Women, as Ìyánífá, are automatically Elégán and must never see Odù, but male babalawo can also be Babalawo Elégán. (A rare few who do not have Odù have been sanctified to see her for certain ritual purposes.) Male Ifá priests who have not seen Odù before or have not undergone a special ceremony must not see her at all. Female Ìyánífá never receive and must never see Odù, because of who she is and her relationship to Ifá himself. There is no question whatsoever as to the gender of the backbone of Ifá, the master of the secrets of the wisdom of Ifá, the keeper of the key to divination, and the very foundation of Ifá religion. She is a woman. Although other women cannot see her, Odù possesses something that she shares with all women, and especially with all female Ifá priests. Odù is female intuition; she is the Knowing that happens before knowledge is revealed on this earthly plane. She is kept in the deepest crevices of the house of Orunmila and in the most private cavities of babalawos' shrines. Ìyánífá around the world huddle together sometimes and meditate upon the fact that this cavity is a metaphor for the womb, the uterus, and that although women cannot see Odù, to some extent Ìyánífá *are* Odù. The case of Odù is not a justification to disallow women from the priesthood of Ifá. Women are always Babalawo Elegan, as are the men who do not have Odù. Only babalawo who have Odù are known as Babalawo Olodu. So, although women as well as uninitiated men are excluded from seeing Odù, no male or female Ifá priest is excluded from the responsibility of learning *odù Ifá*, the literature. The concept of inclusion is again paramount to the discussion, as the very survival of Odù the woman depends upon her exclusion as well as her seclusion.

Odù the woman can be considered the embodiment of *odù* the literature in the sense that every Ifá priest, babalawo or Ìyánífá, on his or her initiation day at the end of a seven-day ritual, is born into a new person, an Iyawo who meets the earth guided by a particular *odù Ifá*. There is no babalawo or Ìyánífá who does not know his or her *odù*, as that is the very foundation of the life and work of the Ifá priest, whether he or she possesses the icons of Odù the woman or not. This centrality of an *odù* to the identity of an Ifá priest is interesting to note in the context of Ifá initiation itself and in relation to the role Ìyánífá must play in the initiation of an Ifá priest. In fact, while this most important divination is cast for the would-be Ifá priest, it is an Ìyánífá who must hold the *ibo*, the implements of Ifá that answer questions by indicating Ifá's response. An Ìyánífá must always play a central role in the initiation ceremony of any Ifá priest, whether they are male or female. The procession to the sacred grove of Ifá, the *igbodu*, is always led by an Ìyánífá who is carrying an image of Èsù on her head. The recession as the new initiate emerges from the *igbodu* is also led by an Ìyánífá carrying an image of Èsù. Traditionally, while the initiation is taking place, the Ìyánífá is sitting opposite the *igbodu* cracking nuts of *egusi*, presumably both for sacrifice and for nourishment. There has been some debate among Ifá priests whether Ìyánífá can perform initiations at all; some assert that women cannot ever perform Ifá initiations, even if they are initiating someone as another Ìyánífá. The fact is that if women were to initiate someone into Ifá, they would have to initiate that person as a babalawo or an Ìyánífá Elegan, as discussed above. The traditional involvement of Ìyánífá in the Ifá initiation ceremony speaks again to the centrality of women in Yorùbá life in general and particularly in the Ifá priesthood.

In the case of every Yorùbá priest, there are certain taboos which the initiate of one day or one hundred years must observe. I sought permission from my Oluwo to reveal some basic taboos here. Some of these taboos are common to all babalawos and Ìyánífás, while some are quite specific to the individual, the *odù* that bore him or her as an Ifá priest, and other Ifá that are cast during initiation. For instance, every babalawo must be a peaceful person whose life is guided by Ifá. They must not disrespect any other Ifá priest. If there is rioting or fighting, they must not get involved. They should not participate in wicked gossip. All women and most men, including Babalawo Elegan, must not see Odù. Ìyánífá and other women must also observe a taboo not to touch the implements of Ifá (or other òrìsà) during the time of their menstruation. They also should not touch birds or blood at this time. In Oyo, they can be present during spiritual work such as divination and *ebo* while observing the restrictions mentioned above, although certain very particular *ebos* may be affected by the presence of a menstruating woman. The efficaciousness of some medicines may also be affected if a menstruating woman touches them.

In the diaspora, the protocol of the priest or house may forbid the participation of menstruating women to varying degrees. For some, a woman on her cycle may not be present for any spiritual work at all. For others, she may not even prepare food. Still others allow her to chant and sing, but not to dance or do sacrifices. A respectful practice for menstruating women is to inform the officiating priests of her status and ask the Ifá priests to instruct her on their own protocols. Some will insist that this is a misogynist taboo, while some argue that this taboo originally grew out of a strictly hygienic concern. Many women and some men contend that it is at this time when women are at their most powerful to effect spiritual work and most vulnerable to be affected by spiritual work done in their presence. My own thought is that the founders of this taboo may have been women themselves, who knew that they should use this time as a spiritual and physical rejuvenation. Also, women in ancient Yorùbáland and in most parts of the world today would be happy to arrange a break for themselves once a month in light of the fierce energy that they put into their work on a regular basis.

A similar vein of thought to that which prohibits women from the Ifá priesthood imagines certain taboos for Ìyánífá that are not founded in Ifá literature, such as the idea that Ìyánífá must not divine with *ikin* but must always use *opele*. With no disrespect intended to any indigenous Oluwo who may follow this taboo, I have not heard of this restriction from my own elders, nor has any credible evidence based in Ifá been put forth to this effect. Also, some babalawos feel that a woman cannot hold an *opon Ifá* or divining board on the ground between her legs, as is most natural to do when divining. A Cuban comrade in Ifá asserts that the *opon Ifá* cannot face a woman's vagina. This too demeans the position not only of Ìyánífá but of Ifá in its relationship to women, and we have not found evidence within the Ifá corpus that supports this prohibition. Also, in some cases Olofin or Odùduwà, the progenitor of the Yorùbá people and great ancestor of the Ooni, is referred to in the same terms as Odù. But it should be noted that Odùduwà or Olofin is not the same divinity as Odù. Although both are extremely powerful and sacrosanct, the relationship that Ifá mandates between women and Odù is not the same as that between women and Odùduwà.

One can conclude that Yorùbá religion in West Africa is more respectful of women's power, and also more empowering to women, than western traditions and Yorùbá traditions in the African diaspora. In a personal communication in February 2008, Professor Jacob Olupona aptly notes: "It is in the area of resilience and change that African traditional religion has demonstrated its most important contribution to contemporary knowledge. African traditional religion has been quite receptive to change. For example, its encounter with the two monotheistic religions which have come to Africa, Christianity and Islam, as well as with modernity, has transformed the religion and triggered various kinds of responses to the encounter."

One likely logical response to the "encounter" mentioned above is a change in relation to women's participation in the Ifá priesthood. That change may have been triggered by the brutal experience of slavery and the attempted erasure of African identity from African people in the diaspora. The long-term forced encounters between African indigenous religions, Christianity, and Islam that occurred outside the African continent certainly would have distorted the role of women in Ifá at least as much as they affected other aspects of social life. One might even argue that the prohibition on women's involvement as Ifá priests that is found in the diaspora is a direct result of the influence of western religions where women are forbidden from entering the priesthood. Women cannot be Catholic priests, nor can they be Muslim imams; so to insist that women can and should be permitted to serve as Ifá priests is, in fact, a revolutionary and anti-imperialist idea.

I have the utmost respect for all manifestations of Yorùbá religion, and I believe that its every form is in fact a testimony to the very truth and endurance of Ifá. The dynamic capacity of the Yorùbá religion has allowed it to survive slavery, desecration, fear, hatred, and every imaginable brutality that African people have suffered in the world. It is important in this time of rapid growth of the Yorùbá religion and dissemination of Ifá to emphasize that there is no realm of Yorùbá religion from which women are entirely excluded. The exclusion of women is a practice of imperialism that is not part of Ifá practice in Africa, although it is widely practiced among Ifá devotees in the African diaspora.

I would like to close with a verse of Ifá in which it is not clear whether the diviner is male or female, but it is clear that all humans in general and Ifá priests in particular—even Òrunmílà himself—will do well to commit themselves to the veneration and study of their ancestors from most recent to most ancient. If more of us would commit ourselves to the study and implementation of the wisdom found within the Ifá literary corpus, the world would be further along on its way to healing the wounds of the past. We should all make a covenant with our ancestors, and like Ifá himself and Odù Ifá herself, we would not die anymore. And we would never allow any African culture, language, or people to die again:

> Báá báá ró lórò eni
> Sòròsòrò làá dà.
> A dífá fún Òrúnmìlà
> Ifá ńlo lèé begúngún mulè
> Mo diwin o
> Mo begúngún mulè
> Òrúnmìlà, Èlà Sòdè
> Ifá, ńlo bégúngún mulè
> Lagabalá
> Mo begúngún mulè
> Mo diwin.

> When someone meets with a trusted friend
> One becomes very talkative
> When Òrunmílà performed divination
> Ifá was going to make a sacred pact with the ancestors
> I have become a spirit
> I have made a secret pact with the ancestors
> I have become a spirit
> Òrunmílà, Èlà Sòdè
> Ifá was going to make a pact with the Ancestors
> Truly so, I have made a pact with the Ancestors
> I have become a spirit.

The verse above states that those of us who would go into the sacred grove of *Egúngún* to make a covenant with our ancestors, as Orunmila himself did, will live forever. To make a covenant with our ancestors, to practice our religion as they taught us to do, and to honor our ancestors while doing so, is so that we ourselves and our religion may become immortal. *Àse wa!*

Notes

1. Olúògbògbò is the title of the ruler of the town of Ógbògbò whose gender is not specified.
2. Aátàgbórí is probably the name of the title of the king of Ìgbórí.

3. Mokélùúgbè is a person's name.
4. Alápìíni is the chief priest of *Egúngún*, the ancestral divinity.
5. Òfòríipáà okùn is the nickname of Alápìíni.
6. All translations are mine unless otherwise indicated.

References

Abímbọ́lá, Kola. 2006. *Yorùbá Culture: A Philosophical Account.* Birmingham, UK: Ìrókò Academic Publishers.

Abímbọ́lá, Wándé. 1977. *Ifá Divination Poetry.* New York: Nok.

——. 2001. "The Bag of Wisdom: Osun and the Origins of the If a Divination." In *Osun Across the Waters: A Yoruba Goddess in Africa and the Americas.* Edited by Joseph M. Murphy and Mei-Mei Sanford. Bloomington: Indiana University Press. 141–154.

Beier, Ulli, ed. 1967. *Introduction to African Literature: An Anthology of Critical Writing on African and Afro-American Literature and Oral Tradition.* Evanston, IL: Northwestern University Press.

Cabrera, Lydia. 1974. *Yemayá y Ochún: Kariocha, Iyalorichas y Olorichas.* Madrid: Forma Gráfica.

Kamara, Jemadari, and Tony Menelik Van Der Meer, eds. 2004. *State of the Race Creating Our 21st Century: Where Do We Go From Here?* Boston: Diaspora Press.

Kaplan, Flora Edouwaye S., ed. 1997. *Queens, Queen Mothers, Priestesses and Power: Case Studies in African Gender.* New York: New York Academy of Sciences.

Murphy, Joseph M., and Mei-Mei Sanford, eds. 2001. *Òsun Across the Waters: A Yorùbá Goddess in Africa and the Americas.* Bloomington: Indiana University Press.

Olupona, Jacob K., ed. 1991. *African Traditional Religions in Contemporary Society.* New York: Paragon House.

Oyewùmí, Oyèrónké. 1997. *The Invention of Women: Making an African Sense of Western Gender Discourses.* Minneapolis: University of Minnesota Press.

Rich, Adrienne, 1971. *The Will to Change: Poems 1968–1970.* New York: Norton.

19 Transnational Ifá

The "Readings of the Year" and Contemporary Economies of Orisa Knowledge

Kamari Maxine Clarke

On January 1, 2008, the second generation of Orisa-voodoo leadership in Oyotunji African Village in South Carolina gathered in the Afin (king's quarters) adorned in white, with all eyes focused on the Ifá oracle's annual prophecy—the communication with the gods to procure the reading of the year. This annual ceremony in Oyotunji, like that in Cuba and among *santeros* in the United States, has become increasingly critical to various national and international communities as the yearly message used to circumvent and prevent disasters, undermine hardships, and maximize social and economic opportunities. But this time the interpretation focused on diasporic concerns—diasporic realities and political challenges. Such forms of civic prophecy have their roots in West African rituals in the Americas, where the history of slavery in the Americas led to relegation of divinatory practices to private and secretive realms (Stewart 2005). However, what we are seeing today, with the political expansion of such forms of public divination in new diasporic formations in Oyotunji African voodoo religious practices and beyond, is the move from a ritual practice embedded in African Ifá referents to new civic interpretive constellations reflective of the contemporary growth of a religious metapolitics of transnational Ifá.

Today, despite the movement of large numbers of African immigrants in the United States and the spread and resurgence of African charismatic religious participation in Africa and the West, we have witnessed a rapid religious recomposition in the engagement with Yorùbá religious traditional practices. Marked by new scales of religious organization, new directional flows of influence, assertive new theologies, and intensified public presences, the reality today is that

Orisa-Voodoo practitioners are engaged in a renewed and growing interest in religion in Africa. But Africa merely represents a symbolic domain, or the basis of enchantment for the marking of originary roots and legitimizing histories. The new African-based religious resurgences are intersubjective yet taking shape in political, economic, and cultural constellations that have less to do with modalities of African religious consciousness than with the ways these new Ifá diasporic ritual resurgences are being engaged in altered spheres of practice and power. In the United States, these new spheres of practice in Ifá diasporic rituals are increasingly producing modalities of religious consciousness that are deeply responsive to black American social and political domains—from the campaigning and election of Barack Obama to the growing popularity of various forms of oratory, such as the reading of the year and various acts of prophecy. And as such, they are increasingly becoming a critical domain for the reformulation of African-based practices in an increasingly American social space.

In these Americanist domains, various religious cosmologies are playing increasingly expansive roles in the replication of American concerns and the reproduction of increasingly Americanist sensibilities. In exploring one aspect of this context, this chapter explores the growth and changing significance of the reading of the year in Oyotunji Village and highlights the development of this form of Ifá divination as a mechanism for prophecy among African American practitioners engaged in African reclamation movements. How we make sense of various ritual mechanisms for procuring knowledge about the future, about hope, and about the development of alliances with institutions of power outside of their "traditional" sites remains understudied. The context for understanding such African-based rituals in histories of American slavery is among the most controversial issues unfolding in diaspora studies today.

The controversy has involved two competing lines of argumentation. The first is that the notion of the African diasporic religion and its religious formations should be imagined within the history of African ritual cosmologies and that we can understand the structural transformation of black religious change today only in that light (Abímbọlá 1976, 2006). The second is the assumption that the history of black Atlantic slavery represents the turning point for the development of new religious formations and that contemporary religious formations should be understood in relation to this history of religious loss (Ayorinde 2000; Brandon 1993; Gonzales-Wippler 1992). My line of argumentation makes clear that neither the history of African ritual cosmologies nor the history of slavery is foundational for understanding the reenchantment of new forms of Ifá religious consciousness. Rather, the reality of emergent political and economic and cultural domains, coupled with a new global social imaginary around which Ifá divination is taking shape, has more to do with a range of new forces whose constellations represent the diversity of African pasts and futures and thus the various genealogies of formation. In this regard, I call for the recasting of transatlantic slavery as a central metaphor in black Atlantic imaginaries, in order to rethink the politics of Orisa prophecy as a form of public praxis being brokered today by U.S. Orisa practitioners, and in order to predict, to diagnose, and to accord hope.

Rather than assuming that the expansion of public divinatory mechanisms such as the reading of the year should be examined based on histories of slavery, I show that various readings of the year by U.S.-based babalawos are new claims to diasporic linkages that are forward looking and that seek to be relevant in international and national affairs. These new formations have taken shape as a result of histories of slavery that have led to predominantly black American excursions to West African regions such as Benin, Nigeria, Ghana, and Senegal to engage in roots tourism as well as to procure new technologies for the recalibration of black subjectivity.

These new technologies of knowledge are taking the form of packages of knowledge that are procured through divination and marketed through various electronic and interpersonal spheres. The reading of the year is one such technology. But as I argue, practitioners perform Ifá divinatory readings in relation to post–Berlin Wall discourses of neoliberal governance in which what we see operative is not simply dialogues about the scattering of enslaved Africans transported from Africa to the Americas, the Indian Ocean, and elsewhere. Rather, the establishment of modern capitalism and the building of the modern world have involved the ironic decentering of slavery and the recalibration of knowledge in relation to new technologies for understanding and striving for a future of inclusion of democratic participation.

I now turn to the use of new divinatory readings in a large movement in the United States known as the Oyotunji African Village, and among their followers spread throughout the United States What is important to note here is that when Orisa practices were exported with Afro-Cuban practitioners to the United States in the 1960s, the popular mode of knowledge production was not Ifá divination performed by babalawos, but *Èrìndínlógún* performed by Orisa priests and priestesses. In the 1960s and 1970s histories of the development of the Orisa-Voodoo movement, Santería-based divinatory techniques were incorporated by many Orisa-Voodoo Yorùbá revivalists and provided adherents with the necessary tools to produce Yorùbá ritual knowledge about the past and to predict the future.

From the late 1980s to the early 1990s, as more priests traveled to West Africa to pursue *Igbó odù* (the initiation procedure of obtaining a primary divinatory *odù* for Ifá), increasing numbers of Orisa followers became equipped to conduct this new form of Yorùbá divination known as Ifá divination. My objective is to demonstrate not only how Orisa devotees have used Ifá divination to manage the political economy of American hegemonic power, but also how they use contemporary and cutting-edge technologies of knowledge to enhance their own socio-political capital in U.S. contexts. I show that transnational Yorùbá revivalists are innovating with Ifá knowledge technologies to reproduce new relations in their world through the establishment of normative values and bundles of divinatory typologies. These relations are diasporic in their breadth and far-reaching in their ability to engage issues of international and global concern. What we see is that the new technologies of divinatory hope being deployed today are much unlike earlier forms. These contemporary divinatory technologies draw on metaprag-matic domains in which divinatory speech is both referential and pragmatic. As a referential form of knowledge, it articulates meaning through prediction. Its pragmatic function highlights the key goal of such utterances—to regulate core domains of the possible by calling on the prestige of the symbolic power of the American presidency, not of African empires.

New Technologies of Hope: Ifá Divination

Divination is often represented by Orisa practitioners as an application of sa-cred knowledge. It operates as a mechanism through which canonical divinatory structures enable priests to transport information about the otherwise unknown future, past, and present. A range of anthropologists have studied the centrality of divinatory knowledge in the lives of individuals and demonstrated that divi-nation provides a means by which individuals can understand their world and interpret their role in it (Bascom 1969a, 1969b, 1980; Abímbọ́lá 1976, 1977; Akin-naso 1995). Contemporary studies of transnational Orisa formations have tended to focus on the mechanics of divinatory ritual practices in the context of the his-tories West African slave migrations. They have paid less attention to the specific processes by which changing divinatory interpretations are both incorporated into a particular divinatory canon, thereby changing the canon itself, and the mechanisms by which new forms of global power are being allied.

As we shall see, examinations of the spread of the reading of the year high-light how divinatory change is being brokered through new public channels. As always, in order for these forms of divinatory communication to be seen as ef-ficacious, the process must involve the systematic repetition of ritual protocol, particular utterances, and projections about the future and the assumption of possession, through which the body of the babalawo becomes a conduit for the communication of the message. In Oyotunji Village, the specialized knowledge derived is characterized by a performative language, which the diviner engages in creating the ritual process. Through Ifá divination, not only do diviners offer practitioners the ability to control their fate and therefore empower themselves with transformative acts, they also allow them to promote an underground econ-omy within which like-minded practitioners can form various alliances toward the procurement of new knowledge about the world and their place in it.

Yet even as divination involves the repetition of formal acts and utterances through which sacred knowledge is derived, it is also a highly interpretive act, embedded in particular relations of power and holding with it the power of hope and innovation for new futures. In this regard, Ifá divination is represented among most Oyotunji Village practitioners as the most sophisticated and ancient form of divinatory knowledge. It is believed to have sustained its ancient and traditional form over longer periods than the other system, *Èrìndínlógún* (Brandon 1993, 142).

Èrìndínlógún divination, on the other hand, is the most common form of divination among recently initiated priests in Oyotunji and throughout U.S.-affiliated and Santería communities. It tends to be more inclusive in its potential for priestly participation. For example, both women and men can function equally as *Èrìndínlógún* priests.[1] Although gendered involvement is changing, women's participation in particular is not a widespread assumption of Ifá divinatory practices. What is relevant here is that the successful completion of an initiation in *Igbó odù* raises the initiate to the highest rank of priesthood—a babalawo.

In the 1990s, Oyotunji-centered revivalists as well as increasing numbers of affiliated Orisa-Voodoo practitioners attempted to radically adapt their divinatory rituals in order to produce new mechanisms through which the ancestral past could be known.[2] They not only developed Ifá ritual institutions to explain the logic of slavery through "roots readings," but they also developed a range of divinatory tools for widespread public consumption. As such, various divination readings have circulated for both individual/private and public uses. I classify the public and private Orisa divination readings into two categories: (1) standard individual reading (which incorporates the ancestral family), and (2) what I refer to as the civic society reading. Whereas different divinatory methods involving both *èrìndínlógún* and Ifá are used for the standard individual reading, only Ifá methods are used for readings in civic contexts.

Individual readings are the most common in both Yorùbáland and the Americas, and are conducted between a client and a diviner. In Nigeria, they tend to take place in the presence of the client. In the United States, although in most cases the presence of the client is necessary, there are innovations in which absentee divinatory readings can be derived and communicated by telephone or the Internet.[3] Nevertheless, the standard interaction is organized as a private consultation in which the priest functions as a conduit for messages from the ancestors and orisas. The priest interprets the configuration of the divinatory tools and is then expected to verbalize these interpretations for the client.

Individual divination readings can also be a necessary part of social activities. Some examples of the creative incorporation of standard readings in Oyotunji revivalist movements are the river reading, designed to ritualize the process of initiation of new Oyotunji residents, and the family reading, *orò ìdílé*, otherwise known as the "roots reading."[4] Divinatory roots readings follow the same logic and format as both standard and civic readings but their goal is to recover client ancestral histories. By tracing family lineage, determining kin occupations, and endowing the client with new Yorùbá names, these individual readings are meant to uncover the past that has been lost as a result of transatlantic slavery. Thus, the goal is to obtain knowledge about Yorùbá or West African ancestors. The exchange of knowledge between the client and diviner is made possible through the ritualization of the Ifá canon.

The individual and civic forms of divinatory processes share the same methods but serve different functions. The civic reading, although structurally similar to the individual reading, is conducted for the purposes of group instruction; it is within the group that the reading of the year falls. Types of civic readings popular in Oyotunji include the reading of the week, the reading of the month, the reading of the year, and the annual Orisa cult (*egbë*) readings.[5]

Yorùbá Civic Divinatory Readings: The Reading of the Year

Often civic readings are performed by a group of two or more priests from a designated cult group and occur in incrementally consistent periods. Both in Nigerian locations and in Oyotunji Village, head priests conduct readings in an attempt to alert the leadership, the community, or the nation of the Oracle's predictions. The reading of the year is one such civic divinatory ritual, representing a set of predictions for the new year. Although delivered orally, and traditionally committed to memory, the production of these divination "readings" has shifted in the late twentieth and early twenty-first century from the oral transmission of narratives, to the translation of oral narratives, to the written documentation of these predictions and postings on email and the World Wide Web.

The key to these readings involves establishing the lead or head *odù*, and determining whether it is in *Ire* (positive) or *Osobo* (negative). Then readings are divided into various sectors: (1) a reading for the world, (2) a reading for the United States, and (3) a reading for African Americans. The interpretation reflects the vantage point of the babalawos and their audience. In this case, themes dealing with turmoil, struggle, blessings, family, and the adherence to law are relevant. The reading offers African Americans hope and locates them in an important economy of involvement in their own disenfranchisement. As noted below:

> *Reading for the World, the United States, and African Americans*
> *Dafa fun Aiye* [World]
> *Oworin Sa/Olori odu*
> *Eji Ogbe/Ire*
> *Irosun Rete/Osobo*
> *Iwori Sa/Mojale*
> *Ogunda rete/kotojale*

Oworin Sa says there is likely to be upheaval and turmoil, which will come like a storm and will in fact usher in the changes that bring things together. The young people will help to foster these changes and will have a great impact on world events this year.

Eji Ogbe says that this type of momentum brings expansion and creativity. There will be more talk on saving the world, living green, and the like, and a discussion of new plans about how to get these things done. They will not happen overnight. It talks about a flash flood of activity and information that will work slower under levels. It will take an extended period—be patient or actively passive.

Iwori Sa says some of the nations "on top" are slipping, or may take a fall. The destiny of the world is changing. There are those who want more, and those who do not want all the natural resources used up before it is their turn. Many in the world seeking their destiny without knowing what they are looking for will be brought right to the door of priests. Those with spiritual knowledge and power must come together, work together, or the world will pay the price. Without this unity it would be like writing your name at the edge of the ocean and seeing it washed away without a trace.

We must use the energy of honesty and ability of Ogun to organize with those of like mind. Law enforcement will be big this year. Stay legal—don't get caught in tricks and traps because you don't have the right fee or piece of paper!

Dafa fun [United States]
Iwori worin/Olori odu
Oturapon gunda/Ire
Ogunda Meji/osobo
Obara Sa/kotojale

Iwori worin with *Ogunda Meji* as the *osobo* is almost the complete opposite of the world. Insanity, fights at every turn, rather chaotic in the United States, as they are undecided about what to do!

Ogunda Meji tells us of wars and rumors of wars concerning the United States. A lot will be due to the United States' lack of honesty—overthrowing democracy, supporting dictators, and the like. More U.S. officials will have problems with the law. Overseas assassinations that involve the United States may happen. There could be another dramatic attack on the United States this year!

Eji Ogbe tells us that there will be procrastinators in the United States, in regards to discussions around ideas. . . . Big talk, little action! Big plans will be frustrated this year. The best thing for the United States would be to bring troops home, though this is unlikely because there is too big an investment.

Oturapon gunda says honesty could help the United States resolve disputes. This year is a good year for the United States to have a diet of strict humility, as it may be forced to eat crow! There is likely to be a continued loss of prestige . . . more troops being sacrificed . . . and billions of dollars going to support a futile effort. Misdirected focus. The United States needs a change of image . . . not just public relations, but down to the basics of how the nation formulates.

Dafa fun [African Americans]
Ogbe worin/Olori Odu
Ogunda worin/ire *
Otura wori/osobo
IworiMeji/mojale *
Irosun tura/kotojale

The African Americans have a good reading this year. *Ogbe worin* says there's a lot going on in the African American community. Young people are greatly involved in working these plans. They may not yet be the leaders, but they contribute to the energy of creativity and expansiveness. It is a good year to start good projects for African Americans that address what the race needs.

Ogunda worin says things will move quickly with great energy and drive. This will not be a time for procrastination—one could get run over by this movement. African Americans are coming into their own destiny realizing who they are and what they bring to the table! It will be a good year for educational programs. There are those who will be coming searching for answers.

Otura wori says it is not a good year to ego trip, thinking you are more than you are. Communication will not be well thought out or grounded. Truth must be what is put out there! There are likely to be a few pretenders . . . who may not even have a clue.

Kotojale, Irosun tura tells us that having a spiritual ego is good as long as you don't go overboard. It is a good year for the priesthood to sell a "good" bag of goods. It is a good year for spiritual education, because people will be seeking spiritual information.

Reading for the World

As noted, the message for the world is that of change and youth. The destiny of the world is changing. The idea that many in the world will be in a position to seek their destiny and that they will be "brought right to the door of priests" offers hope to believers whose world depends on conversion and change. The message is that of unity and change.

Also included is a message about honesty. It provides warnings to those otherwise oblivious to the implications of breaking the law: "We must use the energy of honesty and ability of Ogun to organize with those of like mind. Law enforcement will be big this year. Stay legal—don't get caught in tricks and traps because you don't have the right fee or piece of paper!"

Reading for the United States

For the United States, the message is that of chaos, since the Ogunda Meji is in *osobo*. It describes wars and rumors of wars with the United States. This is a result of the United States's lack of honesty—overthrowing democracies, supporting dictators. As noted, "Big plans will be frustrated this year. The best thing for the United States would be to bring troops home,"

This message points to the war on terror and the seemingly dismal place of the United States in the world. Dishonesty is identified as a part of the problem, and as a result there will be a "continued loss of prestige."

Reading for African Americans

Finally, the reading for African Americans highlights the most positive part of the prophecy. As noted, "*Ogbe worin* says there's a lot going on in the African American community. Young people are greatly involved in working these plans. They may not yet be the leaders, but they contribute to energy of creativity and expansiveness."

We are told that it is a "good year to start good projects for African Americans that address what the race needs." Here, the projects should be taken on according to racial group needs, and it will be a time to "move quickly with great energy and drive." It is a "good year for educational programs. There are those who will be coming searching for answers." Thus, it will be a time of plenty and those with spiritual egos kept in check will reap the economic gains from others seeking spiritual information.

Economization of Divinatory Knowledge: A New Generation

Oyotunji Village's changing divinatory practices are reflective of the forms of change in the community's own social realities. In the 1970s, Oba Oseijeman Adefumi I forged ahead to create Oyotunji Village; on February 11, 2005 he passed on and was succeeded by his son, the now-reigning Oba (king) of the diasporic world of Orisa-Voodoo black nationalist practitioners. Where once divinatory knowledge in Oyotunji Village was shared freely with community members and, more broadly, with affiliates or nonmembers, technological advances have enabled the inclusion of a YouTube excerpt of the reading. Since this writing, the video and has been removed from Oyotunji Village's website. I commented in my field notes, however, that at the end of the video the listener is told to make a donation in order to acquire a copy of this entire reading: "This year these video proceedings are available to those who want to make a purchase. By logging onto www.oyotunji.org you can obtain a copy."

Alongside the development of this new marketing strategy we are also seeing the emergence of a centralized authority—an institutionalized authority of divination, reflecting the move from a personal and individualized packaging of interpretive knowledge about lost dispersed Africans to a more bureaucratic formulation that seems conscious of state concerns and that is allowing practitioners to recalibrate their practices alongside predominant hegemonic forms.

This process of transformation has led to the packaging of particular forms of Ifá divinatory authority by which various religious movements and their constituents create ways of arranging, structuring, and resolving social challenges connected to how practitioners come to terms with significant changes in global events. These oracular mechanisms highlight the new marketing techniques of Orisa-Voodoo's new religious formations. And as such, the entry of these new spheres of divinatory power represent a kind of recalibration in which the once marginal forms of subject making that involved particular valences outside of state mechanisms and alliances have shifted to take on a new form of calibration—which I call new "diasporic technologies of religious consciousness"—in which the nature of engagement is actually less about the movement of vernacular forms of homeland divinatory knowledge than about recalibration of social consciousness in new global domains.

This recalibration of diasporic formations is not only a departure from earlier uses of diaspora, as embedded in marginal formations of identity politics; it involves particular extranational forms of community making unlike earlier forms that were deeply embedded in global knowledge about international relations, widespread Rule of Law mechanisms, and supranational institutions such as the United Nations. As an international body, the United Nations is also involved in the fostering of transnational diasporic community formation. Thus, the invention and application of Ifá divinatory readings such as the reading of the year highlights the incorporation of the form and structure of Ifá divination and the recalibration of older knowledge domains into new sociopolitical forms that call on us to ask, What are the new ways that notions of diasporic linkages to Africa are being deployed, and what does that deployment say about the growing merger between the religious and the political, belief, and consumerism?

Answering this inquiry has implications for how social science scholarship approaches the fiction of race and its relationship to African diasporic linkages to slavery as the central component of that dispersal. What it highlights is that new Oyotunji-American Orisa networks of knowledge and hope are being articulated within new public constellations of kinship and linkage, politics, and international consciousness. In this regard, there is a need to rethink the social and political histories of these formations in relation to the ways that particular practices move from discourses of marginality and powerlessness to discourses of international power and self-help. Thus, today's uses of Ifá divination highlight the brokering of hope and the desire to lay claim to the West and its resources—to have the ability to know the future and to spread ideas about present practices.

My goal here has been to highlight how the reading of the year ceremony is not only used to facilitate a vision for the future but to redirect the relevance of slavery to such prophetic knowledge. Thus, this moment of new technologies of prophecy marks the shift in the North American academy from the fiction of racial linkage as a result of the transatlantic slave trade as the founding moment for the formation of the African diaspora to a new space of linkage that is being held up by larger internationalist concerns. Analytically, we can observe a shift from diaspora as specters of loss, as dispersal, and as earlier conceptualizations embedded in more personal divinatory concerns, to the extraordinariness of new diasporic formations emerging through interesting alliances with significantly powerful state and suprastate support.

The new diasporic formations being mobilized involve the development of contemporary alliances with and observations of fields of global capital and power. These relationships are connected to the post–Cold War democratization movements, which are propelling a new language of diaspora that has little resemblance to earlier articulations.

Notes

1. Within Ifa divination, everyone does not have equal access to the Ifá priesthood. Although both women and men can undergo the preliminary stages of initiation, granting them tools to legitimately conduct Ifá divination, in Oyotunji, only men are permitted to pursue the secondary, more complex level of Ifá initiation in which they are said to go to Igbó *odù* and become babalawos.

2. The majority of prominent priests in Oyotunji are now babalawos; therefore much of what follows in this essay will be based on my observations of Ifá divination.

3. Otherwise known as divination by phone.

4. Unlike the other forms of divinatory rituals, clients tend to only conduct one roots reading in a lifetime. The diviner performs this ritual in order to provide the client with knowledge of his or her paternal or maternal lineage, the specific historical explanations of his or her family's pre-slavery status, and the major calamities that led to the enslavement of the client's ancestors. Most importantly, the roots reading ritualizes the transformation of the client from an individual whose preslavery past was unknown and whose name reflected the legacy of being designated as chattel to the diviner's assignment of a new Yorùbá name to an otherwise American identity. Through the divinatory process of the roots reading, divining priests uncover the client's past and designate new Yorùbá names to mark the end of a sacrificial cycle.

5. There are twelve cult groups in Oyotunji and during different times of the year each of the groups organize a festival in order to venerate the òrìsà that bears its name (for example, the Ọsun festival every April is organized to celebrate the òrìsà Ọsun). Members of that cult group conduct both a prefestival reading in order to ascertain the type of offerings that should accompany the festival celebrations, and a postfestival reading in order to establish whether the offerings were well received by the venerated Òrìsà. There are a total of twelve cult groups, and with the direction of the divinatory interpretations each group organizes one festival during a different month each year.

References

Abímbọ́lá, Wándé. 1976. *Ifá: An Exposition of Ifá Literary Corpus*. Ibadan: Oxford University Press.

———. 1977. *Ifá Divination Poetry*. New York: Nok.

———. 2006. *Ìjìnlẹ̀ Ohùn Ẹnu Ifá: Apá Kejì*. Ibadan: University Press PLC.

Abu-Lughod, Lila. 1989. "Bedouins, Cassettes and Technologies of Public Culture." *Middle East Report* 165 (July/August): 7–11, 47.

———. 1993. "Finding a Place for Islam: Egyptian Television and the National Interest." *Public Culture* 5: 493–513.

Akinnaso, F. Niyi. 1995. "Bourdieu and the Diviner: Knowledge and Symbolic Power in Yoruba Divination." In *The Pursuit of Certainty: Religious and Cultural Formulations*, edited by Wendy James, 234–258. London: Routledge.

Anderson, Benedict R. 1983. *Imagined Communities: Reflections on the Origin and Spread of Nationalism*. London: Verso.

Appadurai, Arjun. 1995. "The Production of Locality." In *Counterworks: Managing the Diversity of Knowledge*, edited by R. Fardon, 205–225. London: Routledge.

Apter, Andrew. 1992. *Black Critics and Kings: The Hermeneutics of Power in Yoruba Society*. Chicago: University of Chicago Press.

Ayorinde, Christine. "Afrocuban Religiosity, Revolution, and National Identity (Cubanidad/Cubanía)." PhD diss., 2000. University of Birmingham.

———. 2009. "*Regla de Ocha-Ifa* and the Construction of Cuban Identity." In *Identity in the Shadow of Slavery*, edited by P. E. Lovejoy, 72–85. London: Continuum.

Bakhtin, Mikhail M. 1981. *The Dialogic Imagination: Four Essays*. Austin: University of Texas Press.

Barber, Karin. 1991. *I Could Speak Until Tomorrow: Oriki, Women, and the Past in a Yoruba Town*. Edinburgh: Edinburgh University Press.

Barthes, Roland. 1982. *Empire of Signs*. New York: Hill and Wang.

Bascom, William. 1969a. *The Yoruba of Southwestern Nigeria*. New York: Holt, Rinehart, and Winston.

———. 1969b. *Ifá Divination: Communication between Gods and Men in West Africa*. Bloomington: Indiana University Press.

———. 1980. *Sixteen Cowries: Yoruba Divination from Africa to the New World*. Bloomington: Indiana University Press.

———. 1992. *African Folktales in the New World*. Bloomington: Indiana University Press.

Bastide, Roger. 1971. *African Civilisations in the New World*. Translated by Peter Green. New York: Harper & Row.

———. 1978. *The African Religions of Brazil: Toward a Sociology of the Interpretation of Civilizations*. Baltimore: John Hopkins University Press.

Bourdieu, Pierre. 1990. *The Logic of Practice*. Stanford, CA: Stanford University Press.

———. 1991. *Language and Symbolic Power*. Cambridge, MA: Harvard University Press.

Brandon, George. 1993. *Santería from Africa to the New World: The Dead Sell Memories*. Bloomington: Indiana University Press.

Capone, Stefania. 1999a. "L'Afrique réinventée ou la construction de la tradition dans les cultes afro-brésiliens." *Archives européennes de sociologie* 40, no. 1: 1–25.

———. 1999b. "Les dieux sur le Net: l'essor des religions d'origine africaine aux Etats-Unis." *L'Homme* 151: 47–74.

Clarke, Kamari Maxine. 2002. "Governmentality, Modernity, and the Historical Politics of Oyo-Hegemony in Yoruba Transnational Revivalism." *Anthropologica: The Journal of the Canadian Anthropology Society* 44 (2): 271–293.

Connerton, Paul. 1989. *How Societies Remember.* Cambridge: Cambridge University Press.

De Moraes Farias, P. F. and Karin Barber, eds. 1990. *Self-Assertion and Brokerage: Early Cultural Nationalism in West Africa.* Birmingham, UK: University of Birmingham Press.

Drewal, Margaret Thompson. 1994. *Yoruba Ritual: Performers, Play, Agency.* Bloomington: Indiana University Press.

———. 1997. "Dancing for Ògun in Yorubaland and in Brazil." In *Africa's Ogun: Old World and New,* 2nd ed., edited by S. T. Barnes, 199–234. Bloomington: Indiana University Press.

Ellis, A. B. 1894. *The Yoruba-Speaking Peoples of the Slave Coast of West Africa: Their Religion, Manners, Customs, Laws, Language, etc.* London: Chapman and Hall.

Eltis, David. 1987. *Economic Growth and the Ending of the Transatlantic Slave Trade.* New York: Oxford University Press.

Fadipe, N. A. 1970. *The Sociology of the Yoruba.* Ibadan: University Press.

Falola, Toyin, ed. 1993. *Pioneer, Patriot and Patriarch: Samuel Johnson and the Yoruba People.* Madison: University of Wisconsin.

Forde, Cyril Daryll. 1951. *Yoruba-Speaking Peoples of South-Western Nigeria.* London: International African Institute.

Gonzalez-Wippler, Migene. 1992. *Powers of the Orishas: Santería and the Worship of Saints.* New York: Original Publications.

Hernandez-Reguant, Ariana. 1999. "Kwanzaa and the U.S. Ethnic Mosaic." In *Representations of Blackness and the Performance of Identities,* edited by J. Muteba Rahier, 101–122. London: Bergin & Garvey.

Laitin, David. D. 1986. *Hegemony and Culture: Politics and Religious Change Among the Yoruba.* Chicago: University of Chicago Press.

Larkin, Brian. 1997. "Indian Films and Nigerian Lovers: Media and the Creation of Parallel Modernities." *Africa* 67, no. 3: 406–440.

Lovejoy, Paul E. 1983. *Transformations in Slavery: A History of Slavery in Africa.* Cambridge: Cambridge University Press.

Mason, John. 1985. *Four New World Yoruba Rituals.* Brooklyn: Yoruba Theological Archministry.

Mason, John, and Gary Edwards. 1985. *Black Gods: Orisa Studies in the New World.* Brooklyn: Yoruba Theological Archministry.

Matory, James Lorand 1994. *Sex and the Empire that Is No More: Gender and the Politics of Metaphor in Oyo Yoruba Religion.* Minneapolis: University of Minnesota Press.

———. 1999. "The English Professors of Brazil: On the Diasporic Roots of the Yoruba Nation." *Comparative Studies in Society and History* 41, no. 1: 72–103.

McCarthy Brown, Karen. 1991. *Mama Lola: A Vodou Priestess in Brooklyn.* Berkeley: University of California Press.

Olupona, Jacob K., ed. 2000. *African Spirituality: Forms, Meanings, and Expressions.* New York: Crossroad.

———. 1991. *Kingship, Religion, and Rituals in a Nigerian Community: A Phenomenological Study of Ondo Yoruba Festivals.* Stockholm: Almquist & Wiksell International.

Park, Robert Ezra. 1950. *Race and Culture.* New York: Free Press.

Scott, David. 1991. "That Event, This Memory: Notes on the Anthropology of African Diasporas in the New World." *Diaspora* 1 no. 3: 261–284.

Skinner, Elliott Percival. 1992. *African Americans and U.S. Policy Toward Africa, 1850–1924: In Defense of Black Nationality*. Washington, DC: Howard University Press.

Stewart, Dianne M. 2005. *Three Eyes for the Journey: The African Dimensions of the Jamaican Religious Experience*. New York: Oxford University Press.

Sutton, Constance R. 1992. "Some Thoughts on Gendering and Internationalizing Our Thinking about Transnational Migrations." In *Towards a Transnational Perspective on Migration: Race, Class, Ethnicity, and Nationalism Reconsidered*, edited by Nina Glick-Schiller, Linda Basch, and Cristina Blanc-Szanton, 241–251. New York: New York Academy of Sciences.

Szwed, John F., ed. 1970. *Black America*. New York: Basic Books.

Thompson, Robert Farris. 1983. *Flash of the Spirit: African and Afro-American Art and Philosophy*. New York: Vintage.

Wipper, Audrey. 1972. "African Women, Fashion, and Scapegoating." *Canadian Journal of African Studies* 6, no. 2: 329–349.

Yái, Ọlábíyí Babalọlá. 2001. "Yoruba Religion and Globalization: Some Reflections." *Cuadernos Digitales* 15: 1–21.

PART IV.
SACRED ART IN IFÁ

20 The Creatures of Ifá

Philip M. Peek

IF ANYONE EVER doubted the centrality of divination to a culture, even a superficial glance at Ifá studies demonstrates the essential nature of this system for the Yorùbá peoples everywhere. Ifá was present at the creation of the world; it is the articulator of "destiny" and its successful implementation; and very simply, it aids millions daily. Ifá has perhaps always guided the Yorùbá but we know positively it has been utilized for hundreds of years, as proven by the spectacular Ifá divination tray acquired circa 1650 by the Ulmer Museum. Now Ifá is a key element of the African—not just Yorùbá—diaspora, as life in the Americas demonstrates.

The importance of "creatures" in connection with cultural systems seems without question. African studies have a wealth of magnificent studies of how important various animals, birds, and reptiles are in worldviews and religious beliefs and practices throughout the continent (Peek 2000a). Major ethnographic studies such as those by Mary Douglas (1984), Marcel Griaule and Germaine Deiterlen (1986), Roy Willis (1974), Paula Ben-Amos (1976), Ben-Amos and Arnold Rubin (1983), and Allen Roberts (1995) have established the centrality of selected creatures to the worldviews of different peoples.

As I began my study of African systems of divination, I found instance after instance of the participation of animals, birds, and reptiles in the divinatory enterprise (Peek 1982, 1991a, 2000a). Often they appear as agents of divination, such as spider divination in Cameroon (Gebauer 1964) and the fox among the Dogon (Griaule and Deiterlen 1986). Parts of creatures may be utilized, as with animal bones in the divination tablets or in the diviner's baskets throughout southern Africa. In other cases, we find symbolic use of animals, as with the diviners' headdresses with pangolin designs among the Luba (M. Roberts 2000) or small wooden carvings of swamp dwellers used as rubbing oracles of central Africa (Mack 1981). The list is long and inevitably presents us with a variety of interesting, often puzzling, issues. Why, for example, do we find tortoise shells used by diviners in various ways literally from one corner of the continent to another?

For these reasons, I fully expected to find much in the vast corpus of Ifá studies to explain the frequent presence of animals, birds, and reptiles in the arts and artifacts of Ifá divination. In fact, one of the earliest studies of Ifá by a European, Leo Frobenius, who traveled in Yorùbá country from 1910 to 1912, commented extensively on the decorations of Ifá trays (2007). Surely there are clear reasons for the creatures on the divination implements such as the diviner's tray (*opon Ifá*), tapper (*iroke Ifá*), the closed box containing emblems of the diviner's destiny that he receives at his initiation (*igba odu*), the carved wooden cup with lid for the *ikin Ifá*, the divination bowl (*agere Ifá*) for ritual materials (*apoti Ifá*), bags (*apo Ifá* or *apo jerugbe*; beaded bag, *ikolaba Ifá*), staffs (*opa orere* or *osun babalawo*, the iron staff topped with bird forms; *ikute Ifá*, beaded staff), the ritual iron cutlass with a bell handle (*ada oosa/Talabi*), the Ifá priest's crown (*ade babalawo*), beaded shoulder pieces (*ikunpa Ifá*), and the beaded horsetail fly whisk (*irukere*) (Abiodun 1975, 431–432). Equally, there must be good reasons for the creatures often cited in *odu* verses and used for sacrifices (Bascom 1969; Gleason 1973; Abímbọ́lá 1975, 1976, 1977). But I was not to find easy answers to my query. Representations of creatures are abundant but explanations proved hard to come by. Why is that the case?

The Evidence of Creatures

The dramatic presence of various creatures in African divination systems provides an intriguing perspective on those cultures, their worldviews, epistemologies, and value systems. Some creatures may be represented (and thus utilized symbolically) for their diagnostic abilities, such as dogs in Central Africa where their olfactory sensitivities aid in the hunt for wild game, as well as for evildoers. The famous Pale Fox of the Dogon of Mali is key to their divination system for reasons pertaining to the origin myths of the people, and thus provides insight into their whole worldview. Other instances of "mythical" or primordial creatures are readily encountered, such as the chameleon, one of the world's most ancient creatures, for much of West Africa. Perhaps we can offer one more example, to illustrate avoidance as opposed to incorporation of an animal in order to enhance the oracular enterprise. In some cultures, diviners avoid spotted or stripe-skinned animals because they would confuse the search for answers (Peek 1991, 207, n.13).

When I visited with diviners in Maputo, Mozambique, the evidence of creatures was abundant. Hung behind the diviners were the standard black, red, and white cloths picturing guinea fowl, cobras, and roosters. The cast objects were primarily in groupings of sea shells (dominated by *cosenana*, the obligatory "Great Mother" shell), crocodile and pangolin scales, and the shells of tree seeds. Diviners freely explained the "opposition" of land and water demonstrated by the shells and the mediating role of the separated crocodile scales. In other words, the presence of specific creatures was critical to the divination process and readily articulated.

Of course, the list of divinatory creatures could be much longer, and we will return to comparative examples momentarily. But the basic point is clear: African divination systems make careful and calculated choices of the creatures that are brought into or excluded from their divination systems. With so much evidence from other African peoples, we would expect some reflection of such concerns in the exceptionally complex and well-studied Ifá divination system of the Yorùbá of Nigeria, as well as those systems derived from Ifá among West African neighbors and in the Americas, which have such an abundance of creatures represented throughout Ifá practices. However, this does not appear to be the case. I will survey the evidence and discuss the creatures of Ifá and how they may aid us in understanding this divination system. Within this current investigation, I am limited to what scholars of Ifá have already published.

First, it is necessary to establish which creatures are found. As an indication of the problems to anticipate, even Roache's (1974) identification of the creatures portrayed is often only a vague impression that might be contradicted by another source. Nevertheless, the animals discussed in published Ifá research include: antelopes, though they are never identified specifically, and are often mixed with other quadrupeds; birds, which are also often unidentifiable though a few are specifically cited, such as pigeons, hornbills, vultures, doves, ducks, hens, "witchbirds," and the West African grey parrot's red tail feathers for babalawos; chameleons; crabs, which sometimes appear opposite Eshu's face on the divining tray; dogs; fish, usually identified as mudfish but occasionally referred to simply as coiled fish as for market sales; goats; hens, which are usually portrayed with snakes in their beaks in Yorùbá art; insects, though less frequently and usually limited to the butterfly, centipede, and scorpion; monkeys; hares, infrequently; reptiles such as lizards or crocodiles, although they often remain indistinguishable; snakes, usually either being devoured by or devouring hens but in some instances depicted as emerging from human nostrils (the python and Gabon viper are the only ones cited specifically); snails; and tortoises and turtles.

Prince (1966) offers a rough tabulation of some fifty Ifá trays and reports that the most frequent representations are he-goats, rams, fowls, and pigeons. I would add hens and snakes, "witchbirds," crabs, snails, and reptiles as very popular. But again there are no clearly dominant creatures in terms of numbers of representations on Ifá artifacts.

Contexts

From the studies reviewed, contexts do not appear to matter. For instance, there do not appear to be consistent correlations between Ifá diviners' beaded bags and the creatures represented on them. Chameleons, for example, can appear on the *opon Ifá* as well as the diviner's bag. A thorough study that included the *odu* verses (Bascom 1969; Gleason 1973; Abímbọ́lá 1976) and closer attention to sacrificial animals would no doubt give us more information about animals and Ifá, as virtually every creature is present in the verses. Presumably this type of evidence from the *odu* would correlate with the orisha involved, but it could also reveal the associations common for various creatures and thus possibly clarify their use in Ifá paraphernalia. Careful review of the creatures that play roles in the initiations of babalawos might prove valuable as well (Bascom 1969, 4).

Birds often appear on Ifá paraphernalia, and some interpretation related to context seems possible because one figure does seem to be strictly limited in representation. This is the highly stylized bird form that tops the staffs (*osun*) held by babalawo and placed in their shrines. These seem to be generally agreed to be for appeasement of the negative powers of women, the "witches' aspect." They seem to appear only on the staffs and nowhere else. The only other commonly identifiable birds are hens, most often with snakes in their beaks. This is a common motif for the *agere* (divination bowl) and *opon* (divination tray). Both birds will be discussed further.

The Meanings of Creatures

One would expect that the Yorùbá worldview would incorporate significant creatures in their visual and verbal arts, especially in those related to Ifá divination. This is certainly the case elsewhere, where divination systems provide symbolic summations of their larger cultures through their imagery. But the situation may be different with the Yorùbá, as Witte observes: "Neither the individual animals nor the group, or groups as a whole, should be burdened with profound symbolic meanings. Nevertheless, some of the animals merit our attention" (1994, 62). And yet, beyond simply listing creatures observed, usually those on the rims of Ifá divination trays (see Fagg and Pemberton 1982, 114–115, 172–173; Witte 1994), little explanation is available. While it is possible to find meaningful creatures indicating aspects of the Yorùbá worldview generally, our concern is their link to Ifá.

Background

The selection of creatures in African expressive behaviors usually seems to rely on their symbolic importance, whether that links to widely observed "natural" characteristics, anomalous aspects (whether locally or universally acknowledged), or truly unique culture-specific considerations. The choices in the case of our present problem are not immediately obvious, though it is possible to find a variety of rationales. We will briefly review the most obvious paths to follow and comment on their efficacy.

Part of the discussion necessarily enters that murky water of the rationales for symbolic representation. And as always, we are caught in the conundrum of whether creatures are chosen as a result of observations of "natural" behavior or the attribution of "cultural" behavior. For example, inevitably the depiction of the chameleon, seemingly anywhere it appears, is interpreted as being due to its changeability. The wonder of its ability to alter its color is then "rationally" linked to the cultural frame in which it is found. Does that then give us chameleons on the *opon Ifá* (divination tray), because of Eshu's presence and the randomness of his changes, or is it due to the chameleon's "primordial" associations (Abímbọ́lá 1977, 1–2)? Another puzzle about the depiction of chameleons extends beyond Ifá and the Yorùbá. Why are their tails always "incorrectly" curled upwards in art works, while in nature they curl downwards?

Abnormality is surely in the eyes of the beholder, and thus one assumes culture trumps nature in most cases. Nevertheless, we have continent-wide recognition of chameleons, pangolins, and tortoises, all of which offer unique physical characteristics that seem sufficient to make them noteworthy.

While the physical context of the creatures' representations does not appear to help us understand their presence, perhaps there is evidence in other aspects of Yorùbá culture that will clarify matters. Mere frequency of representation might indicate relative importance, but one still needs to know why a certain creature is selected. Some possibilities include whether or not a creature is closely linked to one or more orisha, as a standard bearer or as a sacrifice. Or could the creature be associated with some skill or quality linked to the enterprise of divination—perhaps as an excellent communicator and link to the ancestors or powers that hold the information Ifá reveals, as with spiders and crabs in Cameroon? Or could these simply be prestige representations, as with the equestrian figure that often bears *agere Ifá,* the divination bowl that holds the palm nuts?

Evidence for the Yorùbá Worldview as Demonstrated outside of Ifá Material

The scholarship on Ifá alone gives us little evidence to start our investigation of its creature embellishments, so we will consider the meanings of creatures in related aspects of Yorùbá culture to determine whether or not they aid us with our study of Ifá. This seems logical, since several scholars have noted that Ifá trays and containers are de facto models of the Universe (Witte 1994, 59–60; La-Gamma 2000, 36–37).

Perhaps the creatures found on Ifá's elaborate paraphernalia are part of the general Yorùbá cosmos and actually identify links to the most important orisha. For example, Ogun seems to be linked to the tortoise, which is represented; but dogs, which are Ogun's favorite sacrifice, are seldom depicted in the artworks. In addition, I have found many other creatures associated with Ogun in addition to dogs and turtles: snails, alligators, lizards, chameleons, ostriches, vultures, doves, snakes, centipedes, and even butterflies (H. Drewal 1980b, 248–251). Bascom (1980, 42) reports that Orunmila's prinicipal sacrifice is a she-goat.

In *The Religion of the Yorùbás,* Venerable J. Olumide Lucas lists various major orisha and their most common sacrifices, but there is no explanation of why these choices are made (1948, 208). "Through Ifá divination an Ori might demand a particular sacrifice, for example, a billy-goat, a cock or a duck, each being symbolic of specific needs to be met" (Abiodun 1987, 260). One would hope that the needs met would direct us towards the valued aspects of that creature and help explain its presence (or absence) on Ifá paraphernalia. Abiodun does offer a few tantalizing examples. He notes that snails are among the objects that "soften" Ori and the sacrifice of cocks and ducks serve "to gain favor in one's community and pacify those who harbor grievances against the devotee without his knowing it" (ibid.). Keith Nicklin cites the catfish, crocodile, and crab on the rim of an Ifá tray as a reference to the "Goddess of the Waters," Olokun (1991, 24–25, plate 22).

Another aspect that may be relevant to the representations on Ifá regalia is how spirit possession is depicted. It may be that the occasional portrayals of snakes or arms with hands emerging from nostrils of human faces may be an attempt to visualize the "invisible" spiritual presences.

Another important aspect of Ifá's creatures is their use in the initiation ceremonies for diviners. Presumably, desirable qualities are transferred to the initiate through the sacrifice or incorporation of these beasts. Bascom notes that for Salako's initiation into the use of the sixteen-cowrie form of divination, sponsors brought fish, rat, Tulberg's rat, pangolin, tortoise, elephant meat, guinea fowl, hen, pigeon, snail, cock, and ram (1980, 10). Most of these items were prepared as a medicine that was then applied to a cut on Salako's head, but no further details about specific qualities are provided.

In terms of creatures per se, as there is relatively more about birds in Yorùbá expressive culture, we will treat them first. As noted earlier in this discussion, exact identifications are hard to make. In his groundbreaking article "The Sign of the Divine King," Thompson (1970) develops the importance of birds on kings' beaded crowns, but is at a loss to identify them specifically. In Ifá iconography, *Igun,* the vulture, seems to be the single most important creature related to divination, for the most obvious of reasons. Abímbọ́lá gives *Igun*'s appellation: "*Igun,* nicknamed Etie, whose garment is a symbol of sacrifice"; and as one Ifá poem states, "without *Igun,* nobody performs sacrifices" (1975, 28). All sacrifices must be gone within a day or it means that they were not accepted by the spiritual powers to whom they are offered; thus, without the scavenging vulture, there would be no evidence that sacrifices had been taken. With their bald heads, symbols of their old age, vultures are respected and are not allowed to be killed (73).

Hornbills are given special recognition in many West African cultures. Among the Fon of Benin, the presence of a hornbill at the tip of an Ifá (or Fa, in this case) tapper is explained as a reference to the hornbill's status as "one of nature's best diviners"; "the tapper signifies revelatory knowledge in both its use and imagery" (Blier 1998, 90). Intriguingly, Drewal seems to represent the hornbill in a different light. Commenting on a hornbill-topped tapper, he refers to *agbigbo*, the hornbill, as "an infamous character in Ifá divination orature who serves as a reminder that only proper rituals and offerings can avert disaster" (H. Drewal 1992, 187). In his study of Gelede masquerades, Lawal provides some helpful clarification as he distinguishes two different hornbills: *Agbigbo*, the big-headed grey hornbill that is sent by witches to bring death to individuals, and *Akala*, the ground hornbill which is a carrier of messages and sacrifices (1996, 239, 244; see also Abímbólá 1975, 75). In earlier publications, Abímbólá offers more dramatic descriptions using two different spellings of, apparently, the same type of hornbill. In *Sixteen Great Poems of Ifá* (1975) he identifies *Agbigbo*, the main character in a long Ifá poem that recounts the misbehavior of an Ifá priest of that name as the "symbol of unfaithfulness in Ifá priests, a negation of the strict sanctions of the Ifá divination system" and further, "a symbol of death and evil" (210, 233). In *Ifá Divination Poetry* (1977), Abímbólá uses a more complete name for this bird— *Agbigboniwonran*—and offers the same identification (161–162). While these accounts differ somewhat, it is clear that this hornbill is an important topic in Ifá divination though it plays no role in divination per se.

Another type of bird, the so-called witchbird, is seldom clearly identified in the literature beyond its association with witches. For example, McClelland notes: "A witch is visualized as a white bird with a long red beak and claws" (1982, 29). Is this why "witchbirds" are depicted on Ifá trays? Lawal notes that "the 'powerful mothers' change into birds at night" (1996, 239). Unfortunately, he offers no insights about the creature. Abímbólá (1975, 322), identifies *Ehuru*, "a mythical bird believed to be the bird of the witches," as what they can become when they fly about at night, but no further description is provided. Are these depicted on Ifá trays and other paraphernalia? If so, why?

Blier (1998, 91) reports that the *opa* (staff) Osanyin are surmounted by birds that allude to the forest as a source for medicines and to witchcraft, "a gathering of birds," which diviners counteract. Osanyin staffs are of course linked to the orisha of medicine, but are part of a babalawo's regalia due to the healing in which diviners are engaged. Keith Nicklin underscores this aspect when he writes of the sixteen birds surrounding a larger bird ("bird of the elders of Orunmila, god of divination") at the top of these staffs (1991, 17). Perhaps the larger point here is the "kill or cure" dichotomy that identifies so many ritual specialists everywhere: those with knowledge to cure by definition have knowledge to kill.

Henry Drewal presents a more complex analysis of a diviner's *osun* staff with a single bird on top. This is a depiction of *asa*, the hawk, which acts quickly with determination: "Once it has grabbed its prey with its feet, nothing drops from the hawk's claws" (H. Drewal 1987, 141–142; see also M. Drewal and H. Drewal 1983, 66; M. Drewal 1988, 49). But the staff is more complicated because its true power is in its "tail" which is stuck into the ground and "it is likened to the power of the spiny anteater (pangolin), which curls its tail around its body to make it impervious to attack" (H. Drewal 1987, 142). Here is an example of the classic problem of the symbolic association with no apparent reference, demonstrating the value of careful questioning.

It might be quickly noted that in Benin City, the capital of the Benin Kingdom that has historical ties to the Yorùbá, such staffs are topped by a representation of the grey heron, "king of the night birds," "lord of the witches" (Ben-Amos 1976, 248–249). While the grey heron is not noted as being significant among the Yorùbá, here is yet another fearsome bird that reflects the kill-or-cure powers of healers and diviners.

Lawal's study of Gelede presents more valuable information about other birds in the Yorùbá worldview that might aid our study of Ifá symbols. One example is the pigeon. "In Ifá divination rituals, the bird [pigeon] symbolizes honor and prosperity" and will bring both when sacrificed to. Pigeons are also associated with twins, because they lay two eggs at a time (1996, 240). The red tail feathers of the West African grey parrot are common additions to priestly and kingly regalia throughout southern Nigeria, but seldom do we learn why the bird is so noteworthy. Curiously, the fact that it is one of the best mimics of human speech is seldom noted. One who notes it is Lawal, who comments on the red tail feathers' association with fertility and menstrual blood due to the color, but he also reports other qualities that relate to the bird's "speaking" abilities (241): "One other reason for the popularity of the parrot among the Yorùbá is the bird's ability to imitate human speech and so to report to its owner whatever transpired in his absence" (242). This role as "spy" becomes one of a "reporter" who is thought to be the "moral conscience of the community" (242). Here we have the type of evidence that can easily be linked to Ifá: the parrot as reporter, moral conscience, and articulator can be associated with divination. But what is critical is that we do not find such a clear identification in the Ifá scholarship itself—we must look elsewhere.

Reptiles of all types are frequently associated with divination systems elsewhere in Africa, and Ifá may be no exception in this regard because snakes, tortoises, and various similar creatures appear on the babalawo's regalia and equipment. One would expect to find chameleons, and indeed they do appear, but there is nothing directly related to Ifá that explains their presence. Elsewhere they serve as messengers between worlds, are noted for their color-changing ability, have rotating eyeballs, and are often included among the world's primordial creatures. Thompson (1970) discusses the chameleon and the Agemo cult devoted to it in Ijebu, an important Yorùbá city. Based on work in the same area, Pemberton provides a comprehensive description of chameleon's powers: "Treading gently upon the earth, intimate in its relationship with nature, possessing the knowledge of nature's secrets, and capable of absorbing the color, the power, of others, while not losing its own power, the chameleon images a covert power" (1988–1989, 630). Certainly this describes a powerfully significant creature—indeed, one of the few recognized throughout Africa—but there is still nothing to directly connect the chameleon to Ifá divination.

Tortoises appear on the Ifá trays and bowls, but seldom is any explanation readily available. For example, while describing the decoration on an Ifá bowl, Witte declares "the opele chains and the tortoise clearly indicate the Ifá oracle " (1982, 163), but why? Grillo (1995) notes the trickster role of tortoise in many folk tales as well as that of a messenger; thus, there is a correlation with Eshu's function in relation to Ifá divination. Perhaps tortoise is present as a mediator (234). The tortoise is clearly a creature that attracts contrary characterizations, which is often the sign of a true trickster—ambivalence is felt about a creature whose characteristics are ambiguous.

John Mason (2004), for example, refers to the "crafty, trouble-making peddler Tortoise," but why is tortoise so characterized? McClelland, in a similar vein, assures us that tortoise is considered "the enfant terrible of the animal world" and is associated by the Yorùbá with Eshu (1982, 16). Again, the question one finds oneself asking is why.

This matter is especially frustrating because tortoise shells are found in association with diviners among peoples all over Africa, from the Baule and Senufo of Cote d'Ivoire to the Yorùbá and Igbo of Nigeria. There are also references found among Central and Southern African peoples. While some folks reckon the tortoise as a trickster, others count him as among the wisest of creatures. This is a confusing matter that requires further research and examination.

One final observation about tortoises (or turtles): I have always wondered why there is so little consistency in terminology in Africanists' references to this creature—tortoise and turtle seem to be used interchangeably. According to Professor Olasope Oyelaran, the Yorùbá do distinguish between the land-based tortoise, *ahun*, and the "virtually non-terrestial" water-based turtle, *ireere* (pers. comm. 2008).

Pangolins truly epitomize the anomalous creature—there are so many ways in which they are "betwixt and between." Several scholars have noted the possible depiction of pangolin scales on Ifá tray rims (e.g., H. Drewal 1980a, 37) and pangolin scales may be used for the *opele* chain. Lawal summarizes the variety of meaningful associations of pangolins due to their unique defensive posture and their use in medicines (1996, 249).

The last of the creatures in this general category is the snail. Snail's "water" (a phrase never fully explained) is an important element in diviners' initiation ceremonies and the preparation of palm nuts, and is frequently cited in sacrificial lists. But its function is still unclear, although there are other Yorùbá traditions that note its calming effects. Several sources comment that snails do not bleed (Abímbọ́lá 1975, 386), and therein may lie their secret and the reason for their importance in a variety of rituals.

And then there is the seemingly most unlikely of sacred symbols: the mudfish. Witte's "Fishes of the Earth" (1982) provides an excellent review of the anomalous characteristics of the mudfish and traces its representation in various contexts. It is such a large fish of curious appearance (with its "whiskers"), able to live on land and water, some species capable of delivering an electric shock, that it is easily placed in anyone's anomalous creatures category.[1] Witte's study is an excellent example of the multivocal/multivalent symbol because the mudfish means so much to so many. There are visual and verbal references to this creature throughout southern Nigeria. Yet we still do not have any direct links to Ifá, although the mudfish clearly appears on many *opon Ifá*.

In such an extraordinarily mixed list of creatures, one wonders what if anything links them together. One possibility is that a number of them are frequently viewed, given their ambivalent and anomalous characteristics, as messengers, as cross-world communicators; thus this curious grouping of mudfish, turtles, and chameleons represents those most important of creatures in many cosmologies (Peek 1991a). Nevertheless, we have little concrete evidence that links such associations to Ifá divination.

Another approach in our study of "Ifá's creatures" is to consider the historical evidence for these animals found related to Ifá. Perhaps a look at the evidence from Nok, ancient Ife, Owo, even Benin City may help us. Snails figure prominently in various aspects of Ifá initiations, for example. Does that large bronze snail with a tiny leopard on top from Igbo Ukwu tell us anything about the historical importance of snails? As Witte notes (1982), the mudfish representations as fish-legged creatures seem to carry associations with Owo and Benin and possibly the Ogboni society. This is another area of research that demands further inquiry.

Another historical association might lie with the related and possibly older divining chain forms of *opele* and *agbiba* (Peek 1982). In fact, it was the explicit presence of animal associations on divining chains that first drew me to the current study of Ifá. Throughout southern Nigeria, where one finds the divining chain one also finds the use of a wild boar's tusk as the "tapper." Less widely practiced but still significant is the tradition that the shells used for the chain must come from wild mango seeds found in elephant dung. But we find no such associations in the Ifá traditions. Certainly historical research might reveal important information about Ifá but there are no immediate indications of success in clarifying Ifá's creatures.

Wealth and prestige were often noted in catalogs' descriptions of the artistic elaborations of Ifá apparatuses. Ivory tappers seem more related to the prestige of ivory than the elephant. Drewal also notes the prestige of ivory for Ifá ritual art works such as the ivory *agere* (divination bowl) with an equestrian figure holding the small bowl (H. Drewal 1992, 194). One can readily understand the elephant's ivory as a step up from the warthog's tusk used throughout southern Nigeria.

The association with wealth could also be spiritual, in that water and the orisha associated with the rivers and the sea, such as Olokun, may be cited as the sources of wealth, and representations of mudfish and crabs elicit that linkage. Equestrian figures, frequently the basic design of Ifá cups, are usually considered symbols of wealth.

Several sources cite "the cycle of life" as a rationale for the individual portrayals on bowls and trays and bags. The Drewals, for example, portray this cycle as depicted on one of many similar Gelede masks: "pig devours monkey, who devours corn, and, on top, snake devours tortoise" (H. Drewal and M. Drewal 1990, 209). Indeed, the number of hens killing snakes, snakes killing birds, animals ready for sacrifice, Eshu devotees with pipes, and so on Yoruba religious objects represent life's continuity and celebrate the interconnectedness of all beings in the world. Again, this may well be the case, but given Ifá's centrality to the daily life of the individual and the well-being of the universe, mere happenstance seems an inadequate response to my question about the significance of animals in Ifá. But it seems that these animal images are too pedestrian to embellish the lofty enterprise of Ifá—or is the perpetuation of the daily round the real point? Lawal offers an alternative to the assumption of a life full of aggression and competition, suggesting that the bird and snake motif is really a reminder to act cautiously (1996, 248–249). This approach has further internal problems. Is the depiction of a chicken an indication of the most common of sacrifices and thus a reference to the sacred, or is it just a chicken with a simple association to domestic life? Or is this depiction in relation to Ifá a reminder that, by many accounts, Ifá was present at the creation of the world?

Elsewhere I have noted the coincidence of a range of animals that act as divinatory agents that seem to have absolutely nothing in common. The Pale Fox of the Dogon, crabs and spiders among Cameroonian peoples, mice for the Baule, and tortoises, ubiquitous in various forms, are absolutely essential elements of numerous divination systems. Snails are also prominent in various aspects of Ifá. That they share the characteristic of silence may be significant (Peek 1994, 2000b). Most African peoples value the elder who can speak well, who speaks slowly with carefully chosen words. Those who speak rapidly, loudly, too often, and so on are little regarded. The ground-dwelling spider carries the ancestors' message to the divining arena but it may be that it was chosen from among other creatures because the ancestors trusted its abilities to carry the correct message—to remember the message and to speak carefully with well-chosen words.

Actually there are significant associations of sound and Ifá, starting with the construction of the Ifá tray with its hollowed base and the use of the tapper, which is frequently embellished with a clapper bell. Many cite the jingling of the Osun/Osanyin/Ifá staffs when carried by babalawo. And of course there are the *odu* verses that must be narrated so effectively. Further indicating the importance of sound, a tantalizing anecdote in one of the Drewals's publications refers to the sacrifice of a chicken and the removal of the esophagus for a medicine to enhance *emi*, breath or "vital force" (M. Drewal and H. Drewal 1987, 226).

Far too many studies of Ifá, even if there is comment on the creatures depicted, cite "tradition" as the cause of the representations. Far be it for me to deny such a response by Yorùbá informants—maybe these representations are simply decorative, incidental, and idiosyncratic. But if so, this fact would make the Yorùbá unique among African cultures in a rather unexpected way. Embellishments of the most central institution in Yorùbá culture, which has served its people for hundreds of years and has survived throughout the African diaspora, can hardly be just "decorations." No other divination system can claim a similar legacy. Nevertheless, this seems to be the case. Margaret Drewal writes about the images on a divination container: "Often these images are simply part of the artist's repertoire and are reproduced on any number of different types of objects he carves, such as doors, divination trays, drums, and so on" (M. Drewal 1988, 46). If indeed there are no essential associations of certain birds or animals and their representation on Ifá trays and so on, why are they there at all? No creature explicitly aids Ifá in the divinatory enterprise.

In my study of the divining chain in southern Nigeria (Peek 1982), I suggested that the elaborated form of Ifá with the palm nuts may be more recent. Possibly an existing system of casting, in a sense, whole phrases via the *opele* chain was "refined" into a more complex system in which one "casts" a "word" at a time via Ifá's palm nuts. The latter form gained more prestige over what came to be called a shortcut due to that degree of elaboration. Then, as the *opele* chain had a diminished status, it came to seen as derivative from Ifá "proper." We can never assume the direction of borrowing or adaptation—a tradition can trickle down just as easily as it can percolate upwards.

I readily grant that this can only be speculation at this point, but I was drawn back to my earlier suggestion concerning the divining chain complex when I realized that the meaningfulness of the creatures linked, very loosely it seems, to Ifá had their importance elsewhere. For example, many animals, birds, and reptiles are more associated with the orisa than with Ifá—or simply with the general Yorùbá worldview. And it is the *opele* chain system that has the absolutely required links to the natural world through the boar's tusk and the origin of the shells used in the chain. I did not anticipate that I would return to this idea when I started this chapter.

There is also the intriguing link to Muslim sand divination—*Khatt al-raml*—which has no associated creatures but does have clear associations with Ifá as we know it today (Brenner 2000a, 2000b) but could only have come to the

Yorùbá centuries after their establishment. Given divination's importance to human activity, it seems reasonable to think that another system preceded Ifá as it is practiced today.

And as some note, Ifá could be done in the sand—the elaboration of the tray and the special termite-produced dust is not essential. When I have observed sand divination practiced in Mali and Cote d'Ivoire, there are seemingly random markings in the sand that are then read in a more general fashion, but they do not initially have the "shape" of the *odu*. Nevertheless, recent studies of apparently related systems, such as Bamana sand divination, do generate patterns comparable to Ifá.[2] I must hasten to add that I have not had time to study sand divination per se more closely and have no idea if there are supportive data or not for what I am suggesting. I do know that diviners using sand divination seem to develop very "intuitive" responses rather than work from a developed geometric pattern with set interpretations.

In addition to the formal similarities of a base-four system with sixteen major configurations, one also wonders if the matter of reading cast configurations left to right, right to left (and even up/down) may have origins outside of Yorùbá culture, perhaps in reading Arabic. And perhaps one could speculate further whether the occasionally noted tradition of the diviner facing eastward also relates to an "eastern" orientation of adaptations.

Whatever the case, in the end it would appear that Ifá is sufficient in and of itself, needing no aid from "animal helpers" as found in so many divination systems. No creatures serve as oracular agents, as in Baule mouse divination, nor as facilitators, as with dogs in Central Africa. At this point we are clearly in the dangerous neighborhood of speculation, since there is an absence of clear links to the creatures that figure so prominently in Yorùbá cosmology. In other words, the Yorùbá obviously use animals, birds, and reptiles to symbolize a variety of human values and actions, but there seem to be no "creatures of Ifá" like those I initially sought. There are no primary and causal relationships such as we find elsewhere. This is not to posit that all divination systems must have creatures with which they are associated, but strikingly most do.

Indeed, perhaps, though I first doubted it, animals are just decorative for Ifá. When animals are presented and discussed, the references are always to other, non-Ifá orisha, behaviors, values, and so on. Obviously various rationales can be found—and I would welcome them—for example, the liminality of the divinatory enterprise and the presence of liminal creatures such as chameleons and pangolins. I was initially anticipating associations with silent creatures such as crabs and spiders that are observable on Ifá trays, but this does not appear to be a factor in their choice.

If my comparative study of divination systems of African peoples has taught me anything, it is that these systems are deeply imbedded in their cultures. There is always a wealth of literal and symbolic associations manifest in the divinatory enterprise—this is what makes this such a valuable approach to study these cultures. For Ifá, the associations of this type are found in the *odu* verses, the texts of Ifá, but not in the mechanics or regalia. For the latter, the associations are always secondary with reference to other aspects of Yorùbá culture. Also, there are frequent allusions to the *odu* as being folktales, despite the conflict here between "true" versus "fictional" narratives—a dilemma Bascom (1943) noted long ago.

Could it be that Ifá is indeed related to Muslim sand divination and was melded centuries ago with an existing divining chain system, which was deeply rooted in Yorùbá tradition? Perhaps Ifá palm nut divination provides a "refinement" of the *opele* and *agbigba* approaches that provides full ideas and phrases by revealing the truth word by word as the marks appear in the sand and, now, on an Ifá tray? Such a synthesis of borrowed and indigenous divination traditions has been proposed for the Sikidy system of Madagascar (Verin and Rajaonarimananana 1991) and Hakata of southern African peoples (Brenner 2000a, 58). Perhaps a similar process occurred with Ifá. Indeed, this seems to be exactly what Louis Brenner is suggesting in several detailed articles about *khatt al-raml* vis-à-vis Ifá and the other systems just noted, as well as Mande divination (2000a, 2000b). Brenner's detailed studies present excellent cases for intra-Muslim dynamics as well as intercultural variables in the process of culture contact and the possible adaptation of systems such as divination. The most far-reaching and profound speculation is to be found in Wim van Binsbergen's (2005) brilliant comparative study, which ultimately suggests that the reason for the striking similarities of these divination systems is that a "proto-African form" diffused out of Africa and then was reintroduced by Muslims. Whatever the final decision about origins, if there can be any, there is no question that Ifá's heart and soul will always be Yorùbá.

Notes

1. For evidence from Benin City, see also Ben-Amos and Rubin (1983).
2. See Hooser (2006) for a solid critical comparative discussion.

References

Abímbọ́lá, Wándé. 1975. *Sixteen Great Poems of Ifá*. Paris: UNESCO.
———. 1976. *Ifá: An Exposition of Ifá Literary Corpus*. Ibadan: Oxford University Press.
———. 1977. *Ifá Divination Poetry*. New York: Nok Publishers.
Abiodun, Rowland. 1975. "Ifá Art Objects: An Interpretation Base on Oral Traditions," in *Yorùbá Oral Tradition*, edited by W. Abimbola, 421–469. Ile-Ife: Department of African Languages and Literatures, University of Ife.

———. 1987. "Verbal and Visual Metaphors: Mythical Allusions in Yorùbá Ritualistic Art of Ori." *Word and Image* 3, no. 3: 252–270.

Bascom, William R. 1943. "The Relationship of Yorùbá Folklore to Divining." *Journal of American Folklore* 46: 127–131.

———. 1969. *Ifá Divination: Communication Between Gods and Men in West Africa*. Bloomington: Indiana University Press.

———. 1980. *Sixteen Cowries: Yorùbá Divination from Africa to the New World*. Bloomington: Indiana University Press.

Ben-Amos, Paula Girshick. 1976. "Men and Animals in Benin Art." *Man* 11, no. 2: 243–52.

Ben-Amos, Paula, and Arnold Rubin, eds. 1983. *The Art of Power, The Power of Art*. Los Angeles: Fowler Museum of Cultural History.

Blier, Suzanne. 1998. *Royal Arts of Africa: The Majesty of Form*. Upper Saddle River, NJ: Laurence King.

Brenner, Louis. 2000a. "Histories of Religion in Africa." *Journal of Religion in Africa* 3, no. 2: 143–167.

———. 2000b. "Muslim Divination and the History of Relgion in Sub-Saharan Africa," in *Insight and Artistry in African Divination*, edited by John Pemberton III, 45–59. Washington, DC: Smithsonian Institution Press.

Douglas, Mary. 1984. "Animals in Lele Religious Symbolism," in *Implicit Meanings: Essays in Anthropology*, 27–46. London: Routledge and Kegan Paul.

Drewal, Henry J. 1980a. *African Artistry: Technique and Aesthetics in Yorùbá Culture*. Atlanta: High Museum of Art.

———. 1980b. "Art or Accident: Yorùbá Body Artists and Their Deity Ogun." In *Africa's Ogun: Old World and New*, edited by S. Barnes, 235–260. Bloomington: Indiana University Press.

———. 1987. "Art and Divination Among the Yorùbá: Design and Myth." *Africana Journal* 14: 139–156.

———. 1992. "Image and Indeterminacy: Elephants and Ivory Among the Yorùbá." In *Elephant: The Animal and Its Ivory in African Culture*, edited by D. Ross, 187–207. Los Angeles: Fowler Museum of Cultural History.

Drewal, Henry J., and Margaret T. Drewal. 1990. *Gelede: Art and Female Power Among the Yorùbá*. Bloomington: Indiana University Press.

Drewal, Margaret T. 1988. *Yorùbá Art in Life and Thought*. Bundoora, AU: African Studies Center, La Trobe University.

Drewal, Margaret T., and H. J. Drewal. 1983. "An Ifá Diviner's Shrine in Ijebuland." *African Arts* 16, no. 2: 60–67, 99–100.

———. 1987. "Composing Time and Space in Yorùbá Art." *Word and Image* 3, no. 3: 225–251.

Fagg, William, and John Pemberton III. 1982. *Yorùbá Sculpture of West Africa*. London: Collins.

Frobenius, Leo. 2007. "The Religion of the Yorùbá." In *Leo Frobenius on African History, Art, and Culture: An Anthology*, edited by E. Haberland, 160–191. Princeton, NJ: Markus Weiner Publishers.

Gebauer, Paul. 1964. *Spider Divination in the Cameroons*. Milwaukee: Milwaukee Public Museum.

Gleason, Judith. 1973. *A Recitation of Ifá, Oracle of the Yorùbá*. New York: Grossman.

Griaule, M., and G. Dieterlen. 1986. *The Pale Fox (Le Renard Pale)*. Translated by S. C. Infantino. Chino Valley, AZ: Continuum Foundation.

Grillo, Laura S. "Divination in the Religious Systems of West Africa." PhD diss., University of Chicago, 1995.

Hooser, Aubrey Morrow. "Divining a Pattern: Exploring Commonalities in the Ifá and Yijing Methods of Mathematico-Generative Bibliomancy." MA thesis, Boston University, 2006.

LaGamma, Alisa. 2000. *Art and Oracle: African Art and Rituals of Divination*. New York: Metropolitan Museum of Art.

Lawal, Babatunde. 1996. *The Gelede Spectacle: Art, Gender, and Social Harmony in an African Culture*. Seattle: University of Washington Press.

Lucas, J. O. 1948. *The Religion of the Yorùbás*. Lagos: C. M. S. Bookshop.

Mack, John. 1981. "Animal Representations in Kuba Art: An Anthropological Interpretation." *Oxford Art Journal* 4, no. 2: 50–56.

Mason, John. 2004. *IYIN PIPE: Praise of Completeness. Yorùbá Art from the Danny Simmons Collection*. Brooklyn: Yorùbá Theological Archministry.

McClelland, E. M. 1982. *Folk Practice and the Art*. Vol. 1, *The Cult of Ifá among the Yorùbá*. London: Ethographica.

Nicklin, Keith. 1991. *Yorùbá: A Celebration of African Art*. London: Horniman Museum.

Peek, Philip M. 1982. "The Divining Chain in Southern Nigeria." In *African Religious Groups and Beliefs*, edited by S. Ottenberg, 187–205. Meerut, IND: Folklore Institute.

———. 1991a. "The Study of Divination, Present and Past." In *African Divination Systems*, edited by P. M. Peek, 1–22. Bloomington: Indiana University Press.

———. 1991b. "African Systems of Divination: Non-Normal Modes of Cognition" In *African Divination Systems*, edited by P. M. Peek, 193–212. Bloomington: Indiana University Press.

———. 1994. "The Sounds of Silence: Cross-World Communication and the Auditory Arts in African Societies." *American Ethnologist* 21, no. 3: 474–494.

———. 2000a. "Recasting Divination Research." In *Insight and Artistry in African Divination*, edited by John Pemberton III, 25–33. Washington, DC: Smithsonian Institution Press.

———. 2000b. "Re-Sounding Silences." In *Sound*, edited by P. Kruth and H. Stobart, 16–33. Cambridge: Cambridge University Press.

Pemberton, John, III. 1988–1989. "The King and the Chameleon: *odun* Agemo." *Ife: Annals of the Institute of Cultural Studies* 2: 47–64.

Prince, Raymond. 1966. *Ifá: Yorùbá Divination and Sacrifice*. Ibadan: University of Ibadan Press.

Roache, Evelyn. 1974. "The Art of the Ifá Oracle." *African Arts* 8, no. 1: 20–25, 87.

Roberts, Allen F. 1995. *Animals in African Art: From the Familiar to the Marvelous*. New York: Museum for African Art; Munich: Prestel-Verlag.

Roberts, Mary Nooter. 2000. "Proofs and Promises: Setting Meaning Before the Eyes." In *Insight and Artistry in African Divination*, edited by J. Pemberton III, 63–82. Washington: Smithsonian Institution Press.

Thompson, Robert Farris. 1970. "The Sign of the Divine King." *African Arts* 3, no. 3: 8–17, 74–80.

van Binsbergen, Wim. 2005. "African Divination Across Time and Space." Keynote Address for Realities Re-viewed/Revealed: Divination in Sub-Saharan Africa, National Museum of Ethnology, Leiden, July 4–5. http://shikanda.net/ancient_models/divination_space_time_2008 .pdfhttp://www.shikanda.net.

Verin, Pierre, and N. Rajaonarimanana. 1991. "Divination in Madagascar: The Antemoro Case and the Diffusion of Divination." In *African Divination Systems: Ways of Knowing*, edited by P. M. Peek, 53–68. Bloomington: Indiana University Press.

Willis, Roy. 1974. *Man and Beast*. New York: Basic Books.

Witte, Hans. 1982. "Fishes of the Earth: Mudfish Symbolism in Yorùbá Iconography," *Visible Religion* 1: 154–174.

———. 1994. "Ifá Trays from the Osogbo and Ijebu Regions." In *The Yorùbá Artist,* edited by R. Abiodun, H. J. Drewal, and J. Pemberton III, 58–77. Washington, DC: Smithsonian Institution Press.

21 Of Color, Character, Attributes, and Values of Orunmila

Bolaji Campbell

In the summer of 1995, I accompanied two visiting American students, Ed Pavlic and David Doris, to the famous cloth market in Ede in southwestern Nigeria to purchase *adire eleko,* the Yorùbá indigo-dyed fabrics. I had the shock of my life when I heard a comment from one of the market women who had noticed a yellow and green beaded bracelet on David's wrist.

The woman had spontaneously remarked: *"ah, awo ti e ni eleyi"* ("So this individual is even an Ifá initiate"). I was unprepared for this kind of reaction largely because the bracelet was not very significant or much of an issue for me until then. As a result of that incident, I realized that colorful beads not only confer certain social privileges but are also an important marker of social distinction, selectively transforming the ordinary into the extraordinary, and the novices into the knowledgeable. The recognition of David's membership in the cult of *awo* (esoteric knowledge) meant that we began to have special treatment in the market, eventually going home with a good bargain.

This past summer, in a similar but quite unrelated circumstance twelve years after the initial incident, I saw a brownish-red-and-green beaded bracelet on the wrist of Lukman Akinleye-Asoleke, and I wanted to know what his beaded bracelet indicated. He informed me that he was "an initiate of Ifá." This further reaffirmed the argument that these colors had a socially prescribed code that commanded recognition and respect and that had been quite unfamiliar to me previously. This is despite the fact that I am a scholar of Yorùbá art and culture and a practicing artist who knows the nuances, symbolism, and meaning of color. Yet I grew up in the postcolonial Yorùbá society of the 1960s and 1970s where the thought or desire of identifying with traditional values was sometimes fraught with a lot of baggage, often creating an inferiority complex or the syndrome of the less cosmopolitan and unsophisticated known as the *araoko* complex. The negation of that complex was the more seductive, brazenly patronizing trope of the "enlightened, literate, or trendy" implicated in the notion of *olaaju,* which those marginalized sought to embrace without question. Regrettably, the complicated situation created by the tension between these two complexes was consistent with the narrative of the colonizer whose credo appeared to be the only worthy tool of social mobility, a determinant and index for modernity. The result is a postcolonial psyche, which conditions a certain sense of alienation from some facets of Yorùbá culture, given the fact that I am *alakowe*—elite with a characteristic distance and arrogance from certain aspects of Yorùbá culture.[1] For me, these incidents marked a remarkable turning point, first in my perception and understanding of color, and subsequently in my scholarly approach and interpretation in the field of African art history.

Yorùbá folk narratives and the Ifá divination corpus abound with many fascinating glimpses of the immeasurable influence and potency of color in Yorùbá social and religious life. One of the most intriguing of these concerns Esu, the Yorùbá trickster divinity. Whenever Esu sought to create confusion, dialogue, intrigue or altercation, he wore his colorful four-sided hat, each side with its distinct color of red, yellow, black, and white. The hat was created to cause confusion, while challenging and bewildering any and all who encountered it.

Once, Esu deliberately initiated a fight between two bosom friends, who had their farmlands next to each other. While taking a walk one evening, Esu encountered the two friends on their farms. The first person Alao, greeted the man with the peculiar hat. As soon as he was out of earshot, Alao called out to his friend Areo, wondering if he had seen the man with the peculiarly patterned hat of black. Yes, Alao answered, but corrected his friend: the man's hat was red and not black. To this Areo said, "You must be mistaken, my friend, the man wore a black hat, your eyes must be deceiving you." Soon this degenerated into a very intense argument followed by a mindless exchange of blows. At the height of this altercation, the man with the colorful hat returned and in amusement separated the bosom friends.

This narrative underscores the need for tolerance, patience, communication, and dialogue as important ingredients in fostering amicable and peaceful coexistence in every facet of Yorùbá social life. Indeed, for our purposes, the narrative raises the fundamental role of the symbolism and the affective power, influence, and potency of color in every aspect of Yorùbá social organization. Color, as on the mythical hat of Esu, is shaped by the angle, condition, and perspective of one's vision, which invariably is influenced by an indeterminate array of multifaceted variables.

Citing Christian Missionary Society records, John Peel (1997) reported that during the Yorùbá civil wars (1793–1886) members of Orisa Oko cult in Abeokuta, who had their faces painted in *pupa* and *funfun* colors as a mark of their membership in the group, enjoyed many social privileges. They were able to cross the war zones without fear of molestation or reprisals. Despite the chaotic nature of the civil society during this period, they were not permitted to be taken into captivity or sold into slavery. In addition, they were also exempt from paying the poll tax. This tradition continues today, in faraway Ijero Ekiti, where members of the Orisa Oko cult paint their faces not only as a mark of membership but also as a kind of inoculation to protect themselves against strange ailments.

So strong is their belief in the ritual efficacy of this practice that they are proud to proclaim: *akii k'efun, ka j'ejo, aki k'osun ka gb'arun we* (one does not paint *efun* on the body and be summoned for interrogation in a court of law; neither could one apply *osun* on one's body and begin to nurse strange ailments).[2] Further, as Orisa Oko was connected with the punishment and rehabilitation of witches in the past, its members were accorded many social privileges because they were deemed progressive members of the Yorùbá societies of their day. Clearly, the foregoing demonstrates that colors are used in many complex manners, including to reinforce identity, confer social privileges, beautify, and honor, while also serving as protection against social reprisals. Color at times functions as a thing of honor, often devised to imbue the living and the dead as well as the sacred and the secular with beauty, in order to harness their inherent qualities for the good of human society.

Like most cultures in Africa, the Yorùbá have three distinct color categories, into which all the colors of the spectrum are classified. These categories are *awo dudu* (black), *awo pupa* (red), and *awo funfun* (white). The categories are named after individual colors but each category consists of an array of primary, secondary and tertiary colors, which share the same analogous affinities with one another within the triadic harmonies. *Funfun*, for instance, embraces all the hues, shades, and tints of white, including, cream, silver, light grey, sky blue, and shimmering transparencies.

According to the lyrics of a Yorùbá folksong, the metaphoric ownership of dyes and the three-color categories of *pupa, funfun,* and *dudu* are conferred on three primordial birds: *agbe, aluko,* and *lekeleke.* Clearly, this was born out of the recognition of the sheer beauty of the birds' plumage and the significant position that bird imagery occupies in Yorùbá thought.

Agbe lo l'aro, Aluko lo l'osun Lekeleke lo l'efun.

Agbe (the blue turaco) owns the dark indigo dyes,
Aluko (woodcock) owns the camwood dyes,
Lekeleke (the cattle egret) has the ownership of the white chalk.
(My translation)[3]

A critical analysis of the lyrics reveals that the three birds represent the potentials and possibilities for transformation even in the seemingly ordinary matter of the ownership and use of color. The importance of bird imagery in Yorùbá thought cannot be overemphasized, given the mythical power of birds as the embodiment of spiritual power and transformation in many aspects of Yorùbá social institutions.

In a fascinating essay entitled "Yorùbá Pidgin Chromacy," Moyo Okediji (1991) explores the multiple dimensions of indigenous Yorùbá perceptions of color while drawing attention to the hybridization and extension of the vocabulary of color arising from colonial contacts. Okediji argues that much of the hybridization has given rise to the Yorùbánization of certain key English terms and color nomenclature in Nigeria. We will cite a few examples here to buttress his argument. According to Okediji, blue is referred to as *buluu*, red is termed *reedi*, and green is sometimes called *girinii* while yellow is called *yelo*. These examples are merely suggestive of the creative and dynamic ways Yorùbá culture continues to respond to changes mediated by increasing Westernization and other foreign religious influences discernible in many aspects of Yorùbá social organizations. In spite of this new trend, however, the tricolor categorization of old still holds true.[4]

While elaborating on Okediji's theories, Henry Drewal surmises that Yorùbá perceptions are influenced by "evocative associations with temperature and, by temperaments," an attitude that "distinguishes one chromatic group from another" (Drewal and Mason 1998, 18). A further amplification of this theory suggests that color is also about transformation and how it is used in providing visually stimulating images or sacrifices in honor and veneration of the orisa.

Within the Ifá divination corpus, black, which translates as *dudu*, is semantically used in placatory modes—"to invest," "to imbue," "to beg," and "to appeal to"—in a very subtle manner. According to Rowland Abiodun, the notion of conveying and conceding to an individual the essence of their existence, character, and being is implicated within the sacred ritual of imbuing with dyes, an act first performed by Obatala at the dawn of creation. Thus to invest in dyes (*ree l'aro*) is to imbue an individual with character, purpose, and beauty. In essence, the sacred aestheticians of the orisa are merely reenacting the rituals first initiated and perfected by Obatala at the dawn of existence. In order to foreground this argument, let us turn to the pertinent divination text dealing with the rituals of investing with dyes:

Orisa-nla daro meta Oda kan ni dudu Oda ka ni pupa
Oda ka ni funfun
Dudu ni o re mi
O o gbodo re mi ni pupa
Dudu ni o re mi
O o gbodo re mi ni funfun
Iwaa mi ni k'o tete re ni kutukutu obarisa. . . .

Orisa-nla prepared three dyes
He made one black
He made one red
He made one white Make me black
Do not make me red
Make me black
Do not make me white
Dye me with my Iwa first
At the dawn of creation. . . .
(Abiodun 1990, 67)

Taking inspiration from this important Ifá divination poetry, my essay focuses on the transforming potentials of color used mythically in the selection of destiny, and more philosophically as a palpable medium of veneration and control in the hands of contemporary Yorùbá artists. In this manner, colors on Yorùbá images and on African art in general are employed to foster communication between the worshippers and the worshipped. These colors belong to a complex cultural tradition involving religion, history, music, aesthetic evaluation, and philosophical ethos.

Although Ifá admonishes that there is hardly any fate that is irreparable or that cannot be changed or influenced with sacrifice, Ifá also recognizes the centrality of individual choices as the only mitigating constraints to attaining the full potentials of our natural abilities, endowments, and selected destinies, often conceptualized as our character (*iwa*).

Beyond the seemingly mundane notion of identifying and beautifying, colors on sacred and secular spaces imbue people, objects,and things with character (*iwa*) while simultaneously conveying the notion of transcendence. Many verses within the divination corpus demonstrate ways in which colors are used to evoke the character, values, and attributes of Orunmila in particular. Furthermore, the colors used on certain Ifá ritual objects and those employed on the vestments of the diviners who are custodians, philosophers, and agents of the sacred institution communicate Yoruba beliefs about this diviniation god.

Coming of age in Nigeria during the oil boom era, it was rather challenging making sense of a society in the throes of several radical and fundamental changes. It was an era with discernible contradictions in the fabric of Nigerian society. The transformation from a rural and semisedentary economy into a global and cosmopolitan polity was marked by rural-urban migrations, shifting values, healthcare delivery, and the introduction of new religious practices and beliefs. The sudden changes precipitated a social crisis and transformation unprecedented in Yorùbá history. These changes had far-reaching implications for every facet of Yorùbá social institutions. Yet the adoption of a Western worldview further complicated by Christianity and Islam continues to exert an immeasurable impact on the social-religious dynamics of Nigerian society. The deliberate cultivation of the *alakowe* syndrome mentioned earlier, together with my academic training and orientation, had sufficiently distanced me from exploring the meaning, symbolism, and potency of color from this unique and no less intriguing perspective. Though the practice of wearing beads is no longer prominent, I recall that I observed at very close quarters how colorful beads had functioned as a kind of protection against unwanted pregnancies, as prophylaxis against hemorrhoids, and as talisman and control against libidinal instincts, particularly when worn on the waist, wrists, and necks of young women.

Despite my earlier prejudice and cynicism about the efficacy of color in matters related to health and healing, I continue to marvel at the degree to which color permeates every aspect of Yorùbá culture. One might be able to pursue the full potential of this line of inquiry if only one were willing to abandon certain Western-based paradigms, attitudes, and empirical definitional models, no matter how foundational they might appear. However, in order to engage the fascinating dimension and perception of color fully in relation to Orunmila's character, values, and attributes as enshrined in the oral literature, let us now turn to his *oriki:*

Bara Petu
Baba kekere Oke Igeti
Eleeri ipin
Ibikeji Olodumare
Orisa ti o fi gbogbo aye f'oju orori si patapata
A b' ara'lu bi ajere
Orisa ti ngbe nkan ole gun Fagunwa, oko Oyeku Olomu nla, a bo ni ma ru
    Baba Esu Odara
Orisa ti ngba'ni l'owo eni t'o ni ika ninu
Baba akere fi inu se ogbon
Opitan Ife
A fun ni da
Odudu tii du ori ilemere, ki ori ilemere ma ba a fo
A tun ori eni ti ko sunwon se
Fonron owu kan soso
Ajeju oogun
Opoki a mu ide s' oju
Baba Agbonniregun
Ara Iwonran ni ibi ti oju rere ti nmo wa
Baba elepo pupo ko gbudo je adin
Baba eleran pupo, ko gbudo je eran t'o l'eegun
A yoo teere gbara san'le, ma fi ara pa
A soro dayo
Ki a mo o ki a la
Oba Alade Olodu Meridinlogun Oni'le ori oke ti nri afopin eye S'aye s'orun
    Ibini
A ji pa ojo 'ku da

Baba mi Agboniregun, a to i fi ara ti bi oke
A to i ba j'aye Ogege, a gba'yegun Agiri ile Ilogbon Amoi motan
Omo Ado baba ti i w'ewu oogun
Ajana eta ti i m'ori ekun i se'bo suuru suuru
Orisa oko aje
Olojomba a ri apa eran s'ogun
Olagbayegun Ojolugbedu orun Oniwaaye aiku
Oropoto n'iyun Ajituu ma ka'ni Baba a f'ede f'eyo
A se eyi ti o soro i se
Edu Oloja Oribujo
Oba a tun omo da be ewu Okinkin a to eyin erin ni fifon Iku dudu atewo
Oro, ajepo ma pon on
Erigialo
Iba to to to . . .

Honorable one from the ancient town of Petu[5]
Smallish one from the hills of Igeti
Witness to the selection of destiny
Deputy of Olodumare, the supreme creator
Orisa with its satellite all over the world
Whose body is extra sensitive as a sieve
The god who straightens things for the weak, the indolent and the lazy
Fagunwa, husband of Oyeku
One with huge breasts, who nurtures without ever losing weight
Father of Esu, also known as Odara, the trickster
The god who saves us from our adversary, the evil intentioned
Small and mighty one, with a mind-full-of-wisdom
The great historian of Ife
One who makes it possible to recreate
Savior and redeemer of the head of *Ilemere*[6]
Repairer of bad fate or destiny
The mythical thread
Who operates more effectively than medicinal charms
Opoki, with brass-eyes
Esteemed father, owner of the sacred palm tree, Agboniregun
Indigene of Iwonran, where day dawns
One with a vast reservoir of palmoil, who has no need for palm kernel oil
One with abundant meat supply, who has no need for bony meat
One who glides elegantly on the floor without sustaining injuries
One who understands how to make all our problems disappear
To know how to praise and honor him is to be saved
King of the sixteen-divination corpus
Owner of the elevated home, who sees the limits of the flight of birds
One who understands the earthly and otherworldly fate of Ibini
One who wards off imminent and sudden death
My father, Agboniregun, whom we could lean on for support and survival
    like the hill

A dependable one to associate with
Ogege, who maintains the equilibrium of the world
Agiri, of the house of wisdom
One who cannot fully be comprehended
Offspring of Ado-baba, who wears the brass studded shirt of medicine
Ajana, the fearless one who uses the head of the leopard in sacrifice
Tamer of the excesses of witches
Olojomba, who sacrifices with animal fore limbs
One who mediates the balance of the universe
Gbedu drummer of the otherworld
The immortal one
With a vast storage of choral beads
One who has no need to roll up his mat in the morning
The great one who speaks in many languages
Tending to the most mysterious of human problems
Most accomplished dark-skinned one
The mighty king who refashions the child as a tailor
Okinkin, the powerful one who blows the elephant tusk as trumpets
Awesome one who resides in the palm
Enigmatic one who takes a lot of palmoil, yet it does not affect his
    complexion
Formidable one we cling to for survival
Iba, great reverence and homage are your dues!
(Adewale-Somadhi 1993)

From the foregoing, Orunmila is *ogege agbayegun*: the mighty one who maintains the principle of balance and equilibrium in the universe. His other attributes include *Eleriipin* (witness to the choices made by each individual at the dawn of existence) and *Okitibiri, Apa ojo iku da* (the great changer, who alters the date of death) (Idowu 1995, 76). Orunmila is *Afedefeyo*, the great linguist who speaks in many languages and tongues; according to Bolaji Idowu, this implies that he understands all languages spoken on earth. So it is easy for him to understand and give counsel to all (ibid.). Further, Orunmila is *adani n'imoran bi iyekan eni* (the great counsel who advises one as one's relative) (Abimbola 1975). Orunmila is also *okunrin kekere oke Igeti* (the short one that dwells on the hills of Igeti). Perhaps the most remarkable is the epithet *akerefinusogbon* (the smallish one with a mind full of wisdom)—a misnomer given the enormous proportions and high esteem in which the orisa is held within Yorùbá religious and cultural institutions. According to E. M. Lijadu (1972), Orunmila's wisdom surpasses all the other orisa; hence Olodumare appointed him as the repairer and negotiator who understands the principles with which to maintain social equilibrium in all spheres of human endeavor. Thus, his preeminent position is further reinforced by the praise name of *Gbolajoko omo okinkin tii meriniifo* (the most esteemed one who blows the tusks of the elephant for honor and beauty).

How do these accolades, as the embodiment of Orunmila's articulated values and character, translate into concrete visual forms? The answers can be found in some of Ifá's honorific ritual objects, including the staff of office of the diviner, *opa orere* or *opa osooro*—typically surmounted with a lone bird (*eye'kan*) on its summit; the divination tray, *opon Ifá*; the tapper, *iroke*, often made in ivory, beads, brass, or wood; the divination chain, *opele*; and the divination dust, *iyerosun*. All of these items are kept inside a wooden bowl, *agere Ifá*, when not in use. Last but not least is the collection of beaded objects, including *apo Ifá*, the diviner's bag; *okute Ifá*, scepter of Ifá; *ade babalawo*, the diviner's coronet; *ikolaba Ifá*, the diviner's shoulder piece; *irukere*, the horsetail fly whisk, and *odigba*, the beaded necklaces or pectoral—typically the symbol of a successful professional practice. Apart from the bag, coronet, necklaces, flywhisk, and tapper, very few objects have any colors on them.

There is hardly any relationship between the verbal artistry of Ifá and the colorful materials used in invoking the essential nature of Orunmila. All this praise poetry hardly ever accounts for the colorful palettes typically used in creating the vestments worn by Orunmila's priests and followers or even those found on the ritual objects used in honor of the orisa.

Colors associated with Orunmila fall within the *dudu* and *pupa* category, a duality mirroring the notion of cooperation and balance needed in apprehending the dynamic forces controlling Yorùbá social institutions. On a more general level, these colors range from the brilliant yellows and the greens to the darker shades of blue, purple, and brown. Others include bright red, pink, and white. The white hues refer to the ethical purity of Orunmila, who symbolizes a certain dimension of truth by being the proverbial witness to the choices made by each individual at the dawn of creation. The same color is associated with the ivory *iroke* used in striking the divination board, invoking the presence of the deity at the commencement of every divination. Thus the color is a visual articulation of the cognomen of Orunmila as a witness to the choices made by individuals at that singular moment of the selection of destiny prior to their arrival in the tangible world of the living. The role of Orunmila as a witness is made concretely visible in the face adorning the borders of the divination tray, although many scholars have argued that this is the face of Esu, Orunmila's most trusted ally and faithful messenger.[7] I like to assert that Esu and Orunmila are two sides of the same coin. While Orunmila represents the principle of order and balance, Esu is its more ambivalent and indecisive aspect. Both represent the binary of opposition (*tibi tire*) integral to understanding the mystery of life within the Yorùbá universe, and only through Orunmila could the individual cautiously navigate its convoluted course. While Orunmila is responsible for proffering solutions to problems of existence, Esu is the "approver and bearer of sacrifices to heaven [especially to the divinities and to the malevolent forces, *ajogun* in particular]" (Idowu 1995, 80). In consideration of this, Esu has the right to retain a portion of all sacrifices.

Consequently, one must constantly acknowledge Esu because he is the lord of the mythical crossroads, custodian of *ase* (sacred power), divine mediator, messenger-policeman, agent provocateur, and the "divine enforcer who punishes those who fail to make the sacrifices prescribed by the diviners and rewards those who do" (Bascom 1980, 40). In order to continue their worship of this all-important divinity, descendants of enslaved Yorùbá peoples, particularly in the former Spanish colony of Cuba and in the former Portuguese colony of Brazil, subverted the Catholic Church during the period of plantation slavery by identifying and disguising Esu, also known as Elegbara/Elegua, with twenty-one catholic saints. This is certainly consistent with Bolaji Idowu's opinion that: "Esu has two hundred names, by which it is meant that he is an elusive, slippery character whom it is not easy to fix. He is called *Logemo Orun; A-nla-ka 'luu; Papa wara; A-tuka-ma-see-sa*—'The indulgent child of heaven; He whose greatness is manifested all over the place; the hurrying, sudden one; He who breaks into fragments and cannot be gathered together!'" (Idowu 1995, 83).

The specific colors of Esu remain as intriguing, if not as downright confusing and elusive, as the divinity. In Yorùbáland, most ritual objects of Esu are usually in the four colors—red, black, yellow, and white. Whether laterite or earthen mound, stone or knife, cowries or cudgel, flute or pipe, these colors represent the different manifestations and tendencies of the orisa of unpredictability. And these tendencies suggest ways in which the ritual objects are mediated and re-inscribed even in the African diaspora while revealing the proclivity, taste, and aesthetic preferences of most of his ardent devotees in the new world. Sacred candles used in honor of Esu reveal and exhibit intriguing tendencies, insamuch as they are created in nearly all colors of the rainbow, and are reflective of Esu's multivalent attributes, tendencies, roads, and manifestations.

To engage the services of this ambivalent divinity and avatar of fate, one merely needed to specify the particular errand. To incur Esu's wrath, one only needed to offer the wrong ritual item. Offering *adin* (dark palm kernel oil) instead of *epo pupa* (red palm oil), for instance, is enough to trigger the wrath of Esu (Idowu 1995). Conceptualized and used in the same manner, the ritual candles are made in particular colors. Some of these candles have single colors—black or red—or a combination of both. Others have many hues, depending on the need of the devotees.

We return to Orunmila by exploring the symbolism, meaning, and attributive qualities of colors on the ritual objects and the vestments of its priests and devotees. *Dudu* is the preferred color of the babalawo—owners and repositories of esoteric knowledge, ritual leaders and devotees of Ifá Orunmila. In addition, *dudu* is also the color of the sacred nuts of divination. The important position that the color occupies is made more apparent by the fact that when new babalawo are undergoing their final initiation ceremony before starting their professional practice, those who are ranked highest are given blue *segi* beads. Those

304 | Bolaji Campbell

in the second category receive *akun* (red coral beads), while those in the third category are presented with a necklace of brown colored kernel nuts (Abiodun 2000). It is apparent that there is some hierarchy with regard to colors. This same perception is extended to *etu*, the dark indigo dyed cloth often regarded as *baba aso*, literally "the father of cloth" and the most highly coveted fabric, which is the favorite of Yorùbá elders.

The dark colors of *dudu* include blue, black, grey, purple, and green; by association, *dudu* refers to the depth of Orunmila's knowledge and wisdom, and to the enduring quality of the ancient divination system still regarded as the most dependable body of knowledge for unraveling the mysteries and problems of existence. Those dark hues personify the dark glowing qualities of *ikin* seeds—a reliable means of decoding and unraveling the mystery of *odu*, the sacred text of divination. Additionally, the dark hues are equally suggestive of the complexion of the orisa Orunmila, a very dark-skinned person whose color could not be affected even by the consumption of red palm oil, as contained in his *oriki*: *Oro Ajepo ma pon* (the enigmatic one who takes a lot of palm oil yet it does not affect his complexion).

Further, the yellow color refers by association to *iyerosun* (the divination dust), on which the important marks of divination are inscribed. Like the *ikin*, the *iyerosun* constitutes a means of revealing, disentangling, discerning, and illuminating the intentions of Orunmila while apprehending the complexities and mysteries of life. Yellow also refers to the color of *ado baba*, the glowing warm color of brass used as storage for medicinal ingredients by the divination priests. Yellow brings light out of inscrutable darkness, an ability expected of every babalawo. Red, on the other hand, is the color of palm oil, one of Orunmila's favorite ritual offerings, used in dousing and placating the ambivalent tempers of Esu Odara. It is also the color of coral beads, *iyun* or *akun*, which Orunmila uses for beauty and honor. Red symbolizes *ase*, the catalytic power held in trust by Esu. All the other orisa periodically obtain but a tiny aspect of this vital energy from Esu in order to effect changes in the world. Thus, red is a most auspicious color used in pacifying, placating, and honoring Orunmila.

At a cursory glance, these colors span the entire gamut of the Yorùbá chromatic universe. They sometimes reveal the ambivalent nature of the principle of divination, suggestive of the nuances and temperaments of the orisa, which by extension mirrors all of our human susceptibilities and foibles. The variegated colors (*awo alarabara*) used in honor of Orunmila are apparently the same palette used for Egungun, which embodies the spirit of the ancestors as well as the Yorùbá rulers (*oba*), who are earthly representatives of the gods. These colors are in essence neutralizers and are expressive of the principle of cooperation, balance, and objectivity expected of the deputy of the orisa—whose roles and influences place them way beyond the realm of partisanship, in order for them to maintain their neutrality in all spheres of human endeavors. These colors reflect both the ambivalent and benevolent nature of the orisa. They are in that respect expressive of their temperaments as either cool, cold, and detached or perhaps warm, temperamental, and volatile. The multifaceted nature of these colors in essence replicates and mirrors the synergistic powers and attributes of the orisa, which continue to find expression in the ways in which their earthly representatives, the *oba*, are arrayed.

I would like to conclude this essay with a rigorous culture-based analysis and interpretation by examining one diviner's bag, showing how all the preceding philosophical ideals are articulated in the selection, use, and arrangement of colorful beads on the object. In the Ifá divination bag, we see the remarkable way in which the bead artist has created a visual *oriki* for Orunmila, while employing colorful beads as an appropriate and viable lexicon for its realization. Made with the proverbially dual face of Orunmila centrally positioned in the upper middle of the bag, this object is the mark of a highly successful professional practice. The significance of the placement, symbolism, and meaning of Orunmila's face on the bag could be likened to the significance it it carries on Ifá divination trays, where it is a presence usually invoked at the start of every divination. On each side of the face are interlocking chains in *funfun* and *dudu* colors, over a pink or light-red background.

Immediately below the face is the image of a reptile, which represents Esu, Orunmila's most trusted ally. Its head is tangentially placed below the face's lips, which are the portal for the evocative utterance of *ase*, the catalytic energy that makes things happen. The reptile could be a lizard (*alangba*), crocodile (*onii*), or wood gecko (*tewogbeji*), all of which represent the performative power—*ase*—employed by Esu while triggering the activities of the temperamental orisa of the Yorùbá pantheon. The reptile is appropriately depicted in a glowing warm palette (*pupa*), is occasionally interspersed with carefully arranged rolls of white (*funfun*) as a means of dousing the temperament of one fully charged with action, power, and energy.

By presenting visual images that are *oriki* concretized, defined by Olabiyi Yai, as an "unfinished generative art enterprise" (1994, 107), we can better appreciate the dialogic role visuals serve in fostering communication between god and man while providing the orisa with sacrifices that are meant to move, evoke, and energize their spiritual powers for the benefit of human society. Art as *oriki* concretized strives to bring out the beauty and character of the orisa in their bifurcated potentials for the benefit of human society. Character (*iwa*) is of the essence.

Notes

1. I was preoccupied, like most people in my generation, with the need to embrace Western culture as a natural process of socialization in postcolonial Yorùbá society. I recall how one of my aunts would reprimand me constantly each time I wore my favorite red shorts outside of our home in Lagos. Her concern was that I might be mistaken for a Sango worshipper. This might appear somewhat ridiculous to me today, but given the history and legacy of my forebears as perhaps the first generation of educated Christian elites in colonial Nigeria, one could better understand her sense of apprehension.

2. *Osun* here refers to camwood dyes, a kind of cosmetic applied on the bodies of babies by Yorùbá women.

3. All translations are mine unless otherwise indicated.

4. In a bid to test the veracity of Okediji's hypothesis, I created a 120-hue color wheel insisting that respondents use only Yorùbá words in naming each of the hues. In the summer of 1993, with the assistance of students of Obafemi Awolowo University, this research was carried out in the urban centers and rural communities throughout Yorùbáland. It is interesting that their responses came back to the same three basic color categories of *pupa*, *funfun*, and *dudu*, with slight adjectival modifications.

5. Other divination texts refer to Orunmila as indigene of Usi-Ekiti, Ado, Ijesa Obokun, Owo, Ibini, and Ife or Iwonran among many other places. In this instance, Petu might be a shortened form of Ipetumodu. It appears all of these were places where Orunmila might have practiced before finally settling on the hills of Igeti in Ife.

6. *Ilemere* refers to the *abiku* (born-to-die) syndrome or the familiar spirit of gnomes—the *enfant terrible*.

7. For further elaboration of Esu's face or imagery on the divination board, see Abiodun (1975) and Lawal (2008).

References

Abímbọ́lá, Wándé. 1975. *Sixteen Great Poems of Ifá*. Paris: UNESCO.

Abiodun, Rowland. 1975. "Ifá Art Objects: An Interpretation Based on Oral Traditions." In *Yorùbá Oral Tradition: Poetry in Music, Dance and Drama*, edited by Wándé Abímbọ́lá, 421–469. Ile Ife: Department of African Languages and Literatures, University of Ife.

———. 1990. "The Future of African Art Studies: An African Perspective." In *African Art Studies: The State of the Discipline*, edited by Rowland Abiodun, 63–89. Washington, DC: National Museum of African Art.

———. 2000. "Beads: The Ultimate Yorùbá Adornment." Lecture at the University of Wisconsin—Madison, April 27.

Adewale-Somadhi, F. 1993. *Fundamentals of Yorùbá Religion (Orisa Worship)*. Lagos: Ile Orunmila Communications.

Bascom, William. 1980. *Sixteen Cowries: Yorùbá Divination from Africa to the New World*. Bloomington: Indiana University Press.

Campbell, Bolaji. 2008. *Painting for the Gods: Art and Aesthetics of Yorùbá Religious Murals*. Trenton, NJ: Africa World Press.

———. 2001. "Yorùbá Shrine Painting Tradition: Color, Cosmos, Process and Aesthetics." PhD diss., University of Wisconsin-Madison.

Drewal, Henry, and John Mason. 1998. *Beads, Body and Soul: Art and Light in the Yorùbá Universe.* Los Angeles: Fowler Museum of Cultural History.

Idowu, Bolaji. 1995. *Olodumare: God in Yorùbá Belief.* New York: Original Publications.

Lawal, Babatunde. 2008. "Ejiwapo: the Dialectics of Twoness in Yorùbá Art and Culture." *African Arts* 41, no. 1: 24–39.

Lijadu, E. M. 1972. *Orunmila! Nipa.* Ado-Ekiti, Nigeria: Omolayo Standard Press.

Okediji, Moyo. 1991. "Yorùbá Pidgin Chromacy." In *ORITAMETA: Proceedings of the First International Conference on Yorùbá Art,* 122–130. Ile Ife: Dept. of Fine Arts, Obafemi Awolowo University.

Peel, John. 1997. "A Comparative Analysis of Ogun in Pre-Colonial Yorùbáland." In *Africa's Ogun: Old World and New,* edited by Sandra T. Barnes, 263–289. Bloomington: Indiana University Press.

Yai, Olabiyi. 1994. "In Praise of Metonymy: The Concepts of 'Tradition' and 'Creativity' in the Transmission of Yorùbá Artistry over Time and Space." In *The Yorùbá Artist,* edited by Rowland Abiodun, Henry John Drewal, and John Pemberton III, 107–115. Washington: Smithsonian Institution Press.

22 Signs, Doors, and Games

Divination's Dynamic Visual Canon

Laura S. Grillo

The Signs: A Visual Canon

One of the foremost interpreters of Yorùbá divination, William Bascom, boldly asserted that the verses associated with the signs of Ifá and recited by the babala-wo are the critical interpretive standard of this system. Bascom gives the verses the status of a canon for Yorùbá culture, claiming that "these verses constitute their unwritten scriptures" (1969a, 11). I suggest that as rich and valuable as this oral literature is, it would nevertheless be a mistake to ascribe to the verses the status of a fixed and authoritative canon. Rather, I contend that it is the set of 256 signs, the *odu* "signatures of Ifá" themselves, that comprise Ifá's canon. They fix in concrete visual form a catalogue of the normative. While the verses are num-berless and open to innovation, Ifá's set of signs is closed and unchanging. As a *visual canon,* Ifá encodes fundamental principles, ideals, and norms of culture in the material emblems of its art.

Because sacred scriptures generally are held in the highest esteem by schol-ars of religion, who look to these written texts as the definitive articulations of a tradition's self-understanding and the basis for its moral philosophy, it is natural that those wishing to redeem African religious traditions from the secondary place to which they were mistakenly relegated would wish to promote the anal-ogy between the Christian canon and the Ifá verses. However, "the overreliance on 'text' as the genre privileged with unique intelligibility severely restricts" the interpretation of other, equally expressive religious realities, such as ritual per-formance (Sullivan 1987, 772–773n169). Properly understood, the words spoken in a ritual context—and the Ifá verses in particular—should not be treated as "text"; "they are stylized semantic fields whose specific forms of expression are themselves symbolic and significant" (ibid.). Certainly in Ifá the verbal and visual components do work in conjunction. My point is that the "textual" coherence of the verses is only apparent in the performance of the divinatory ritual, as commentary on the dynamic interplay of the signs.

In applying the term "canon" to the visual iconography of divinatory practices, I aim to blur the distinction between "texts" and "objects" in order to underscore how, in West Africa, critical discourse about the nature of divinity, the dynamics of the cosmos, and the place of the person in it is forcefully embodied in the plastic arts and ritual practice.

In what follows, I draw analogies between Ifá and the divinatory system of the Dogon of Mali to show how these two equally well-documented though very disparate forms of West African divination both operate on the basis of a dynamic, visual canon. My object is not to promote the primacy of one over the other, nor to explore the possibility of a mutual influence or common source. Rather, the comparison lends weight to the idea that the signs constitute the divinatory canon. A comparative analysis strengthens the argument, even as it opens avenues for reflection on a foundational West African epistemology that I suggest undergirds both systems.[1]

The Dynamics of Divination: The Fixed and the Random

Iconography of an Enigma

Divination is sought at moments of crisis, when a person experiences an acute disjunction between an ideal model of reality and the real contingencies of experience, when what "is" does not conform to what "ought" to be. Clients come to diviners seeking clarity, insight, and guidance. However, divination proceeds along a paradoxical course. Rather than offering explicit explanation, divination responds with another puzzle. The divinatory "word" comes in the form of an image, a conjunction of symbols physically cast into new combination: palm nuts, cowries, stones, and bones are beaten, cast, tossed, and shaken into recombining arrangements in various divinatory practices. Moreover, the arrangement of these elements does not encode a one-to-one symbolic correspondence (in which, for example, heads means "yes" and tails "no"). Rather, bundles of meaning with various referents are conveyed simultaneously, like visual poems. To further complicate matters, these configurations are superimposed upon templates, such as a divining tray or table, which are themselves replete with visual imagery, rich with significance. These palimpsests graphically represent the world while the signs indicate the complex nature of experience within it. Together, they construct what anthropologist James W. Fernandez (1986, 206) calls an "argument of images," one that is, even without the embellishment of words, verses or other "text," richly suggestive.

The Origin of the Signs: Making Order

The order and arrangement of the divinatory signs as a complete system is a critical aspect of a Yorùbá diviner's training, for knowledge about their construction and relative placement is fundamental for determining their meaning. The sheer abundance of stories and myths explaining and commenting upon the visual structure and arrangement of the signs is one clear indicator that the *odu* system, as an entity in its own right, is critical. In fact, mythology traces the origins of the *odu* to the very inception of the world.[2]

Among the many mythic accounts of the origin of the *odu* and Ifá divination, all show the sixteen principal *odu* to be consubstantial with powerful primordial beings. McClelland called them "the earthly counterparts of heavenly beings" (1966, 424). One tells how the supreme divinity, Olodumare, hatched from an enormous egg, the first of sixteen divine beings to emerge from it.[3] Being the senior in rank, Olodumare, the Supreme Being, sent the younger divinity Orunmila to make the earth and to set human beings upon it. All sixteen (eight pairs of twins) eventually descended to do Olodumare's bidding. In a sort of reverse apotheosis, all of the divinities in this pantheon are said to have become Yorùbá ancestral kings and culture heroes whose personal trials and adventures established the precedent for all human experience. Orunmila initiated the original sixteen twins as Ifá diviners. These world-defining entities left their "signature" upon the practice, the *odu*.

The order of the *odu* figures in the divinatory schema indicates the order in which each divinity is said to have arrived in Ile-Ife, the mythic center of the world, birthplace of humanity, and the first Yorùbá city.[4] Bascom (1969b) calls this Yorùbá cosmology "charmingly ethnocentric," for it identifies Ile-Ife not only as the first city but as the axis mundi itself. Here, it is said, divination was first established as the means by which humans would maintain access to the divinities after they retreated into the heavens. Only at this point were human beings initiated as practitioners of Ifá and able to become the first babalawos, the "fathers of secrets."

Another version says that Olodumare himself settled in Ile-Ife and was its first inhabitant. There he set in the earth a palm nut tree with sixteen branches.[5] Sixteen holes were dug around the tree, and into each fell sixteen palm nuts. This yielded the 256 (or 16^2) possible outcomes of Ifá divination, the number of signs in the system (Maupoil 1981, 36). The signs are subsequently identified with each of the divinities to descend to the earthly city.

A particularly vivid representation of this schema shows all 256 possible variations of the *odu* as a succession of royal visits. The first and most important *odu*, Eji Ogbe, makes fifteen visits to other less powerful kingdoms, and is visited fifteen times in turn. Each lesser-ranking figure only visits those of inferior rank, and therefore makes fewer total rounds. "One [informant] explained that Orunmila arranged this scheme *so that 'all the world' could come into contact* . . . before they went back to heaven" (McClelland 1966, 425, emphasis mine). Plotting out the *odu* in this way one can see the entire order and arrangement of the signs as a progression forward and back, a journey that establishes the world.[6]

Other myths, as well as elements of the verses associated with the *odu*, depict the primordial beings fighting among themselves for rank and place, and the order of the *odu* in the Ifá system as the outcome of their struggles for standing within the pantheon.[7] In this way, the system of the signs, even in its seemingly static canonical arrangement, bears evidence that tension and strife are the essence of a dynamic universe.

Of course, the characterization of the original primordial beings as twins refers to the structure of the *odu* configurations themselves, composed of two identical parallel columns of four markings each, made up of either a double or a single stroke. However, twinship is a ubiquitous symbol of extraordinary spiritual power. Twinship is a mode of being replete with the fullness of the primordium and in keeping with the complete nature of the Divine. It is interesting to note, therefore, that the iconography of divination suggests a twinning or doubling of the mythic primordial inaugurators of Ifá and diviners.

Among other Yorùbá tales of the origin of divination is one that makes the primordial trickster, Eshu, the originator of Ifá: "Once the gods were hungry because men stopped sacrificing . . . Eshu arranged that knowledge should be given to men that they might know the gods' will and how to escape evil by offering sacrifice." (Pelton 1980, 136). Here Ifá is a mirror of the twin need and mutual indebtedness between gods and mortals. Iconography upholds this idea even more forcefully. Without exception, the border of every Yorùbá divining tray bears the carved image of at least one face of Eshu. At the time of a divinatory reading, the Yorùbá Ifá tray (*opon*) is always placed between the diviner and the client and oriented so that the face of Eshu is opposite the diviner, as if it were his mirror image. In this way, Eshu and the babalawo are twinned, and serve as double mediators between gods and humans.[8]

Another indicator that the system of signs is paramount in Ifá is the notable parallel with the role of the signs in other West African divination systems, and in particular that of the Dogon of Mali, known as "divination by the fox." The Dogon divinatory system involves the reading of actual paw prints left across a divining table that have been traced in sand. The table used to instruct and initiate diviners makes explicit how the signs reflect the mythology of the origin of the world and the inauguration of divination itself.[9]

According to Dogon mythology, the cosmic egg was the container of all the original elements and order; the first divining table re-presents it. Called "the belly of all the signs of the world," the cosmic egg is depicted as being divided into four quadrants, marking the four cardinal directions and the four elements (Griaule and Dieterlen 1965, 64).

> Each of these sectors . . . originally contained eight figures, each of which in turn produced eight . . . thus 8 × 8 × 4, or 256 signs, to which were added 8 (two for each quadrant) which represent the mythic ancestors, and 2 for the center, representing the primordial couple, the original Nommo. This yields a total of 266 "signs of Amma" (*amma bummo*). (72)

However, as Griaule and Dieterlen note, "the 256 core signs are called the 'complete signs of the world' (*aduno liga bummo*)" (65). The parallels of the number of Dogon and Yorùbá divinatory signs, their divine origin, and their significance as the seminal ingredients composing the world is striking. So too is the common notion of primordial existence originating from a complete, self-contained source. Here I reiterate that according to Yorùbá cosmology too, "Olodumare, the supreme being, is said to have been the son of a Boa called Ere who hatched him, in the beginning of the world, from an enormous egg, [and this was likened to] a great water pot (*odu*)" (McClelland 1966, 423). This full and fecund container is reproduced in the complete system of the signs; significantly, the symbol of *odu* *Ifá* is a closed calabash.[10]

In Dogon mythology, the supreme being, Amma, stirred the primordial elements and from this motion, the first beings, called Nommo, were formed as four pairs of twins. Interestingly, while the original Yorùbá beings were eight pairs of twins (the sixteen principal *odu*), Ifá makes clear that the first four are significantly more powerful. For example, Ogbe Meji, the first *odu*, is said to be the son of Orunmila, founder of the earth, and Osun, the divinity who reigns over the heavens.[11] As the figure issuing from the binding of the twin entities of the cosmos itself, this *odu* reigns supreme. Within Ifá procedings, these signs elicit ritual response; according to Bascom (1969a, 47), Ofun Meji, the last of the twinned figures, is so powerful in its own right that "it is tabu for a fly to alight upon it, [so] it is 'closed' immediately by turning over one of the shells of the divining chain when it is cast." However, the power of the first four *odu* is such that these signs are used alone, and independent of Ifá proper or the verses associated with them, as the transformative ingredient in "ayajo," protective or retaliatory "medicines." The signs are themselves forceful and reality defining.

For the Dogon, too, the sign itself is a generative force: "the sign [is a] means of acting upon the future. The ritual execution of suggestive graphic signs is efficacious, active [*agissante*]: it promotes the existence of the thing represented, re-edits it" (Griaule and Dieterlen 1965, 79). Therefore, drawing a sign has a catalytic effect. Since the iconic image is an actual constubstantial double of that which it models, its manifestation provokes a new way of being. The ritual efficacy of divination is that it carries the germ of the symbolized being in its symbolic forms, a being who is made both visible and active in divinatory representation.

The idea present in both traditions that the very inscription of the sign generates and sanctions change substantiates my hypothesis that the signs of divination themselves bear the authorizing power of canon.

The Dogon signs are arranged on the divining table in a hierarchy, referred to as the "articulated signs of the world in descent," an allusion to their mythic descent from heaven to earth in an ark (Griaule 1986, 84). (This is reminiscent of the *odu*'s descent to Ile-Ife). According to Dogon mythology, however, they were stolen from that realm. The myths recount that one of the primordial twins, Ogo, in an act of restless rebellion, broke away from the womb of Amma.[12] Tearing away a piece of the placenta, Ogo fashioned an ark. In it, he made several voyages between heaven and earth, vain attempts to bring into existence a rival world of his own making. The divinatory table is called "kala," meaning "torn," because it too was originally made from this piece of placenta.[13] Ascending back to the womb, Ogo stole the primordial grain; descending again, he danced on the placenta and his pounding steps shaped the world. Ogo is therefore known as the "iconographer of the cosmos."[14] After each of Ogo's efforts, Amma punished him, thwarted his action and reestablished control. First Amma cut out his tongue, then broke his teeth, then slit his throat—all to deprive Ogo of the creative faculty of speech. In final punishment, Amma reduced him to the abased form of the fox (*yurugu*). But in a last effort to retain a creative role, the fox begged Amma to be allowed to speak to human beings through signs. Amma relented and made the mute fox the bearer of divination. Of course, we recognize the similarity between Ogo and Eshu, the defiant Yorùbá trickster and overseer of divination.[15]

On the original Dogon divinatory table, the signs relate this cosmology: the first quadrant represents the womb of God, the second shows Ogo breaking away, the third depicts the creation of heaven and earth, while the fourth quadrant contains the sign of the original placenta spread out as the first agricultural field, the microcosmic arena in which men bind the cosmic forces.[16] The table is, in the words of Robert Pelton, "quite simply an *imago mundi,* an icon of the cosmos in its spatial and temporal movements, which are in turn images of the sacred history of the Dogon" (Pelton 1980, 198).

More significant for this study is that the order of signs on the Dogon divinatory table mirrors the signs in the Yorùbá system as a depiction of cosmogony. These figures represent the entire repository of knowledge about the world and the place of humans in it in iconic form. The stylized semantic fields of the *odu* themselves are the closed canon of divination. In the Dogon case, because of the completeness and sacrosanct status of the signs, "no one would invent a *bummo* nor modify the traditional arrangement. To draw a new sign would be [to create] a new thing, and therefore considered 'to go beyond' Amma. . . . One would say of anyone who would do such a thing: 'He has gone beyond (lacked respect for) Amma'" (Griaule and Dieterlen 1965, 100). Similarly, in Yorùbá divination only a portion of that huge literary corpus can ever be known by any one diviner, and it is expected that the number and form of the verses will change. One early interpreter of Ifá, J. D. Clarke, asserted that the verses connected with the *odu* figures "must not suggest an Ifá canon. No one man knows the whole tradition. I am told that babalawo 'swap stories' over their palm wine to demonstrate good fellowship" (1939, 246). By contrast, the iconographic signs remain constant.

The Play of the Random

To this point, I have been focusing on the divine origin of the signs to underscore their sanctity, and the fixed number of the signs to show them to be a closed set. I have shown that the signs represent the defining precedents of the cosmogony and therefore the totality of ordered existence. And we have seen how divination fixes a catalogue of the normative in concrete visual form. Divination is pivotal in West African religions precisely because it is an instantiation of the underlying cosmogonic mythologies upon which their traditions are premised. The divinatory trays and tables on which the signs are inscribed are microcosmic arenas, and the signs themselves represent "a resumé of a whole social order" (Werbner 1989, 20, quoting H. Junod). At the same time, divination situates the individual within the web of this social and cosmic order by literally tracing experience onto the "map" of prototypical cosmic events. In this way, divination turns seemingly chaotic and random occurences into significant events. It allows individual experience to be compared, measured, analyzed, and reinterpreted against these defining patterns and precedents. In short, it allows experience to be understood.

However, divination is more than a static code. It is a dynamic process. First, despite the canonical nature of the signs, within the divinatory ritual the signs are determined by some random occurence (for example, the remainder of palm nuts left in the hand of an Ifá diviner or the paw prints left by a fox on a Dogon divining table). This activity introduces a dynamic element into the process. Divination recasts experience not only in terms of its fixed set of signs but also through the dynamic of their reconfiguration. This is the critical juncture when the intermediating forces are at play, when Eshu opens the way to usher in a message from the orisha (divinities) and when the mute Ogo speaks through the signs of the fox. The active process of obtaining the divinatory sign itself recapitulates the cosmic dynamics that these primordial beings set in motion; neither allowed order to remain fixed, but overturned it and thus introduced new, generative possibility. In arriving at the signs by seemingly random means, divination reproduces the mythic tension between the ordained order of the cosmos and its chaotic disruption. The process reflects the ongoing interplay between the ideal model of reality and the fraught reality of day-to-day experience—the kind that brings one to confer with a diviner in the first place.

The geomantic forms of West African divination systems (whether etched in wood dust on a Yorùbá divining tray or traced on the sand of a Dogon divinatory table) literally re-recast the idiosyncratic situation of a client into the more interpretable idioms of culture. But interpretation of the signs is not rigidly scripted, even by the verses of Ifá. Rather, the recombining arrangements of the system's symbolic repertoire are key, even for understanding the often cryptic references of the *odu* verses. As the signs are reconfigured on the tray or table, juxtaposed images obtain new, enriched meaning.[17] The visual ideograms not only afford the participants the opportunity to "see" what is at play, but also to play with it, as interpretation is imaginatively applied. The visual metaphors of divination evoke a re-vision of experience.

In Dogon divination, the principle of interpretation consists in observing how the paw prints of the fox "meet or avoid the various shapes on the chart," the divinatory table (Calame-Griaule 1965, 524). The tracks constitute the moving parts of the Dogon divinatory system, which introduce the aleatory. Diviners decipher the trajectory of the fox tracks because their direction and rotation within a given segment of the table and their proximity to the signs inscribed on it indicate the meaning. For example, if the fox's prints circle an emblem indicating the inquiry is about an animal to be purchased, and then lead to a sector of the table containing the sign of the funerary blanket, this indicates the animal will die. Here we see how meaning is embedded not only in the fixed forms (canonical signs) alone, but emerges with the changing configurations that result from the aleatory. Situational complexity is embodied in the moving parts of the divinatory canon—in this case, the fox's prints.

In Ifá, the babalawo beats the palm nuts to introduce the element of the random. According to the number of palm nuts that remain in his hand at each turn, he draws the series of marks to shape the *odu* that will speak to the particular situation of the inquirer. Therefore the Ifá signs themselves are the "moving part" of the process. Moreover, the resulting double configuration (two columns of four markings) represents a struggle between principal figures, and the *odu* is interpreted in terms of this depiction. In this way dynamism is inherent in the sign itself.

As the babalawo traces the figure of the *odu* sign in wood dust on the divining tray, he uses a back-and-forth motion. Rather than constructing the octogram by configuring one side of the double figure and then the other, he determines both simultaneously, drawing the parallel figures from right to left and top to bottom. This pattern is reminiscent of the way the original twinned *odu* "paired off" until they had made an entire circuit of royal visits. In that primordial perambulation, half of one of the original twinned signs met half of another to form a new coupling, until arriving "home" to the twin.[18]

A Dogon diviner reads the six segments of the oblong divinatory table in a similar trajectory, first from left to right, then top to bottom and then back again, from right to left. This pattern is reminiscent of Ogo's zigzagging series of ascents and descents and his circumambulation on earth in search of his twin. In both cases, I suggest the pattern of the divinatory action reiterates the back-and-forth journeys of the primordial beings at the beginning of time, even as it reflects the ongoing dynamism of this world for which they established all precedents. This dynamism is what leads me to see not just another cultural icon but a living document in divination, a visual discourse—about the universe, culture, and the nature of experience.

Once cast in terms of the visual canon, the client's experience can be revised—both in the literal sense of 'being seen anew" and in the figurative sense of enabling them to be transformed. However, the interpretation of the visual metaphors created by these recombining patterns and juxtapositions is not prescribed by the diviner nor by any oral literature associated with a given pattern. Nor is interpretation made in strict conformity with a fixed code; rather, the divinatory process relies on a hermeneutical exegesis in which the client takes part as much as the diviner.

Puzzling out the significance of the new recombined patterns that unfold during the course of divinatory consultation draws participants into a deeper level of engagement with the visual canon. The genius of the divinatory enterprise is this ludic quality that promotes a deeply edifying imaginative interplay with the visual canon. The interpretation of the signs invites a kind of visionary theorizing on the meaning of the canon, and demonstrates what Jonathan Z. Smith calls a "canonical-interpretive enterprise" (1982, 50), which I will suggest is a form of serious play.

Doors and Games:
The Play of the Canon and the Creative Elaboration of Culture

In this concluding section, I demonstrate that divination's visual canon extends into the material forms surrounding its practice and into culture at large. Continuing my comparative study of Dogon and Yorùbá iconography, I will illustrate this innovative use of divination's lexicon.

Doors

Both Yorùbá and Dogon have a tradition of sculpting doors in low relief. For the Yorùbá, such decorated doors "signal places frequented by persons of some distinction—rulers, elders, and priests—or spiritual forces—gods and ancestors. They publicize as well as restrict entrances to special spaces" (H. Drewal 1980, 25).

Griaule and Dieterlen (1965, 85) described a sculpted door of a Dogon Hogon, the religious and temporal leader of a clan, and its iconography. It shows the 266 primordial elements referred to in the cosmogonic mythology arranged in multiple columns of short lines, an image that calls to mind the 256 Yorùbá *odu*; these geometric patterns or "signs" also appear on Dogon shrine walls. They refer to "the basic ontological properties of the world" (Pemberton 1987, 8). On the opposite panel of this door is sculpted a broken spiral moving from a central point out towards the periphery and turning back in on itself. It reportedly represents the mixing of the primordial elements, an activity that brought the world into existence, and is called "a day's work of Amma" (Griaule and Dieterlen 1965, 84).

A sculpted door of a Yorùbá diviner presented by art historian Hans Witte (1984, 33, plate 2) reiterates many of the same visual themes traditionally seen on Yorùbá divining trays. In its center is a divining tray with the face of Eshu on right and left. Whenever "Ifá trays are represented on sculptured doors, the head of Eshu is always on the right side, so that when the door stands open, Eshu indicates the way" (ibid. 33). Four *opele* chains are arranged around the Ifá tray.[19] Their cowries are positioned to form the signatures of the four principal *odu*. Together their sequence signifies "the most terrible spell of all" (ibid. 24).

Bascom refers to such a configuration as well, stating that it represents "pure ayajo," or medicine associated with the Ifá figures, consisting of instructions for herbs and incantations:

> The figures of Ogbe Meji, Oyeku Meji, Iwori Meji, and Edi Meji set at right angles to each other as reported by Frobenius (1913, I, 255), Maupoil (1943, 187–188), and Mercier (1954, 255) was recognized by informants as part of Ifá, but only as medicine and without any orientation to the cardinal points of the compass. An Ife diviner . . . identified it as "mediator" (oniata), a very strong medicine to spoil the work of one's enemy. (Bascom 1969a, 61)

The appearance of this configuration on a diviner's door shows the signs themselves to be emblems of communication and bearers of power in their own right.

Above this configuration on the door is a round wheel-like image: two concentric circles with the space between them divided into four segments. It depicts the compartments of an open Ifá container used to store divining materials.[20] The form of this container is, incidentally, not unlike the description of the original Dogon divining table, which was also round. It, too, contained all the elemental signs of the world.

On either side of the container is a tortoise, a commonly reiterated symbol of Ifá (Orunmila or Eshu). Its propensity to retreat into the protective camouflage of its shell metaphorically represents the closely guarded "secret" knowledge of Ifá. This is the case for the Dogon, who also see in the tortoise shell an inscription of the primal field and the divinatory table.

The undulating messenger-snake also embellishes either side of the door, as two sinuous columns. Because tortoises, like snakes, bind water and land, they are also considered messengers between realms, just as Ifá is a messenger between realms. Also depicted is the elongated flute of Eshu, a well-known icon of this trickster's status as messenger of the gods.[21] At either end of the door are wide bands of the complex interlaced pattern, *ibo,* the ubiquitous symbol of the interwoven aspects of existence.

On one end of this figure is an extension, a sort of handle, in the shape of the classic Yorùbá icon of the double-headed ax of Shango, the Oyo God of Thunder, who is described in the divinatory poetry as "the great avenger." It is said that "Shango fights with troublemakers and those who use bad medicine to harm others, as well as with his worshipers who offend him in other ways" (Bascom 1969b, 84). The evocation of a punishing avenger reiterates the message of the *opele* configuration ("the most terrible spell of all"), for certainly there is no force more threatening than an avenging spirit.

The Game of Ayo

Most interesting of all is a figure in the lower quadrants of the door, not commented on by Witte, which seems obviously to be the board of a popular game known by many names but which the Yorùbá call Ayo. However, what is to be made of the Ayo gameboard itself? Ayo is a game played throughout Africa, with versions of it found as far to the south and east as Madagascar and as far to the north and west as Mauritania. It is popular throughout sub-Saharan West Africa, where it might be played for idle amusement during siesta, or turn into a serious tournament between fierce competitors surrounded by spectators admiring the players' skill.

The game is based on the random distribution of seeds (like random patterns of the diviner's palm nuts) and requires attention to the constant reconfiguration of their arrangements as they are played. A player must devise a strategy of action on the basis of emerging patterns, a process much like the search for guidance within the context of divination. Before extending the analogy much further, let us turn our attention to the structure of Ayo, its concrete form and its rule of operation.

The wooden game board is an elongated form into which are carved twelve cups, six on each side. At the start of the game, each of these cups holds four game pieces, usually large seeds resembling palm nuts. One proceeds by distributing the seeds from a cup on one's own side of the game board, always moving the seeds from left to right. When it is a player's turn he or she scoops up a cup of seeds and distributes them, dropping them one at a time into successive cups, always proceeding in the same circulating direction. The gesture of scooping up the playing pieces and casting them around the board is not unlike that of the diviner, who in "beating the palm nuts" attempts to grasp them all with one swipe of the hand but expects and allows one or two to fall or remain behind. The object is to land in a cup on the opponent's side containing only one or two seeds, so that the drop of the final seed makes a new total of two or three seeds.[22] These are the winning combinations that allow the player to "capture" those seeds (as one would capture pieces after jumping them in a game of checkers). An alternative way of playing is to make the winning combination either a three or a four.[23] At the end of the game, when all the pieces have been won, the player who has the greatest number of pieces wins the game.

Ayo is often said to be a game of chance, but is in fact one of skill. A player must calculate and devise a strategy of action on the basis of the emerging patterns on the board, a process much like the search for insight and guidance on the basis of the emerging signs in divination. In a fast game between competing players, it also requires psychological cunning. I suggest that these are the same skills required to work out one's destiny, for destiny is considered more a matter of careful deliberation and bold action than a fixed fate.

A game is the engagement of a complex interplay between rules and chance. In this way, too, Ayo is not unlike divination, which explores the tension between the ideal order and real experience. To play is to intervene in the sequence of events, in order to transform a situation. This is also what divination does.

The manipulation of the palm nuts on a divining tray follows strict rules, but the interpretive processes promotes the application of skills and involves the active engagement of its participants—not only the diviner but also the inquirer, whose concerns it graphically depicts. The aim of the divinatory engagement is not to predict a fixed fate but to enable the individual to perceive options and maximize possibilities. In this way, the game of Ayo and the practice of divination follow a parallel course.

Ayo in Ifá Divination and Yorùbá Ritual

In her documentation of Yorùbá ritual, Margaret Drewal (1992) elaborates upon a series of rituals called *Itefa*, the "Establishment of the Self," which are explicitly concerned with fixing the identity of an individual within the community. Divination plays a critical part in *Itefa*; the babalawo performs divination to determine the Ifá texts that will function "as models for self-examination and self-interpretation [that will enable the individual to] embark on a lifelong program of searching, reflexivity and interpretation" (63). *Itefa* also prepares a personal set of palm nuts consecrated for the sole use of an initiate throughout his or her lifetime.

Drewal recounts that during her observations of *Itefa* ceremonies held for the sons of Oshitola, a diviner and Drewal's principal informant, the *odu* verse obtained for one of the children referred to a culture hero who played Ayo. This ancestor-hero made conscious use of the game to draw people to him, gain from their knowledge, and learn how to rule. While the reference to Ayo in the *odu* corpus itself is not particularly telling, for there are many references to banal activities in the verses, what is significant is that the verse recognizes that Ayo is an exercise of strategy, requiring social grace, cunning, careful observation, and calculated action. From its practice, the hero learns to be king. The game is a metaphor for all that is necessary to succeed in life. Oshitola interpreted the *odu* as indicating that "the gathering and exchanging of views will be beneficial to Olofin," his son (M. Drewal 1992, 84). Accordingly, an improvised ritual segment was devised in light of the reading, and the children were made to play a perfunctory game of Ayo. From this example of a game embedded in a ritual, we see the interwoven nature of visual and verbal "text." The improvised game becomes part of a ritual act that will engender the qualities associated with its practice in the initiate. The enactment of game playing in this ritual context is itself an imaginative play of the cultural canon.

Ayo and the Ark

The speculation that there is a conscious correlation between divination and Ayo is also borne out by the association that the Dogon make between the game board and the "ark" of Ogo. According to various mythic accounts, the Dogon trickster journeyed to and from heaven in this ark to gather the primordial grain. The ark is represented as a small square box, "*yurugu koro sibe nay,* 'ark of the *yurugu* with four corners'" (Griaule and Dieterlen 1965, 204). A drawing of Ogo's ark that appears in Germaine Dieterlen and Marcel Griaule's *Le renard pâle* (1986) exhibits a clear physical correlation with the game board: both are elongated three-dimensional wooden blocks in which are carved two parallel rows of cups.

The nuts or seeds used to play Ayo suggest the palm nuts that fell from Olodumare's primordial tree, and also primeval grains Ogo stole from heaven and bore away in the ark. Their displacement on the game board would correspond to the movement of the first spiral stirrings of creation within the cosmic egg, as well as the ongoing fecund permutations of the cosmos. During the game, the Dogon orient the board from east to west, the direction in which the ark supposedly progressed when it first came to earth. (This is also the direction associated with Eshu). The game board's allusion to greater cosmic dynamics was suggested by its association with the Dogon calendrical system, in which each of the holes stood for a month. The whole of the game reproduces the workings of the universe in time and space. It also represents the fecund activity of the dynamic cosmos in which the human being holds a central place: one half of the board represents women, the other side men, while the distribution of grains connotes the union of the sexes and the proliferation of the human species. This may lend further insight into the significance of the fact that half the *odu* configuration is considered the male side and the other half female. We see that like the diviner's tray or table, the game is nothing less than a microcosm of the world and that the seeds moving on it, like the changing configurations of the signs, represent its dynamic action.

The Play of the Visual Canon

Extending the metaphor between the game and the process of divination, I contend that divination demonstrates a concern for both the rules that govern its operation and inventive engagement that makes the process rewarding. The signs constitute the normative order, but they are constantly put into play.

Through the recombining arrangements of its symbolic repertoire, divination literally recasts experience. The interpretation of the signs allows for an imaginative interplay with that canon. In this way, divination orchestrates a full immersion in a compelling interactive experience in which meaning is constructed in the playful engagement of its lexicon. Divination offers more than rigid prescription or mute enactment; it is a playful transaction, a strategy for negotiating meaning. It is this ludic quality that makes divination both a powerful vehicle for personal transformation and an effective medium for conveying the significance of the canon. Divination is serious play—the play of the visual canon.

Notes

1. I developed this argument on divination as West African epistemology elsewhere, notably in my dissertation (Grillo 1995) and in Grillo (2006).

2. There are many accounts of the origin, nature and function of the *odu*. Among those cited by McClelland (1966) are Johnson (1921), Bascom (1942), Lucas (1948), and Parrinder (1961). McClelland warns "It is by no means easy to arrive at a clear conception from the complex and mystifying stories that overwhelm the inquirer" (1966, 423).

3. Like Ogo, the first to emerge from the "primodial egg," also known as the "womb" of Amma, in Dogon mythology.

4. The Fon of Benin who adopted the Yorùbá system of Ifá divination also trace its origins to the city of Ife. This city, while an actual administrative center of a southern Nigerian province, about fifty miles east of Ibadan, evokes a "mystical homeland" where "the supreme creator God passed" (Maupoil 1981, 32). Maupoil cites A. B. Ellis (1894, 89) saying "Ife is considered the cradle of the human race" (1981, 32).

5. Mircea Eliade would have seen the archetype of the *axis mundi* in this tree. Maupoil relates the Fon legend surrounding this tree, named *Fe-de* (palm nut tree of Fe), showing it to follow the celestial movement: "And since its creation one can see it standing straight up in the morning, inclined toward the middle during the day, and touching the earth with its branches . . . at nightfall. It rises again the next day, and its movement continues in this way to the present day" (1981, 36).

6. Bascom established that the names of the sixteen basic figures are standard, but that the order varies within Yorùbá country, as well as in practices of Ifá in Dahomey, Togo, Ghana, Cuba, and Brazil. Though twenty-one rankings were recorded, Bascom (1969a, 47) noted that one order predominates.

7. The whole arrangement of the 256 *odu* as a system emphasizes the primacy of order for interpretation. In "Two Studies of Ifá Divination" (Morton-Williams 1966), this issue is discussed from two different points of view. Bascom (1966) presents an empirical survey of the order as recorded by informants not only among the Yorùbá but elsewhere in West Africa and among the practitioners of Ifá in Cuba to assess the reliability of anthropological descriptions. Bascom ascertains a remarkable consistency of the structure across traditions that attests to the important symbolic significance of the order itself. E. M. McClelland's associated piece (1966) confirms the uniformity of structure and explains its consistent internal logic as a pairing off of twin elements.

8. In both Dogon and Yorùbá divination the diviner is a twin of the primordial trickster, inextricably associated with the technique. Dogon mythology suggests that we are the twins of Ogo, restless to find completion, to make a world of our own meaning, unwilling merely to submit to our fate, always looking to negotiate our destiny—beginning with a trip to the diviner to peek into the path set before us in the hopes of taking another, shorter, better route to our own ends. Diviners and clients alike are twins of Ogo, *cocreators of this world*, pushing against what is stirring things up, making new things happen in the imaginative interplay with the world.

9. Michel-Jones suggests that the myth and common Dogon oral literature such as fables and stories should not be categorically differentiated. Moreover, she indicates that she would not distinguish between the esoteric and exoteric variations of the myth, since the versions are not incompatible for the individuals for whom they have significance. "If the myth is 'living,' that is to say efficacious, if it possesses an integrating character as a conceptual framework and interpretive grid of the whole sensible world, as the 'word of old' in which all the elements of social life are theoretically prefigured, it is susceptible to various 'transcriptions'" (1978, 37).

10. The iconography of broken pottery that decorates the altars erected to Eshu is in striking contrast to the closed calabash, the symbol of Odu Ifá. Whereas Ifá is the closed system of order and the calabash the container of the contents of destiny, the broken pottery indicates the force of Eshu to break open and upset this contained order. Whereas the Odu represent structure, Eshu willfully injects the energy of "antistructure" and the uncontainable. The Ifá tray circumbscribes this energy, and shows that the very order of the cosmos that it represents holds a place for the unpredictable and the means to negotiate destiny. In Dogon divination, the table serves this purpose.

11. These figures are like a primordial couple. In striking parallel to the Dogon myth, they would have made an incestuous couple. In the Dogon myth, however, the son issuing from such a union is the trickster Ogo.

12. In breaking away from his twin, Ogo is an exceptional being, a loner who is forever after in search of his twin. In the mythology associated with Ifá, too, there is reference to a primordial being who is exceptional in that he was not a twin, *Osetua*. Osetua is said to be the son of Eshu, the primordial trickster, and Osun, who as a witch is by definition a transformer associated with reversals of order. With such a parentage, *Osetua* necessarily embodies a provocative force: "The son of such parents inspired dread and could not be wholly disregarded. He . . . acted as a special courier from earth to Ifá in heaven" (McClelland 1966, 424).

13. "*Kala sibe nay*" ("torn at the four corners") (Griaule and Dieterlen 1965, 274).

14. In this way, Ogo is like Eshu, known for his vigorous energy, insatiable libido, and agility. Eshu's notorious dancing similarly shapes the world. One of his praise songs says, "if there are no drums / he will dance to the pounding of mortars" (Pelton 1980, 132, quoting Wescott 1962, 352).

15. Eshu is the mediator between the divinities and human beings, the principal messenger of Ifá and the figure around whom divination pivots. As a trickster, he stirs up the unpredictable, interjects the unexpected, and thereby opens the way to an unknown destiny, replete with possibility. Eshu represents reversals and transformation, the very object of the divinatory enterprise.

16. According to Griaule and Dieterlen (1965, 86), before planting an "ancestral field," a schematic representation of the 266 primordial signs is inscribed on the ground. This image, called the *vagea minne*, is comprised of two concentric circles and a central point. Between the two circles are four or five jagged lines, a dynamic image of vibrant motion. Outside this circle, the four cardinal points of the cosmos are marked with grains. In this way the ancestral field is correlated with the arrangement of the primordial egg and its elements. The image suggests the dynamic and generative forces.

17. As the fixed templates of order, the tray or table represent the boundaries within which the chaos of the random is safely entertained. These palimpsests serve as the container of the unleashed disorder.

18. "[The signs] are set under the names of two Odu in each case. . . . Conceiving [the basic sixteen Odu figures] first as personages and referring to the supporting myth [their structure can be seen as] *a stately choreographic movement of which the basic features are a constant pairing off,* a regular change in partners, and a fixed path to tread until the measure, having worked itself out, comes to a natural end" (McClelland 1966, 425, emphasis mine).

19. The Ifá *opele* is a divining instrument that offers an alternative to the use of the palm nuts, and conveys the *odu* more rapidly. It consists of a double chain on which are strung four elements such as cowrie shells or pieces of calabash each. The chain is held at one end and thrust away from the diviner. The pieces land in either a concave/convex position corresponding to a single or double mark of the *odu.* Yorùbá myths point to the chain as a vehicle for the original descent of Oduduwa to earth. It is therefore the corollary of the ark in which Ogo descends from the primordial egg to create the earth, according to Dogon mythology.

20. Also said to contain substances representing the four primordial elements. This is similar to the Dogon *vagea minne* (see note 16).

21. The association of the world-creating trickster and the flute reinforces the idea that sound breaks the homogeneity of silence, marks time with its rhythm, and is a powerful generative force.

22. Here we see that a winning move in Ayo is like the determinative action of the beating of the palm nuts in Ifá divination: when one or two palm nuts remain in his hand, the babalawo inscribes one of the marks that comprises the *odu* sign.

23. The numbers three and four have symbolic significance in Dogon cosmology as well as Ifá iconography, representing male and female principles respectively. Bascom (1969a, 27) notes that palm nuts with three "eyes," indentations at their bases, are considered male; only those those with four "eyes," considered female, are appropriate for ritual use. These are called *awenren Ifá.*

References

Bascom, William 1942. "Ifá Divination." *Man* 42, no. 21: 41–43.

——. 1966. "Odu Ifá: The Names of the Signs." *Africa* 36, no. 4: 408–421.

——. 1969a. *Ifá Divination: Communication Between Gods and Men in West Africa.* Bloomington: Indiana University Press.

——. 1969b. *The Yoruba of Southwestern Nigeria.* New York: Holt, Rinehart & Winston.

Calame-Griaule, Geneviève. 1965. *Ethnologie et langage: la parole chez les Dogon.* Paris: Editions Gallimard.

Clarke, J. D. 1939. "Ifá Divination." *Journal of the Royal Anthropological Institute* 69: 235–256.

Drewal, Henry John. 1980. *African Artistry: Technique and Aesthetics in Yoruba Sculpture.* Atlanta: High Museum of Art.

Drewal, Margaret Thompson. 1992. *Yoruba Ritual: Performers, Play, Agency.* Bloomington: Indiana University Press.

Ellis, A. B. 1894. *The Yoruba-Speaking Peoples of the Slave Coast of West Africa: Their Religion, Manners, Customs, Laws, Language.* London: Chipman and Hall, Ltd.

Fernandez, James W. 1986. *Persuasions and Performances: The Play of Tropes in Culture.* Bloomington: Indiana University Press.

Griaule, Marcel, and Germaine Dieterlen. 1986. *Le renard pâle*. Translated by Stephen C. Infantino. Paris: Institut d'Ethnologie

Grillo, Laura. "Divination in the Religious Systems of West Africa." PhD diss., University of Chicago, 1995.

———. 2006. "Divination: The Innovation and Adaptation of Traditional Religions in Response to the Contingencies of Contemporary Urban West Africa." In *The Histories, Languages and Cultures of West Africa: Interdisciplinary Essays,* edited by Akura Sarr, Amadou T. Fofana, Edris Makward, and C. Frederick. 377–386. Lewiston, NY: Edwin Mellen Press

Johnson, Samuel. 1921. *The History of the Yoruba*. London: Routledge.

Junod, Henri A. 1924. "La divination au moyen de tablettes d'ivoire chez les Pedis." Bulletin of the Societe neuchateloise de geographie.

Lucas, J. Olumide. 1961. *The Religion of the Yoruba*. Oxford: Oxford University Press.

Maupoil, Bernard. 1981 *La Géomancie à l'ancienne Côte des Esclaves*. Paris: Institut d'Ethnologie.

McClelland, E. M. 1966. "The Significance of Number in the Odu of Ifá." *Africa* 36, no. 4: 421–431.

Michel-Jones, Françoise. 1978. *Retour aux Dogon: figure du double et ambivalence*. Paris: Le Sycomore.

Morton-Williams, Peter. 1966. "Two Studies of Ifá Divination: Introduction—The Mode of Divination." *Africa* 36, no. 4: 406–408.

Parrinder, G. 1949. *West African Religion*. London: Epworth Press.

Pelton, Robert D. 1980. *The Trickster in West Africa: A Study of Mythic Irony and Sacred Delight*. Berkeley: University of California Press.

Pemberton, John, III. 1987. "Traditional African Iconography." In *Encyclopedia of Religion* vol. 7, edited by Mircea Eliade, 8–14. New York: Macmillan.

Smith, Jonathan Z. 1982. *Imagining Religion: From Babylon to Jonestown*. Chicago: University of Chicago Press.

Sullivan, Lawrence E. 1987. "Tricksters: An Overview." In *Encyclopedia of Religion* vol. 15, edited byMircea Eliade, 45–46. New York: Macmillan.

Werbner, Richard. 1989. *Ritual Passage, Sacred Journey: The Process and Organization of Religious Movement*. Washington, DC: Smithsonian Institution Press.

Wescott, Joan. 1962. "The Sculpture and Myths of Eshu-Elegba, the Yoruba Trickster: Definition and Interpretation in Yoruba Iconography." *Africa* 32, no. 4: 336–354.

Witte, Hans. 1984. *Ifá and Esu: Iconography of Order and Disorder*. Soest, NL: Kunsthandel Luttik.

23 Ifá

Visual and Sensorial Aspects

Henry John Drewal

Introduction: Sensiotics

The senses are crucial to understandings of the arts, not only in Africa, but of arts everywhere.[1] I have been writing on this matter since about 1990, but my first encounter with such issues goes back much further. My earliest lesson, though I did not know it at the time, dates to my very first attempt at African art research—my apprenticeships with the Yorùbá artist Sanusi of the Adigbologe Atelier in Abeokuta, Nigeria in 1965, and a second, mask-making apprenticeship with Ogundipe of Ilaro in 1978 when I made a Gelede mask for the impending festival. I believe that work still dances in Gelede performances (Okediji 2003, 182). What I learned from those apprenticeships was that "the actions of artists teach us as much about style and aesthetics as their words" (H. Drewal 1980, 7). I gained insights into Yorùbá artistic concepts, not only in discussing them with artists and observing them as they emerged from the creative process, but also in attempting to achieve them in my own carving under the tutelage of Yorùbá artists. In other words, my own bodily, multisensorial experience was crucial to a more profound understanding (oye) of Yorùbá art and the culture and history that shape it. This process of watching, listening, carving, making mistakes, being corrected by example, and trying again was a transformative sensorial experience for me. Slowly my body learned to carve as my adze strokes became more precise and effective and the image in my mind took shape through the actions of my body. Yorùbá people understand this kind of experience and explain it with a sensory metaphor: "the outsider or uninitiated usually sees through the nose" ("imu ni alejo fi i reran") (Abiodun 1990, 75). This saying has two different yet complementary connotations: that an outsider understands little because he or she confuses sensing organs, and at the same time that understanding requires multiple senses

(Abiodun 2008; Abayomi Ola, pers. comm. 2005). In addition to wisdom (*ogbon*) and knowledge (*imo*), we struggle to achieve understanding (*oye*).

A similar orientation, a fascination with arts (both visual and performance) and their impact on audiences, led me to Efe/Gelede masquerades as the subject of my PhD field research in 1970–1971. I chose Efe/Gelede because it epitomizes for Yorùbá people a deeply moving multimedia and multisensorial spectacle of sights, sounds, smells, tastes, touches, and movements captured in the praise "the eyes that have seen Gelede, have seen the ultimate spectacle" (*"oju to ba ri Gelede, ti de opin iran"*). While this saying seems to privilege the sense of sight ("eyes" and "spectacle"), it implies an experience that comes from more than just sight: Efe/Gelede is about the dance movements of masqueraders, the sounds of complex drum rhythms, the sound of leg rattles, and the songs of Oro Efe at night when sounds dominate sights, not to mention the smells of *akara/moi-moi* and the tastes of other dishes one would find in the marketplace. For remember, the market is the place of the performances, the space commanded by powerful women who are the very ones honored in Efe/Gelede.

These are examples of what I call "body-mind work" and what Paul Stoller (1997) evocatively calls "sensuous scholarship." Here one no longer aspires to achieve the impossible "distanced objectivity" of a so-called participant-observer (which historically emphasizes observation). Rather one works as a sensorially engaged participant, using all his or her senses in order to open the multiple sensory paths to knowledge and understanding. Granted, the differences between cultural insiders and outsiders will always remain, yet within those groups there are significant differences in cultural knowledge, wisdom and understanding, perspectives that provide different insights. And perhaps most of us are cultural "inbetweeners" (Okediji 2008). The engagement of the senses is crucial to such understanding.[2]

This initial exposition of an approach I call *sensiotics* outlines a theoretical perspective, proposes a specific methodology, and gives a few examples from the world of Ifá to illustrate this approach. I argue that Yorùbá artists (working in all forms and media—song, sculpture, painting, tattooing, dance, and so on) and audiences use the senses (sight, taste, hearing, speaking, touch, motion, and extrasensory perception) to create and respond to the affective and aesthetic qualities of art and design or *ona*, here defined as "evocative form." As you will note, I consider seven senses—the usual five plus two others I believe are distinct and equally important: motion and ESP. Motion has to do with our relation to gravitational forces and our sense of balance. It is interesting to note that among the Anglo-Ewe, a sense of balance (*agbagbadodo*), when a child first learns to rise up on two feet and not fall over, is "an essential part of what it means to be human" (Geurts 2002, 49–50). A similar idea may be present in the Yorùbá term *dogba*, "to balance." I extend the notion of balance/spatial orientation to encompass motion, with its sensing organ, the labyrinth of the inner ear.

The seventh sense, what some call "the sixth sense," has to do with ESP that seems related to the notion of intuition. I would suggest that when we try to understand the concept of trance or altered states of consciousness, when one's head "swells" (*ori wu*) as Yorùbá say—a phenomenon that is certainly widespread in the artistic and religious traditions of Africa and its diasporas (and probably a universal human experience)—we are dealing with issues of ESP, the supplement, the indeterminate.[3] This is much like the trance experiences of followers of Shango. This seventh sense is related to synesthesia—the simultaneous body-mind interplay of multiple senses that has a profound effect on how we experience things in this world and what we imagine might be beyond—as expressed by A. M. Opoku urging us to "see the music, hear the dance" (Lamp 2004, 15). This notion of indeterminacy is fundamental to Yorùbá thinking. It is expressed in the notion of "four hundred plus one orisa"—a pantheon that is without limit, forever in flux. As Olabiyi Yai (pers. comm. 2006) has remarked, this indeterminacy is expressed in the concept of *okanlenirinwo* orisa which translates as "something that is ever-unpredictable and does not admit of limitation or ceiling." And as Wọlé Ṣóyinká reminds us, "Ifá emphasizes for us the perpetual elasticity of knowledge" (2008, 41).

The arts (sculpture, dance, song, chant, poetry, incantations, and the rest), as Rowland Abiodun (1987, 2008) posits, are all classifiable as *owe* (figures of speech), matters that are the subject of discussion, concern, or action (*oro*). *Oro* should be interpreted as the embodiment of *ogbon, imo ati oye* (the one and indivisible combination of wisdom, knowledge, and understanding)—a concept that precedes speech, visual and verbal arts, performance, touch and smell but includes them all and more in the sense of *okanlenirinwo* (literally "401," but conveying the sense of multiplicity).

If these insights are valid, then I believe we need to rethink our ways of working. Language-based approaches, such as semiotics, structuralism, and poststructuralism, are not vision based. Such linguistic or logocentric approaches to the arts have tended to distort or blur understandings of art on its own terms (H. Drewal 1990, 35). When we consider art, it becomes form webbed by words. Granted, we cannot avoid using words—our discipline is basically words about images. But we need to go beyond this. As W. J. T. Mitchell has observed, "'visual experience' or 'visual literacy' might not be fully explicable in the model of textuality" (1994, 16). Malcolm Gladwell (2005, 119–120), drawing on the work of Jonathan W. Schooler, notes that visual perception is "clouded" and "overshadowed" by the verbal; that visual cognition is "immediate, holistic, and instinctive" whereas verbal cognition is linear and consciously constructed. It seems clear, then, that we need to explore how art communicates and evokes by means of its own unique sensorial modes (H. Drewal 2002, 200). As I have argued before, "while the study of language is a means, it is not an end. Language-based approaches, such as semiotics, are just that—language-based, not vision-based.

Art communicates and evokes by means of its own unique codes, and these need our attention" (H. Drewal 1990, 35). Such a vision-based approach is being developed by Moyo Okediji (1992, 119–123; forthcoming) that he calls "semioptics"—an approach that recognizes the limitations of the linguistic thrust of semiotics and seeks to uncover the ways in which the sense of sight shapes our perceptions and understandings of the world.[4]

Yet vision-based approaches would be only an important first step in a more inclusive and comprehensive project of developing the theories and methods to reveal the bodily, multisensorial basis of understanding of arts, an approach I term "sensiotics" that I have been feeling, thinking, and working on (and that has been working on me) since my first apprenticeships with Yorùbá sculptors in the 1960s–1970s. I would contend that while language, for example, is one of the ways we re-present the world, before language we began by perceiving, reasoning, theorizing, and understanding through all our senses. Sight, hearing, touch, smell, taste, and motion continually participate, though we may often be unconscious of them, in the ways we literally make sense of the world, and art. Seeing (hearing, tasting, and so on) is thinking. Sensing is theorizing. In the beginning, there was no word, only sensations.

Ifá: Visual and Sensorial Dimensions

The remainder of this essay illustrates my sensiotics approach with a few examples of the visual and sensorial aspects of Ifá material and immaterial culture.[5] Seriate composition and mythic allusions characterize Ifá art. In divination trays (*opon Ifá*), low relief images encircle the divining surface. An Ifá/Fa divination tray in the Ulm Museum, West Germany (Weickmann Collection, inventory no. 46), collected at Allada during the first half of the seventeenth century, documents the antiquity of seriate composition.[6] A large frontal face centered at the top may refer to Esu/Elegba, the divine mediator/messenger between humans and spiritual forces. Three medicine gourds crown the brow. Two profile figures, one with a gourd at the end of a tailed coiffure, may also be Esu/Elegba references. Arranged around the border is a myriad of images: quadrupeds, cowrie shells, birds, reptiles, women, men, and cultural items such as pipes, tools, swords, sheaths, axes, cups, brooms, shackles (?), drums, gourds, guns, market goods, and divination tappers. Things present in the world crowd the space and express a wide variety of themes: leadership, warfare, survival, fertility, protection, sacrifice, and so forth. No narrative unifies these diverse depictions; rather, they convey the autonomous forces operating in the Yorùbá cosmos that affect and concern the diviner and his clients. Each is given approximately equal visual importance, thus evoking a dynamic and fluid cosmos of forces, the same forces that "speak" through the *ese Ifá* recited by the diviner. Notice also the marked shifts in perspective and proportion throughout the figured border. In keeping with the seriate form any visual element may be enlarged or reduced at the discretion of the artist. Such a compositional mode documents the autonomy of individual motifs. Even when the motifs on a divination tray are nonrepresentational, their arrangement remains serial/seriate—distinct sectors with contrasting geometric or organic configurations frequently separated and delimited by borders—thereby conveying through nonobjective patterns the idea of unique, separate powers.

But seriality and multiple proportions and perspectives are not the only features of composition in Ifá divination trays. There is also an explicit orientation and emphasis on four directions, the four quadrants between these, and the center of the tray. The four directions refer to the cardinal points, for the diviner sits facing the east with the frontal face of the tray sited opposite him. Research in Ijebu Yorùbáland revealed that Ifá shrines and rituals are oriented ideally on an eastwest axis: entrances to shrines and groves must face east, the direction from which Orunmila (Ifá) is said to have come.[7] The importance of these cardinal points and Yorùbá astronomical concepts requires serious study, for they are deeply rooted in Ifá and other Yorùbá beliefs. All this is about positioning and movement—orienting oneself in order to move forward in life's journey through a cosmos of complex competing forces that must be continually negotiated.

In divination trays, then, there is a compositional interplay of a circle and intersecting lines, the former reflecting the unity of the Yorùbá cosmos consisting of the world (*aye*) and the otherworld (*orun*) populated by diverse, autonomous forces, and the latter expressing the intersection of cosmic realms at the metaphorical crossroads (*orita meta*) and the cardinal points.

In addition to its articulation of a cosmos of autonomous forces, the divination tray evokes legendary diviners and their exploits. These accounts from the past are precedents for actions and remedies in the present. One old tray, discussed by its owner Kolawole Oshitola, has eight sections plus one, all said to represent ancient diviners. The diviner invokes each section as he "opens" the tray at the beginning of a consultation. The main, or largest "face of the tray" (*oju opon*) (1), is oriented opposite the diviner. The part nearest the diviner (2) is the *ese opon*, "foot of the tray." At the right hand side (3) is *ona kanran*, a "straight path," while the left (4) is *ona murun*, also a "direct path." As Oshitola explains: "These are ancient forefathers . . . when you work, work, work, your name will remain in history. That *ona murun* is one of the hardworking, ancient diviners, and he became so famous that we shall always remember his name forever." *Ona kanran* (straight path) was also famous. His way was straight, meaning he was "a straightforward person . . . a good man." Straightness is a metaphor for openness, honesty, and trustworthiness. The upper right quadrant of the tray (5) is *alabalotun*, "the-onewhoproposeswiththeright"; the upper left (6) is *alaselosi*, "the-onewhoimplementswiththeleft." On the lower right (7) is *ajiletepowo*, "anearlyriserwhositsdownandprospers," and on the lower left (8) is *afurukeresayo*, "theonewhohasadiviner'sfly-whiskandishappy." The center and "leader" of the tray (9), where the verses of Ifá are marked, is the *erilade opon*, "thecenterofthet-raythe-meeting place-that-crowns-all."

After the diviner "greets" these nine ancients, he may then pay homage to his forefathers, the deities, and certain birds. These birds are metaphors for the diviner's ability to chant and also, according to Ifá lore, ancient diviners. As Oshitola explains, "all the birds and animals have the knowledge of Ifá in the ancient times." Many stories recount the trials and tribulations of these bird diviners. Their victories presage the success of the diviner who invokes their memory.

In praising all the sections of the tray, the diviner alerts its spiritual essences, readies it for action, and at the same time, focuses the attention of all those present at the divining session. It is also a means by which the diviner collects himself and establishes his own concentration. But the diviner's most important task is to invoke famous past diviners, bringing them to the consultation in the world from the otherworld and into the present from the past. The divination session is then like all Yorùbá rituals in that the invocation temporarily makes manifest an otherworldly reality (H. Drewal and M. Drewal 1983, 4). In effect, the divination tray is a crossroads where the otherworldly and worldly realms communicate, a metaphor made visible by the diviner when he inscribes lines in *iyerosun* (camwood powder) on the tray, thereby "opening" it just before beginning his work.

Each section of the tray is a path and simultaneously a personified entity. All ways are recognized and invoked separately, some with attributes that distinguish their roles. For example, the diviners whose praise names are "theone-whoproposeswiththeright" and the "one-whoimplementswiththeleft" refer to the Yorùbá belief about the use of the right hand in social or worldly matters and the use of the left in sacred, mystical affairs. The diviner orients himself facing east toward an open doorway or path. This direction must be kept clear during invocations to give free access to the forces called. The invocation and the presence of these forces assure success; their neglect courts disaster.

Compare this marking of paths/lines on the tray by a babalawo with the lines, dots, and colors marked on the head of a newly initiated orisa devotee (*adosu*). The reason I have described the opening of the diviner's tray in detail and compared it to the marking of an *adosu*'s head is the importance of gesture or motion—one of the seven senses involved in understandings of art. It is the action of the diviner or priest that acknowledges and activates spirit to create evocative form or *ona*.

Colors and Ifá

I want to now join the sense of motion with that of sight, specifically the perception of color, which I will argue involves three senses simultaneously—sight, motion, and touch. A divination session engages multiple senses. Divination is an *etutu*, a "cooling," soothing, placating act. And as its name implies, it evokes a change in temperature, that is, temperament. Those present, humans and spirits, must feel the cooling, calming moment. In this way, the sense of touch is part of the perception of color. But more than this, I would argue that color cognition among Yorùbá (and others) is not solely a matter of sight and touch, but also of motion.

The Yorùbá distinguish three chromatic groupings: *pupa, funfun,* and *dudu*—inadequately translated as "reds," "whites," and "blacks/dark hues" respectively (Okediji 1991; Campbell 2008).[8] Remember, colors provoke the sensation of temperature, experienced through the sense of touch. Reds (*pupa*) are hot (*gbigbona*), whites (*funfun*) are cool (*tutu*), and dark colors (*dudu*)—black, blue, green, brown—mediate between these two extremes. Such colors evoke temperature and by extension temperament—the character of the gods. Thus the cool of white invites the presence of Obatala and the heat of red evokes the warrior Shango.[9]

Colors also evoke a sense of motion. We know that reds and other warm or hot hues seem to advance toward us due to the length of their light waves hitting the retina of our eyes. Blues, purples, greens tend to recede, move away from us. Thus our perception of color engages three senses simultaneously: sight, touch, and motion.

Now in much of the world of Ifá, the colors yellow and green tend to dominate, especially in the beadwork of diviners. According to Yorùbá chromatics, yellow and green are mediating colors—they are not the hot (*gbigbona*) hues, and they are not the cool ones (*tutu*). They fall between these two extremes, moderating and mediating them. And this, I would suggest, is symbolic of the position of Ifá (and the diviner) in the Yorùbá cosmos; to serve as a cosmic bridge between *aye* and *orun,* between humans and divine forces. These mediating beads are known as *otutuopon.* As Oshitola explained to me: "They are either green and yellow or green and brown. [They say] 'When we perform a ceremony for someone, it will be alright [it will succeed]'" (pers. comm. 1982, 1986). And the full range of colors in the beaded necklace of diviners (*odigba*) signals the fact that Ifá must work with *all* forces in *aye* and *orun.*

Black or dark hues (*dudu*) are other important colors in Ifá that are related to the *ikin Ifá,* the sixteen palm oil nuts—the most important objects in a diviner's possession. They are vehicles of illumination. Very dark, black, and shiny from age and handling, they evoke the aesthetic beauty of Ifá whose blackness is praised in the name given to ebony children, Adubiifa, "Black-as-the-ikin-Ifá." (Abiodun 2008, 54). Blackness, as Abiodun reminds us, is symbolic of the infinite knowledge and wisdom of Ifá and its diviners in penetrating the vast unknown, the forces operating in the cosmos, and providing illumination. Blackness also references the unfathomable depths of the ocean, the realm of Olokun to which diviners travel when they leave *aye* for *orun* (Oshitola pers. comm. 1982, 1986)—a journey referenced in the double fish-tailed figure of Olokun on an Ifá tray.

Hearing/Sound

Along with the senses of sight, touch, and motion, an Ifá divination session demands hearing. Of primary importance are of course the invocations of the diviner and the recitation of the *ese* and *odu Ifá*. But in conjunction with these powerful words (*afose*) that can "make things come to pass" are other sounds that are essential for the efficacy of the session.

Hearing, a sense that has great value, especially on a continent where oral traditions are essential to the production and reproduction of social, cultural, and artistic practices, is an extremely important sensorial mode of understanding in Yorùbá society. As Abiodun (1983) notes, in Yorùbá society, a multisensorial mode of understanding is embedded in the concept of *iluti*: the ability to hear, communicate, and remember—in other words, the capacity to learn, to be educated. And significantly, *iluti* determines whether or not a work of art is alive and responding, in other words, effectively evocative.

Thus sounds, a very important mode of appreciation, are often ignored or devalued in discussions of the visual arts. Consider what I wrote above about Ifá divination trays. While I explored the complex composition and imagery of the tray and waxed eloquent about such sights, I did not mention that the hollow area carved into the underside of the tray creates a sound chamber. The tray is a wooden drum—imagery plus sound.[10] When an Ifá priest strikes the center of the front surface (*erinladeopon*) with the pointed end of a divination tapper (*iroke*), the sound reverberates in order to "communicate between this world and the next" as the diviner Kolawole Oshitola explained to me (pers. comm. 1982, 1986). Then comes the sound that follows when the diviner strikes or "beats" together (*pa'kin*) the sixteen *ikin Ifá* and marks the *odu Ifá* signature in the camwood powder (*iyerosun*) on the tray. The sound of the tapper on drum-tray, followed by the sharp clack of the *ikin*, alerts cosmic forces. Sacred sounds, not just images, create a transcendent, evocative experience of art.[11]

Taste also figures in another aspect of a divination session. The camwood powder (*iyerosun*) that covers the "crown" of the tray is later incorporated into empowering packets by the diviner for his clients. The clients must ingest (that is, taste and swallow) some of the *iyerosun* for the ritual to be effective in activating cosmic forces. Tasting the *iyerosun* ensures that the client embodies the empowering *ase* of the forces revealed by Ifá. Too, taste (and touch) are engaged when, in the early morning, a diviner or Ifá follower "wakes up" his deity before invocations by loudly spraying *oti* (schnapps/liquor) on the *ikin*. Tasting, touching, and hearing are essential elements in sensorially evocative practices of belief.

The Diviner and his Staff (opa osun Orunmila)

Symbolizing the diviner and his work is the *osun* staff, one of the diviner's most important possessions (Drewal and Drewal 1983). Made of iron, the *osun* staff stands erect next to an *akoko* tree [*Newboldia laevis bignoniaceae*] (Abraham 1958, 44) in front of a diviner's house. *Akoko* leaves, among their various functions, are used in bestowing titles. Besides marking a residence of a diviner, the staff stands for the first diviner and deity of divination, Orunmila, and Orunmila's friendship with the goddess of the sea, Olokun. The relationship between the *akoko* tree and the staff symbolizing Orunmila and his friendship with Olokun is synthesized in Orunmila's epithet, "TheAkokoTreebytheSea" (Akoko'lokun). One story recounts how Orunmila was such a good friend to Olokun that she gave him her daughter, Ajesina, as a wife. Represented by an exceptionally large cowrie, Ajesina, literally "WealthOpenstheWay" (Ajesiona), is often honored on diviners' shrines (H. Drewal and M. Drewal 1983). But besides this, Olokun holds a special place in the world of Ifá. The goddess of the sea controls the entire universe, for water surrounds all land. The sea is vast and encompassing, and more importantly, it is where a diviner's spirit is thought to go when he departs the world. Certain accounts illuminate other aspects of the staff's ritual significance. Once, three warrior deities, Ogun, Ija, and Osoosi, went to Death (Iku) and told him to kill Orunmila because they suspected that he wanted to steal their wives. Death prepared to strike. Afraid, Orunmila went to consult another diviner, who instructed him to give a cock to Death. Orunmila pulled the cock's tail feathers, and it cried, "Kooo, kooo, kooo." When Death heard the suffering cry of the cock, it sounded so wonderful that he took the cry and went away. In the Ifá rite that establishes a man's shrine (*itefa*), a cock is sacrificed at the site of the staff as an act to ward off Death. The diviner attaches the head, wings, and feet of the cock to the staff to serve as evidence of the sacrifice. Death is satisfied to take the breath or spirit of the cock, while the spirit residing in the staff receives the nourishment of its blood.

The staff represents the power of the diviner to conquer death; it possesses performative power (*ase*). When used with incantations, the staff acts as a weapon against death and other destructive forces. Its medium, iron, reinforces its aspect as a weapon and recalls Orunmila's victory over three warriors noted for their own mastery of iron. The substances that give the staff much of its power are buried at its base, or tail (*iru*). The staff's tail is stuck into the ground, and it absorbs power through its tip. As one diviner explains, "any powerful enemy that stands in the way of *osun* is ready to die." Thus, when going on an "Ifá journey," that is, when performing an important divinatory ceremony that involves a procession, the staff leads the way. True to its position in front of the house it must also be in front of a procession. At crossroads the Ifá entourage stops and chants incantations, while the one in the lead swings the end of the staff outward to drive away destructive forces. Because the power of the staff is in its tail, it is likened to the power of the spiny anteater (pangolin), which curls its tail around its body to make it impervious to attack. Enemies cannot destroy it. The staff is also quickacting and efficient. It has the power of the hawk (*asa*), which is represented at the top of the *osun*. Thus, according to the diviner Oshitola, "history told us that if we want something to act quickly, we should do it in the name of the hawk." (pers. comm. 1982, 1986) Once a hawk has grabbed its prey with its feet, nothing drops—unless, of course, the hawk chooses to let go. Thus, if a diviner wants to take the staff along in procession, he chants, "Stand up, let's go because the hawk is alert: he acts quickly."

In addition to its identities as Orunmila, weapon, anteater, and hawk, the staff also symbolizes the diviner himself. There is a prayer for the staff that goes, "*Osun duro, maa subule*" ("Osun stand, don't fall down")—meaning that the diviner should live long. When a diviner dies, the staff is laid down on its side and the diviner's journey to the watery realm of Olokun commences. After two to three months his successor will offer a number of large sacrifices to the staff, and then it will be re-erected. It stands again to assert that although the father has fallen, his successor has taken over; he is prepared. Thus the staff not only marks the presence of Orunmila and protects the diviner's house, it also represents the diviner himself—his life, his power and resilience, his quickness and tenacity in conquering enemies, and ultimately his departure from the world to the realm of Olokun. The diviner must possess the powers of the spiny anteater and the hawk, not just for his own protection in dealing with a myriad of autonomous, potentially destructive forces, but also for the protection of his clients, who seek his help.

The Importance of Enactment

Like the divination tray, the diviner's staff is at the center of many important rituals involving the senses—processions, sacrifices, initiations, and funerals. The sight of the staff may provoke evocative associations (weapon, imperious pangolin, swift hawk, cock sacrifice, stalwart diviner, and so on), but it equally conjures up gestures (swinging the staff in processions, covering it with the head and feathers of a sacrifice, laying it down at the passing of a diviner), sounds (prayers and songs, the cry of the cock), smells and tastes (of an offering), and touch (of hard, cold iron). All these are essential elements that contribute to a deeply affective, evocative ritual experience, like the experience of art, *ona*. The reason these multisensorial elements and enactments in rituals are so important may explained by recent discoveries in neuroscience, more specifically the role of "mirror neurons." Stated briefly, when we see an action being performed, our neural networks fire and our brains actually perform the action we are seeing—

our body-minds *do* what we *see* (Rarey 2008). So then, when we physically do what our mirror neurons did when we first saw an action, we are learning, reinforcing, deepening, embedding bodily, sensorial experiences, and making them a part of us both mentally and physically. In this way lessons stick—they become a part of us, since multiple neural-paths make for stronger memories. What is performance but a way to enact—that is, embody—knowledge and understanding. And there are many stages in the very complex *itefa* ceremonies that require enactment—the engagement of songs, music, movement, taste, touch, hearing, and the processional journey led by the *osun* staff that clears the way of any obstacles to success. All the senses are engaged to deepen the evocative qualities of the experience.

Envoi

While these few examples focus on the arts of Ifá passed down and shaped over countless generations, I believe sensiotics can also inform our understandings of contemporary Yorùbá (and African) arts and the global reach of arts associated with Ifá. These twentieth- and twenty-first century forms are shaping and responding to wider worlds—a spinning globe of complex, competing images, sensations, and ideas that constantly bombard us. Out of these, artists create and audiences respond using their senses and sensibilities. If we want to understand the creativity of artists and the responses of audiences, then we must understand how the senses shape and guide us from *orun* to *aye* (and back to *orun*). Let our body-minds soar with *imo, ogbon, at'oye* as we create words to represent the evocative, sensuous experiences called *ona—ASE!*

Notes

1. These ideas about the senses result from many years of living among Yorùbá-speaking people in West Africa and their descendants in Brazil since 1964. At various times this work has been generously funded by the following: Institute of Intercultural Studies, New York; the African Studies Institute, Columbia University; Cleveland State University; the National Endowment for the Humanities; the Nigerian National Museum; Universities of Ibadan and Ife/Obafemi Awolowo; the Fulbright Fellowship Program; the Guggenheim Foundation; and University of Wisconsin-Madison. I express my deep gratitude to these institutions and especially to certain individuals: Samuel Akinfenwa, Raimi Akaki Taiwo, J. R. O. Ojo, 'Wándé Abímbọ́lá, Oyin Ogunba, Rowland Abiodun, Kolawole Oshitola, the Longe and Abiodun families, 'Sope Oyelaran, and Margaret Thompson Drewal, whose assistance and friendship have sustained my efforts over many years. Their wisdom, insights, and probing questions helped shape this paper. Some sections of this essay are revisions and expansions of my 1987 article, "Art and Divination: Design and Myth."

2. There is now a rapidly growing interest in aspects of this multisensorial approach. In anthropology, the seminal work has been done by Paul Stoller (1984, 1989, 1997), Michael

Taussig (1993, 2004) and Kathryn Geurts (2002). In the field of African art history/visual culture, Roach and Eicher (1973); Eicher (1995); Robert Farris Thompson (1974), Herbert Cole (1970, 1974), and Simon Ottenberg (1975) were among the first to open more than our eyes to the importance of the senses. Now others are exploring this topic (Peek 1994; Strother 1998, 2000; Lamp 2004; Blier 2004; Cooksey 2004). In September 2005, the University of Minnesota held a symposium called "The Senses and Sentiments of Dress," honoring the work of Joanne Eicher. Diane Ackerman's (1990) poetic evocation of the "natural history of the senses" has inspired wide audiences beyond the academy. Much of this work reflects a renewed interest in the body as an important site of investigation, for the senses are about bodily experience and knowledge. It is no mystery, then, that the often exquisitely poetic writing of Robert Farris Thompson comes from his roots as an ethnomusicologist and mambo freak; that Margaret Thompson Drewal (1992) and Frederick Lamp understand performance so well because they were dancers, and Daniel Reed music because he had to learn from his Dan master singing instructor how to "heat up" a Dan Ge masquerade performance with a loud voice, high register, and tight timbre (Reed 2003, 126); for more examples of multisensory approaches, see also Philip Peek (1994) on the "Sounds of Silence," as well as René Devisch (1993) on the importance of smell among the Yaka of Central Africa; and Sylvia Boone (1986) on the senses in Sande initiations.

3. See H. Drewal (1993).

4. Moyo Okediji's critique of semiotics and its impact on visual culture and art-historical studies is the focus of a forthcoming book that will revolutionize how we think about language and images.

5. The richness and complexity of Ifá divination have fascinated scholars for quite some time. Most notable of the pioneers are Frobenius (1913, 1973), Maupoil (1943), and Bascom (1969, 1980). They were followed by such major scholars as Abimbola (1968, 1969, 1975, 1976, 1977, 1980), Beyiokii (1971), McClelland (1966, 1982), and Adedeji (1970). Abiodun (1975, 1980), and Witte (1984) have illuminated imagery in Ifá art (see also Pemberton 2000).

6. While Yorùbá people (and Ifá/Fa) were certainly present in Allada in the seventeenth century, the style and iconography of this divination tray suggest Aja or Fon work rather than Yorùbá. See Merlo (1974) for nineteenthcentury Aja/Kota/Fon and Ewe work in a style strikingly similar to the Ulm tray. Regardless of the exact provenance of this piece, it is certain that Ifá (Fa) was widely practiced in this area as a result of (Oyo) Yorùbá cultural influence. The composition and iconography, therefore, can be said to reflect Yorùbá cosmological ideas.

7. Frobenius (1973, 188–189), citing information received early in this century from diviners in Ibadan, Ife, and Lokoja (Lokoya), collected the following myth at Lokoja: "Long, long ago, when everything was in confusion and young and old died, Olodumare (God) summoned Eshuogbe and said: 'Create order in the region of the sunrise.' To OyakoMedyi: 'Create order in the region of the sunset.' Next morning Edshuogbe created order in the east and in the evening OyakoMedyi created order in the west."

8. Campbell (2008) offers more elaboration on this.

9. These same color temperament connotations carry over to Yorùbá descendants in Cuba as well. John Mason (pers. comm. 1989) notes: "when a diviner warns of a 'red' enemy, a violent, unpredictable, explosive person is being described."

10. See Abiodun (1975).

11. There are many dents in the surface of the seventeenth-century Ulm tray—marks left by the diviner while communicating "between this world and the next."

References

Abímbọ́lá, Wándé. 1968. *Ijinle Ohun Eni Ifá, Apa Kiini.* Glasgow: Collins.

——. 1969. *Ijinle Ohun Enu Ifá, Apa Keji.* Glasgow: Collins.

——. 1975. *Sixteen Great Poems of Ifá.* Paris: UNESCO.

——. 1976. *Ifá: An Exposition of Ifá Literary Corpus.* Ibadan: Oxford University Press.

——. 1977. *Ifá Divination Poetry.* New York: Nok.

——. 1980. "Verbal and Visual Symbolism in Ifá Divination." Paper presented at the Conference on the Relations between the Verbal and Visual Arts in Africa, Philadelphia, October 10–14.

Abiodun, Rowland. 1975. "Ifá Art Objects: An Interpretation Based on Oral Traditions." In *Yorùbá Oral Tradition: Poetry in Music, Dance and Drama,* edited by W. Abimbola, 421–469. IleIfe: Department of African Languages and Literatures, University of Ife.

——. 1980. "Ritual Allusions in Yorùbá Ritualistic Art: Oriinu, Visual and Verbal Metaphor." Paper read at the Conference on the Relations Between the Verbal and Visual Arts in Africa, Philadelphia, October 10–14.

——. 1983. "Identity and the Artistic Process in the Yorùbá Aesthetic Concept of Iwa." *Journal of Cultures and Ideas,* 1: 13–30.

——. 1987. "Verbal and Visual Metaphors: Mythical Allusions in Yorùbá Ritualistic Art of Ori." *Word and Image: A Journal of Verbal/Visual Inquiry,* 3, no. 3: 252–270.

——, ed. 1990. "The Future of African Art Studies: An African Perspective." In *African Art Studies: The State of the Discipline,* 63–89. Washington, DC: National Museum of African Art.

——. 2008. "Who was the First to Speak?" In *Orisa Devotion as World Religion,* edited by Jacob Olupona and Terry Rey, 51–69. Madison: The University of Wisconsin Press.

Abraham, Roy C. 1958. *Dictionary of Modern Yorùbá.* London: University of London Press.

Ackerman, Diane. 1990. *A Natural History of the Senses.* New York: Vintage.

Adedeji, Joel A. 1970. "The Origin of the Yorùbá Masque Theatre: The Use of Ifá Divination Corpus as Historical Evidence." *African Notes* 6, no. 1: 70–86.

Bascom, William. 1969. *Ifá Divination: Communication between Gods and Men in West Africa.* Bloomington: Indiana University Press.

——. 1980. *Sixteen Cowries: Yorùbá Divination from Africa to the New World.* Bloomington: Indiana University Press.

Beyiokii, A. F. 1971. *Ifá, Its Worship and Proverbs.* Lagos: Salako Printing Works.

Blier, Suzanne Preston, ed. 2004. *Art of the Senses: African Masterpieces from the Teel Collection.* Boston: Museum of Fine Arts.

Boone, Sylvia. 1986. *Radiance from the Waters.* New Haven, CT: Yale University Press.

Campbell, Bolaji. 2008. *Painting for the Gods: Art and Aesthetics of Yorùbá Religious Murals.* Trenton, NJ: Africa World Press.

Cole, Herbert. 1970. *African Arts of Transformation.* Santa Barbara, CA: University of California Press.

——. 1974. "The Art of Festival in Ghana." *African Arts* 8, no. 3: 12–23, 60–62, 90.

Cooksey, Susan, ed. 2004. *Sense, Style, Presence: African Arts of Personal Adornment.* Gainesville, FL: Samuel P. Harn Museum of Art.

Devisch, René. 1993. *Weaving the Threads of Life.* Chicago: University of Chicago Press.

Drewal, Henry John. 1987. "Art and Divination among the Yorùbá: Design and Myth." *Africana Journal* 14, no. 2/3: 139–156.

——. 1980. *African Artistry: Technique and Aesthetics in Yorùbá Sculpture.* Atlanta: High Museum of Art.

——. 1988. "Beauty and Being: Aesthetics and Ontology in Yorùbá Body Art." In *Marks of Civilization,* edited by A. Rubin, 83–96. Los Angeles: Fowler Museum of Cultural History.

——. 1990. "African Art Studies Today," *African Art Studies: The State of the Discipline,* edited by Rowland Abiodun, 29–62. Washington: National Museum of African Art.

——. 1993. "Image and Indeterminacy: The Significances of Elephants and Ivory among the Yorùbá." In *Elephant: The Animal and its Ivory in African Culture,* edited by D. Ross, 186–207. Los Angeles: Fowler Museum of Cultural History.

——. 2002. "Celebrating Water Spirits: Influence, Confluence, and Difference in Ijebu-Yorùbá and Delta Masquerades," In *Ways of the River: Arts and Environment of the Niger Delta,* edited by Philip M. Peek and Martha G. Anderson, 193–215, 353. Los Angeles: Fowler Museum of Cultural History.

Drewal, Henry John, and Margaret Thompson Drewal. 1983. *Gelede: Art and Female Power among the Yorùbá.* Bloomington: Indiana University Press.

Drewal, Margaret Thompson. 1992. *Yorùbá Ritual: Performers, Play, Agency.* Bloomington: Indiana University Press.

Drewal, Margaret Thompson, and Henry John Drewal. 1983. "An Ifá Diviner's Shrine in Ijebuland." *African Arts* 16, no. 2: 60–67, 99–100.

Eicher, Joanne B., ed. 1995. *Dress and Ethnicity: Change Across Space and Time.* Washington, DC: Berg.

Eicher, Joanne B., and Sandra Lee Evenson, eds. 2000. *The Visible Self: Global Perspectives on Dress, Culture, and Society.* New York: Fairchild Publications.

Frobenius, Leo. 1913. *The Voice of Africa,* vol. 2. London: Hutchinson.

——. 1973. "The Religion of the Yorùbá." In *Leo Frobenius, 1873–1973: An Anthology,* edited by E. Naberland, 160–191. Wiesbaden, DE: Franz Steiner Verlag.

Geurts, Kathryn. 2002. *Culture and the Senses: Bodily Ways of Knowledge in an African Community.* Berkeley: University of California Press.

Gladwell, Malcolm. 2005. *Blink.* New York: Little, Brown.

Lamp, Frederick, ed. 2004. *See the Music, Hear the Dance: Rethinking African Art at the Baltimore Museum of Art.* Munich: Prestel.

Maupoil, Bernard. 1943. *La géomancie a l'ancienne cote des esclaves.* Paris: Travaux et Mémoires de l'Institut d'Ethnologie.

McClelland. E. M. 1966. "The Significance of Number in the Odu of Ifa." *Africa* 36, no. 4: 421–431.

——. 1982. *The Cult of Ifá among the Yorùbá.* London: Ethnographica.

Merlo, Christian. 1974. "Statuettes of the Abiku Cult." *African Arts* 8, no. 4: 30–35, 84.

Mitchell, William John Thomas. 1994. *Picture Theory.* Chicago: University of Chicago Press.

Okediji, Moyosore B. 1991. "Yorùbá Pidgin Chromacy." In *Oritameta: Proceedings of the 1990 Conference on Yorùbá Art,* edited by Moyo Okediji, 16–28. Ile-Ife: Department of Fine Arts, Obafemi Awolowo University.

——, ed. 1992. *Principles of "Traditional" African Art.* Ibadan: Bard Book.

——. Forthcoming. *Crossing the T.*

——. 2003. *The Shattered Gourd: Yorùbá Forms in Twentieth-Century American Art.* Seattle: University of Washington Press.

——. 2008. "Inbetweeners: Mamiwata and the Hybridity of Contemporary African Art." In *Sacred Waters: Arts for Mami Wata and other Divinities in Africa and the Diaspora,* edited by H. J. Drewal, 479–491. Bloomington: Indiana University Press.

Olupona, Jacob K., and Terry Rey, eds. 2008. *Orisa Devotion as World Religion.* Madison: University of Wisconsin Press.

Ottenberg, Simon. 1975. *Masked Rituals of Afikpo: The Context of an African Art*. Seattle: University of Washington Press.

Peek, Philip. 1994. "The Sounds of Silence: Cross-World Communication and the Auditory Arts." *American Ethnologist* 21, no. 3: 474–494.

Pemberton, John, III, ed. 2000. *Insight and Artistry in African Divination*. Washington, DC: Smithsonian Institution Press.

Rarey, Matthew. "The Mirrors of Mardi Gras" (unpublished seminar paper, University of Wisconsin—Madison, 2008).

Reed, Daniel B. 2003. *Dan Ge Performance: Masks and Music in Contemporary Cote d'Ivoire*. Bloomington: Indiana University Press.

Roach, Mary Ellen, and Joanne Bubolz Eicher. 1973. *The Visible Self: Perspectives on Dress*. Englewood Cliffs, NJ: Prentice Hall.

Ṣóyinká, Wọlé. 2008. "The Tolerant Gods," In *Orisa Devotion as World Religion*, edited by Jacob Olupona and Terry Rey, 31–50. Madison: University of Wisconsin Press.

Stoller, Paul. 1984. "Sound in Songhay Cultural Experience." *American Ethnologist* 11, no. 3: 559–570.

——. 1989. *The Taste of Ethnographic Things: The Senses in Anthropology*. Philadelphia: University of Pennsylvania Press.

——. 1997. *Sensual Scholarship*. Philadelphia: University of Pennsylvania Press.

Strother, Zoe. 1998. *Inventing Masks: Agency and History in the Art of the Central Pende*. Chicago: University of Chicago Press.

——. 2000. "Smells and Bells: The Role of Skepticism in Pende Divination," In *Insight and Artistry in African Divination*, edited by John Pemberton, 99–115. Washington, DC: Smithsonian Institution Press.

Taussig, Michael. 1993. *Mimesis and Alterity: A Particular History of the Senses*. New York: Routledge.

——. 2004. *My Cocaine Museum*. Chicago: University of Chicago Press.

Thompson, Robert Farris. 1974. *African Art in Motion*. Los Angeles: University of California Press.

Witte, Hans. 1984. *Ifá and Eshu: Iconography of Order and Disorder*. Soest, NE: Kunsthandel Luttik.

24 Art, Culture, and Creativity

The Representation of Ifá in Yorùbá Video Films

Akintunde Akinyemi

THE FIRST SERIOUS attempt to dramatize the practice of Yorùbá Ifá tradition in motion pictures in Nigeria started in the late 1970s with the production of the late Hubert Ogunde's series *Aiyé* (1979), *Jáíyésinmi* (1980), *Àròpin N Tènìyàn* (1982), and *Àyànmó* (1988) on film and Ifáyemí Elebuìbon's popular weekly primetime television series, *Ifá Olókun Asòròdayò*, on the television service of the Broadcasting Corporation of Oyo State, Ìbàdàn. Today, video is the dominant technological medium of popular culture and entertainment in many Nigerian urban centers. The ubiquitous presence and popularity of video in Nigeria point to its importance as a new medium for the production, dissemination, and consumption of one specific form of popular culture, with its ideology and aesthetic. With the popularity of video film production in Nigeria today, Ifá has once again become an instrument of creativity—in the hands of video screenwriters. The representation of Ifá in Yorùbá video films manifests in different forms: the exhibition of the iconic objects of Ifá divination, the characterization of the Ifá diviner-priests by actor-diviners, the recreation of the Ifá divination process and the accompanying sacrifices, and the reinvention of the performance of *ìyèrè* (Ifá chants). However, it should be stated from the outset that my concern in this chapter is not just about the preservation and survival of Ifá oracular tradition in video films; I also examine the ways in which the Ifá corpus has been adjusted by video screenwriters to address contemporary interests and concerns in modern society. Consequently, on several occasions Ifá folkloric materials have become instruments that video screenwriters manipulate easily to raise social consciousness in the minds of their audiences.

Exhibition of the Paraphernalia of Ifá

Ifá, as a Yorùbá divination god, has his own iconic objects of divination. The most prominent are the divination tray (*opón Ifá*);[1] the sacred divination palm nuts (*ikin*); the sacred divining powder (*ìyèrè òsùn* or *ìyèròsùn*);[2] the sacred chain of divination (*òpèlè*);[3] the carved club-like object used by Ifá priests for the invocation of the spirit of Ifá during the process of divination (*ìróké* or *ìrófá*);[4] and objects used to cast lots (*ìbò*) and quickly select the probable "stories" in the Ifá corpus that could apply to a client, which Bascom refers to as "symbols of specific alternatives" (1969, 32). However, not all these divination instruments of Ifá receive attention in Yorùbá videos. For instance, *ikin*, *ìyèròsùn*, and *ìbò*, the most important and ancient of these divination instruments, are sparingly used for divination in videos. Of the more than fifty Yorùbá videos in which Ifá is represented, the use of *ikin*, *ìyèròsùn*, and *ìbò* feature in only two: *Ti Olúwa ni Ilè* and *Erin Lákátabú*. This comports with Yorùbá tradition, wherein Ifá priests are selective in their use of the sixteen sacred palm nuts, the divining powder, and the lot-casting objects, when consulting for their clients.

Ifá priests use the sixteen sacred palm nuts more often for divination when making very important or special religious consultations for their communities, in their own homes for members of their families, or for themselves, especially on ceremonial occasions. This, according to Abímbọ́lá, is probably due to the considerable trouble and rather long time that this particular process of divination entails. The process that he describes as follows:

> For purposes of divination, the priest of Ifá puts the sixteen palm nuts in one hand of his hands and tries to take all of them out at once with the other hand. If one palm-nut is left in his hand, he makes two marks in the yellow powder of divination (*ìyèrè*) but if two palm-nuts are left in his hand, he makes one mark. If none of the palm-nuts is left, or if more than two palm-nuts are left, he makes no marks at all. This process is repeated until an *Odù* signature is obtained. (Abímbọ́lá 1976, 11)

Therefore, most actor-Ifá-diviner-priests in Yorùbá video films, such as *Àfònjá, Ilé Dúdú, Saworoide*, and *Agogo Èèwò*, use the less stressful Ifá divining chain (*òpèlè*) for their consultation instead of the sacred nuts. In reality, *òpèlè* is the most popular instrument of Ifá divination among the Yorùbá people. The divining chain is probably used more often than the sixteen sacred nuts because it is easier to manipulate and quicker to get the signature of Ifá known as the *odù* by using it, and because its process is not as cumbersome as that of the sacred nuts. Most actor-Ifá-diviner-priests in Yorùbá video films use an authentic *òpèlè* divining chain, but rarely do they use the most valuable divining chain, made of brass plates.

As for the minimal representation of lot-casting objects (*ìbò*) in Yorùbá videos, the long process of the casting of the lots must also have contributed to its negligible depiction in films. Again, Abímbọ́lá gives a detailed account of the complicated process of *ìbò* as follows:

> The Ifá priest gives the set of *ìbò* (which could be a piece of cowry-shell or seashell to communicate "yes" or positive response from Ifá, and a piece of stone or animal bone to stand for "no" or negative response from Ifá) to his client and asks him to put to it a question requiring the answer "yes" or "no" . . . the client then whispers a statement to the set of *ìbò* . . . , drops the set of *ìbò* on the paraphernalia of divination while the Ifá priest picks it up immediately and gives it back to the client after using it to touch the paraphernalia. . . . The client then picks up the *ìbò* and keeps the cowries in one of his hands and the bone in the other. The priest of Ifá then takes up the divining chain again and casts it twice. If the *Odù* obtained during the first casting is senior to the *Odù* of the second casting, the priest asks the client to produce the piece of *ìbò* in his right hand. But, if the *Odù* obtained during the first casting is junior to the one obtained during the second casting, he asks the client to produce the piece of *ìbò* on the left hand . . . the process described above is usually followed until all answers are obtained. *Therefore, the Ifá priest may have to cast the divining chain many times when using the ìbò to find out a specific point . . . if at the end, the client is not satisfied, the Ifá priest may ask him or her to come back to repeat the process the next day. In this way, the process may take several hours or days to complete.* (1976, 33–35, emphasis mine)

Since the time allocated to scenes of any film is controlled, it will be practically impossible to have the description paraphrased above represented in video. The most common representation of lot-casting elements in Yorùbá videos is to have cowrie shell and a piece of bone simply put on the divination mat by actor-Ifá-diviner-priests.

The other important instrument of Ifá divination that is prominently used by actor-Ifá-diviner-priests in Yorùbá videos is *ìróké* or *ìrófá*, the carved clublike object used by Ifá priests for the invocation of the spirit of Ifá during the process of divination. Most *ìróké* are made of wood but some are made of ivory, and these are very attractive and precious instruments of the Ifá divination system. Ifá diviner-priests carry *ìróké* as a symbol of the high status they enjoy in their respective communities. A major characteristic feature of the art on *ìróké* is the figure of a kneeling woman, a posture that stands for *ìkúnlè abiyamo* (the kneeling posture of a woman in labor) in the Yorùbá worldview. This position is a pleading, begging posture, calling on Ifá to give the correct answer to the client's request or requests. For instance, the actor-Ifá-diviner-priest in *Erin Lákatabú* performs the invocation of Ifá by knocking the *ìróké* against the ornamented divining tray (*opón Ifá*) with its pointed head—as in a real-life situation—to produce a sonorous sound while he simultaneously chanted the praise of Ifá as follows:

Ifá o gbó o!
Ará Adó Èwí
Ará Èkìtì Èfòn
Ará òtá Gbèdu
Ará Òwonràn níbi ojúmó rere ti n mó wale ayé
Ìwo leégún Olú-Ifè tíí sán Màrìwòo pàko
Kò gbeni tì, kò lani tì
Òkinkin tíí méyín erin-ín fon
Òsèsé, a-sè-bí ègà . . .

Ifá, you hear [me]
One who hails from Adó [Èkìtì town where their king] Èwí [reigns]
One who hails from the hills of Èfòn
One from the land where they value the sound of *gbèdu* drum
One from [the ancient town of] Ìwonràn where the beauty of the dawn
    descends on the earth
You are the masquerader of the ruler of Ifè who dresses himself in palm fronts
One who never fails to protect, one who never fails to prosper (his worshippers)
The king who blows the tusk of the elephant
Òsèsé, one who imitates the call of the weaver bird
(My translation)[5]

However, one common misrepresentation of the objects of Ifá divination in Yorùbá video is the presentation of sixteen cowries as Ifá divining paraphernalia. For instance, one of the two actor-Ifá-diviner-priests in the video-film *Ilè Dúdú* makes his consultation by casting sixteen cowries. While it is true that a system of divination known as *Eérìndínlógún*, which involves the casting of sixteen cowries, exists among the Yorùbá people in West Africa and their descendants in the diaspora, it is odd for an Ifá diviner-priest to use cowries for divination. Divination with sixteen cowries, according to Bascom, "is employed (solely) in the cults of Òrìshàlá and other 'white deities,' and in the cults of Èshù, Shàngó, Oya, Òshun, Obà, Yemoja, Yewa, Nàná Bùrùkú, and in some towns, Òshósì and Shòpòná" (1993, 4). Although *Eérìndínlógún* is similar to Ifá in many instances (such as in the names of the *odù* and the stories in each of them), it is simpler than Ifá divination and held in less esteem—except in the Americas where this system is seen as more important than Ifá because it is more widely known and more frequently employed. Bascom speculates that this may be due to the relative simplicity of the system, to the popularity of Shàngó, Yemoja, Òshun, and other Yorùbá gods with whom sixteen-cowrie divination is associated, and to the fact that it can be practiced by both men and women; women outnumber men in these cults, whereas for the most part, only men practice Ifá (1993, 3).

Acting the Priests of Ifá in Videos

I will now proceed to examine how Ifá diviners are represented in video films through the different actor-Ifá-diviner-priests. In his seminal work on Ifá, Wándé Abímbọ́lá identifies five categories of Ifá diviner-priests (1976, 13). The first and most important group, known as *Babalawo Olódù*, consists of Ifá diviner-priests already initiated into the secrets of *odù*. These are the most qualified Ifá priests, being at once both diviners and healers. The second class consists of Ifá priests who, though not initiated into the secrets of *odù*, the mythical wife of Ifá, still have all the paraphernalia of Ifá divination and are fully authorized to practice the art of divination. The third group is made up of Ifá priests who have all the paraphernalia of Ifá divination but who are not authorized to use them to divine for people outside their own households. In the fourth group are the Ifá priests who divine solely for healing purposes. The last group consists of nonpracticing Ifá priests. These are trained Ifá priests who have all the paraphernalia of Ifá but rarely use them for divination because they are gainfully employed in other full-time jobs. Such priests attend the regular assemblies of Ifá priests and maintain a disciplined attitude to life that is characteristics of all Ifá priests. Most actor-Ifá-diviner-priests in Yorùbá videos are presented both as diviners and as healers. They act the role of the priests known as Babaláwo Olódù.

One important attribute of Ifá diviner-priests is humility, which manifests in both their appearance and their manners. This is demonstrated, for instance, in the attitude of high chief Amawomárò, the Ifá diviner-priest in the film *Saworoide*, who refused to succumb to the antics of King Lápite when the king wrongfully accused him of being the brain behind the disappearance of Àyàngalú from Jogbo. Instead of trading words with the king, the Ifá priest simply counseled him on the way out of the crisis. One may argue, therefore, that the scriptwriter uses attitudes like this to demonstrate the great discipline and perseverance common to Ifá priests in real-life situations. Thus, it can hardly be gainsaid that the Ifá cult, comprising as it does properly disciplined, humble, and well-informed priests, is one of the most important and most useful cults of the Yorùbá people.

Another significant representation of Ifá priests in Yorùbá films is their mode of dress. The elaborate dress of some actor-Ifá-diviner-priests in Yorùba video film is a major departure from the modest dress of Yorùbá Ifá priests, described by Abímbọ́lá as "usually very poor" (1976, 17). The majority of Ifá diviner-priests in Yorùbá video films, unlike those described by Abímbọ́lá, are presented in predominantly white garments and wearing assorted beads known as *ìdè Ifá*, tied around the neck and wrist. It is not unusual for Yorùbá Ifá diviner-priests to appear in white; what is strange is the adornment of actor-Ifá-priests with elaborate and expensive traditional Yorùbá fabric materials of *aso òkè* (hand-woven cloth) such as *agbádá etù* (a billowing men's garment) used by the original Ifá priest in the films *Saworoide* and *Agogo Èèwò*, or the *gbárìyè* (a pleated gown worn when dancing) used by the babalawo in the film *Máyégún*, or the *età* (voluminous, elaborately emboridered fabric) wrapper tied on the left shoulder (*pakájà*) over a white *dànsíkí* (a wide-sleeve gown) with matching *abetí ajá* cap (a cap with two brims) by Ifá priests in the films *Àfònjá, Saworoide,* and *Agogo Èèwò*. In our opinion, screenwriters adopt expensive adornment of Ifá priests as a strategy to exhibit the aesthetics and richness of the Yorùbá traditional textile industry. This is in line with what Akínwùmí Ìṣọla, the scriptwriter of the films *Saworoide* and *Agogo Èèwò*, said in a July 2006 interview with me:

> what informs my use of oral tradition in general is to emphasize my debt to our heritage. . . . Therefore, as a creative writer, I go back to the bank of images anytime that I am writing my scripts to retrieve stored pictures . . . My position as a writer, therefore, is that we should go back to the teachings in our culture, especially now that many people are alienated because we have refused to teach the values in our culture. (Akinyemi 2008, 439–442)

In a number of Yorùbá video films, such as *Ìfura* and *Àpésìn*, Ifá priests are mistakenly dressed as members of the *ògbóni* or *òsùgbó* secret societies with a *sàkì* shawl on their left shoulder. *Sàkì* are major paraphernalia of the *ògbóni* or *òsùgbó* council, not that of Ifá. Although the Olúwo, one of the high priests of Ifá, sits on the *ògbóni* council, the other members of the council are not necessarily Ifá priests (see Fadipe 1970; Morton-Williams 1960). In addition, in a couple of films, actor-Ifá-diviner-priests prescribe sacrifices to their clients without any form of consultation with or guidance from Ifá, thus presenting Ifá diviner-priests as magicians, clairvoyants, or mind readers. An example of this form of misrepresentation occurs in the film entitled *Mágbe,* in which an Ifá diviner-priest attends to a poor and barren couple in search of wealth and children without any form of consultation with Ifá for guidance. Some scholars have expressed suspicion about Ifá diviner-priests and skepticism about their method of divination. For instance, some argue that the priests possess a hypertrophied sense of hearing; a few think that Ifá is probably an esoteric system. To my mind, more work still needs to be done on the question of the accuracy of the diviner-priests' predictions, because personal testimonies on this matter will always be subjective or impressionistic. Without further research, it will be difficult to agree with the suggestion that Ifá divination is a mystical system.

Recreation of Ifá Divination Process in Yorùbá Video Films

One other documented feature of Ifá in Yorùbá films is the recreation of the process of divination itself. This is a fairly long and complicated process that starts with the client confiding his secret problem to Ifá. This could take different forms. The most popular method is for the client to whisper his or her problems to a sum of money, in the form of bill or coin, which he or she throws into the paraphernalia of Ifá divination laid out by the priest of Ifá. Incidentally, this method is not common in Yorùbá videos. This is a true reflection of the situation in contemporary society, wherein modern Ifá priests expect higher monetary gains from their consultation. Two common methods are for the client either to hold the paraphernalia of divination in his or her hands and whisper his or her mind to it to prevent the Ifá diviner-priest from hearing his or her voice (as in the second Ifá consultation in *Erin Lákátabú*), or to divulge his or her problems directly to the priest of Ifá ahead of consultation (as in the early part of the same film). It is also possible for this stage of the consultation to be skipped completely in films. However, in such a situation, there will be reference to the method adopted by the client in relaying his or her problem to Ifá as the consultation progresses. For instance, a statement like *"Ifá ní e n l'álàákáláá"* ("Ifá says you are having nightmares/bad dreams") from the Ifá priest in *Àfònjá* confirms that the client's problem was not revealed to the priest ahead of consultation. In contrast, the statement *"àlá tí kábíyèsí lá mójúmó òní, ó jáyé, ó jórun"* ("will the nightmare/ bad dream that the king had overnight lead to death or not?") in *Erin Lákátabú* shows that the client (the king) had already divulged his problem to the diviner-priest ahead of the priest's consultation of the Ifá oracle.

The next stage of the divination process begins when the priest of Ifá takes up the divination instruments and starts to eulogize Ifá to invoke the spirit of the deity and plead with him to be clear and precise in his response to the requests of the client. These chants usually include a salute to Ifá/Òrúnmìlà and sometimes salutes to the Almighty God and certain other authorities. Below is a typical example of such introductory poetry, taken from *Agogo Èèwò*:

> *Iwájú opón,*
> *Èyìn opón*
> *Olòfún lótùún*
> *Olòkànràn losì*
> *Ààrin opón, ìta òrun*
> *Bó bá ti rí ni o wí o!*
> *Má fibi pere, má fire pebi;*
> *Má mómùú lómùú, má fòlòlò fohùn*
> *Wàá báyìí lògeereé ta*
> *Báa fémo lójú, a rína . . .*

Homage to the front side of the divination tray
Homage to the back side of the divination tray
Homage to the controller of the divination tray on the right side
Homage to the controller of the divination tray on the left side
Homage to the central part of the divination tray where nothing is hidden
Be factual (and address the problems of the client directly)!
Please don't lie,
Don't misrepresent yourself
Speak clearly to us about what you see

The proper performance of divination with *ikin* or *òpèlè* follows this introductory chant. Both the sacred palm nuts (*ikin*) and the divining chain (*òpèlè*) are used by actor-Ifá-diviner-priests in Yorùbá videos to arrive at the signature of an *odù*, although the divining chain is used more than the sacred palm nuts, probably because of its simplicity. Whichever divining instrument an actor-Ifá-diviner-priest decides to use in a film, his control of the instrument conforms to that of an authentic Ifá priest in Yorùbá society. For instance, whenever the divining chain is used in videos, the actor-Ifá-diviner-priest holds the chain in the middle and throws it before himself. As mentioned earlier, the divining chain has four half nuts of the *òpèlè* tree tied to each side of it. Each one of these half nuts has a concave and convex surface. When the divining chain is thrown forward, all or some or none of the half nuts may come to rest with their concave surfaces facing upwards; similarly for their convex surfaces. The pattern so formed on each occasion by the half nuts on the chain is regarded as an *odù*. For the sixteen sacred palm nuts, however, the actor-Ifá-diviner-priest, like a real diviner-priest of Ifá uses the method described by Abímbólá, which I cited earlier.

There are two categories of *odù*: the principal *odù* (*ojú odù*), sixteen in number and the minor *odù* (*omo odù* or *àmúlù odù*), 240 in number. Each of the 256 *odù* has its own specific divination signature and numerous chapters of stories known as *ese Ifá*. Once the actor-Ifá-diviner-priest recognizes the signature of the *odù* that appears, he identifies it by name, gives a short summary of the message from Ifá, chants the *ese Ifá* he considers to be most representative of the character of the *odù* that appeared, and rounds up the divination by relating the recited verse to the client's problem. The excerpt below from the *Àfònjá* illustrates this tripartite process:

> Ifá Diviner-Priest (after casting his divining chain, *òpèlè*, twice on the divining mat—a piece of white cloth): *Ire lo bá wá? Odù àbáwáyé yín ló jade yìíi! Odù Òsédìwòrì. Ifá ní è n lá àlákálàá, àlárándanràndan. Ifá ní kí e sì gbó ìkìlò àwon àgbà, kí e má baà sìse. Bífá yìí ti wí nùun nínú Òsépopo-Ìwòrìpopo. E è rí bí Òrúnmìlà sòrò bèè sí:*
>
> *Àfòn-ón so, àfòn ò là, àfòn ò wò,*
> *Bèè ni àfòn ò já;*
> *A díá fún Ayígbiribákújà*
> *Èyí tíí somo bíbí inúu Láderin.*
> *Láderin ló bí Pàsán,*
> *Pàsán ló bí alùgbìn,*
> *Alùgbìn ló b'Àfònjá,*
> *Enu tí won ó yà n'Ifè,*
> *Orin awo ló kó sí won lénu.*
> *Wón n wí pé:*
> *Àfòn, lara kaka so o!*
> *Àfòn, lara kaka so o!*
> *Àfòn, lara kaka so o!*

Àfòn, lara kaka so o!
Ifá, kaka káwo mó là
Àfòn, lara kaka so o!

Ifá ní e ó là láyé, won ó sì gbó lode òrun; e ó sì lókìkí jákèjádò ilè Yorùbá. Sùgbón kí e gbó ìkìlò, bí béè kó, gbogbo ìran yín ni yóò derú! Ifá ló wí béè o.

Ifá Diviner-Priest [after casting his divining chain, *òpèlè*, twice on the divining mat—a piece of white cloth] Do you have a good message [for the client]? What we have here is the *odù* of your forefathers! Odù Òsédìwòrì. The oracle says that you are having nightmares and bad dreams. Ifá cautions that you must heed his warning lest you go astray. That is the message from Ifá through Odù Òsépopo-Ìwòrìpopo. This is what the oracle says [in the *odù*]:

The *àfòn* tree bears fruit that does not burst open nor falls off,
The *àfòn* fruit will not even snap off from the tree,
Divination was performed for Ayígbiribákújà,
Who is the biological child of Láderin.
Láderin gave birth to Pàsán.
Pàsán gave birth to Alùgbìn.
Alùgbìn gave birth to Àfònjá.
When they open their mouth to sing in Ifè,
It's the religious song of Ifá that they sang.
They started singing:
Àfòn, please bear some fruits quickly
Àfòn, please bear some fruits quickly
Àfòn, please bear some fruits quickly
Àfòn, please bear some fruits quickly
Even if this will not prosper the [Ifá] priest
Àfòn, please bear some fruits quickly!

The Ifá oracle says that you will be rich and that the news of your wealth will spread all over the world. Your fame shall be known all over Yorùbáland and even beyond. But you must heed the warnings or else you and your unborn generations will be enslaved. That is what the Ifá oracle says.

One may rightly conclude that the whole of the literary corpus of Ifá known as *ese Ifá* is based on the *odù*. What a priest of Ifá tells his client either in reality or in a film is usually taken directly from the *odù* corpus. This is contrary to the occasional presentation of Ifá priests in some films, like *Mágbe*, as clever psychologists and spiritualists who read problems of their clients from their general appearance, not through consultation with Ifá. While the *odù* are important for the divination aspect of Ifá, the *ese Ifá* form the main bulk of chants in the Ifá literary corpus. At the same time, the *ese Ifá* are quite important for the divination aspect of Ifá because the pronouncements and predictions of the Ifá diviner-priests are based on the content of *ese Ifá*. Each *ese Ifá* presents an archetypal situation, a legendary character who consults a diviner-priest on specific problems. He or she is asked to do something, usually a sacrifice, in order to have a solution to the problems. The client either obeys or disobeys the directive. When s/he obeys, the problems are solved and the client will show his/her happiness, but the client suffers if s/he refuses to obey.

The diviner-priest presents these situations to the client, who may stop the diviner the moment the priest comes to an *ese Ifá* which he or she considers to be relevant to his or her problem, or may sit silently as the diviner recites one *ese Ifá* after the other. The client may seek further clarification with the *ibò* lots-casting objects. The client then identifies him- or herself in a total and symbolic manner with the protagonist or legendary character in the story of *ese Ifá*, carrying out whatever the diviner-priest advises. The client believes at that moment that the fate of the disobedient character would befall him or her while the good fortune of the obedient one would be his or hers, depending on whether he or she obeys or disobeys the diviner. The basic function of Ifá, therefore, is to resolve everyday human problems. Its role as a molder that tends the whole world with its great knowledge is characterized in this excerpt of Ifá verse:

> *Pá bí osán já*
> *Osán já*
> *Awo won lode ìtórí*
> *Àkàtànpò jákùn, ó dìkàlè*
> *A díá fún Òrúnmìlà*
> *Ifá n lo táyé Olúfè se*
> *Bí ení sogbá*
> *Ta ni yòó báni táyé se?*
> *Ewé òpèpè tile so*
> *Ifá ni yòó bá wa táyé so*
> *Ewé òpèpè tile so*

> Sudden as the snap of leather string,
> Leather string snaps
> They are the original Ifá diviners in the city of Ìtórí
> When the catapult loses its ground
> Divination was performed for Òrúnmìlà
> Ifá was going to mend the life of the king of Ifè
> As one mends broken calabash
> Who will help us mend our lives?
> Mend our lives perfectly
> It is Ifá who will help mend our lives
> (Abímbólá 1976, 56–57).

In *Ilè Dúdú*, for instance, a nursing mother who had lost four children in infancy in quick succession visits the actor-Ifá-diviner-priest with her fifth sick child to seek protection so that the child will not die like the others before him. After listening to the woman's complaint, the actor-Ifá-diviner-priest quickly consults his Ifá, recites a relevant verse from Odù Òyèkú Méjì, which in reality normally "denotes that death and all other evil will disappear" (Abímbólá 1976: 30), and

350 | Akintunde Akinyemi

informs the woman that the sick child will not survive but that he can prevent
future recurrences of infant death in her family:

BABALÁWO: *Òyèkú Alápà:*

> *Afínjú, tolórò, egbèra*
> *Òbùn ràìràì òun asìèrè egbèfà*
> *Pansàgà òun àbíkú ogboogba ni wón jé*
> *A dífá fún Alápà-níràwé*
> *Omo agbólú-oká sebo nítorí omo*
> *Òògùn yòówù e fi de àbíkú,*
> *Omo ó relé rè bó dòla . . .*
> *Àríké, omo yìí ó tún wá*

ÀRÍKÉ: *Baba, e gbà mí, e má jé ó wá móò*

BABALÁWO: *Só o wá rí i, wíwá tó bá tún wá léèkefà yìí, àtilo rè kò wá ní seé se
mó fún un. Yóò wá dúró, tí ó sojú tí ó sèyìn re. Bí ó se wá dúró, ó kù sówó
èmi àti ìwo, sùgbón yóò ná o lówó díè nítorí bómodé bá gbóngbón-on kíkú
léèrùn, Ìyá rè a sì gbóngbó-on sísin sípadò. Kò tún lo mó.*

IFÁ DIVINER: *Òyèkú Alápà:*

> A person of fastidious cleanliness is similar to the affluent
> A dirty person is also similar to the mentally unbalanced
> A child who dies at infancy is like an adulterous person
> Divination was made for Alápà-níràwé
> The child of the one who sacrifices a cobra for his children's sake
> No matter the efficacy of the medication one adopts
> To prevent an *àbíkú* child from dying in infancy,
> The child will die eventually . . .
> Àríké, this child will return after his death

ÀRÍKÉ: Old man, please help, let him not come back.

IFÁ DIVINER: What you have to understand is this, when he makes a comeback
the sixth time, it will be difficult for him to die again. He will live till your
old age. However, we both have some responsibilities to perform to ensure
that this come to pass. Therefore, you will spend some money, and we
must act fast and wisely too.

Similarly in *Agogo Èèwò,* when the new king of Jogbo seeks the guidance of Ifá
for direction on how to check the corruption among members of his council of
chiefs, the actor-Ifá-diviner-priest recites two relevant verses of Ifá from the Odù
Ògúndá Méjì and Ìrosùn Méjì before giving specific instruction to the king on
what he has to do to purge his council of advisers of corruption:

BABALÁWO: *Ògúndá Méjì—Afipá lówó, won kì í kádún*
> *Afiwàràwàrà-lówó, tí sológun, won kì í dòla*
> *Bó pé títí n ó lówó*
> *Wón n be lábà tí n jèsun isu*

Ojó èsan ò lo títí, kò jórò ó dun ni
A dífá fún Adigunlà, tí á digun sèse
Kèèpé o, kèè jìnnà
E wá wofá awó kì, bó ti n se
Ifá dé, aláse,
Òpè, abìse-wàrà

Ìròsùn Méjì tè lé e
Bómodé kan n jèèwò, bénìkan ò bi í
Bó pé títí, ohun tí n bini a máa bini
Èèwò a sì béèrè
A dífá fún eni tí bàbá rè ó kú,
Tí ó jogún ìyá è
A ì í se é o! Èèwò
Bí bá bi ni, e jòwó è!

Ifá ní a ó ro agogo kan, a ó máa pè é ní 'agogo èèwò'. Yóò tóbi díè. A ó sa Ògúndá sí i légbèé òtún, a ó sa Ìròsùn sí i légbèé òsì. Bí enìkan bá fé joyè, yóò wá jéjèé pé òun ò níí dale ìlú Jogbo. A ó wá mú ewé olúdù, a ó gbo ó mó èèpo ìròsùn. A ó wá da àgbo yìí sínú agogo èèwò; olóyè yóò wá mu nínú rè tó bá di ojó keje . . . Bí olóyè kan bá wá dalè, inú ni yóò run olóyè béè pa. Èlà ború o, èlà boyè o.

Those who get rich forcefully hardly last a year
Those who acquire instant wealth like warriors hardly last a day
The tolerant one is still alive in their farmstead enjoying a life of bliss
The day of retribution is at hand
That should be our consolation
Divination was made for Adigunla (One-who-wages-war-to-make-wealth)
Who will hurt himself sooner than later.
Before long
See how Ifá predictions are coming to pass
Ifá is here, the one who speaks authoritatively
Òpè, whose prediction must come to pass.

This is closely followed by Ìròsùn Méjì
If a youngster violates the taboo and gets away with it
Eventually, he will face the law of retribution
And will be punished for violating the norms of the society
Divination was made for the one who will inherit his mother after his father's
    death.
It is not done, discard it

Ifá oracle instructs us to fashion a gong to be called "the gong of taboo." It will be big a little bit. We will inscribe the Ògúndá marks on the right side, and Ìròsùn on the left. We will then prepare herbal drink from the leaves of *olúdù* and the back of the *ìyèrè* tree. We will pour the herbal drink in the gong and all chiefs will take oath and drink the herbal preparation on the seventh day. If any chief breaks the oath by behaving treacherously, such a chief will die of stomach upset.

It is clear from our discussion so far that each *ese Ifá* has a structural pattern, which distinguishes it from other forms of Yorùbá oral literature. The form of *ese Ifá* is predominantly poetic. The poems of *ese Ifá* are of varying lengths; some, known as *Ifá Kékèké*—short poems of Ifá—are as short as four sentences while others, known as *Ifá Nlánlá*—long poems of Ifá—could be as long as six hundred sentences. Since *ese Ifá* is historical in content, its structure is also based on its historical nature. Earlier scholars have commented upon or described the structure of *ese Ifá*. Raymond Prince outlines four sections for each complete *ese Ifá:* the introductory lines, the presentation of the protagonist and his or her problem, the sacrifice, and the key to the understanding of the foregoing, the resolution (1964, 2–6). On the other hand, Bascom has a threefold division into the mythological case that serves as a precedent, the resolution or outcome of this case, and its application to the Ifá client (which he admits does not occur within the story in the *ese Ifá*). Bascom's third section constitutes the personal interpretation of the *ese Ifá* (1969, 122–127). Abímbọ́lá posits a more detailed eight-part structure for an *ese Ifá* (1976, 43).

The shorter poems of Ifá, which are usually shortened versions of the eight-part type, make use of only parts 1–3 and part 8 but not parts 4–7. It is this shorter form of *ese Ifá* that most actor-Ifá-diviner-priests use in video films because actors can memorize them with relative ease. Even when a screenwriter uses creative ingenuity to create an *ese Ifá*, the writer ensures that it falls within the standard structure of *ese Ifá*. For instance, the opening Ifá verse supposedly taken from Odù Òtúá in *Saworoide* and rendered by the first diviner shortly before the death of the first king of Jogbo town is the screenwriter's own creation, which looks very much like an authentic *ese Ifá*:

> Aso funfun níí sunkún aró
> Ìpìlè òrò níí sunkún èkejì tan-tan-tan
> A díá fún Adéròmókùn, omo Oòni
> Àlànàkàn Èsùrú
> Níjó tí n mékún sèráhùn ire gbogbo
> Bóká bá yo nigbó,
> A bónà wá
> Ire gbogbo, mama wá Jogbo wá ò
> Ire gbogbo.
> Báa bá dami sórí, a bésè wá
> Ire gbogbo, mama wá Jogbo wá ò
> Ire gbogbo
> Ire gbogbo níí sojú owó
> Ire gbogbo, mama wá Jogbo wá ò
> Ire gbogbo

It is the white cloth that cries for indigo
The discussion held at the commencement of an issue cries for its partner
    persistently

Divination was made for Adéròmókùn, child of the Oòni (king of Ilé-Ifè)
Whose appellation is Àlànàkàn Èsùrú
When he was crying for good things of life
When the cobra comes out of the bush,
It follows an existing path
May all good things come the way of Jogbo
All good things
If we pour water on the head,
It takes the downward path until it reaches the feet
May all good things come the way of Jogbo
All good things
All good things come the way of money
May all good things come the way of Jogbo
All good things

Ese Ifá, whether long or short, lifted verbatim from the Ifá corpus or composed by a screenwriter, make use of very interesting poetic devices such as personification, allegory, and metaphor that must be decoded appropriately by the diviner-priest in order to resolve the client's problems accurately.

Prescription of Ifá Divination Sacrifices and Medicines (Ebo Ifá)

To every complete Ifá divination process there is always a prescribed sacrifice (*ẹbọ*) to be performed by the client. Whether the prescription of Ifá is good or bad, the client must always perform one form of sacrifice or another. It is the belief of the Yorùbá that if the prediction of Ifá is good, a sacrifice will help to make it come to pass, and that if the prediction is bad, a sacrifice will help the client to dispel the evil. Consequently, it is part of the training of Ifá diviner-priests to learn by heart the sacrifice that goes with every *ese Ifá*. Therefore, after the long process of divination, the Ifá diviner-priest will tell the client the sacrifice or medicinal preparation that goes with the prediction. The sacrifice could be as simple as the following excerpt from *Erin Lákátabú:*

"*Ifá ní kí e ní òpòlopò sùúrù àti ìfura. Kò gbebo, kò gbòògùn*"

"Ifá says that you have to be patient and observant. No real sacrifice or offering"

On the other hand, the *ẹbọ Ifá* could come with very detailed instructions similar to what we have in the beginning of *Saworoide*, in which the Ifá priest gives the following instruction to the people of Jogbo town on the religious ceremonies that must be performed during installation of a new king:

Kí e ro adé ide kan, saworo etí ìlù, àti àdó ide kan, kí e fi òmò gbé igi ìlùu dùndún kan, kí e fi se ìlù. A ó wá kó ewé Ifá jo, a ó se é bó ti ye sínú orù. A ó mú awé àgbáàrín kan, a ó fi sínú ihò tí n be lórí adé ide. A ó mú awé àgbáàrín kejì, a ó jù ú sínú igi ìlùu saworoide. A ó wá jó gbogbo ewé Ifá tó kù ní èjíjó. A ó ro ó sínú àdó ide. Èjíjó yìí ni a ó fi sín gbéré fún Àyàngalú àti gbogbo àwon Oníjogbo tó bá n je. A ó wá fó orù tí a lò mólè

Fashion out a brass crown, drum jingle bells, and a small container. Carve a drum frame and make a drum. We will gather the prescribed herbs into a small pot. We will put one half of an *àgbáàrín* nut in the hole on the king's crown. The other half of the *àgbáàrín* nut will be kept inside the drum frame. We will then burn the herbs in the pot into powder and pour it into the pot-like brass container. The powder is to be rubbed into the incisions made on *Àyàngalú* [the master drummer], and all future kings. We will then break the pot into pieces.

When properly done, *ebo Ifá* is believed to be very effective and, any attempt to treat it with contempt could lead to serious repercussions. For instance, the condescending attitude of Làgàta (the usurper of the Oníjogbo kingship title) and his lack of respect for the royal institution of Jogbo in *Agogo Èèwò* portend his untimely death the moment he wears the beaded crown of Jogbo without taking all necessary precautions laid down in the *ebo Ifá* described above. Normally, the sacrifice does not form part of the literary corpus of Ifá, but there are a number of instances in which Ifá divination sacrifice is included.

Reinventing the Performance of *Ìyèrè Ifá*

The chanting of *Ìyèrè* (*ìyèrè sísun*) is a common occurrence at the weekly Ifá worship known as *ojó awo* and the annual *molè* festival usually held in honor of Yorùbá paramount rulers. There is an excellent recreation of the performance of this Ifá text (*ìyèrè Ifá sísun*) by Akinwumi Ìṣọla in *Agogo Èèwò*. In the early part of the film, the Ifá diviners of Jogbo town assemble at the house of their chief priest (Amawomárò), chanting and making sacrifices to Ifá. As they chant, some of them produce special dance music on the traditional Ifá drum of *àràn* and its accompaniment of *agogo* (the gong) and dance merrily in front of the chief diviner-priest's house.

> *Ifá ló nílé ayé, Olódùmarè ló lòrun,*
> *Ifá ló nílé ayé oò, Olódùmarè ló lòrun,*
> *Ènìyàn-án gò lágò jù, wón se báwon gbón*
> *Wón se báwon gbón*
> *Ifá ló nílé ayé, Olódùmarè ló lòrun,*
> *Ifá ló nílé ayé oò, Olódùmarè ló lòrun,*
> *Ènìyàn-án gò lágò jù, wón se báwon gbón*

> Ifá owns this world but it is Olúdùmarè who owns heaven
> Ifá owns this world, but it is Olúdùmarè who owns heaven
> Men, though stupid, think they are wise
> Think they are wise
> Ifá owns this world but it is Olúdùmarè who owns heaven
> Ifá owns this world, but it is Olúdùmarè who owns heaven
> Men, though stupid, think they are wise

The chanting of *ìyèrè Ifá* is a well-developed art among Ifá priests, usually done in choral form and led by a good chanter. To every complete sentence chanted correctly by the leader of the chant, the other priests chant "*hain-in,*" meaning "yes," which represents "correct." However, if the leader has chanted a sentence wrongly, the other priests will not respond with "*hain-in*" but rather inform the leader of the mistake. According to Abímbọ́lá, "where a priest makes serious mistakes while chanting and refuses to stop chanting in defiance of the expressed wishes of the congregation, he might even be thrown out of the meeting in shame" (1976, 15).

Akínwùmí Ìṣọla, the screenwriter of *Agogo Èèwò*, is aware that the *ìyèrè Ifá* text embraces certain internal symbolic essences that are useful to a writer seeking materials to construct a model social vision. He is also aware that *ìyèrè Ifá* embodies the cultural values and visions of a people and offers itself as one of the most enduring intellectual and philosophical symbols of the Yorùbá worldview. It is for this reason that he manipulates the *ìyèrè Ifá* delivery mode in his criticism of the Jogbo chiefs, in which he castigates the chiefs and refers to them as "*agò*" (stupid or unintelligent) and "*alábòsí*" (hypocrites). Thus, while employing lampoon—the most scathing satiric genre—we see Ìṣọla lashing out at the chiefs of Jogbo to criticize and expose their shortcomings:

E wá wayé òsèlú, òsèlú alábòsí,
E wá wayé òsèlú, òsèlú alábòsí,
Wón kówó ìlú sápò, wón fowó mutí.
Wón fowó mutí.
Wón fowó mutí
E wá wayé òsèlú, òsèlú alábòsí,
E wá wayé òsèlú, òsèlú alábòsí,
Wón kówó ìlú sápò, wón fowó mutí.

Watch these hypocrites called politicians,
Watch these hypocrites called politicians,
They stole the nation's wealth and squandered it.
They squandered it.
They squandered it
Watch these hypocrites called politicians,
Watch these hypocrites called politicians,
They stole the nation's wealth and squandered it.

What this discussion has revealed is that the intersection of Ifá tradition and Yoruba films manifests at two levels: documentation and manipulation. By documentation, I mean the adoption of specific aspects of Ifá tradition, which Yorùbá screenwriters lift verbatim and insert edited or unedited in appropriate places in their films. We see this as the writers' modest way of preserving Yorùbá Ifá tradition. Contemporary Yorùbá culture differs so drastically from what it used to be. The old social institutions that ensured the continuity of certain cultural practices have become irrelevant, and the discontinuation of ceremonies connected with them has also led to the loss of the tradition associated with them. Akínwùmí Ìṣọla, one of the foremost Yorùbá screenwriters and a leading Yorùbá cultural revivalist, has personally expressed his worry over the destruction of what he refers to as the "African literary ecosystem" and the "bastardization" of the traditional purpose of literature in contemporary society (1992, 18). In order to arrest the deterioration, Ìṣọla and other screenwriters like Adebayo Faleti and Jimoh Aliu have devised various means of preserving oral tradition in their films.

By contrast, with manipulation screenwriters only make selective use of elements of oral tradition, which they exploit to advance their ideological positions. What appeals to such writers in oral tradition is not just the preservation of the material itself but also the ideas contained in it, which are seen as having enduring relevance. At the level of *iyèrè*, for instance, the writer of *Agogo Èèwò* turns that aspect of Ifá tradition to metaphorical or symbolic use to articulate a political vision. He thereby succeeds in converting the genre into a complex set of symbols that is only partly indigenous. The major aspects of the traditional symbols are now encoded to articulate a modern meaning. In this case, the screenwriter's technique frees *iyèrè* from the encumbrances of *Ifá*, a strict form of oral tradition. The instance of video as a medium of popular culture in Yorùbá society affords us an opportunity to look at what happens when modern technology meets a society that is at best still groping its way toward modernity. For despite modern technology's ubiquitous presence in Yorùbá society, the society still retains worldviews and mental attitudes that exist side by side with science and technology. Such attitudes and worldviews inform not just daily socioeconomic and political life but also the reception and utilization of foreign technology. Even then, we still witness a mutually beneficial and dynamic interaction between technology and tradition. The best thing about Ifá tradition may be, indeed, that in spite of all odds the tradition is moving on and maintaining its essence even while changing some of its outer form when in contact with film. As Ogundele submits, "what we are witnessing now is not so much technology at the service of tradition, but its opposite: tradition at the service of technology" (2000, 98). What one would have wished for is a mutual beneficial and dynamic interaction between the two, but the cash nexus—the driving force behind the video productions—prevents this. The situation is further reinforced by the power of the new technological medium of production and consumption: its inherent ability to mass produce and to transform what it produces. One can only hope for a reciprocal interaction between the two sooner than later.

Notes

1. Ifá divining trays are usually made of wood. They are available in circular, semicircular, and rectangular forms. The edges of the divining trays are normally decorated with different kinds of designs, including animal figures. The divining powder (*iyèròsùn*) is usually sprinkled on the tray and the diviner-priests print their divination marks on the powder during the process of divination.

2. This yellow divining powder is produced by the *ìròsùn* tree (*Baphia nitida*).

3. These are nuts obtained from the seeds of the *òpèlè* tree (*Schrebera golungensis*). The divining chain itself is shaped like a tuning fork. Tied at regular intervals to the chain are eight half-nuts of the *òpèlè* tree. Four half-nuts are tied to each arm of the chain. At each end of the chain, the Ifá priest ties a number of objects such as small beads, coins, and cowries, for aesthetics. The material of which the genuine *òpèlè* chain is made is tough leather, but sometimes cotton string or brass is used.

4. Carved on *ìróké* is the figure of a kneeling woman, which is characteristic of Yoruba ritual art. It is used to tap the divination tray during divination to invoke the spirit of Ifá. This kneeling posture of a woman during labor (*ikúnlè abiyamo*) represents a pleading, begging posture, calling on Ifá to give the correct answer to the client's request. The greatest symbol of pleading among the Yoruba even today is to say "*Mo fi ìkúnlè abiyami bè* (I invoke the kneeling posture of a woman in labor to plead for leniency)." Only the hard-hearted will not forgive after hearing that statement.

5. All translations are mine unless otherwise stated.

References

Abímbólá, Wándé. 1976. *Ifá: An Exposition of Ifá Literary Corpus*. Ibadan: Oxford University Press.

Akinyemi, Akintunde. 2008. "A Conversation with Akinwumi Isola on His Writing Life." In *Emerging Perspectives on Akinwumi Isola,* edited by Akintunde Akinyemi and Toyin Falola, 429–452. Trenton, NJ: Africa World Press.

Bascom, William. 1969. *Ifá Divination: Communication Between Gods and Men in West Africa*. Bloomington: Indiana University Press.

———. 1993. *Sixteen Cowries: Yoruba Divination from Africa to the New World*. Bloomington: Indiana University Press.

Epega, Afolabi, and Philip John Neimark. 1995. *The Sacred Ifá Oracle*. San Francisco: Harper San Francisco.

Fadipe, N. A. 1970. *The Sociology of the Yoruba*. Ibadan: University Press.

Ìsọla, Akinwumi. 1992. "The African Writer's Tongue." *Research in African Literature* 23, no. 1: 17–26.

Meyer, Birgit. 2005. "Mediating Tradition: Pentecostal Pastor, African Priests, and Chiefs in Ghanaian Popular Films." In *Christianity and Social Change in Africa: Essays in Honor of J. D. Y. Peel,* edited by Toyin Falola, 275–306. Durham, NC: Carolina Academic Press.

Morton-Williams, Peter. 1960. "The Ogboni Cult in Oyo." *Africa* 30, no. 4: 362–374.

Ogundele, Wole. 2000. "Folk Opera to Soap Opera: Improvisations and Transformations in Yoruba Popular Theater." In *Nigerian Video Films,* edited by Jonathan Haynes, 89–147. Athens: Ohio State University Center for International Studies.

Prince, R. 1964. *Ifa: Yoruba Divination and Sacrifice*. Ibadan: Ibadan University Press.

List of Selected Video Films Cited

Àfònjá, produced by Remdel Optimum Communications Limited, 2003.

Agogo Èèwò, produced by Mainframe Film and TV Productions 2002.

Àpésìn, produced by Epsalum Productions (n.d.).

Erin Lákátabú, produced by Corporate Pictures and Sound Image (n. d.).

Ìfura, produced by T. J. Olaoluwa Commercial Enterprises in Conjunction with Afonja Presentations (n.d.).

Ilè Dúdú, produced by Solid Productions (n.d.).

Mágbe, produced by Solid Productions (n.d.).

Máyégún, produced by Yinka Quadri Productions (n.d.).

Saworoide, produced by Mainframe Film and TV Productions 2000.

Ti Olúwa Ni Ilè (parts 1–3), produced by Mainframe Film and TV Productions 2003.

Contributors

Wándé Abímbọ́lá taught in three Nigerian universities and also at many universities in the United States, including Harvard University. His books include *Ifá: An Exposition of Ifá Literary Corpus* (1976), *Ifá Divination Poetry* (1977), *Awon Oju Odu Mereerindinlogun* (1977), and *Ifá Will Mend Our Broken World: Thoughts on Yoruba Religion and Culture in Africa and the Diaspora* (1997).

M. Ajisebo McElwaine Abimbola coadministered the "Safeguarding the Ifá Divination System" project, which led to the establishment of the Ifá Heritage Institute, Oyo, Nigeria, in 2008. She holds an MA from the University of Massachusetts at Boston and a BA in African Studies, Women's Studies, and Religious Studies from St. Lawrence University.

Rowland O. Abiodun is John C. Newton Professor of Art, the History of Art, and Black Studies at Amherst College. His publications include *Yoruba Art and Language: Seeking the African in African Art* (2014), and *What Follows Six Is More than Seven: Understanding African Art* (1995); he coauthored *Cloth Only Wears to Shreds: Yoruba Textiles and Photographs from the Beier Collection* (2004).

Adélékè Adéẹ̀kọ́ authored *Proverbs, Textuality, and Nativism in African Literature* (1998) and *The Slave's Rebellion: Literature, History, Orature* (2005). Adéẹ̀kọ́ guest edited a special issue of *Research in African Literatures* (Winter 2009) on slavery in the African diaspora. He teaches in the Department of African and African American Studies at Ohio State University.

Akintunde Akinyemi teachesYoruba language and literature at the University of Florida. His publications include *Yoruba Royal Poetry: A Socio-historical Exposition and Annotated Translation* (2004); he coauthored *Dictionnaire usual Yoruba-français* (1997); and coedited *Sango in Africa and the African Diaspora* (2009) and *Emerging Perspectives on Akinwumi Isola* (2008).

Andrew Apter is professor of history and anthropology at the University of California, Los Angeles. His books include *Black Critics and Kings: The Hermeneutics of Power in Yoruba Society* (1992); *The Pan-African Nation: Oil and the Spectacle of Culture in Nigeria* (2005), and *Beyond Words: Discourse and Critical Agency in Africa* (2007).

Bolaji Campbell teaches in the Department of History of Art and Visual Culture at Rhode Island School of Design. Bolaji Campbell has published numerous essays in learned journals and as chapters in books. His most recent work is *Painting for the Gods: Art and Aesthetics of Yoruba Religious Murals* (2008).

Stefania Capone is a senior researcher of the French National Center for Scientific Research and teaches at the EHESS, Paris. Her publications include *Searching for Africa in Brazil: Power and Tradition in Candomblé* (2010) and *Les Yoruba du Nouveau Monde: Religion, ethnicité et nationalisme noir aux Etas-Unis* (2005).

Kamari Maxine Clarke is a professor at the University of Pennsylvania. Her publications include *Mapping Yoruba Networks: Power and Agency in the Making of Transnational Communities* (2004), *Fictions of Justice: the International Criminal Court and the Challenge of Legal Pluralism in Sub-Saharan Africa* (2009); she coedited *Transforming Ethnographic Knowledge* (2012).

Henry John Drewal teaches at the University of Wisconsin–Madison. He was the guest curator at the Fowler Museum at UCLA for a major traveling exhibition entitled *Mami Wata: Arts for Water Spirits in Africa and Its Diasporas* and is the editor of *Sacred Waters: Arts for Mami Wata and other Water Divinities in Africa and the Diaspora* (2008).

Ysamur M. Flores-Peña earned a PhD from the University of California, Los Angeles and an MA from the Catholic University of Puerto Rico. His publications include *Santeria Garments and Altars: Speaking Without a Voice* (1994), and "Fit for a Queen: Analysis of a Consecration Outfit in the Cult of Yemaya," *Folklore Forum* (1990).

Laura S. Grillo earned her PhD in history of religions from the University of Chicago. Her current book in progress, *An Intimate Rebuke: Female Genital Power in Ritual and Politics in Côte d'Ivoire*, was generously supported with a postdoctoral fellowship at Harvard Divinity School. Laura teaches at Pacifica Graduate Institute.

Barry Hallen is an Alumni Fellow of the W. E. B. Du Bois Institute for African and African American Research, Harvard University. His publications include *The Good, the Bad, and the Beautiful: Discourse about Values in Yoruba Culture* (2000), *African Philosophy: The Analytic Approach* (2006), and *A Short History of African Philosophy* (2009).

Akínwùmí Ìṣọlá is one of the leading contemporary writers in Yoruba language and literature. His major publications include: *Two Yorùbá Historical Dramas: Efúnṣetán aníwúra, Iyálóde ìbàdàn, and Tinúubú, ìyálóde ẹgbá: Being Translations of Efúnṣetán aníwúra, Iyálóde ìbàdàn and Olú Ọmọ* (Africa World Press, 2005), and *Making Culture Memorable: Essays in Language, Culture and Development* (DB Martoy Books, 2010).

Velma Love teaches at Howard University School of Divinity. Her publications include: *Divining the Self: A Study in Yoruba Myth and Human Consciousness* (2012) and "The Bible and Contemporary African American Culture: Hermeneutical Forays, Observations, and Impressions" in *African Americans and the Bible: Sacred Texts and Social Textures.*

Wyatt MacGaffey is professor of anthropology emeritus at Haverford College. His publications include *Chiefs, Priests, and Praise-Singers: History, Politics, and Land Ownership in Northern Ghana* (2013), *Religion and Society in Central Africa* (1986), *Kongo Political Culture* (2000), and *Custom and Government in the Lower Congo* (1970).

John Mason received a 1999 Guggenheim Fellowship in folklore. His most noted published works include *Baba's Esu-Elegba Tales* (2015), *Araaraara: Wondrous Inhabitor of Thunder* (2012), *Adura Fun Orisa: Prayers for Selected Heads* (2002), and with Henry John Drewal, *Beads, Body and Soul: Art and Light in the Yoruba Universe* (1998).

Joseph M. Murphy is the Paul and Chandler Tagliabue Professor of Interfaith Studies and Dialogue in the Theology Department at Georgetown University. He is the author of *Santería: An African Religion in America* (1993), *Working the Spirit: Ceremonies of the African Diaspora* (1994), and *Botánicas: Sacred Spaces of Healing and Devotion in Urban America* (2015). With Mei-Mei Sanford he has edited the volume *Osun across the Waters: A Yoruba Goddess in Africa and the Americas* (2001).

Jacob K. Olupona is a professor at Harvard University. His books include *City of 201 Gods: Ile-Ife in Time, Space, and the Imagination* (2011) and *Kingship, Religion and Rituals in a Nigerian Community: A Phenomenological Study of Ondo Yoruba Festivals* (1991). Olupona has received prestigious grants from the Guggenheim Foundation, the American Philosophical Society, and the Ford Foundation.

Ayo Opefeyitimi lectures at the Department of Linguistics and African Languages at Obafemi Awolowo University, Ile-Ife, Nigeria. He has over three decades' experience in the teaching and research of orature, stylistic, and Yoruba literary and cultural studies. He has published books in these areas as well. He is a Fulbright Fellow and CODESRIA Laureate.

Olasope O. Oyelaran is a research scholar-in-residence at Kalamazoo College. He served as visiting professor in Arts and Sciences and director of global studies in the Heinecke Institute of Western Michigan University, 2005–2008. He established the Department of African Languages and Literatures at Obafemi Awolowo University in Ile-Ife, Nigeria.

Philip M. Peek is professor emeritus at Drew University. He is editor of *African Divination Systems: Ways of Knowing* (1991) and *Twins in African and Diaspora Cultures: Double Trouble, Twice Blessed* (2011). He coedited *Reviewing Reality: Dynamics of African Divination* (2013), *Divination and Healing: Potent Vision* (2004), and *African Folklore: An Encyclopedia* (2004).

Mei-Mei Sanford is adjunct instructor of Africana studies at the College of William and Mary. She is the coeditor of *Ọṣun Across the Waters: A Yoruba Goddess in Africa and the Americas* (2001).

Olúfẹ́mi Táíwò is professor at Seattle University. He has served as a Ford Foundation visiting postdoctoral research and teaching fellow at the Carter G. Woodson Institute for Afro-American and African Studies, University of Virginia, 2000–2001. He is one of the founders of the International Society for African Philosophy and Studies (ISAPS).

Index

da Silva, Ornato José, 228
da Silva, Ruth Moreira, 228, 230
da Silva, Vagner Gonçalves, 227
de Heusch, Luc, 146, 148
de Odé, Carlinhos, 231–237
de Ogun, Torodê, 229
de Oxalá, Adilson. *See* Martins, Adilson
    Antônio
de Oxalá, Marcos, 233, 234, 235
de Oxoguian, Edeuzuita, 231, 232
development, 161–162
diasporic technologies of religious conscious-
    ness, 269
dilogun. See *merindinlogun*
divination powder, 1, 177, 178, 330, 332, 341
divination tapper, 35, 36, 332, 341; in Nigerian
    video films, 342
divination tray, 1, 35, 36, 70, 120, 277, 280, 302,
    357n1; and animal imagery, 279–281, 286; as
    art, 328–330; and Eṣu, 279, 311; in Nigerian
    video films, 342; and women diviners,
    256–257; and Yoruba worldview, 215, 309; on
    Yoruba carved doors, 317
diviner. See *babalawo*
divining chain: and animal associations, 286,
    288; compared to Christian rosary, 178;
    description and use, 37, 53, 107, 323n19, 357n3;
    historical arrival of, 288; materials of, 36,
    357n3; in Nigerian video films, 341, 342,
    347–348; on Yoruba carved doors, 317
do Bonfim, Martiniano Eliesu, 225, 226
Dogon: cosmology, 320; divination, 12, 278, 287;
    doors, 316–317; visual cannon in, 309, 311–315
dos Santos, Eugenia Ana, 225
dreams, 8, 133, 135–136, 182, 183, 186, 187, 189
Drewal, Henry John, 144, 283, 286
Drewal, Margaret, 9, 188, 288, 319
dùndún, 39, 196
Durkheim, Emile, 146
dyes, 78, 202n4, 296, 297, 298

ẹbo: etymology of the word, 153. *See also*
    sacrifice
eérìndínlógún. See *merindilogun*
Ègbá, 196
Ehuru, 283
Ejibogbe, 194, 102, 217. See also *Òdí Èjìogbé*
Ekiti, 47, 296, 343
Ela, 19, 22, 25
el Cojo, Nõ Juan, 196
Elebuìbon, Ifáyemí, 340
eleerindinlogun, 138

Elegba. *See* Esu
Elegbara. *See* Esu
Elegua. *See* Esu
elekes, 183. See also *Lukumi*
enactment, 320, 321, 334, 335
Enigbè, 194, 196, 197
Epega, D. Onadele, 101
Erin Lákátabú, 341, 342, 346, 353
Esegba of Ilesha, Chief, 27
ẹṣẹ ifá: categories of, 352; content, 35, 72; as
    proverbs, 55–57; structure, 3, 33–35, 51–53;
    variation among, 92
Eshu. *See* Esu
ESP, 12, 326, 327
Estácio de Sá, 228
Esu, 11, 322n15, 343; animal images of, 258, 311,
    317; in Brazil and Cuba, 303; character of,
    295, 303; colors for, 303; compared to Dogon
    trickster, 313, 314, 322n14; Devil as, 171; divi-
    nation tray and, 1, 215, 311, 328; divining bowl
    and, 36; Islam and, 170–173; myths about the
    odù and, 311; narrative about, 295; offerings
    for, 304; relationship to Orunmila, 302, 305;
    women in procession and, 255; on Yoruba
    carved doors, 317
èsúsú, 200–201
ethics, 96–97, 103, 209, 232
Ewe, 34, 326
extrasensory perception, 12. *See also* ESP

Fakeye, Lamidi Olonade, 130
Faleti, Adebayo, 356
Falola, Toyin, 146
Fanti, 198
Fatogun, Babalawo, 170, 176
Federal University of Bahia, 226
feitura do santo, 232, 242n20
Festival Internacional de Tradiciones Af-
    roamericanas, 247
filhos-de-santo, 236
fly whisk, 124, 126, 127, 128, 278, 302
folktales, 164–166
Fon, 34, 282, 321n4, 321n5
Fonseca, Jr., Eduardo, 228
fortune telling, 70, 98, 102, 110
Frobenius, Leo, 124, 278, 317
fundamentos, 230, 232, 233, 240

Gan, 34
Garcia, Nõ Filomeno, 196
Gates, Jr., Henry Louis, xvi, 95
Gbadegesin, Segun, 97, 101

CPSIA information can be obtained
at www.ICGtesting.com
Printed in the USA
BVOW04s1211300517
485505BV00001BB/40/P